Culturally Sp

Open Linguistics Series

Series Editor:

This series is 'open' in two senses. First, it provides a forum for works associated with any school of linguistics or with none. Most practising linguists have long since outgrown the unhealthy assumption that theorizing about language should be left to those working in the generativist-formalist paradigm. Today large and increasing numbers of scholars are seeking to understand the nature of language by exploring one or other of the various cognitive models of language, or in terms of the communicative use of language, or both. This series is playing a valuable part in re-establishing the traditional 'openness' of the study of language. The series includes many studies that are in, or on the borders of, various functional theories of language, and especially (because it has been the most widely used of these) Systemic Functional Linguistics. The general trend of the series has been towards a functional view of language, but this simply reflects the works that have been offered to date. The series continues to be open to all approaches, including works in the generativist-formalist tradition.

The second way in which the series is 'open' is that it encourages studies that open out 'core' linguistics in various ways: to encompass discourse and the description of natural texts; to explore the relationships between linguistics and its neighbouring disciplines – psychology, sociology, philosophy, cultural and literary studies – and to apply it in fields such as education, language pathology and law.

Relations between the fields of linguistics and artificial intelligence are covered in a sister series, Communication in Artificial Intelligence. Studies that are primarily descriptive are published in a new series, Functional Descriptions of Language.

Recent titles in the series

Culturally Speaking

Managing Rapport through Talk across Cultures

Edited by

Helen Spencer-Oatey

continuum
LONDON · NEW YORK

CONTINUUM
The Tower Building, 11 York Road, London SE1 7NX
15 East 26th Street, New York, NY 10010

First published 2000
Reprinted 2002, 2004
© Helen Spencer-Oatey and contributors 2000

British Library Cataloguing-in-Publication Data
A catalogue record for this book is available from the British Library.
ISBN 0-304-70436-9 (hardback)
    0-826-46636-2 (paperback)

Library of Congress Cataloging-in-Publication Data
Culturally speaking: managing rapport through talk across cultures / edited by
   Helen Spencer-Oatey.
      p. cm.
   (Open linguistics series)
   Includes bibliographical references and index.
   1. Intercultural communication. 2. Interpersonal relations. 3. Language and culture.
   I. Spencer-Oatey, Helen, 1952–   II. Series.

   GN345.6.C86 2000
   303.48′2–dc21

                                                                99-049356

Typeset by BookEns, Royston, Herts.
Printed and bound in Great Britain by
Biddles Ltd, King's Lynn, Norfolk

Contents

Figures

Tables

Contributors

Karin Birkner has just completed her PhD and is currently working at the University of Freiburg.

Michael Harris Bond is Professor of Psychology, Chinese University of Hong Kong.

Nikolas Coupland is Professor and Director of the Cardiff Centre for Language and Communication Research.

Ellen Cray is an Assistant Professor, School of Linguistics and Applied Language Studies, Carleton University, Ottawa.

Li Dong is Associate Professor, Translation Institute of Beijing Foreign Studies University.

William B. Gudykunst is Professor of Speech Communication, California State University, Fullerton.

Susanne Günthner is Assistant Professor of Linguistics at the University of Konstanz.

Juliane House is Professor of Applied Linguistics and Head of the English and German Language Programmes, University of Hamburg.

Gabriele Kasper is Professor of Second Language Studies, University of Hawaii at Manoa.

Friederike Kern recently completed her PhD in Linguistics at the University of Hamburg.

Laura Miller is an Assistant Professor in the Department of Sociology and Anthropology, Loyola University of Chicago.

Patrick Ng is Lecturer in the Department of English, City University of Hong Kong.

Theodossia-Soula Pavlidou is Professor of Linguistics, Aristotle University of Thessaloniki.

Martha C. Pennington is Powdrill Professor of English Language Acquisition, University of Luton.

Helen Spencer-Oatey is Principal Research Fellow in Linguistics, University of Luton and is field manager of its degree courses in Intercultural Communication.

Noriko Tanaka teaches in the Faculty of Languages and Cultures and in the Graduate School of Applied Language Studies, Meikai University.

Jianyu Xing is a PhD student in the Department of Linguistics, University of Luton. **Virpi Ylänne-McEwen** is Lecturer at the Centre for Language and Communication, University of Wales, Cardiff.

Vladimir Žegarac is Senior Lecturer in Linguistics at the University of Luton.

Acknowledgements

I would like to thank the many people who have played a part in this book. My interest in the relationship between language and culture was stimulated by students, friends and even strangers in China who brought to my attention many differences between British and Chinese ways of speaking. Without them I would not have started down this road. When I began teaching the subject at the University of Luton, my students stimulated me to explore and re-think issues through their scepticism of existing 'politeness' frameworks and through their comments and questions. They were a tremendous help in developing and refining my ideas.

When the first draft of the book had been completed, members of the Intercultural Discourse Forum at the University of Luton read and discussed each chapter carefully and made very useful suggestions for improvements. They provided me with professional and personal support which was a great encouragement, and I would particularly like to thank John Twitchin and Vladimir Žegarac in this respect.

Finally, I would like to express a big 'thank you' to my husband, Andrew Spencer, for his tremendous support and encouragement throughout the project. He not only provided me with wonderful emotional support, but willingly spent extra time looking after our children and helped me with many tedious parts of the editing process. 'Thank you' to you all.

The publishers and authors wish to thank the following for permission to use copyright material: ABC News for an extract from *World News Tonight*, broadcast by NHK in Tokyo, 20 February 1992; Cambridge University Press for Figures 9.1 and 9.2 which were originally published in N. Coupland, J. Coupland, H. Giles and K. Henwood (1988), Accommodating the elderly: invoking and extending a theory. *Language in Society*, 17: 1–41; Elsevier Science for Tables 6.1, 6.4a and 6.4b which were originally published in T. Pavlidou (1994), Contrasting German–Greek politeness and the consequences *Journal of Pragmatics*, 21: 487–511; *The Guardian* for an extract from material written by Edward Pilkington and published on 15 August 1995; the *Journal of Asian Pacific Communication* for sections 3.2, 3.3, 3.3.1 and 3.3.3, originally published in M.H. Bond (1998), Managing culture in studies of communication: a futurescape. *Journal of Asian*

Pacific Communication 8(1): 31–49; and Sage Publications for Figure 14.1 from W.B. Gudykunst (1998), *Bridging Differences: Effective Intergroup Communication*, 3rd edition, Thousand Oaks: Sage, p. 51.

Transcription Conventions

Meaning	Symbol	Example
The Words Themselves		
Unintelligible text	(???)	(???) I mean natural
Guess at unclear text	(word?)	(leaves?) nothing to the imagination
False start	wo-word	idea is cl-very clear to me now
Omitted segment	word segment'word	es kommt nicht an d'Öffentlichkeit
Links between words or utterances		
Overlapping text	word [word] word	Doris: all men think this is [just great]
	[word] word	Andrea: [of course]
Latching, i.e. two	=	A: D'yuh like it =
Utterances run together with no pause		D: = (hhh) Yes I DO like it
Pausing		
Micropause	(.)	well (.) enjoy (.) hm (.) what do I enjoy
Brief pause	(-)	it (-) eh you can look at other
Pause of indicated length	(0.5)	when (0.2) when in a country
Words spoken differently from surrounding text	word ≪ symbol > word word >	
Loudly	≪ f > >	oh I see ≪ f > then from school >
Softly/very softly	≪ p > > / ≪ pp > >	≪ pp > not as bad as here >
Whispered	≪ wh > >	leaves nothing ≪ wh > to the imagination >
Faster	≪ all > >	and then ≪ all > they also asked me if I > could imagine that
Getting faster	≪ acc > >	because of the files ≪ acc > indeed I thought it's an interesting job >
Vocalizations		
Laugh particles	(hihi)	too (hihi) much?
Outbreaths	(hhh)	(hhh) yes I do like it
Inbreaths	(.hhh)	(.hhh) maybe
Inbreathed fricative	(.hss)	(.hss) is that so?

Prominence

Lengthened/very lengthened segment	wo:rd / wo::rd	it is re:ally cosy
Emphasized syllable/ word	NEver / NEVER	Yang: this is natural Andrea: this is not NATURAL

Intonation

Strongly rising tone	word?	this is from the traditional? or political?
Slightly rising tone	word,	however, if you say, eh they are not equal
Low rising tone	word'	I mean natural'
Slightly falling tone	word;	and come back again in the evening;
Slightly falling, final tone	word.	yes yes right.
Continuing tone	word_	did you ever, have (0.5) well any_
Relevant additional information	{descriptive comment}	{coughs} / {smacks lips}
English translation/ gloss	$English English$	A: *Gut?* $Good?$

(Based on the GAT system, Selting *et al.* 1998)

To my mother

1

Introduction: Language, Culture and Rapport Management

Helen Spencer-Oatey

One afternoon after work, a British teacher of EFL, who had recently started teaching at a college in Hong Kong, decided to visit some friends who lived in a different part of the city. She went to the appropriate bus stop, and as she walked up, a group of her students who were waiting there asked 'Where are you going?' Immediately she felt irritated, and thought to herself, 'What business is it of theirs where I'm going? Why should I tell them about my personal life?' However, she tried to hide her irritation, and simply answered, 'I'm going to visit some friends.'

Several months later this British teacher discovered that 'Where are you going?' is simply a greeting in Chinese. There is no expectation that it should be answered explicitly: a vague response such as 'Over there' or 'Into town' is perfectly adequate. Moreover, according to Chinese conventions, the students were being friendly and polite in giving such a greeting, not intrusive and disrespectful as the British teacher interpreted them to be.

This incident, which I personally experienced during my first overseas teaching post, highlights three features that are important foci of this book:

- people's use of language can influence interpersonal relations (the students' question irritated the teacher and she started to form a negative impression of them);
- people may try to 'manage' their relationships with others (the teacher did not want the students to know that she was irritated, and so she tried to hide her annoyance);
- different cultures may have different conventions as to what is appropriate behaviour in what contexts ('Where are you going?' is

a polite greeting among acquaintances in Chinese, but is an inappropriate explicit question in this context in English).

The main title of this book is *Culturally Speaking*, but, as the subtitle, *Managing Rapport through Talk across Cultures*, suggests, the 'speaking' component focuses on a specific aspect of communication: the management of social relations. People sometimes think of communication as 'the transmission of information' but, as many authors have pointed out, communication also involves 'the management of social relations'. Watzlawick *et al.* (1967), for example, propose that all language has a *content* component and a *relationship* component. If two people have a disagreement, for instance, there will be a *content* aspect to their disagreement, which concerns the *'what'* of the disagreement, such as disagreement over the accuracy of a piece of information, or the suitability of a course of action. However, there will also be a *relationship* aspect to their disagreement; for example, whether the expression of disagreement conveys lack of respect for the other person, whether it is interpreted as a bid for one-upmanship or whether it leads to feelings of resentment or dislike.

Similarly, Brown and Yule (1983) identify two main functions of language: the *transactional* (or information-transferring) function, and the *interactional* (or maintenance of social relationships) function. They suggest that discourse is either primarily transactional in focus, or primarily interactional in focus, and that the goals of these two main types of discourse are different. The goal of transactional language is to convey information coherently and accurately, whereas the goal of interactional speech is to communicate friendliness and good will, and to make the participants feel comfortable and unthreatened. Weather forecasts and academic lectures are typical examples of primarily transactional language, while greetings and small talk are typical examples of primarily interactional language.

One of the main areas of linguistic theory that is relevant to 'relational communication' is politeness theory. However, in this book the term 'politeness' is avoided as much as possible (except when discussing well-known theories of politeness) because the term is so confusing. 'Politeness' is often interpreted as referring to the use of relatively formal and deferential language, such as formal terms of address like *Sir* or *Madam*, request patterns such as *would you be so kind as to ...*, and formal expressions of gratitude and apology. From such a perspective, sentences such as *'Would you mind passing the salt'* would be classified as 'more polite' than *'Pass the salt, will you'*.

However, there are many occasions when it is more appropriate to use '*Pass the salt, will you*' than '*Would you mind passing the salt*' (at home, to a family member, for example). And as Fraser and Nolan (1981: 96) point out, politeness is actually a contextual judgement: 'no sentence is inherently polite or impolite. We often take certain expressions to be impolite, but it is not the expressions themselves but the conditions under which they are used that determine the judgement of politeness.' In other words, sentences or linguistic constructions are not *ipso facto* polite or rude; rather, politeness is a social judgement, and speakers are judged to be polite or rude, depending on what they say in what context. Politeness, in this sense, is a question of appropriateness.

A further limitation of the term 'politeness' is that it emphasizes the harmonious aspect of social relations, and in fact politeness theory has traditionally focused on this aspect. However, people sometimes attack rather than support their interlocutors and, as Turner (1996) and Culpepper (1996) both argue, 'politeness' theory needs to incorporate this component. Tracy (1990) and Penman (1990) maintain that politeness should be studied within the broader framework of facework. Tracy (1990), for example, suggests that people may want to make a variety of identity claims, apart from the claim to be pleasant and likeable (the one she maintains is most closely associated with politeness); for instance, they may want to be seen as competent, trustworthy, intimidating, strong, or reasonable. Tracy proposes, therefore, that politeness theory should be extended to incorporate these notions. However, this would take us into the fields of impression management and self-presentation, and would obviously include far more than the scope of traditional politeness theory: the maintenance and/or promotion of harmonious inter-personal relations. Although such issues certainly need addressing, they are not the focus of this book. This book concentrates on the management of interpersonal relations: the use of language to promote, maintain or threaten harmonious social relations. I suggest the term *rapport management* to refer to this area.

The second component of the title refers to 'culture'. Culture is notoriously difficult to define. In 1952, the American anthropologists, Kroeber and Kluckhohn, critically reviewed concepts and definitions of culture, and compiled a list of 164 different definitions. Apte (1994: 2001), writing in the ten-volume *Encyclopedia of Language and Linguistics*, summarizes the problem as follows: 'Despite a century of efforts to define culture adequately, there was in the early 1990s no agreement among anthropologists regarding its nature.' Despite these problems, I propose the following definition for the purposes of this book:

> Culture is a fuzzy set of attitudes, beliefs, behavioural conventions, and basic assumptions and values that are shared by a group of people, and that influence each member's behaviour and each member's interpretations of the 'meaning' of other people's behaviour.

This definition draws attention to a number of issues. Firstly, culture is manifested at different layers of depth, ranging from inner core basic assumptions and values, through outer core attitudes, beliefs and social conventions, to surface-level behavioural manifestations. Figure 1.1 is a diagrammatic representation of the different layers of culture. Secondly, the sub-surface aspects of culture influence people's behaviour and the meanings they attribute to other people's behaviour (along with other factors such as personality). Thirdly, culture is a 'fuzzy' concept, in that group members are unlikely to share identical sets of attitudes, beliefs and so on, but rather show 'family resemblances', with the result that there is no absolute set of features that can distinguish definitively one cultural group from another. Fourthly, culture is associated with social groups. All people are simultaneously members of a number of different groups and categories; for example, gender groups, ethnic groups, generational groups, national groups, professional groups, and so on. So in many respects, all these different groupings can be seen as different cultural groups. However, in this book, 'culture' is operationalized primarily in terms of ethnolinguistic and/or national or regional political identity; for example, authors analyse and compare the language and behaviour of Greeks, East and West Germans, Canadian English speakers, British English speakers, Hong Kong Chinese, Mainland Chinese, and so on. This is not to deny the cultural element in other types of groupings, nor is it meant to imply that members of these groups are a homogeneous set of people (see Chapters 3 and 9 for discussions of such issues). However, it would obviously be impossible to deal adequately in a single volume with all variables that are associated with different social groups, and so the book is deliberately limited in scope.

Throughout the book, the term 'cross-cultural' is used to refer to comparative data – in other words, data obtained independently from different cultural groups; the term 'intercultural' is used to refer to interactional data – in other words, data obtained when people from two different cultural groups interact with each other (see also note 2,

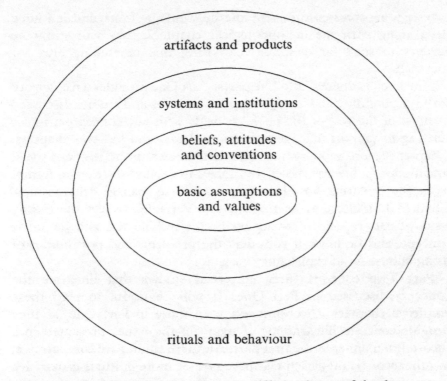

artifacts and products

systems and institutions

beliefs, attitudes
and conventions

basic assumptions
and values

rituals and behaviour

Figure 1.1 Manifestations of culture at differing layers of depth
Source: Adapted from G. Hofstede, *Cultures and Organizations*, New York:
McGraw-Hill, 1991, and F. Trompenaars and C. Hampden-Turner, *Riding the
Waves of Culture*, London: Nicholas Brealey, 1997

Chapter 14). All the chapters of the book revolve round the two main
themes discussed above, rapport management and culture, and
explore the interrelationship between the two.

There are three types of chapter in the book: theoretical chapters
which explore conceptual issues, empirical chapters which report
research results, and methodological chapters which discuss research
procedures. Some readers may find such a combination strange, and
feel that empirical studies belong more naturally in a different kind of
book. I believe it is very important, however, to include them here.
As Hall (1976) points out, 'Most cross-cultural exploration begins
with the annoyance of being lost', and so for readers who have little
experience of living or working with people from different cultural
backgrounds, theoretical discussion of cross-cultural and intercultural issues can be little more than a dry academic exercise. In-
depth studies of cross-cultural differences and intercultural encounters
can help reduce this problem. They also illustrate different ways of

investigating cross-cultural and intercultural questions, and so I hope that, along with the methodological chapters, they will stimulate readers to start (or continue) exploring this fascinating area for themselves.

The book is divided into five parts. Part One provides a framework for understanding and interpreting the theories and studies discussed in most of the rest of the book. It deals with key conceptual issues relating to rapport management and culture, and has two chapters. Chapter 2, on rapport management, draws primarily on social pragmatics, politeness theory and face theory, and develops a framework for exploring how language is used to manage relationships. Chapter 3, 'Culture as an Explanatory Variable', tackles the thorny issue of culture, and, drawing on both psychological and linguistic concepts and findings, it considers the problems and possibilities of using culture as an explanatory variable.

Part Two contains three empirical studies that illustrate the concepts discussed in Part One. It will be useful to read these empirical chapters in conjunction with those in Part One, as they provide concrete illustrations of many of the issues presented in a theoretical manner in the first part. All three studies are comparative; in other words, they each compare two or more cultural groups for selected pragmatic and/or discourse features. Chapter 4 compares the apologizing behaviour of native speakers of Japanese, British English and Canadian English, in terms of both the strategies used and the situations requiring an apology. It questions the widely-held stereotype that 'Japanese are always apologizing'. Chapter 5 explores how British, Mainland Chinese and Hong Kong Chinese evaluate different types of compliment responses. It discusses how people's reactions relate to culturally-dependent maxims for managing rapport, and questions a component of Leech's (1983) maxim of modesty. Chapter 6 moves beyond speech act analysis and examines the opening and closing sections of authentic Greek and German telephone conversations, comparing the preferences of the two groups for attending to the relationship aspect of communication.

Obviously these three studies can only touch on a very small proportion of different features and variables that affect rapport management, and they can only include a limited number of different languages and cultural groups. So Part Two also contains a reading list, suggesting other comparative empirical studies that could be of interest to readers.

By the end of Part Two, readers should have a clear understanding of key concepts and issues associated with rapport management, and should be aware of various types of differences between cultural groups in how they handle relationship issues. However, cross-cultural (i.e. comparative) studies do not tell us how people will necessarily behave or react when they take part in intercultural interactions. Such studies provide useful 'baseline' data but, in analysing intercultural encounters, we need theoretical clarification of the factors that influence people's performance. Part Three, therefore, returns to theoretical issues. Chapter 7 describes the processes involved in comprehending and producing discourse, and illustrates how misunderstandings can occur. It argues that con-trastive discourse studies (i.e. the kind of research presented in Part Two) are of paramount importance in accounting for intercultural misunderstandings. This issue is taken up in the next chapter. Taking a Relevance Theory perspective, Chapter 8 analyses in detail how people draw on pragmatic knowledge in the communication process, and why this can be problematic in intercultural encounters. Chapter 9 provides a very different theoretical perspective on intercultural discourse. Focusing on ways in which speakers can 'attune' their talk more or less to each other, the chapter describes the basic tenets of Communication Accommodation Theory, and describes how intercultural discourse can be explained from this perspective.

Part Four of the book returns once more to empirical studies. As with Part Two, the chapters here illustrate concepts and issues discussed in the theoretical chapters. They attempt to put flesh on the bones and to bring the issues to life. Chapter 10 analyses an authentic conversation between German and Chinese students who meet for the first time. It illustrates how different styles and beliefs about argumentation in initial encounters can negatively affect people's evaluations of an interaction. Chapter 11 analyses authentic conversations between Japanese and American members of staff of Japanese companies who work together in the same offices. The analysis focuses on negative assessments, such as disagreement or disapproval, and illustrates similarities and differences in the ways in which such matters are handled and interpreted by people from the two groups. Chapter 12 analyses the self-presentation techniques used by East and West German applicants in job interviews conducted by West German employers, and explores the effects these have on the interviewers' assessments. Chapter 13 analyses an authentic business visit to Britain by Chinese business people during a promotional visit to the UK. It focuses on the problems that occurred, and analyses them from a face theory perspective. As with

Part Two, Part Four contains a reading list of other studies that analyse authentic intercultural interactions and that may therefore be of interest to readers.

The final section, Part Five, discusses methodological issues, and is therefore applicable to all the other parts of the book. It aims to encourage and help readers to start (or continue) exploring the field for themselves. Chapter 14 explains some fundamental research design issues that need to be considered when planning and implementing cross-cultural research. Chapter 15 focuses on the collection of data in pragmatics research, describing the different procedures that can be used for collecting such data, and evaluating their relative strengths and weaknesses.

Each chapter of the book ends with points for discussion, so that the concepts and issues discussed in the chapter can be explored in greater depth if required. The book as a whole attempts to draw together and interrelate as many concepts as possible, especially through cross-referencing and the discussion questions. However, in this comparatively new field of intercultural communication, many issues require further development. More cross-cultural and intercultural data are needed, and theories and concepts need to be refined. This book does not attempt to resolve all the issues, but I hope it will stimulate further interest and research.

PART ONE

FUNDAMENTAL CONCEPTUAL ISSUES

2

Rapport Management: A Framework for Analysis

Helen Spencer-Oatey

2.1 Introduction

One morning, a British teacher of EFL and TEFL trainer was observing a reading class at a university in China. The teacher of the reading class was an experienced Chinese member of staff, and the students were all in-service teachers of English who had previously been taught by the British teacher. It was the Chinese teacher's first lesson with the class. During the course of the lesson, she asked the students in turn to read part of the passage aloud and to answer the questions she posed. If students tried to query her feedback to their answers, she avoided any discussion and simply moved on to the next student. The class became increasingly uncomfortable with this style of teaching, and eventually one student challenged the teacher, asking 'Why do we have to read the passage aloud? And why don't you discuss our queries? What you're doing is not at all useful for us!' Both the teacher and the students were shocked by the remarks, and the atmosphere was extremely strained for the rest of the lesson. During the following weeks and months, both the students and the British teacher failed to develop a harmonious relationship with this teacher, despite repeated efforts.

This incident illustrates the crucial importance of *face* in our interactions with people. The Chinese teacher felt she had lost face, not only in front of her students, but also in front of the 'foreigner' who was observing her. Her authority and teaching expertise had been challenged, in a society where such incidents are extremely rare in that context. The British teacher was 'blamed' for allowing such an incident to occur, and neither the British teacher nor the students were ever able to fully repair the relational damage that had been done.

Needless to say, words can have a dramatic effect, both positive and negative, on our relationships with people. As explained in Chapter 1, all language has a dual function: the transfer of information, and the management of social relations. This book focuses on the management of social relations, an aspect of language use that I call 'rapport management'. In this chapter, basic concepts and issues within the field of rapport management are explained, in order to provide a framework for the analysis of language use from this perspective. From a theoretical point of view, the material is based primarily on politeness theory and draws particular attention to the notion of face. However, I use the term 'rapport management' rather than 'face management' because the term 'face' seems to focus on concerns for self, whereas rapport management suggests more of a balance between self and other. The concern of rapport management is also broader: it examines the way that language is used to construct, maintain and/or threaten social relationships and, as explained below, includes the management of sociality rights as well as of face.

This chapter deals with the following issues:

- rapport management, including face needs and sociality rights;
- strategies for managing rapport;
- factors influencing strategy use (rapport orientation, contextual variables, pragmatic conventions);
- rapport management outcomes;
- rapport management across cultures.

2.2 The universal need for 'face'

Face is a concept that is intuitively meaningful to people, but one that is difficult to define precisely. It is concerned with people's sense of worth, dignity and identity, and is associated with issues such as respect, honour, status, reputation and competence (cf. Ting-Toomey and Kurogi 1998). As Lim (1994: 210) points out, the claim for face relates to positive social values: 'people do not claim face for what they think are negative'. Along with other theorists (e.g. Brown and Levinson 1987; Leech 1983), I believe face to be a universal phenomenon: everyone has the same fundamental face concerns. However, culture can affect the relative sensitivity of different aspects of people's face, as well as which strategies are most appropriate for managing face (cf. Ting-Toomey and Kurogi 1998; Gudykunst, writing here in Chapter 14).

Brown and Levinson (1987), in their seminal work on politeness, propose that face is the key motivating force for politeness, and they maintain that it consists of two related aspects, negative face and positive face. In their model, negative face is a person's want to be unimpeded by others, the desire to be free to act as she/he chooses and not be imposed upon; and positive face is a person's want to be appreciated and approved of by selected others, in terms of personality, desires, behaviour, values, and so on. In other words, negative face represents a desire for autonomy, and positive face represents a desire for approval.

Other linguists have challenged Brown and Levinson's (1987) conceptualization of face. For example, Matsumoto (1988), Ide (1989) and Mao (1994) all refer to the importance of 'social identity' as a concept in Japanese and Chinese society. Matsumoto (1988: 405), for instance, argues as follows:

> What is of paramount concern to a Japanese is not his/her own territory, but the position in relation to the others in the group and his/her acceptance by those others. Loss of face is associated with the perception by others that one has not comprehended and acknowledged the structure and hierarchy of the group ... A Japanese generally must understand where s/he stands in relation to other members of the group or society, and must acknowledge his/her dependence on the others. Acknowledgement and main-tenance of the relative position of others, rather than preservation of an individual's proper territory, governs all social interaction.

In other words, Matsumoto's (1988) criticisms of Brown and Levinson (1987) are twofold: that they have ignored the interpersonal or social perspective on face, and that they have overemphasized the notion of individual freedom and autonomy. As Gu (1998) points out, it is not that concerns about autonomy, imposition, and so on do not exist in Eastern cultures, but rather that they are not regarded as face concerns.

Taking these arguments into consideration, I propose a modified framework for conceptualizing face and rapport. I maintain that Brown and Levinson's (1987) conceptualization of positive face has been underspecified, and that the concerns they identify as negative face issues are not necessarily face concerns at all. I propose instead that rapport management (the management of harmony–disharmony among people) involves two main components: the management of face and the management of sociality rights. Face management, as the term indicates, involves the management of face needs and, following Goffman (1972: 5), I define face as 'the positive social *value* a person effectively claims for himself [sic] by the line others assume he has taken during a particular contact' (my emphasis). The management of sociality rights, on the other hand, involves the management of social expectancies, which I define as 'fundamental personal/social *entitlements* that individuals effectively claim for themselves in their interactions with others'. In other words, face is associated with personal/social value, and is concerned with people's sense of worth, dignity, honour, reputation, competence and so on. Sociality rights, on the other hand, are concerned with personal/social expectancies, and reflect people's concerns over fairness, consideration, social inclusion/exclusion and so on.

I suggest that face has the following two interrelated aspects:

(1) *Quality face*: we have a fundamental desire for people to evaluate us positively in terms of our personal qualities, e.g. our competence, abilities, appearance etc. Quality face is concerned with the value that we effectively claim for ourselves in terms of such personal qualities as these, and so is closely associated with our sense of personal self-esteem.

(2) *Identity face*: we have a fundamental desire for people to acknowledge and uphold our social identities or roles, e.g. as group leader, valued customer, close friend. Identity face is concerned with the value that we effectively claim for ourselves in terms of social or group roles, and is closely associated with our sense of public worth. (See Chapter 13 for a more detailed discussion of identity face.)

Similarly, I suggest that sociality rights have two interrelated aspects:

(3) *Equity rights*: we have a fundamental belief that we are entitled to personal consideration from others, so that we are treated fairly: that we are not unduly imposed upon, that we are not unfairly ordered about, and that we are not taken advantage of or exploited. There seem to be two components to this equity entitlement: the notion of *cost–benefit* (the extent to which we are exploited or disadvantaged, and the belief that costs and benefits should be kept roughly in balance through the principle of reciprocity), and the related issue of *autonomy–imposition* (the extent to which people control us or impose on us).

(4) *Association rights*: we have a fundamental belief that we are entitled to an association with others that is in keeping with the type of relationship that we have with them. These association

rights relate partly to *interactional association–dissociation* (the type and extent of our involvement with others), so that we feel, for example, that we are entitled to an appropriate amount of conversational interaction and social chit-chat with others (e.g. not ignored on the one hand, but not overwhelmed on the other). They also relate to *affective association–dissociation* (the extent to which we share concerns, feelings and interests). Naturally, what counts as 'an appropriate amount' depends on the nature of the relationship, as well as sociocultural norms and personal preferences.

As can be seen, the management of both face and sociality rights has a personal component (quality face and equity rights, respectively), and a social component (identity face and association rights, respectively). The framework thus differs from Brown and Levinson's (1987) model of politeness in two main ways. Firstly, unlike Brown and Levinson's model, which is primarily a personal or individual conceptualization of face, it incorporates a social or interdependent perspective to the management of relations (cf. Morisaki and Gudykunst 1994; see also Chapters 13 and 14). Secondly, it draws a distinction between face needs (where our sense of personal/social *value* is at stake), and sociality rights (where our sense of personal/social *entitlements* is at stake). Thus in this model Brown and Levinson's (1987) concept of 'negative face' is not treated as a face need but rather as a sociality right. This is shown diagrammatically in Table 2.1. As I discuss in section 2.9, different cultures may place different emphases on these various components of rapport management. Firstly, there may be differing sensitivities to the varying components, so that more rapport management work is necessary for certain aspects than for others. Secondly, there may be different ways of addressing or orienting towards these different

Table 2.1 Components of rapport management

	face management (personal/social value)	sociality rights management (personal/social entitlements)
personal/independent perspective	quality face (cf. Brown and Levinson's positive face)	equity rights (cf. Brown and Levinson's negative face)
social/interdependent perspective	identity face	association rights

sensitivities; some cultures may prefer one type of strategy to mitigate a potential threat to rapport, whereas other cultures may prefer another type of strategy. These differences are taken up again towards the end of this chapter.

2.3 Rapport-threatening behaviour: managing face and sociality rights

As the popular phrase 'lose face' conveys, we do not always receive the respect from others that we would like. People may criticize us or boss us around, insult us and call us names; and when they do, we typically feel embarrassed or uncomfortable. Brown and Levinson (1987), in their politeness model, propose the notion of *face-threatening acts* to explain this phenomenon. They claim that certain communicative acts inherently threaten the face needs of the interlocutors, and that these illocutionary acts can be called *face-threatening acts* (FTAs). How then does this concept of face-threatening acts apply to the framework outlined above?

I suggest that rapport (harmony) between people can be threatened in two main ways: through face-threatening behaviour and through rights-threatening behaviour. When people threaten our rights, they infringe our sense of personal/social entitlements; for example, if someone tries to force us to do something, but we feel they have no right to expect us to do this, they threaten our equity rights. Similarly, if someone speaks to us in a way that is too personal for our liking, we may feel that person has threatened our (dis)association rights. The result is that we feel offended, uncomfortable, annoyed or angry; however, we do not necessarily feel a loss of face. Sometimes, though, people's treatment of us may not simply irritate or annoy us; it may go a step further and make us feel as though we have lost credibility or have been personally devalued in some way. When this happens we talk of 'losing face'. This can happen when people criticize us or oppose us, or make us 'look small' in some way.

To clarify some of these concepts, let us think back to the incident described at the beginning of this chapter. When the student said to the teacher, in front of all the other students, 'Why do we have to read the passage aloud? And why don't you discuss our queries? What you're doing is not at all useful for us!', these comments were very threatening to the teacher's quality face. They challenged her sense of competence as a teacher, making her doubt her ability to teach well, and thus making her lose quality face. At the same time, the fact that the student challenged her at all, and especially in public, can also be seen (in the Chinese context) as a threat to her identity face. The comments threatened her authority as a teacher, and her superior position to the students. The student did not give her the deference she expected, especially in a public context, and in this sense threatened her identity face. In other words, this incident was clearly face-threatening. However, a more minor incident might not have threatened face, but rather just have infringed sociality rights. For example, if the teacher had asked two students to go and get her something, the students could have felt imposed upon, and thus felt that their equity rights had been threatened (for instance, because they felt that it would take up too much of their time, would cause them to miss class, and so on). However, they would probably not have found the request face-threatening; it would probably have been irritating rather than degrading to them. In fact, they might even have found it face-enhancing if they felt honoured to be chosen by the teacher. (See the discussion below on orders/requests.)

Brown and Levinson (1987) discuss FTAs primarily in relation to speech acts, such as requests, offers, compliments, criticism, and so on, so let us first consider how a selection of common speech acts can be viewed from a rapport management perspective.

(1) *Orders and requests* can easily threaten rapport, because they can affect our autonomy, freedom of choice, and freedom from imposition, and thus threaten our sense of equity rights (our entitlement to considerate treatment). They need to be worded, therefore, in such a way that we feel our rights to fair treatment have been adequately addressed, otherwise they may make us feel irritated or annoyed. However, orders/requests are not necessarily face-threatening: they *may* be face-threatening, but need not always be. For example, if we are ordered to do something menial that we feel is 'below us', and we feel devalued in some way, then we may perceive the order to be threatening to our identity face. On the other hand, on a different occasion, we may feel pleased or even honoured if someone asks us for help, feeling that it shows trust in our abilities and/or acceptance as a close friend. In this case, the request can 'give' us face (quality face if it relates to our sense of ability, and identity face if it relates to our relationship with the person). At other times, though, when people ask us to do something, we simply feel inconvenienced or imposed upon, but do not feel we have lost credibility or been devalued. In this case, the request has simply infringed our sense of equity rights.

In other words, orders and requests are rapport-sensitive speech acts, and thus need to be managed appropriately. However, whether they are perceived to be threatening/enhancing of face or infringing/supporting of sociality rights (or a combination of these), depends on a range of circumstantial and personal factors.

(2) *Apologies* are typically post-event speech acts, in the sense that some kind of offence or violation of social norms has taken place. In other words, people's sociality rights have been infringed in some way (e.g. if they have been kept waiting for an hour, their equity rights have been infringed through the 'cost' of wasting their time; or if they have been excluded from a conversation because of others using a language they do not know or because of their choice of an unfamiliar topic, their association rights have been infringed), and there is a need to restore the 'balance' through giving an apology. If the offence is minor, the apology will be routine and is unlikely to be face-threatening to the person apologizing. However, if the offence is more substantial, the act of apologizing can be very face-threatening to the apologizer: it can threaten his/her quality face (sense of personal competence), and if the apology is very public, it can also threaten his/her identity face (sense of standing among others). On the other hand, if no apology is forthcoming, this can be rapport-threatening to the offended person. It can aggravate his/her sense of equity rights, because no (verbal) repair has been made for the infringement that occurred through the offence. And if the offended person feels that s/he has been treated with too much contempt, this can also result in a sense of face loss.

(3) *Compliments* are typically face-enhancing speech acts, in that they are usually intended to have a positive effect on interpersonal relations. Personal compliments typically enhance people's quality face. They can also boost identity face, if they are perceived as enhancing the complimentee's position or role within a group. On the other hand, if the receiver feels that a compliment is too personal, and reflects a more intimate relationship with the complimenter than s/he feels comfortable with, the compliment can have a different effect: it can threaten the receiver's sense of association rights. In this case, the overall effect of the compliment could be rapport-threatening, because the person being complimented might be annoyed at the unwarranted level of assumed intimacy, and hence feel that his/her association rights (entitlements regarding appropriate degree of affective involvement–detachment) have been infringed.

These examples illustrate (but not exhaustively) how complex it is to manage rapport effectively. Rapport threat and rapport enhancement are subjective evaluations, which depend not simply on the content of the message, but on people's interpretations and reactions to who says what under what circumstances.

To complicate matters further, rapport management is not only a matter of handling selected speech acts appropriately. Brown and Levinson's (1987) conceptualization of FTAs could be interpreted as implying that certain communicative acts intrinsically threaten face whereas others do not. So Matsumoto (1989: 219) argues in relation to Japanese that *all* use of language is potentially face-threatening:

> Since any Japanese utterance conveys information about the social context, there is always the possibility that the speaker may, by the choice of an inappropriate form, offend the audience and thus embarrass him/herself. In this sense, any utterance, even a simple declarative, could be face-threatening.

Perhaps a more balanced way of considering this is to say that all use of language (in other words, not only the performance of certain speech acts, but other aspects too) can affect people's interpretations of how appropriately face and sociality rights are managed, and can thereby affect rapport. Tsuruta (1998) takes Matsumoto's argument a step further by suggesting that Brown and Levinson (1987) and Matsumoto (1989) are each discussing different 'domains' of politeness. She argues that Brown and Levinson's model deals primarily with 'illocutionary politeness', whereas Matsumoto's discussion of Japanese honorifics deals primarily with 'stylistic politeness'. Research by Spencer-Oatey and Xing (1998 and Chapter 13 of this book) supports this notion of domains of politeness. Analysis of authentic interactions between British and Chinese business people suggests that the following interrelated domains all play important roles in the management of rapport:

(1) *Illocutionary domain.* This is the domain that Brown and Levinson (1987) deal primarily with. It concerns the rapport-threatening/rapport-enhancing implications of performing speech acts, such as apologies, requests, compliments, and so on. Speech acts such as these need to be handled appropriately if harmonious relations are to be created and/or maintained.

(2) *Discourse domain.* This domain concerns the discourse content and discourse structure of an interchange. It includes issues such as topic choice and topic management (for example, the

inclusion/exclusion of personal topics), and the organization and sequencing of information. These issues need to be handled appropriately if harmonious relations are to be created and/or maintained, because the raising of sensitive topics, for example, can be rapport-threatening, as can frequent, sudden changes of topic.

(3) *Participation domain*. This domain concerns the procedural aspects of an interchange, such as turn-taking (overlaps and inter-turn pauses, turn-taking rights and obligations), the inclusion/exclusion of people present, and the use/non-use of listener responses (verbal and non-verbal). These procedural aspects need to be handled appropriately if harmonious relations are to be created and/or maintained.

(4) *Stylistic domain*. This domain concerns the stylistic aspects of an interchange, such as choice of tone (for example, serious or joking), choice of genre-appropriate lexis and syntax, and choice of genre-appropriate terms of address or use of honorifics. These stylistic aspects need to be handled appropriately if harmonious relations are to be created and/or maintained.

(5) *Non-verbal domain*. This domain concerns the non-verbal aspects of an interchange, such as gestures and other body movements, eye contact, and proxemics. These non-verbal aspects also need to be handled appropriately if harmonious relations are to be created and/or maintained.

Clearly, as Brown and Levinson (1987) point out, the illocutionary force of many speech acts is inherently threatening to rapport. However, as Spencer-Oatey and Xing (1998 and Chapter 13 of this book) illustrate, the appropriate management of other domains also plays a vital role.

2.4 Rapport-management strategies

As explained in section 2.3, losing face is a painful experience and for this reason Brown and Levinson (1987) suggest that it is generally in every participant's best interest to maintain each other's face. Every language, therefore, provides a very wide range of linguistic options that can be used for managing face and sociality rights, and hence for managing rapport. Naturally, the exact range of options, and their social significance, varies from language to language. However, in all languages, every level of language can play a role in each of the rapport management domains. For example, in the illocutionary domain, the following (to name just a few) can each have highly significant effects on interpersonal relations: choice of intonation and tone of voice, choice of lexis, choice of morphology and syntax, choice of terms of address and honorifics. And within the participation and stylistic domains, choice of code and/or dialect, speed of speech, choice of lexis, choice of syntax, and so on, can also each have major effects on interpersonal relations. This section describes some of the main strategies that have been identified so far.

2.4.1 Illocutionary domain: speech act strategies

Up to now, a very large proportion of work on politeness, and hence rapport management, has focused on the illocutionary domain. As a result, considerable attention has been paid to the wording of speech acts, and three important types of features have been analysed in a wide range of studies: the selection of speech act components, the degree of directness/indirectness, and the type and amount of upgraders/downgraders. Let us consider the following examples:

(a) *Do you mind if I ask you a big favour? I know you don't like lending your car, but I was wondering if I could possibly borrow it just for an hour or so on Tuesday afternoon, if you're not using it then. I need to take my mother to the hospital and it's difficult getting there by bus.*
(b) *Thanks ever so much for lending me your car. It was really extremely kind of you, and I very much appreciate it. If I can ever help you out like that, be sure and let me know.*

One way of analysing speech act utterances like these is to examine their main semantic components. Speech acts typically have a range of semantic formulae or components associated with them (often known as 'speech act sets' (Olshtain and Cohen 1983)). Naturally, exactly what these components are varies from one speech act to another. Normally, there is a head act, which conveys the main illocutionary force of the set of utterances; and before or after the head act (or both), there may be additional components (these additional components are often not essential, though). Analysing the above examples in this way provides us with the following descriptions:

Request

Do you mind if I ask you a big favour?	Mitigating supportive move (preparator)

I know you don't like lending your car,	Mitigating supportive move (disarmer)
but I was wondering if I could possibly borrow it just for an hour or so on Tuesday afternoon,	Head act
if you're not using it then.	Mitigating supportive move (imposition downgrader)
I need to take my mother to the hospital and it's difficult getting there by bus.	Mitigating supportive move (grounder)

Expression of gratitude

Thanks ever so much for lending me your car.	Head act
It was really extremely kind of you, and I very much appreciate it.	Complimenting of other person / Expression of appreciation
If I can ever help you out like that, be sure and let me know.	Promise of repayment/ reciprocation

Table 2.2 lists the main semantic components of five common speech acts. Speakers normally select one or more of these speech act formulae in order to reflect their rapport orientation (see section 2.5) in a given situation. However, cultures may differ in both the frequency of use of a given formula in a given situation, and also in the rapport-management value associated with the use or omission of a given formula in a given situation. So in cross-cultural speech act studies, it is common to compare different groups for the use of the different semantic components. Chapters 4 and 5 illustrate this approach.

Another way of analysing speech acts, especially ones such as requests and disagreements, is in terms of directness/indirectness. If we want someone to do the washing up, for example, we can choose from a range of options such as the following:

- Wash the dishes!
- I want you to wash the dishes.
- How about washing the dishes?
- Can you wash the dishes?
- What a lot of dishes there are!

All of these utterances differ in the degree of directness with which the illocutionary force of requesting is conveyed, and choosing one form rather than another can have a major impact on social relations. For reference purposes, Table 2.3 shows the range of direct and

Table 2.2 Semantic components of five common speech acts

Requests (based on Blum-Kulka *et. al.* 1989; list is non-exhaustive)

1. Head act, which can be modified
2. Alerter, e.g. *Excuse me* ...; *Mary* ...
3. Mitigating supportive move
    3.1 Preparator, e.g. *I'd like to ask you something,* ...
    3.2 Getting a precommitment, e.g. *Could you do me a favour?*
    3.3 Grounder, e.g. *Judith, I missed class yesterday. Could I borrow your notes?*
    3.4 Disarmer, e.g. *I know you don't like to lend out your notes, but could* ...
    3.5 Promise of reward, e.g. *Could you give me a lift home? I'll give you something for the petrol.*
    3.6 Imposition downgrader, e.g. *Could you lend me that book, if you're not using it at present?*
4. Aggravating supportive move
    4.1 Insult, e.g. *You've always been a dirty pig, so clear up!*
    4.2 Threat, e.g. *Move that car if you don't want a ticket!*
    4.3 Moralizing, e.g. *If one shares a flat one should be prepared to pull one's weight in cleaning it, so get on with the washing up!*

Refusals of invitations (based on Kinjo 1987)

1. Explicit refusal, e.g. *I can't make it..*
2. Expression of appreciation, e.g. *Thanks for the invitation.*
3. Excuse or explanation, e.g. *I'm busy.*
4. Expression of regret, e.g. *I'm sorry.*
5. Expression of positive feelings or wishes, e.g. *It sounds like fun/I wish I could make it.*
6. A conditional, e.g. *If you had told me earlier, I could have gone with you.*
7. Offer of an alternative, e.g. *How about Sunday?*
8. Request for further information, e.g. *Who'll be there?*
9. Repetition, e.g. *Dinner on Sunday. Well, thanks very much, but* ...

Apologies (based on Blum-Kulka *et al.* 1989)

1. Illocutionary Force Indicating Device (IFID),* e.g. *I'm sorry.*
2. Taking on responsibility, e.g. *I'm sorry, my mistake!*
3. Explanation or account, e.g. *I'm sorry I missed the meeting. I was off sick.*
4. Offer of repair, e.g. *I'm very sorry. I'll buy you another one.*
5. Promise of forbearance, e.g. *I'm so sorry. I promise you it won't happen again.*

Gratitude (based on Eisenstein and Bodman 1986)

1. IFID,* e.g. *Thank you.*
2. Complimenting of other person, action or object, e.g. *Thanks a lot. That was great.*

Table 2.2 cont'd

---

3. Expression of surprise or delight, e.g. *Oh wow. Thank you so much.*
4. Expression of appreciation, e.g. *Thanks, I really appreciate it.*
5. Promise of repayment or reciprocation, e.g. *Thanks, I'll give it back to you on Monday.*
6. Expression of lack of necessity or obligation, e.g. *It's lovely, but you didn't have to get me anything.*
7. Reassurance, e.g. *Just what I wanted.*

Disagreement (based on Beebe and Takahashi 1989a)

1. Explicit disagreement, e.g. *I'm afraid I don't agree.*
2. Criticism or negative evaluation, e.g. *That's not practical.*
3. Question, e.g. *Do you think that would work smoothly?*
4. Alternative suggestion, e.g. *How about trying ...?*
5. Gratitude, e.g. *Thanks very much for your suggestion, ...*
6. Positive remark, e.g. *You've obviously put a lot of work into this, ...*
7. Token agreement, e.g. *I agree with you, but ...*

---

* 'IFIDs [Illocutionary Force Indicating Devices] are formulaic, routinized expressions in which the speaker's apology [gratitude] is made explicit.' Blum-Kulka *et al.* 1989: 290.

indirect strategies identified by Blum-Kulka *et al.* (1989) for conveying requests.

Needless to say, as with speech act components, cultures may differ in both the frequency of use of given levels of directness in given situations, and also in the rapport-management value associated with the level of directness chosen for a given situation. In Greek (Sifianou 1992a) and Chinese, for example, direct strategies (mood derivable utterances) are used more frequently than in English, and are often used in situations where a conventionally indirect form would be likely in English. However, such utterances are not usually interpreted as 'rude' in Greek and Chinese, because they are normally softened with particles, affixes and/or tone of voice.

A third way of analysing speech acts is in terms of upgraders/ downgraders or, as they are also called, boosters/hedges or intensifiers/downtoners. Upgraders increase the force of the speech act, whereas downgraders reduce or weaken the force. For speech acts such as requests and disagreements, downgraders have a mitigating effect; in other words, they function to reduce any negative impact associated with the speech act. Upgraders have the opposite effect, and usually function to strengthen the negative

Table 2.3 Strategy types for making requests, on a scale of directness/indirectness

Direct strategies

1. **Mood derivable**: utterances in which the grammatical mood of the verb signals illocutionary force, e.g. *Leave me alone/Clean up that mess.*
2. **Performatives**: utterances in which the illocutionary force is explicitly named, e.g. *I'm asking you to clean up the mess.*
3. **Hedged performatives**: utterances in which the naming of the illocutionary force is modified by hedging expressions, e.g. *I would like to ask you to give your presentation a week earlier than scheduled.*
4. **Obligation statements**: utterances which state the obligation of the hearer to carry out the act, e.g. *You'll have to move that car.*
5. **Want statements**: utterances which state the speaker's desire that the hearer carries out the act, e.g. *I really wish you'd stop bothering me.*

Conventionally indirect strategies

6. **Suggestory formulae**: utterances which contain a suggestion to do something, e.g. *How about cleaning up?*
7. **Query preparatory**: utterances containing reference to preparatory conditions (e.g. ability, willingness) as conventionalized in any specific language, e.g. *Could you clear up the kitchen, please?/ Would you mind moving your car?*

Non-conventionally indirect strategies

8. **Strong hints**: utterances containing partial reference to object or elements needed for the implementation of the act, e.g. *You have left the kitchen in a right mess.*
9. **Mild hints**: utterances that make no reference to the request proper (or any of its elements) but are interpretable as requests by context, e.g. *I am a nun* in response to a persistent hassler.

Source: Blum-Kulka *et al.* 1989: 18

impact of the speech act. On the other hand, for speech acts such as apologies, expressions of gratitude, and compliments, the reverse is the case. Upgraders strengthen the positive impact associated with the speech act, and downgraders weaken it. In other words, whether the use of upgraders improves or worsens social relations depends on the speech act concerned. For reference purposes, Table 2.4 lists some common upgraders and downgraders associated with requests and apologies.

Table 2.4 Types of downgrader/upgraders commonly associated with requests and apologies

Downgraders/upgraders for requests (selected examples)	Downgraders/upgraders for apologies (selected examples)
Can you tidy up your desk?	*I'm sorry.*
Syntactic downgraders	**Downgraders**
Negation of preparatory condition, e.g. *You couldn't tidy up your desk, could you?*	Query precondition, e.g. *Are you sure we were supposed to meet at 10?*
Aspect, e.g. *I'm wondering if you could tidy up your desk?*	Act innocent, e.g. *Am I late?*
Tense, e.g. *I was wondering if you could tidy up your desk?*	Future/task-oriented remark, e.g. *Let's get to work then.*
	Appeaser, e.g. *Let me get you a cup of tea.*
Lexical and phrasal downgraders	**Upgraders**
Politeness marker, e.g. *Can you tidy up your desk, please?*	Intensifying adverbial, e.g. *I'm terribly sorry!*
Understater, e.g. *Can you tidy up your desk a bit?*	Emotional expression, e.g. *Oh no.*
Hedge, e.g. *Can you sort of tidy up your desk?*	Expressions marked for register, e.g. *I do apologize …*
Subjectivizer, e.g. *I wonder if you could tidy up your desk/I'm afraid you're going to have to tidy up …*	Double intensifier or repetition, e.g. *I'm really dreadfully sorry/I'm very very sorry/I'm sorry, please forgive me.*
Downtoner, e.g. *Could you possibly tidy up your desk?*	Concern for hearer, e.g. *I hope you weren't worried about me.*
Cajoler, e.g. *You know, you really need to tidy up …*	
Appealer, e.g. *Tidy up your desk, will you?*	
Upgraders	
Intensifier, e.g. *Your desk is in a terrible mess.*	
Expletive, e.g. *Tidy up your bloody desk!*	
Time intensifier, e.g. *Tidy up your desk right now!*	

Source: Derived from Blum-Kulka *et al.* 1989: Appendix

If we return to the request and apology examples given near the beginning of this section, the role of the upgraders and downgraders can be seen more clearly. The request in the example is a major one, so the head act contains four different types of downgraders in an attempt to reduce the negative impact of the request on the other person. Similarly, the expression of gratitude relates to a major act of helping, and the utterances contain three different upgraders. Analysing them in terms of downgraders/upgraders gives the following descriptions:

Request

I was wondering	Syntactic downgrader (tense and aspect)
if I could possibly borrow it	Lexical and phrasal downgrader (downtoner)
just for an hour or so on Tuesday afternoon.	Lexical and phrasal downgrader (understater)

Expression of gratitude

Thanks ever so much for lending me your car.	Upgrader (intensifying adverbial)
It was really extremely kind of you,	Upgrader (double intensifier)
and I very much appreciate it.	Upgrader (intensifying adverbial)

Needless to say, the range and precise forms of upgraders/downgraders available in one language differ from those available in another language. And as with the other choices of wording, cultures probably vary in both the frequency of use of upgraders/downgraders in given situations, and also in the rapport-management value associated with their use in these contexts. Furthermore, there may be differences in the ways in which the three types of wording choices[1] (selection of semantic components, degree of directness/indirectness, and use of upgraders/downgraders) interact with each other, and in the rapport-management value of these combined choices. More research is needed on these combinations of choices.

2.4.2 Other rapport-management domains

Research into the strategies used in other rapport-management domains has been less systematic, although individual researchers have explored certain components. For example, within the discourse domain, Pavlidou (1994; and Chapter 6 in this book) has investigated phatic talk in the opening and closing sections of telephone conversations. She reports that Greek speakers use a greater amount of phatic talk than Germans do, and that in German–Greek telephone conversations, this can lead to negative evaluations of the other speaker. Within the participation domain, Wieland (1991), for example, has examined turn-taking in French and American dinner conversations. She focused particularly on overlaps, and counted the frequencies with which each interlocutor attempted to take a turn without waiting for the other speaker to finish. She found that French speakers overlapped much more frequently than American speakers did, and that this had a significant effect on participants' evaluations of each other.

Spencer-Oatey and Xing (1998; and Chapter 13 in this book) are currently investigating all five rapport management domains in their analysis of Chinese–British business discourse and, within each domain, they are seeking to identify strategies that are used to manage rapport.

2.4.3 Superstrategies and dimensions of communicative style

All of the linguistic strategies discussed so far are relatively specific, and do not easily enable us to form an overall impression of someone's communicative style. Are there, therefore, some more general superstrategies, or are there dimensions of communicative style along which people (and cultural groups) can vary?

Brown and Levinson (1987) identify four superstrategies for managing face (primarily within the illocutionary domain):

- bald, without redress (clear, unambiguous and concise speech);
- positive politeness (speech which is 'approach-based' and treats the hearer as an in-group member);
- negative politeness (speech which is 'avoidance-based' and respects the hearer's desire for freedom and autonomy);
- off-record (indirect and comparatively ambiguous speech).

Communication Accommodation Theory also suggests four global strategies: approximation, interpretability, discourse management and interpersonal control (see Chapter 9). However, these are very different in type from Brown and Levinson's super-strategies, and seem to correspond more closely to domains of rapport management.

Gudykunst and his colleagues (1996) developed a self-report questionnaire to try and identify universal dimensions of communi-cative style. The questionnaire comprised 158 items measuring many different aspects of communicative style, such as precise versus ambiguous communication, direct versus indirect communication, and communication based on true intentions versus adjusting communication to maintain harmony. A factor analysis revealed eight factors of speech style: ability to infer, indirectness/ambiguity, interpersonal sensitivity, use of dramatic language, affect orientation, openness, precision, and silence. In Chapter 7, House identifies five different dimensions of communicative style on the basis of contrastive analyses of German and English data.

As Bond (1998: 41) points out, researchers have left us with 'a cornucopia of ways in which the speech communication of various cultural groups may differ'. He argues for a synthesis of 'the cultural Babel of speech forms', and this would certainly be a welcome step forward.

2.5 Factors influencing strategy use: (1) rapport orientation

One key factor that influences people's strategy use is their rapport orientation. It is useful first to distinguish between two fundamental orientations: support of one's own face needs and sociality rights, and support of the other person's. Brown and Levinson maintain that it is generally 'in every participant's best interest to maintain each others' [*sic*] face' (1987: 61), because of the mutual vulnerability of face: if person A attacks person B's face, then person B is likely to attack person A's face in return, and the result will be an uncomfortable loss of face for both. So as Ting-Toomey and Cocroft (1994: 323) suggest, a third orientation may be usefully added: mutual support.

Although people may often try to take a 'mutual support' orientation, there are nevertheless occasions when people do attack other people's face. So as Turner (1996) and Culpepper (1996) both argue, 'politeness' theory needs to incorporate this notion.

I suggest, therefore, that speakers can hold any of the following four types of rapport orientation:

1. Rapport-enhancement orientation: a desire to strengthen or enhance harmonious relations between the interlocutors;
2. Rapport-maintenance orientation: a desire to maintain or protect harmonious relations between the interlocutors;
3. Rapport-neglect orientation: a lack of concern or interest in the quality of relations between the interlocutors (perhaps because of a focus on self);

4. Rapport-challenge orientation: a desire to challenge or impair harmonious relations between the interlocutors.[2]

When people hold a rapport-enhancement orientation, they want to enhance the harmony of the relationship. Their motives for holding such an orientation could be various: for example, to start an incipient romantic relationship; to win a lucrative business contract; to show genuine friendliness to someone who is lonely; and so on. But whatever people's motives, their desire is for positive change: to improve the rapport between them. The appropriate 'giving of face' is an important way of doing this.

When people hold a rapport-maintenance orientation, on the other hand, their desire is not so much for change as for preservation. In other words, people simply want to maintain the current quality of relationship and level of rapport. This orientation is often reflected in the choice of appropriate terms of address, honorifics, social indexing markers, and other relevant aspects of register. However, this orientation also relates to the appropriate handling of face-threatening acts. As discussed in section 2.3, Brown and Levinson argue that 'certain kinds of acts intrinsically threaten face, namely those acts that by their nature run contrary to the face wants of the addressee and/or of the speaker' (1987: 65). Examples of such acts are orders, criticisms, complaints, disagreements and threats. When people hold a rapport-maintenance orientation, their aim is to minimize the negative impact of such acts on the hearer by selecting appropriate rapport-management strategies.

When people hold a rapport-neglect orientation, they have little concern for the quality of the relationship between the other speaker(s) and themselves. This may be because their attention is fully focused on task matters (for example, when dealing with an emergency or when trying to convey accurate information); it may be because they genuinely do not care about the relationship for some reason; or it may be because they are more concerned about maintaining their own face than maintaining interpersonal rapport. For example, when a speech act is more face-threatening to the speaker than to the hearer (e.g. an apology), and when the speaker is more concerned about maintaining his/her own face than maintaining or restoring rapport, the speaker's orientation will count as rapport-neglect. (What the effect will be on the hearer is another matter, as we consider in section 2.8.)

When people hold a rapport-challenge orientation, they want to challenge or impair the harmony of the relationship. Once again, people's motives for holding such an orientation could be various: for example, to assert personal independence; to rebuff a romantic advance; to repay a previous offence; and so on. But whatever people's motives, their desire is for negative change: to worsen the rapport between them. Deliberately causing people to lose face is one way of doing this.

Needless to say, people's rapport orientations are not available for open inspection. Unless people talk about them explicitly, they can only be inferred from their choice of rapport-management strategies. Even so, it may still be difficult to distinguish clearly one orientation from another. Nevertheless, the notion of interpersonal intent is an important issue in real-life interaction, and for that reason, I believe it needs to be included in any description of relational management.

Another perspective on rapport orientation is provided by accommodation theory. Accommodation theory proposes that speakers adopt different sociopsychological orientations vis-à-vis their interlocutors, depending on a range of background factors. The theory suggests two main types of orientation:

(1) convergent orientation versus divergent orientation: speakers with a convergent orientation aim to adapt their communicative behaviours to those of the other speaker(s), whereas speakers with a divergent orientation aim to accentuate the differences between their communicative behaviours and those of the other speaker(s) (see Chapter 9);
(2) intergroup orientation versus interpersonal orientation: speakers with an intergroup orientation tend to perceive an encounter primarily in intergroup terms, whereas speakers with an interpersonal orientation tend to perceive an encounter primarily in interpersonal terms (see Gallois *et al*. 1995).

The theory also suggests some of the motives that may underlie both of these types of orientation.

2.6 Factors influencing strategy use: (2) contextual variables

A second set of factors that have a crucial influence on people's choice of rapport management strategies are contextual variables. In this section I discuss four important ones: participant relations, message content, rights and obligations, and communicative activity.

2.6.1 *Participants and their relations*

Participant relations are a very important group of factors that influences use of rapport-management strategies. Several classic studies have helped establish *power* and *distance* as key variables relating to participant relations. For example, Brown and Gilman (1960), in their study of the use of pronouns in French, German and Italian, argue that choice of pronoun is affected by two fundamental dimensions of participant relations: *power* and *solidarity*. And Brown and Levinson (1987) maintain that interlocutors consider the *power* and *distance* of their relationship when choosing among different options for conveying a given speech act.

Moreover, a large number of empirical studies have provided considerable evidence for an association between language use and the variables *power* and *distance*. For example, many linguists have explored the wording of speech acts, such as requests (e.g. Blum-Kulka *et al.* 1985; Holtgraves and Yang 1990; Lim and Bowers 1991), apologies (e.g. Holmes 1990; Olshtain 1989), directives (e.g. Holtgraves *et al.* 1989), and disagreement (e.g. Beebe and Takahashi 1989a), and a very large number of them have found *power* and *distance* to be significant variables.

2.6.1.1 *Power*

This variable has several different labels; for example, *power*, *social power*, *status*, *dominance*, *authority*. Brown and Gilman (1960/1972) define this variable as follows:

> One person may be said to have power over another in the degree that he is able to control the behavior of the other. Power is a relationship between at least two persons, and it is nonreciprocal in the sense that both cannot have power in the same area of behavior. (Brown and Gilman 1972: 255)

In sociolinguistic and pragmatic research, power is typically operationalized in terms of unequal role relations, such as teacher–student or employer–employee. Very often there is no problem with this, but sometimes it can lead to confusion. For example, Blum-Kulka *et al.* (1985) refer to 'driver and passenger' as an unequal relationship, whereas Wood and Kroger (1991) classify 'taxi driver and passenger' as an equal relationship. Similarly, Olshtain (1989) treats 'waiter/customer' as an unequal relationship, whereas Wood and Kroger (1991) classify it as an equal one. It is useful, therefore, to think a little more deeply about the meaning of 'power', and French and Raven's (1959) classic characterization of the five main bases of power is a useful starting point. They argue that there are five main bases of power:

(1) reward power: if a person, A, has control over positive outcomes (such as bonus payments or improved job conditions) that another person, B, desires, A can be said to have reward power over B;

(2) coercive power: if a person, A, has control over negative outcomes (such as demotion or allocation of undesirable tasks) that another person, B, wants to avoid, A can be said to have coercive power over B;

(3) expert power: if a person, A, has some special knowledge or expertise that another person, B, wants or needs, A can be said to have expert power over B;

(4) legitimate power: if a person, A, has the right (because of his/her role, status, or situational circumstances) to prescribe or expect certain things of another person, B, A can be said to have legitimate power over B;

(5) referent power: if a person, B, admires another person, A, and wants to be like him/her in some respect, A can be said to have referent power over B.

Teachers typically have the first four of these types of power (and may have referent power too) in relation to their students, as do employers in relation to their employees. However, the role relations of waiters/customers and taxi drivers/passengers are more complex than this. From one perspective, customers and passengers have power (reward power and coercive power) over waiters/taxi drivers, in that they can choose whether or not to use the restaurant/taxi company again in future, and this may motivate the waiter/taxi driver to provide good service. On the other hand, from another perspective, waiters and taxi drivers have power (legitimate power and coercive power) over customers/passengers, in that they have the right to make certain demands, such as whether people should wait to be seated, or how many people can sit in the taxi, where the luggage should be placed, and so on. In fact, under special circumstances, they can even refuse to accept people's custom if they wish.

2.6.1.2 Distance

This variable also has a number of different labels: *distance, social distance, solidarity, closeness, familiarity, relational intimacy*. Brown and Gilman (1960/1972) describe it as follows:

Now we are concerned with a ... set of relations which are symmetrical. ... Not every personal attribute counts in determining whether two people are solidary enough to use the mutual T.[3] Eye color does not ordinarily matter nor does shoe size. The similarities that matter seem to be those that make for like-mindedness or similar behavior dispositions. ... The T of solidarity can be produced by frequency of contact as well as by objective similarities. However, frequent contact does not necessarily lead to the mutual T. It depends on whether contact results in the discovery or creation of the like-mindedness that seems to be the core of the solidarity semantic. (Brown and Gilman 1972: 258)

Most people have an intuitive understanding of what it means to have a 'close' or 'distant' relationship, but many different strands can be involved. For example, sometimes length of acquaintance seems important; we may classify a stranger, for instance, as distant from us, and a childhood friend as close. On the other hand, we may work with someone for many years, yet dislike them, and so regard them as distant from us. Spencer-Oatey (1996: 7) lists the following possible components (which are often overlapping), based on a review of a range of pragmatic studies:

(1) Social similarity/difference (e.g. Brown and Gilman 1960/1972)
(2) Frequency of contact (e.g. Slugoski and Turnbull 1988)
(3) Length of acquaintance (e.g. Slugoski and Turnbull 1988)
(4) Familiarity, or how well people know each other (e.g. Holmes 1990)
(5) Sense of like-mindedness (e.g. Brown and Gilman 1960/1972)
(6) Positive/negative affect (e.g. Baxter 1984).

It has been suggested (Slugoski and Turnbull 1988, Brown and Gilman 1989) that *distance* and *affect* should be treated as separate parameters, since some research has indicated that *affect* has a separate and differential effect on language use from the influence of *distance*. Social psychological research (see Spencer-Oatey 1996 for a review) also indicates that *distance* may not be a unitary variable, but as yet there is no clear consensus in either field as to how, or whether, the variable should be split.

2.6.1.3 Interrelationship between *power* and *distance*

Thomas (1995) points out that it is sometimes difficult to distinguish between *power* and *distance*, and that in the Cross Cultural Speech Act Realization Project (CCSARP, reported in Blum-Kulka *et al.* 1989), the researchers did not maintain the distinction in practice.

This is because in many cultures the two variables co-occur. However, this is not necessarily the case in all cultures. For example, Spencer-Oatey (1997), in research into British and Chinese conceptions of tutor–postgraduate student relations, found that the variables *power* and *closeness* were significantly negatively correlated for the British respondents, but unrelated for the Chinese respondents. In other words, for the British respondents, the greater the degree of power difference perceived between tutors and postgraduate students, the greater the degree of distance perceived, and vice versa. For the Chinese respondents, on the other hand, there was no link between the two: the degree of power difference perceived between tutors and postgraduate students was not associated with the degree of distance perceived.

2.6.1.4 Number of participants

Another important feature relating to participants is the number of people taking part, either as addressors/addressees or as audience. Rapport-management norms seem to be 'number-sensitive', in that what we say and how we say it is often influenced by the number of people present, and whether they are all listening to what we say. For example, in many cultures, it is much more embarrassing and face-threatening to be criticized in front of one or more other people (for example, in front of a class of students) than to be criticized privately, on a one-to-one basis (for example, in the teacher's office, with no one else present). And similarly, it can be much more embarrassing to be praised in front of other people than to be praised privately, on a one-to-one basis.

2.6.2 *Message content: cost–benefit considerations*

Message content also has a major influence on the choice of rapport-management strategies. Messages can vary in their likely degree of face-threat, and they can also have 'costs' associated with them. These costs are not necessarily financial (although they may be); they can be costs of time, effort, imposition, inconvenience, risk, and so on. For example, asking a friend to drive you to the airport can be costly for the friend in terms of time, inconvenience, financial costs, effort, and so on. And offering to help someone move house can be costly for the offerer in terms of time and effort. Needless to say, some messages are more 'costly' than others. For example, asking a next door neighbour for a lift home from a party you are both attending is less costly (in terms of imposition, effort and inconvenience) than asking them to make a special trip somewhere else. And so normally this difference in the 'costs' associated with the request would result in different wording.

Conversely, messages can have 'benefits' associated with them. For example, offering to drive a friend to the airport can be beneficial to the friend in terms of time, convenience, financial costs, and so on. And as Sifianou (1992b: 160) points out, customers' requests to shop assistants can be beneficial to both parties. Sometimes it may be difficult for a speaker to anticipate whether an addressee will interpret a message as 'costly' or 'beneficial'. For example, a guest may interpret the offer 'Have another sandwich!' as beneficial if s/he is hungry and likes the sandwiches, but as costly if s/he has indigestion and/or dislikes the sandwiches.

In the commercial world, costs lead to debts if the bills are not paid. In the world of social interaction, there is also a sense of indebtedness and a need for book balancing. For example, if someone does a favour for a friend, a slight disequilibrium results, with a greater favour leading to a greater imbalance. Similarly, if someone commits an offence, a disequilibrium results, with a greater offence leading to a greater imbalance. In both cases, balance needs to be restored, and apologies and expressions of gratitude are typical verbal ways respectively of restoring the equilibrium.

2.6.3 Social/Interactional roles

Social/Interactional roles are a third set of factors that can influence the use of rapport-management strategies in that they affect people's assessments of rights and obligations. Thomas (1995: 131) relates the following incident to illustrate the importance of rights and obligations:

> two elderly women [were] travelling on a country bus service. On country routes the driver stops only when requested to do so. The first woman wanted to get off at a scheduled stopping place, and as the bus approached it she simply called out: 'Next stop, driver!' Her companion wanted to get off where there was no official stop, and asked the driver, 'Do you think you could possibly let me out just beyond the traffic lights, please?'

As Thomas goes on to point out, there are no changes between the two 'events' in any of the parameters of power, social distance and size of imposition; they are all held constant. The role relations are the same, and in terms of driving difficulty, it cost the driver no more effort to stop beyond the traffic lights than at the bus stop. The difference simply lies in the rights and obligations of the 'events': in the first case the driver has an obligation to stop, whereas in the second case he has no such obligation.

When people interact with each other, they often take up clearly defined social roles, such as teacher–student, employer–employee, friend–friend, sales assistant–customer, chairperson–committee member. These role relationships not only partially determine the power and distance of the relationship, but also help specify the rights and obligations of each role member. People have the right to expect certain things of the other member and an obligation to carry out certain other things. For example, a teacher has an obligation to handle classroom management issues, and a right to expect the students to comply with classroom management directives. However, there are limits to the scope of teachers' and students' rights and obligations. Whereas it is acceptable for teachers to give directives such as 'Get into groups of four and work on this problem', it is less acceptable (at least in Western societies) to give more personally-oriented directives such as 'Get me a cup of coffee'. The legitimacy of the directive, therefore, depends partly on the nature of the role relationship and partly on the specific content of the message.

2.6.4 Communicative activity

A fourth major factor that can influence the use of rapport management strategies is the type of communicative activity that is taking place: for example, a lecture, a job interview, or a court trial.

Communicative activities often have *communicative genres* associated with them: 'historically and culturally specific, prepatterned and complex solutions to recurrent communicative problems' (Günthner and Knoblauch 1995: 8). These communicative genres may exhibit characteristic patterns in each of the five domains of rapport management (see section 2.3, pp. 19–20), and their 'culturally specific conventions and ideals' (Günthner and Knoblauch 1995: 20) influence how participants compose and interpret talk. For instance, obtaining an appropriate balance between modesty and boasting is a recurrent communicative problem, but what counts as appropriate can vary from one communicative activity to another. For example, in job interviews in Britain, candidates are typically expected to 'sell' themselves, but not appear 'too' proud; yet at an awards ceremony, the persons receiving the awards (actors, writers, etc.) are supposed to minimize their achievements and to give credit to others (the director, fellow actors, supportive spouse, etc.).

Similarly, the communicative 'problems' of speaking rights and turn-taking can vary from one communicative activity to another. For example, in an interview in Britain, it is normally only the panel members who can ask questions, until they pass that right to the interviewee; on the other hand, at a dinner party there is much greater freedom over who can speak when, yet there are still conventions over the fine-tuning of turn-taking (e.g. the acceptability of overlaps).

2.6.5 Overall assessments of context

The contextual features discussed above can play both a 'standing' and a 'dynamic' role in influencing language use. Prior to any speech event, we normally have relatively stable, ongoing conceptions of these various contextual components, based on our relevant previous experience; for example, we have conceptions of the degree of power and distance of given role relationships; of the scope of the rights and obligations of the participants, and of the costs and benefits, face considerations and so on associated with certain speech acts. However, in the course of an interaction, assessment of these variables may change dynamically: for example, a person may be more distant and offhand than expected, or may have differing conceptions of the role-related rights and obligations. If the interaction is to be 'successful' in terms of rapport management, we need to combine these 'dynamic' assessments of context with our 'standing' assessments in making linguistic strategy choices. However, at present we do not fully understand quite how this is done.

Brown and Levinson (1987) propose an additive model of contextual variables, suggesting that speakers make an overall assessment of the amount of facework required by adding up the following: the amount of power difference between hearer and speaker, the amount of distance between speaker and hearer, and the degree of imposition of the message. Holtgraves and Yang (1992: 252), on the other hand, suggest the following:

> When any of the three interpersonal variables reaches a particularly high level, the effects of the remaining variables lessen or drop out completely. For example, if an interactant has committed an extremely offensive act or intends to ask for an extremely large favour, he or she will be polite regardless of the closeness of the relationship with the other person.

Considerable further research is needed in this area to clarify such issues.

2.7 Factors influencing strategy use: (3) pragmatic conventions

A fifth set of factors that play a key role in people's use of rapport-management strategies are pragmatic conventions. Leech (1983) and Thomas (1983) draw a distinction between sociopragmatics (the sociological interface of pragmatics) and pragmalinguistics (the more linguistic end of pragmatics). Both aspects have conventions that can affect how people manage rapport.

2.7.1 Sociopragmatic conventions

It seems that all societies have developed social principles or 'rules' which help to minimize the conflict that might arise from the self-centred pursuit and gratification of face needs and sociality rights. Leech (1983: 132) focuses on this component in his conceptualization of politeness, and specifies the following maxims:

1. TACT MAXIM (in impositives and commissives)
   a. Minimize cost to *other*
   b. Maximize benefit to *other*
2. GENEROSITY MAXIM (in impositives and commissives)
   a. Minimize benefit to *self*
   b. Maximize cost to *self*
3. APPROBATION MAXIM (in expressives and assertives)
   a. Minimize dispraise of *other*
   b. Maximize praise of *other*
4. MODESTY MAXIM (in expressives and assertives)
   a. Minimize praise of *self*
   b. Maximize dispraise of *self*
5. AGREEMENT MAXIM (in assertives)
   a. Minimize disagreement between *self* and *other*
   b. Maximize agreement between *self* and *other*
6. SYMPATHY MAXIM (in assertives)
   a. Minimize antipathy between *self* and *other*
   b. Maximize sympathy between *self* and *other*.

As Thomas (1995) and other authors (e.g. Fraser 1990; Brown and Levinson 1987) have pointed out, a major flaw in Leech's current formulation of politeness is that he provides no motivated way of restricting the number of maxims. One way of reducing this problem would be to regard the maxims as sociocultural conventions governing the pursuit of social goals. The conventions would be rapport-focused, in that they would relate to the rapport-management concerns of face (quality face and identity face) and of sociality rights (equity rights and association rights). So, for example, Leech's (1983) approbation and modesty maxims could be seen as addressing quality face concerns; and his tact and generosity maxims could be seen as addressing concerns over equity rights. But this does not solve the problem as to how many conventions a given rapport-management concern can be addressed by!

Another problem is the universality of the conventions. Although fundamental rapport-management concerns are universal, the sociopragmatic conventions for managing them (and in fact the specific focus of the concerns) may not be. Brown and Levinson (1987), Lim and Bowers (1991) and Leech (1983) all seem to assume that face needs (and 'politeness' maxims, in the case of Leech) have 'universal valences'; in other words, that one pole of a given dimension is always more desirable than the other. For example, with regard to *autonomy–imposition* (qualities associated with equity rights and with the tact and generosity maxims), Brown and Levinson assume that *autonomy* is the desired option. Similarly, with regard to *modesty–pride*, Leech implies 'the more modest the better'. However, I contend that in different circumstances, different options or points on the continuum may be favoured. Which part of the scale is 'optimum' depends partly on the contextual variables discussed in section 2.6, and partly on culturally-based sociopragmatic preferences.

Clearly, much more work needs to be done in this area, perhaps drawing on research in social psychology on social rules (e.g. Argyle *et al.* 1986; see also Chapter 3).

2.7.2 Pragmalinguistic conventions

In addition to sociopragmatic conventions, societies also have pragmalinguistic conventions which affect the management of rapport. These are the conventions of strategy use which affect how a given pragmatic meaning is conveyed in a given context. For example, in British English, it is common (especially among older people) to greet an acquaintance with a remark about the weather such as 'Hello, a bit colder today, isn't it?' in order to show pleasant friendliness. Yet in Chinese, it is more common to ask about meals in such a context and say, for example, 'Hello, have you had lunch?' The functions of the two remarks are virtually identical in the respective languages, but in English the latter remark would probably be interpreted as a preliminary to an invitation. In other words, the two languages have different pragmalinguistic conventions for conveying a friendly greeting to an acquaintance.

Each of the rapport-management domains has pragmalinguistic conventions for conveying given pragmatic meanings in given contexts. For example, there are conventions over topic choice, over the use of listener responses and amount of speaker overlap, over physical proximity, to name just a few. All the conventions are context-specific; in other words, for a given pragmatic message the conventions of strategy use are affected by the contextual factors discussed in section 2.6. Much cross-cultural pragmatic research (e.g. the CCSARP project: see Blum-Kulka *et al.* 1989) has focused on identifying the pragmalinguistic norms associated with the performance of different speech acts in different languages/cultural groups.

2.8 Rapport-management outcomes

Rapport-management outcomes are similar in type to rapport-management orientations. In other words, the degree of rapport between interlocutors can be enhanced, it can be maintained, or it can be reduced. Goffman's (1963: 7) concept of 'negatively eventful' behaviour is useful here. Some types of behaviour (e.g. routine expression of thanks) may pass unperceived as an event when they are performed, but give rise to negative relational outcomes when they are not. Conversely, other types of behaviour (e.g. appropriate degree of unsolicited help given to a stranger) may pass unperceived as an event when they are *not* performed, but give rise to positive relational outcomes when they are.

Needless to say, the perceived relational outcomes of encounters do not always correspond to the initial orientations. Moreover, the perceived outcomes may be different for different interlocutors. There can be various reasons for this, one of which could be cultural differences in ways of managing rapport. (See Chapter 9 for an explanation in terms of Accommodation Theory.)

2.9 Rapport management across cultures

Cultural differences in language use can have a major impact on people's assessments of appropriate language use, and hence rapport-management outcomes. Variation can occur in at least the following aspects:

(1) *Contextual assessment norms*: people from different cultural groups may assess contextual factors somewhat differently. For example, when assessing a role relationship such as teacher–student or employer–employee, people from different cultural groups may have differing expectations regarding the typical degree of power and distance, and/or rights and obligations associated with the role relationship. For example, as explained in Chapter 11, Japanese and American work colleagues sometimes interpreted the purpose of a meeting differently, because they held differing assumptions about their respective roles.

(2) *Sociopragmatic conventions*: people from different cultural groups may hold differing principles for managing rapport in given contexts. For example, some societies may value overt expressions of modesty in interactions with acquaintances and strangers, while others might prefer more 'honest' evaluations. Similarly, some societies may value explicit expression of opinions and permit more open disagreement among new acquaintances than other societies do. For example, Chapter 10 reports differences between Chinese and German students in this respect.

(3) *Pragmalinguistic conventions*: people from different cultural groups may have differing conventions for selecting strategies and interpreting their use in given contexts. For example, two cultural groups may agree that an apology is necessary in a given context (and that the offence is equally severe), but have different conventions for conveying it. For instance, people from one group may typically include an explanation, whereas people from another group may typically use acknowledgement of fault as a key component. Similarly, as pointed out in Chapter 11 'let's think about it' (*kangaete okimashō*) functions as a formulaic preface to a negative assessment in Japanese, but has a more literal meaning in English.

(4) *Fundamental cultural values*: research in cross-cultural psychology has identified a small number of universal dimensions of cultural values (see Chapters 3 and 14), and found that ethnolinguistic groups differ from each other in terms of their mean location on each of these dimensions. More research is needed to explore how these dimensions relate to contextual assessment norms and sociopragmatic conventions.

(5) *Inventory of rapport-management strategies*: every language has a very large inventory of rapport-management strategies. Some of these occur in many languages (e.g. the T/V distinction – the

distinction between a formal form of 'you' such as *vous* and an informal, solidary form of 'you' such as *tu*); others occur in certain languages but are virtually absent in others (e.g. honorific forms in Japanese which are virtually absent in European languages).

Part Two of this book comprises empirical studies which investigate cultural similarities and differences in one or more of the above areas. However, we cannot simply assume that any differences will necessarily affect the way language is used in intercultural encounters, and so Part Three provides some theoretical perspectives on this. Part Four then reports empirical studies of intercultural interactions.

Much more research is still needed, though, on the various potential sources of variation and their interrelationships. Up to now, empirical cross-cultural pragmatic research has focused on investigating pragmalinguistic conventions and, more recently, contextual assessment norms; research in cross-cultural psychology and inter-cultural communication, on the other hand, has focused more on fundamental cultural values. What is now needed is a synthesis of the different perspectives. Bond *et al.* take this issue up in the next chapter, arguing that too exclusive a focus on cultural values is inadequate for explaining the role of culture in intercultural interactions.

Discussion questions

1 For each of the situations given below, consider the following issues:
  - Is the situation likely to affect interpersonal rapport – why/why not?
  - Is the situation likely to be face-threatening to any of the participants, and if so, why?
  - What type of face and/or sociality right is primarily threatened or infringed?

1.1 You are a secretary, and have recently started working for a new boss. One morning she/he storms into the office and shouts at you saying 'Can't you take better minutes than this?'

1.2 Three friends, Paul, Daniel and Matthew, go out for a meal together one evening. During the meal, Paul and Daniel spend nearly all the time talking about a film that Matthew hasn't seen. Matthew is unable to join in the conversation, and any attempts to steer the conversation to a different topic are ignored.

1.3 You are extremely busy with your work/studies at present, and need to work in the evenings and at the weekends to meet your deadlines. However, a good friend needs to decorate his/her new home, and asks you to help for two weekends.

2 During the next week, pay attention to every occasion when someone annoys or upsets you, and you feel offended or hurt in some way. Try to note down what they said or did, how you felt and why. Then try to relate your experiences and feelings to the concepts of face and sociality rights presented in this chapter.

3 Using the information given in Tables 2.2, 2.3 and 2.4, label the semantic components, the level of directness, and the upgraders/downgraders used in the following requests.

3.1 (Asking to borrow lecture notes) *Judith, could I please borrow your notes from the lecture yesterday because I missed it?*

3.2 (Asking to borrow a car) *Hello Paul. Could I possibly borrow your car if you don't need it? My car has broken down. I promise I'll take good care of it.*

3.3 (Asking a student to give his/her presentation a week earlier than scheduled) *I'm sorry to have to ask you this, but could you please do your presentation a week earlier than planned? I'm afraid I have to give all the marks in earlier than I expected.*

3.4 (Asking a younger brother, who is watching TV, to go to the shop) *Phil, do us a favour and get these from the shops for me, will you?*

3.5 (Asking a flatmate to hurry up and get out of the shower) *Come on, get out of the bathroom. You've been in there too long. Don't be selfish.*

4 Suppose you want to thank someone for doing something for you. Choose one variable from each list and work out what you would say or do in each situation and why.

Interlocutor	*Favour done for you*
(1) close friend	(a) picked up your pen
(2) mother	(b) cooked a special dinner for you
(3) new neighbour	(c) paid for your bus ticket
(4) teacher/line manager	(d) gave you a lift home

5 Look at the following true scenario, and discuss the questions that follow.

A Puerto Rican woman, who had been living for many years in the United States, was visited by her father. During his stay, he helped her take care of her son (his grandson). When she thanked him for his help, he became angry and felt hurt.

Her mother called her and said: 'How could you have been so thoughtless? You thanked your father. He was happy to take care of Johnnie. Have you forgotten how to behave? He's your father and he loves you. How could you be so cold – to thank him?' (Eisenstein and Bodman 1993: 74)

5.1 Why did the woman thank her father?
5.2 Why were her father and mother offended?
5.3 What would they have preferred her to say/not say?
5.4 Try to describe the misunderstanding using the concepts given in section 2.9.

Suggestions for further reading

Fraser, B. (1990) Perspectives on politeness. *Journal of Pragmatics*, 14(2): 219–36.

This article provides a useful summary of four key perspectives on politeness: the lay person's social norm view; the conversational-maxim view; the face-saving view; and the conversational-contract view.

Kasper, G. (1990) Linguistic politeness: current research issues. *Journal of Pragmatics*, 14: 193–218.

Kasper, G. (1996) Linguistic etiquette. In F. Coulmas (ed.), *Handbook of Sociolinguistics*. Oxford: Blackwell, 374–85.

These two papers discuss current issues and controversies within politeness theory, and are useful for those who want to start exploring the area in greater depth.

Scollon, R. and Scollon, S.W. (1995) *Intercultural Communication*. Oxford: Blackwell.

Chapters 2 and 3 provide a lively discussion of many of the issues discussed in this chapter.

Thomas, J. (1995) *Meaning in Interaction: An Introduction to Pragmatics*. London: Longman.

Chapters 5, 6 and 7 provide an excellent account of most of the issues discussed in this chapter.

Turner, K. (1996) The principal principles of pragmatic inference: politeness. *Language Teaching*, 29: 1–13.

This 'state of the art' article focuses mainly on Brown and Levinson's model of politeness, and provides a valuable discussion of some of the strengths and weaknesses of the model.

Notes

1. And also other types of wording choices not dealt with here, such as the person-orientation of requests: 'Can I borrow your car' versus 'Can you lend me your car'.
2. Compare Shimanoff's (1987, cited by Ting-Toomey and Cocroft, 1994: 317) categories: face-honouring, face-compensating, face-neutral, and face-threatening.
3. 'Mutual *T*' refers to an 'intimate' form of address. Many languages, such as French and German, require speakers to choose between two types of personal pronoun according to the relationship between the participants.

3

Culture as an Explanatory Variable: Problems and Possibilities[1]

Michael Harris Bond, Vladimir Žegarac and Helen Spencer-Oatey

3.1 Introduction

When the general is weak and without authority;
when his orders are not clear and distinct;
when there are no fixed duties assigned to officers and men;
and the ranks are formed in a slovenly, haphazard manner,
the result is utter disorganization.

Sun Tzu, *The Art of War*

We write this chapter with a practical agenda in mind: we would like to contribute our different experiences and insights towards improving the yield derived from comparative studies of communicative behaviour. We come to such research from different backgrounds (cross-cultural psychology and linguistic pragmatics). Recently, in revising a text on social psychology across cultures, Smith and Bond (1998) decided that its content should include material on differences in communication across cultures along with the traditional topics of social cognition, leadership, intergroup behaviour, and so forth. What they confronted in the literature on such cultural differences, however, was a patchwork quilt of unrelated studies, focusing on a myriad of speech forms and their associated non-verbal behaviours. When these studies invoked culture to explain results, they made opportunistic and speculative forays into the available literature and the concepts unearthed were only loosely linked to individual behaviour. These characteristics of the research and the conceptualization of its results made it difficult to organize the yield. Nor did the authors gain any sense of an emerging paradigm or paradigms (Kuhn 1962) that could help guide future research in this topic area, so important for our twenty-first century.

This chapter attempts to put this current situation into historical perspective, and to use our interdisciplinary experience as a guide for more productive research in the future. We will begin by presenting a representative study of cross-cultural differences in speech during actual business meetings (Yeung, in press). We admire this piece of work, and so feel comfortable using it as a springboard to suggest areas in which our disciplinary efforts could be enlarged and enhanced. These are:

• how cultural differences have so far been conceptualized and measured;
• how cultural concepts have been, and may be, linked to speech behaviour;
• whether more promising ways to conceptualize and measure cultures, especially when studying speech behaviour, can be found by bringing together concepts from different disciplines (including: social psychology, pragmatics, linguistics, the psychology of culture).

3.2 An exemplary case

To see a world in a grain of sand,
And a heaven in a wild flower.

William Blake, *Songs of Innocence*

Yeung (in press) was intrigued by the question of cultural differences in disagreements. It is common for bicultural persons in Hong Kong to observe that local Chinese are more indirect in their speech than Westerners (see, for example, Bilbow 1997), and that avoidance of disagreement is regarded as one component of indirectness (Gudy-kunst and Ting-Toomey 1988: 100–5). So, to assess her hypothesis that Chinese disagreed less, Yeung examined speech samples taken from bank employees in Australia and Hong Kong during actual business meetings convened to develop innovations in banking procedures. This choice of situation ensured that the participants were personally engaged in a situation of high mundane realism, so that their behaviours had external validity (Carlsmith *et al.* 1976).

In designing her speech measures Yeung may have been guided by the spirit of Storti's acute observation that 'The notorious indirect-ness of Asians may, to a certain extent, be nothing more than our inability to recognize Asian-style directness when we see it' (1990: 80–1) (see also Chapter 11). For, in assessing indirectness, she did not merely score various types of disagreement, perhaps a measure of (in)directness obvious to Westerners, but also measured the linguistic formulation of requests and the discourse structures of proposals made by the discussants. She reasoned that variable usage of speech types within each of these verbal categories could increase or decrease the directness of verbal communications. A multi-variate approach could give a more sensitive and comprehensive assessment of hypothesized Chinese indirectness.

After examining her results, however, Yeung drew a more balanced view of Chinese–Western directness in speech: 'The indirect modes of Chinese communication expostulated in the literature are only partially confirmed by the present study.' The Chinese (who were speaking in Cantonese) used relatively more question forms (e.g. making requests, asking for support, etc.) than the Australians, and made fewer assertions of their personal positions. Surprisingly, it was the Australians who hedged *more* by using verbal qualifiers (e.g. 'somewhat', 'perhaps', 'I think', etc.). The Australians actually disagreed *less* with their colleagues of any rank than did the Chinese. The form of that disagreement varied, however, with Australians preferring the 'Yes, but ...' style, the Chinese asking rhetorical questions (e.g. 'Why don't we ...?').

So, a mixed picture of so-called Asian indirectness emerges from this close scrutiny of *in vivo* speech. It raises fascinating questions about the origins of cultural group stereotypes about Chinese indirectness in the communication literature and pushes the thoughtful reader towards innovative strategies for doing future research. We will consider both these issues by using the Yeung study as a talking-piece for the questions about research in cross-cultural communication raised earlier.

3.3 Grappling with culture scientifically

Most cross-cultural exploration begins with
the annoyance of being lost.

Edward Hall, *Beyond Culture*

We believe that it is by encountering difference that most behavioural scientists come to appreciate the necessity of considering the concept of culture in the first place. Typically, we encounter a difference in behaviour, usually arising out of travel to a different place and exchanges with a 'foreigner' who looks or speaks or otherwise behaves differently. *Voilà!* Culture becomes the *deus ex machina* used to account for the observed departures from 'normal' behaviour. 'They do that because they are from Chinese (Serbian, Flemish, etc.) culture' then gets trotted out as an explanation of the observed difference. Of course, the term 'culture' is empty at this stage, completely circular as an explanatory tool until it can be given usable content. The form of that content can be suggested by consulting various definitions of the concept adduced by behavioural scientists. Here one is confronted with *un embarras de richesses* in the literature! Kroeber and Kluckhohn (1952) identified dozens. Of these many, Kluckhohn's (cited in Kroeber and Kluckhohn, p. 86) is widely quoted:

> Culture consists in patterned ways of thinking, feeling and reacting, acquired and transmitted mainly by symbols, constituting the distinctive achievements of human groups, including their embodiments in artifacts; the essential core of culture consists of traditional (i.e. historically derived and selected) ideas and especially their attached values.

Many other definitions of culture have likewise given values a key role in differentiating cultures one from another, and it is to this construct that behavioural scientists have most often turned to explain observed differences between and across cultural groups.

3.3.1 Culture as values

Virtue is the establishing of perfect harmony.

Chuang Tzu

In framing her cross-cultural study of indirectness, Yeung writes, 'There is common agreement that what underlies the Chinese patterns of communication is the Chinese overwhelming desire to maintain harmony in social interactions.' Many would concur (e.g. Gao *et al.* 1996). Indeed, harmony as a motivating end state has assumed mythic status in studies of Asian communication because these cultures all share a common philosophical tradition which stresses interdependency as a fundamental fact of nature (Nakamura 1964). What evidence outside of philosophical texts is there, however, which supports the contention that Chinese or Asian cultures place any more emphasis on harmony as a value than do any other cultural groups?

3.3.1.1 The Hofstede project

In 1980, a Dutch sociologist, Geert Hofstede, published the results from an analysis of 'work-related values' involving stratified samples of more than 100,000 IBM employees in 40 nations. The core of the data consisted of 32 items, most of which assessed the respondent's endorsement of personal goals (e.g. earnings, freedom, cooperation, etc.). Each nation was given a 'culture score' on that item by averaging the scores on that item given by the respondents from that nation. Note that the level of analysis had thereby shifted from the individual to the cultural level; conclusions drawn would hereafter refer to cultures (nations, actually), not to persons.

The resulting culture scores on these 32 items from each of the 40 national samples were then factor analysed. Hofstede (1980) isolated four dimensions of cultural variation from this analysis, viz. Power Distance, Individualism, Uncertainty Avoidance, and Masculinity. Each dimension was exhaustively examined in relation to previous theory in social science and linked to historical, political, social, and economic conditions. Each of the 40 nations was then assigned a set of four scores (out of 100) which constituted its value profile. Hong Kong, for example, scored 68, 25, 29, 57, making it high on Power Distance, low in Individualism, low on Uncertainty Avoidance, and moderate on Masculinity.

Hofstede published the results of this work in a tome entitled *Culture's Consequences*. It took the behavioural sciences by storm. Its depth of scholarship, its range of disciplinary coverage, its multi-national database, its statistical sophistication, its conceptual integration and its empirical mapping of so many 'cultures' lent it great authority. Not surprisingly, it has become one of the most frequently cited texts of the last twenty years in all social science (Hofstede 1997).

The Hofstede project was widely used by many behavioural scientists to support empirical reasoning of this sort: since culture X places greater emphasis on a dimension of valuing, say Power Distance, than culture Y, we should expect to find differences in behaviour Z, say tolerance of insult from a superior (see e.g. Bond *et al.* 1985). In our talking-point case, it could be asked if and how we can use the Hofstede project to support the contention that Chinese culture endorses harmony more strongly than Western culture. That cultural value difference could then be adduced to predict higher levels of Chinese indirectness in speech. Or could it?

Problem 1: Which Chinese nation will be used as a surrogate for Chinese culture?
The Hofstede project mapped three Chinese political entities: Hong Kong, Singapore, and Taiwan. Obviously, one should select the positioning of the Hong Kong Chinese, as Yeung's Chinese participants were from Hong Kong. However, the scores for these three Chinese political units differ in the Hofstede survey, and in other surveys as well (Bond 1996). How then can the social scientist talk about Chinese culture as if it were a unified reality? At least with respect to values, there is no one Chinese culture. Surely we need to define the 'Chineseness' of Chinese cultures using different constructs like, say, beliefs, or confine ourselves to thinking about particular Chinese cultures.

Problem 2: Is a nation a culture?
Many nations appear to be composed of various, different cultural groups, so that treating the nation as a culture is imprecise and misleading. How shall we deal with nations like India or Singapore or Belgium, for example, that are composed of many cultural groups? Schwartz (1994) takes the approach of distinguishing cultural groups within some of his surveyed nations in terms of language used. He typically finds value differences across language communities within a nation (e.g. Israel, Canada). So when political entities are taken as surrogates for culture, we may be in troubled waters if our goal is to learn about particular cultures! In this case, the Hofstede nation score would be an imprecise measure of the culture.

Problem 3: Which of Hofstede's dimensions actually assesses harmony?
Harmony was not measured in the 32-item survey, so one must extrapolate from those values that were used. Cooperation seems similar, but that value (scored negatively) is a part of the Masculinity dimension. And on that dimension, Australia and Hong Kong are in fact very close.

One could argue that preservation of harmony, at least within the in-group, is in fact characteristic of cultures low in Individualism. But the actual values constituting Hofstede's dimension of Individualism were sufficient personal time, freedom, challenge, use of skills on the job, good physical working conditions, and training opportunities.[2] None of these cultural values bears any obvious relationship to harmony, however flexibly defined.

In fact, harmony as a value has been measured in a subsequent value survey of nations (Chinese Culture Connection 1987).

Surprisingly, it entered into a dimension of valuing called Integration on which Australia was considerably *higher* than any of the three Chinese political entities, Taiwan, Singapore, and Hong Kong. Unexpectedly, then, it does not appear that it is in the realm of values at the cultural level that the social scientists' stereotype of greater Chinese harmony will be confirmed.

How then has this stereotype about Chinese harmony arisen? Perhaps the use of the value construct 'harmony' was just a form of social scientist shorthand used to integrate a pattern of observed behavioural differences (including certain types of speech indirectness) which distinguish Chinese from Westerners (Gabrenya and Hwang 1996).

Problem 4: How does one use measures of a culture's values in communication studies?
Linguistically, it seems rather odd to talk about cultures as having values, except perhaps in social scientific discourse. A culture is a social system, not a person. One might instead characterize cultures in terms of the emphases shaped by the institutions and the behavioural norms distinguishing cultural groups from one another.

To measure such emphases, one might proceed as Massimini and Calegari (1979) did, for example. They examined a cultural product, national constitutions, content-analysing their prose for themes relating to individualism and collectivism. Nations were then ranked in terms of the frequency with which these themes were mentioned in their constitutions. Other cultural products with some face-valid connection to valuational aspirations could be examined. Humana (1992), for example, assessed 100 countries for the degree to which they actually practised the conventions constituting the Covenant on Civil and Political Liberties; the Population Crisis Committee (1988) rated 100 nations on the degree to which each had achieved gender equality. Any of these 'cultural products' could arguably be related to the emphases characterizing a cultural group.

These products could then be linked to 'cultural' values, i.e. the average level of various values held by equivalent samples of various cultural groups (see, for example, Bond and Chan 1995). Indeed, Hofstede (1980) did so for each of his cultural dimensions of value. He found, for example, that the Uncertainty Avoidance of a nation was positively related to the average age of political leaders in that country.

Such linkages between culture products and culture-level value endorsements ('cultural' values) are to be expected. As Schwartz (1994: 92) has argued, 'culture-level dimensions [of values] presumably reflect the different solutions that societies evolve to the problems of regulating human activities, the different ways that institutional emphases and investments are patterned and justified in one culture compared with another'.

So, a culture-level value endorsement then becomes a kind of lightning-rod, synthesizing the multifarious societal influences on a sample of the individuals constituting that culture. Use of these culture-level values or dimensions is 'appropriate when one seeks to understand how differences between *cultures* in their symbol systems, institutions, rates and styles of behaviour and so on are related to cultural value emphases' (Schwartz 1994: 117, emphasis added). They are not appropriate, however, 'when one seeks to understand how differences between individual persons in beliefs, attitudes, or behaviour are related to individual differences in value priorities' (Schwartz 1994: 117). But it is precisely these individual-level differences in speech behaviour that we are typically required to explain in cross-cultural studies of communication. Have we been looking in the wrong place for guidance?

Problem 5: How can we use cultural values to explain individual behaviours?

The behaviour of a given person may arise because of values strongly held, which generate motivational pressure for their satisfaction through action by the individual. This is a basic tenet of expectancy-value theories, for example (Feather 1982).

So, when trying to predict why Hong Kong Chinese might be more indirect in speech than Australians, one might simply proceed by arguing that the average Hong Kong Chinese presumably places a higher personal value on Power Distance (Hofstede 1980) or Hierarchy (Schwartz 1994) or Moral Discipline (Chinese Culture Connection 1987) and that this higher value then leads to greater average circumspection in speech. But one cannot do this. 'Culture' values like Power Distance do not apply to individuals, so we cannot argue that the average Hong Kong Chinese is higher in Power Distance than the average Australian. We must instead use values measured at the individual level, e.g. Bond's (1988) value dimension of Social Integration, to predict individual speech indirection. This strategy avoids the 'ecological fallacy' (Hofstede 1980: 29) of shifting from one level (culture) to another level (the individual). (See also Chapter 14.)

It is true that the cultural groups from which our samples have been drawn do differ on Power Distance or on Hierarchy or on Moral

Discipline; it is also true that the average levels of indirectness in speech may differ across the samples. However, the former variables are cultural-level variables; the latter is an individual-level variable. What is missing is a linkage from the cultural-level construct to an individual-level construct like, say, the value dimension of Social Integration. It is this individual-level value that can then be linked to indirectness of speech (see Singelis and Brown 1995 for an elaboration of this argument).

On rare occasions, communication scientists do test their reasoning directly by measuring the individual values of their respondents from a number of different cultural groups and correlating these results with their respondents' speech behaviour (e.g. Nebashi *et al.* 1997). Gudykunst *et al.* (1996) did so and found that the self-ratings of an indirect communication style were negatively related to the endorsement of independence values across all their respondents and in each of their cultural groups. On average, Americans claimed to use less indirect communication than the Japanese, for example, and this difference could then be explained in terms of the tendency for the typical American to endorse the independence values more highly than the typical Japanese.

Here, then, we have an example of a universal or culture-general relationship at the individual level which can be used to explain (or 'unpackage': see Whiting 1976) a cultural difference in a type of speech behaviour. Many would argue that it is the discovery of such universal relationships at the level of the individual that makes cross-cultural research valuable (e.g. Messick 1988).

However, one must be forewarned that results from such research do not always support our reasoning about individual determinants of cross-cultural differences in speech behaviour. Ip and Bond (1995) were interested in explaining cultural differences in the ways people describe themselves. They asked respondents in both Hong Kong and the United States to complete the 'Who Are You' (WAY) questionnaire, originally developed by Kuhn and McPartland (1954), along with the Schwartz (1992) Value Survey (SVS). This procedure enabled the researchers to correlate the frequency with which individuals used categories of descriptor categories from the WAY (e.g. psychological traits, social roles, etc.) with their endorsement of value domains from the SVS, such as power, self-direction, and so forth. That linkage was of interest because some theorists (e.g. Newman 1993) had argued that those persons with an individualistic value orientation would be more likely to describe themselves using trait categories.

The data did not support such a contention. In neither cultural group nor in the sample as a whole was there any link between an individual's values and his or her category usage. So, although there were a number of cultural differences in category frequency, these differences could not be explained in terms of individual values. What other explanatory concepts could be advanced?

3.3.2 Culture as interactional 'rules' or maxims

In linguistics, the most frequent way of 'unpackaging' culture is by drawing on Leech's (1983) Politeness Principle. This comprises a set of six maxims: the Tact Maxim, the Generosity Maxim, the Approbation Maxim, the Modesty Maxim, the Agreement Maxim and the Sympathy Maxim (see Chapter 2, section 2.7.1, for more details). These maxims reflect the norms that people seem to follow in managing rapport. Leech suggests that they work in conjunction with the four conversational maxims of Grice's (1989) Cooperative Principle: the Quantity Maxim (make your contributions as informative as is required); the Quality Maxim (do not say that which you believe to be false or have inadequate evidence for); the Relation Maxim (be relevant); and the Manner Maxim (be brief, be orderly, avoid ambiguity and obscurity of expression). Leech argues that in reality people are often far more indirect than the Cooperative Principle suggests, so he proposes the Politeness Principle to work in conjunction with the Cooperative Principle.

Leech (1983) maintains that, unlike Grice's cooperative maxims that describe universal norms of communicative behaviour, the politeness maxims vary in importance from culture to culture. For example, Leech (1983) suggests that the Modesty Maxim has greater weight in Japanese than in British society, and that conversely the Agreement Maxim is more important in Britain than in Japan. He maintains that such differences can thereby explain why the Japanese typically respond to compliments with greater modesty than the British do. (See Chapter 5 for a discussion of Leech's maxims in relation to British and Chinese responses to compliments.)

Returning to Yeung's study, the Agreement Maxim is clearly of direct relevance to the speech act of disagreement. Perhaps, then, certain societies place greater emphasis on the expression of surface-level agreement than others do; so, if harmony is particularly important in Chinese patterns of communication, maybe this is simply because of the greater weight attached to the notion of agreement. However, once again we run into difficulties with such an explanation because of inconsistency in the argument. In relation to compliment responses, authors (e.g. Chen 1993) maintain that the Modesty Maxim is more important in China than the Agreement Maxim, implying that the Agreement Maxim is not particularly important; yet in relation to disagreement we need to argue (if we want to support the stereotype of Asian indirectness) that the Agreement Maxim is very important in these countries!

To help resolve such difficulties, we need to obtain independent measures of these normative interactional 'rules' – that is, ones that are independent of language use. Only then can we use them to explain any cross-cultural differences in people's use of language. Before we can do this, however, we need to resolve some other problems. Firstly, we need to determine objectively how many fundamental rapport-management maxims exist universally and what they are. Then we need to obtain scores on each maxim for different cultural groups (similar in type to the scores that Hofstede obtained for fundamental cultural values), so that we have objective and independent measures of the relative importance of each rapport maxim in a range of societies. Only then can we use them to try to unpackage culture's effect on rapport-management behaviour in different societies.

Research by Kim (1994) is a step in this direction. Basing her logic on theorizing about culture and communication, she proposed that five key conversational constraints could be extracted from the literature: concerns for (a) clarity, (b) effectiveness, (c) avoiding hurting the other's feelings, (d) minimizing imposition, and (e) avoiding negative evaluation by the hearer.[3] She developed scales to assess the strength of these concerns during conversations with others, and measured self-perceptions of these conversational constraints across a variety of cultural groups. She then related the differences that she found back to fundamental cultural values such as individualism–collectivism.

3.3.3 The reality of context: moving out of subjectivism

It is quite likely, though, that the application of rapport maxims is influenced by the social context of an interaction. So if we are unable to fully unpackage culture's effects using just values and/or maxims, we may be forced to consider the role of the situational context. Linguists pay particular attention to the context, and have identified a large number of contextual factors that affect language use (for an overview, see Chapter 2, section 2.6). Social psychologists, on the other hand, have tended to neglect the situation as a variable and, as Seeman has recently pointed out, research in social psychology has not yet resulted in any 'systematic way of characterizing tasks or environments' (1997: 6).

Several psychological studies, however, have explored an important component of the context – people's conceptions of interpersonal relations. For example, Wish *et al.* (1976) studied both personal and role relationships. They drew up a long list of dyads, such as teacher–student, salesman–regular customer, and personal enemies. Then, using a procedure similar to Kelly's (1955) repertory grid technique, they generated a set of 25 bipolar scales on which these dyads could be rated, e.g. intense–superficial interaction, very friendly–very hostile, exactly equal–extremely unequal power, compatible–incompatible goals and desires, pleasure-oriented–work-oriented, etc. Next they asked 87 university students to use these 25 bipolar scales to rate 20 of their own personal relations (for example, between themselves and their teachers) and 25 role relations (for example, between teacher and student). A multidimensional scaling analysis of the data revealed four dimensions, which they interpreted as follows:

(1) Cooperative and friendly–competitive and hostile
(2) Equal–unequal
(3) Intense–superficial
(4) Socio-emotional/informal–task-oriented/formal.

Marwell and Hage (1970) also investigated role relations. They drew up a list of 100 role relationships, selecting them systematically from eight different sectors of society such as family, education, leisure and commerce. They then noted important similarities and differences which could be applied to all the role relationships, and drew up a list of 16 general variables which could be used to characterize the role relationships, e.g. frequency of interaction, range of locations of interaction, and average degree of occupant choice. Two sets of raters then independently scored these relationships on the 16 general variables. Factor analyses of these two sets of ratings produced very similar factor structures, with three major factors emerging in both. The first factor was labelled Intimacy. Role relationships that scored particularly high on this dimension were husband–wife, father–son, best friend–best friend (same sex), and boyfriend–girlfriend; role relationships that scored particularly low were newspaper vendor–buyer, supermarket cashier–customer and movie customer–usher. The second factor was tentatively labelled Visibility. Role relationships that received high visibility scores were movie customer–usher, guard–

convict, and supermarket cashier–customer; those that received very low visibility scores were abortionist–client, psychiatrist–patient, and confessor–penitent. The third factor was slightly difficult to interpret, but was labelled Regulation. At one end were relationships in which the definition of activities, times and locations are left to the members to decide (e.g. acquaintances, best friends) and at the other extreme are relationships where there is a good deal of specification or scriptedness of what goes on (e.g. judge–defence lawyer, dancer–conductor).

A number of authors (e.g. Lonner 1980, Stiles 1980, Triandis 1978) have commented on the convergence of social psychological studies of interpersonal behaviour. Stiles (1980), for example, maintains that two dimensions are particularly robust: a dominance, control or status dimension, and a dimension relating to friendliness, affect or degree of association. And Spencer-Oatey (1996) suggests that there are close correspondences between linguistic conceptions of participant relations and the dimensions identified by social psychologists. A 'vertical' dimension of interpersonal relations emerges as a single factor in almost all social psychological studies, even though it is labelled in various ways (e.g. equal–unequal, superordination–subordination), and this seems to correspond to the linguistic variable of power. There is slightly less consensus over the other dimensions, but it seems that there are one or more 'horizontal' dimensions which relate to the linguistic variable of distance.

If we try to link other dimensions identified by social psychologists with linguistic concepts, further correspondences can be found:

- *Regulation/Scriptedness–Openness* (Marwell and Hage 1970) can be related to *communicative activities*: some communicative activities are very regulated and scripted, others are much more open;
- *Visible (Public)–Private* (Marwell and Hage 1970) has some links with *number of participants*;
- *Socio-emotional–Task-oriented* (Wish et al. 1976) can be related to linguistic concepts such as the *interactional* versus *transactional* function of language (Brown and Yule 1983; see Chapter 1);
- *Cooperative–Competitive* (Wish et al. 1976) can be related to *rapport orientation*;
- *Intense–Superficial* (Wish et al. 1976) can be related to goals and their relative importance to the individuals involved (cf. Hymes' (1972) concept of *Ends*).

Further research is now needed which can interrelate social psychological and linguistic concepts, and which can identify a set of fundamental dimensions for characterizing the key components of the situational context.

3.3.3.1 The role of culture

Culture enters this labyrinth as a constructor of situations. To take Yeung's research as an example, the 'participative decision-making meeting' she used in gathering speech samples may be a very different situation in Australian than in Hong Kong culture. Using the dimensions identified by Marwell and Hage (1970) and Wish *et al.* (1976) as examples, such a meeting may be high cooperative, medium visible and medium regulation in Hong Kong, but high competitive, medium visible and low regulation in Australia. The observed higher frequency of assertions of personal positions by the Australians could then have arisen because of the meeting's higher competitive quality there, and the greater number of requests for support by the Chinese could be due to the higher cooperative quality in Hong Kong. Both groups could be paying a fair amount of attention to face because of the medium visibility in both countries, but the Chinese use of rhetorical questions could reflect the medium regulation of the situation in Hong Kong, while the frequent hedging by the Australians could reflect the low regulation of such meetings in Australia. So, we could well have a universal theory of speech behaviour in the offing, with situational variation leading to variation in aspects of speech usage across all cultural groups.

The role of culture in this model of behaviour, therefore, is to define what kind of a situation this meeting is in the particular cultures where individual speech is being compared. Unfortunately, very few cross-cultural studies have addressed this essential topic. One exception is research by Forgas and Bond (1985) who examined how Hong Kong Chinese and Australians construed a variety of social situations common to students, like arriving late to a tutorial. They found two dimensions of situational construal to be common to persons from these two cultural groups: degree of involvement and task orientation (cf. Wish *et al.* (1976): Intense/Emotional–Superficial and Task-oriented–Socio-emotional respectively). Not surprisingly, the same situations were slotted at different locations along these two common dimensions by persons from the two cultures. Studying, for example, was more task-oriented for the Hong Kong Chinese than for the Australians. So one could easily predict differences in speech behaviours between these two cultural groups arising in the studying situation because of this difference.

Two programmes of research would now seem called for. First, we need multicultural studies of situations in order to begin teasing out the woof and warp that define a universal taxonomy of situations, objectively defined. Second, we need to adduce some theory which helps explain how persons of given cultures will construe a given situation within this taxonomy. So, for example, if we knew that distance and intimacy (cf. Marwell and Hage 1970) were universal dimensions of role relationships, which are a key feature of many social situations, we could then use Spencer-Oatey's (1997) cross-cultural findings about the tutor–tutee relationship to make predictions for speech behaviour in that relationship. She found that Chinese students from China regarded this relationship as closer and more intimate than did comparable British students. For a start, then, we could expect a wider range of non-academic topics to be included in Chinese tutee speech with their tutors than would be found in British tutee speech with theirs. Other predictions could likewise be made.

With such a universal taxonomy of situations, we could try to unpackage or explain cultural differences in speech behaviour using situational variables. However, these situational variables are likely to interact in very complex ways in their effects on language use, so it is unlikely that we will find many straightforward correspondences between the two. It is possible, though, that the notion of *script* can provide a useful way of linking culturally-based maxims, situational contexts and language use.

3.4 Scripts: maxims, situations, and indirect communication

> Once a word is uttered, a team of four horses cannot drag it back.
> (Chinese proverb) *Anecdotes of Great Men*

Conceptualizing our physical and social environment in terms of categories (rather than merely having particular memories of individual things and events) is useful, because it enables us to make more informed plans about future behaviour in situations which are similar to those we have experienced (or heard about) in the past. A communicative activity (such as a cocktail party, a wedding reception, a job interview, a meeting at work, and even a casual conversation with a friend) is a type of situation. Hence, decisions about how to dress for a wedding reception or a job interview, what to say to your boss in a meeting or over a drink in a pub, etc. depend to a large extent on one's assumptions about these types of situation. Most, if not all, relevant assumptions about taking part in a social situation of a particular type are stored in memory together, so that they can be retrieved and acted upon quickly and easily when the need arises. We will call a set of assumptions which we draw upon in making decisions relating to a particular type of situation a *script* (see Wierzbicka 1994; Goddard 1997).

In the context of this chapter, the notion of script is important because it enables us to explicate the situational dependence of rapport maxims (such as Leech's (1983) politeness maxims). In other words, scripts are ways in which 'rules' or maxims of social behaviour are related to situations. This section has two aims: (a) to illustrate the role of scripts with reference to the communication of disagreement as described in Yeung's study, and (b) to explain the elusive relation between indirectness in communication and the situational dependence of rapport maxims.

3.4.1 The disagreement scripts of Hong Kong Chinese and Australian cultures

Yeung's (in press) study can be seen as an attempt to investigate some of the ways in which the introduction of participative management has been effected in Hong Kong and Australia. She focuses on requests and disagreements. Here we will use the notion of script to characterize what goes on intra/inter-culturally in disagreements. Although Yeung does not define the term 'disagreement', it seems clear that she uses this word in a fairly broad sense. Disagreement can be said to occur if some participant or participants in a situation of communication communicate(s) some belief or beliefs, which are partly or fully inconsistent with some other belief or beliefs publicly held by another participant (or participants) in the same situation. This characterization of disagreement covers both exchanges in which disagreement is communicated explicitly, and those in which it is communicated implicitly.

Manager: That is to say, [the phone] should have a secret code you must press before you can dial an outside number.
Staff: It's very expensive.[4]

The member of staff's utterance communicates partial disagreement implicitly. He does not reject fully the proposal put forward by the manager. Thus, he may well agree that the idea is good in principle, while believing that cost presents an obstacle to its implementation. That is why this is a case of partial disagreement. Furthermore, the member of staff does not actually say that he disagrees: there are no linguistic expressions of disagreement (such as *no, but, I disagree,* etc.). His utterance communicates disagreement implicitly: the observation about the expense involved in implementing the manager's proposal is relevant on this particular occasion only on the assumption that the member of staff intended to communicate the belief that cost might present a problem. So, the conclusion that the member of staff is communicating disagreement is a function of the meaning of the words used and the context.

How disagreement is communicated is determined by a range of factors: the universal norms of communicative behaviour (such as Grice's (1989) Cooperative Principle), the communicator's preferences which follow from culturally variable maxims (such as Leech's (1983) politeness maxims) and the ways in which these maxims are conventionally associated with particular linguistic expressions. So, it is convenient to distinguish these three kinds of factors in formulating and comparing culture-specific scripts for a particular type of situation.

Yeung's study shows that the Chinese and the Australian scripts for communicative interactions in a meeting at work are similar in some respects and different in others. Her findings suggest that the communicative behaviour of the Chinese and the Australians is based on meeting-scripts which share the following assumptions:

(1) In a meeting, active participation of those taking part is required regardless of their relative status: both subordinates and managers should come up with their own opinions, questions, suggestions and new proposals.
(2) In a meeting, if you are making a request or putting forward a proposal, you should do so in a way that does not unduly impose on other participants.
(3) In a meeting, disagreements should be avoided.

It should be reasonably clear that (1) conflicts with (2) and (3). This sort of conflict is to be expected in all societies which have the institution of participative office meetings to which point (1) applies, because assumptions (2) and (3) follow in a fairly straightforward way from considerations of face (see Chapter 2). Cultural differences in the way people behave in business meetings may plausibly be assumed to arise as different solutions to this inherent threat of conflict. It is the more specific rules in the meeting-script which result in the cultural differences observed by researchers. Thus, Yeung observes some cultural differences concerning the relative status of participants and the type of conversational contributions made. For instance, in her sample, 7 per cent of turns taken by the Chinese contained disagreements with the superior, while Australian subordinates disagreed with the superior in only 1 per cent of turns. So, it seems that point (3) in the two meeting-scripts needs to be elaborated in two different ways in the two cultures:

(3a) *The Chinese rule for disagreement*:
It is more important to put forward a constructive suggestion, opinion, etc. than to show respect for the higher status of others, even if this means expressing disagreement.

(3b) *The Australian rule for disagreement*:
It is important not to express disagreement with a superior, even if this means not fulfilling the commitment stated in (1).

It should also be noted that both cultures seem to place greater weight on (1) than on (3). The Chinese and the Australians disagree rather freely (in 19 per cent and 11 per cent of turns, respectively). So, our meeting-script ought to include another assumption (which is shared by both cultures):

(4)   Other things being equal, (1) is more important than (3).

Our scripts for disagreement in meetings are still incomplete. The conflicting assumptions (1) and (3) suggest that a culture should develop set ways in which disagreements are communicated. This is indeed the case. Yeung's findings clearly indicate that the strategies for expressing disagreement used by the Chinese and the Australians are relatively stable. Thus, two-thirds of the Chinese – and only half of the Australian – subordinates' disagreements are prefaced with negative or contrastive markers (such as 'but' or 'no'), and a quarter are unprefaced statements expressing differences of opinion, contrary facts, doubts and reservations. This is broadly consistent with point (4) above (primary importance of the demands of the meeting). Only the Australians' disagreements are characterized by the use of 'yes, but'. Hence, the Australian script for disagreeing in a meeting probably includes an assumption like the following:

(5a) *Australian script for disagreement in meetings*:
Acknowledge the views of the others, and indicate that you disagree only with some implications of their position. You can do this by saying: 'Yes, but ...'

The word 'yes' indicates the speaker's general agreement with other participants, while the meaning of 'but' is, roughly, denial of expectation. So, by saying 'Yes, but ...' the speaker communicates something like this: 'Despite my general agreement with your views, there are some consequences/conclusions/implications that follow from your position; I disagree with them.'

In contrast to Australians, the Chinese tend to use rhetorical questions in a context in which it is evident that the relevant answer supports the speaker's, and contradicts the other participant's, view. The following example from Yeung's study is to the point:

> But this thing is actually very simple. Whether you pass it onto the Liaison Branch or pass it onto us, we say exactly the same things: You want to terminate the bill or renew it? <u>Why doesn't the Bill Centre liaise with clients from their side?</u> It's actually very simple.

In the context set by the preceding utterances, the answer to the second question (underlined) should be obvious: 'There is no good reason for the Bill Centre not to liaise with clients.' From a communicative point of view, this strategy puts the ball in the hearers' court, because the speaker leaves it up to the hearers both to figure out the intended answer and to challenge it by presenting counter-arguments. So, the Chinese script for disagreeing in a meeting probably includes some assumption like the following:

(5b) *Chinese script for disagreement in meetings*:
Present the information that supports your view. Give the hearers a communicative clue that will enable them to figure out your view(s). A rhetorical question is a useful communicative device for achieving this end.

The notion of script provides an intuitive and simple explanation of the observation that people from different cultures behave in different ways in similar situations. This approach also makes it possible to reconcile Yeung's findings with the general view of Chinese culture. It is usually assumed that an Agreement Maxim carries greater weight in the Chinese culture than in Australian culture, and yet Yeung's data point to a different conclusion. The notion of script provides a rather natural and straightforward explanation for this inconsistency. It could be that in the scripts for most types of situations in the Chinese culture, agreement overrides all other (potentially conflicting) considerations. This manifests itself in the form of communicative behaviour that suggests that an Agreement Maxim is operative in this culture. Now, Yeung describes a relatively new type of situation (participative meeting) in Chinese society, and her work lends support to the conclusion that the participative meeting script in Hong Kong presents an exception to the Chinese culture in general: in this script, agreement does not outweigh all other considerations.

If an account along these lines is anything to go by, it suggests a rather elegant way of explaining the relation between interactional 'rules' such as Leech's (1983) Maxims and situational variation. The Maxims could be seen as reflections of the contents of individual scripts for various types of situations used within a given culture. Thus, for the Agreement Maxim to be found to prevail in the Chinese culture, all that is needed is that some rule like 'Avoid disagreement!' should have overriding weight in scripts for most types of situations within the culture. The observable communicative behaviour of the members of this culture would then lend support to the Agreement Maxim, which has the status of an interpretive generalization, rather than of a single criterion that is applied across the board. In this approach, the high weighting of the 'Avoid disagreement' rule across the situation scripts of the Chinese culture could be explained in terms of a social attitude about the importance of agreement, shared by most members of the culture, and this attitude could be seen as derived from a culture-specific manifestation of one of the fundamental value dimensions (perhaps Integration or Individualism). In section 3.3.1.1, we pointed out that neither Hofstede's (1980) study, nor a subsequent values survey of nations (Chinese Culture Connection 1987) supports the view that harmony has a special place in Chinese culture, although hierarchy does (Bond 1996). A descriptive linguistic analysis of situations in terms of scripts could be carried out to provide further evidence bearing on this issue.

Another interesting consequence of the notion of script is that it makes comparisons across cultures reasonably manageable. Scripts are influenced by both interactional 'rules'/maxims and situational factors. Given that 'rules' are measurable cross-culturally, it would be straightforward to assess their variable operation in different cultural groups by examining their strength across, say, a variety of role relationships, conceptualized in culturally equivalent ways (see McAuley et al. 1999). One could then begin theorizing on how culture influences the strength of role-based, conversational maxims, and ally that work with the literature on scripts.

However, an important issue needs to be addressed in this connection. When some interactional 'rules' – for example, 5a and 5b in the participative meeting-scripts in Hong Kong and Australia – are found to be different, the task of comparing the two cultures should not be confined to the observation that Australians are more likely to use the *yes, but...*-strategy and the Chinese the *rhetorical question*-strategy. What needs to be explained is the intuition that the two strategies differ in the degree of (in)directness.

3.4.2 Indirectness

The diagnostic linguistic features of indirectness used in Yeung's (in press) study are: (a) the use of questions instead of statements, (b) the use of degree adverbs and hedges (e.g. 'fairly', 'somewhat', 'rather'), (c) the avoidance of the first person singular pronoun, (d) the tendency to acknowledge the other's previously stated position (say, by repeating it), and (e) the use of rhetorical questions. These features are indeed relevant, and have been used effectively by other researchers (Bond 1991), but they rely on an intuitive notion of indirectness which does not provide a solid basis for measuring indirectness and investigating it across cultures. The main aim of this section is to show how a theoretically motivated comparative notion of indirectness makes the problem more tractable.

Indirectness is a function of the evidence of the communicator's informative intention. Let us explain. Imagine you are in a large room with a few friends. One of them gets up (without explanation) and starts walking. You readily assume that your friend is walking with some intention in mind: to open the door and go out of the room, or perhaps to open the window, or in order to pick up something that he has spotted on the floor. It is only as your friend approaches the door or the window or whatever it is that happens to be lying on the floor that you are in a position to assume confidently that he intends to open the door or the window, or to pick up the object. And when your friend lifts his or her hand towards, say, the door handle, you will be more or less certain of the intention to open the door. The point is this: the assumptions we make about other people's behaviour depend on the available evidence. If the door, the window and the object lying on the floor are to the same side of the room, and if your friend is still at a fair distance from them, you may well not have enough evidence to conclude what it is that your friend is trying to do. Your ability to draw conclusions about your friend's behaviour improves as actions begin to provide more conclusive evidence about his/her intentions.

This observation about the interpretation of behaviour in general carries over to the way acts of communication are understood. The more conclusively a communicative act supports a particular interpretation, the more directly communicated the information in question is; and conversely: the poorer the evidence for a particular interpretation, the more indirect the communication. So, communicative (in)directness can be defined as a function of the evidence for particular interpretations. On this characterization of indirectness, the Chinese *rhetorical question*-strategy for disagreement in meetings is more indirect than the Australian *yes, but*. . .-strategy. Other things being equal, a rhetorical question allows for a wide range of answers, and gives the hearer the opportunity to volunteer a response that goes against the speaker's views. In contrast to the *rhetorical question*-strategy, other things being equal, a 'yes, but. . .' utterance explicitly indicates (a) that the speaker acknowledges the hearer's point of view (this is part of the meaning of 'yes'), and (b) that the speaker disagrees which some assumptions which follow from that view (this is based on the denial of expectation meaning of 'but').

However, in communication things are not always equal! When particular linguistic items are frequently used to perform a particular communicative strategy, they become conventionally associated with that strategy. For example, requests such as 'Can you. . .', 'Could you. . .' and a number of others are *conventional* indicators of polite behaviour. The speaker who uses one of these will not be taken to have communicated anything about his or her politeness, but rather to have simply fulfilled a social convention (except, of course, when the speaker is well-known for lacking good conversational manners, in which case even the observance of a social convention is sufficiently unusual to signal new information worth having). Hence, conventionalization has a direct consequence for the study of indirectness: the more strongly an expression is conventionalized as a marker of indirectness, the less indirectly communicated the message will be. The reason for this should be quite clear: if an expression has become a conventional way for communicating, say, disagreement, then it will provide conclusive evidence that the speaker is in fact expressing disagreement with the hearer, and that he or she is observing a social norm of appropriate linguistic behaviour; the original indirectness of the expression will have been lost.

This characterization of indirectness and conventionalization has important implications for describing and explaining indirect communication across cultures. For example, in order to assess the degree of indirectness of the Chinese and the Australians in expressing disagreements in meetings we need to take into account the extent to which the strategies that they employ have become conventionalized markers of indirectness. But is it possible to measure degrees of conventionalization and indirectness? We do not see why this should not be feasible. Our objective measures could be expressed either fairly loosely by using terms such as 'more or less', or more rigorously, by expressing the findings of careful descriptive and experimental studies on numerical scales of indirectness and conventionalization. Whichever method is adopted, it is important to bear in mind that the judgements of indirectness (and conventionalization) on which people rely in actual spontaneous communicative behaviour are themselves intuitive and comparative, rather than consciously calculated and absolute.

3.5 Conclusion

> Every discovery, every enlargement of the understanding, begins as an imaginative preconception of what the truth might be.
> Peter Medawar, *Advice to a Young Scientist*

Intercultural communication presents researchers with many theoretical and methodological problems. In this chapter we have considered several concepts which play a key role in explaining the complexities of culture and communication: the concept of culture as values (social psychology and anthropology), the analyses of the relation between culture and communication in terms of interactional maxims (linguistic pragmatics), the characterization of communication situations in terms of scripts (psychology of culture; pragmatics), the roles of indirectness and conventionalization in language use (pragmatics; philosophy of language). We have identified a range of problematic issues in the field of intercultural communication, especially with reference to Yeung's (in press) study, and we have explored the possibility of bringing together the notions of values, maxims, situation, script, communicative indirectness and conventionalization in order to provide a coherent approach to these issues. We have argued that the situational context could be characterized in terms of scripts whose content largely reflects particular interactional 'rules'. The widespread distribution of some 'rules' in many situation scripts provides the basis for positing normative maxims. Communicative indirectness is a means of resolving conflicting rules within the same script, and the frequent use of the same solutions gradually leads to conventionalized forms of linguistic behaviour.

Discussion questions

1 Defining culture

1.1 Look up the dictionary entry for 'culture' (consult several dictionaries). Identify the main features of 'culture' in each definition. What differences (if any) do you observe in the definitions?

1.2 Identify and describe any major differences you have observed between the dictionary definitions of 'culture' and the way the notion of culture is characterized in this chapter and Chapter 1.

2 Explaining the effect of culture

2.1 What problems are associated with using 'culture' to explain differences in behaviour between people from different cultural groups?

2.2 What suggestions for overcoming them are made in this chapter? How promising do you think they are?

3 Situations

3.1 Try to characterize each of the following communicative activities in terms of dimensions of situational variation.

Communicative Activity	Dimensions of Situational Variation
(a) University seminar	(i) Regulation/scriptedness–openness
(b) Wedding ceremony	(ii) Visible/public–private
(c) Business negotiation meeting	(iii) Socio-emotional–task-oriented
(d) Job interview	(iv) Cooperative–competitive
(e) Family meal	(v) Intense–superficial

3.2 If you are working with people from different cultures, discuss the similarities and differences in your conceptions.

3.3 Did you experience any difficulties in characterizing communicative activities in this way? If so, what were they and how might they be overcome?

4 Scripts

4.1 Choose one of the communicative activities listed above and try to identify the scripts (i.e. interactional 'rules') that operate in such situations in your culture regarding the expression of one or more of the following: (a) disagreement, (b) modesty, (c) criticism. If you are working with people from different cultures, compare your specifications.

4.2 How could you validate the scripts that you have identified?

Suggestions for further reading

Hofstede, G. (1991) *Cultures and Organizations: Software of the Mind.* London: McGraw Hill.

Matsumoto, D. (1996) *Culture and Psychology.* Pacific Grove, CA: Brooks/Cole.

Smith, P.B. and Bond, M.H. (1998) *Social Psychology across Cultures.* (2nd edition). London: Prentice Hall.

Triandis, H.C. (1994) *Culture and Social Behavior.* New York: McGraw-Hill.

Wierzbicka, A. (1994) Cultural scripts: a semantic approach to cultural analysis and cross-cultural communication. In M. Pütz (ed.), *Language Contact, Language Conflict.* Amsterdam: John Benjamins, 69–87.

Notes

1. Portions of this chapter appeared as an article in the *Journal of Asian Pacific Communication* and it is reprinted by permission.
2. The first three variables were positively correlated with Individualism and the last three were negatively correlated.
3. These seem to draw on both the Cooperative Principle and the Politeness Principle.
4. This example is a translation of an exchange in Cantonese. See Yeung for the Chinese transcription.

PART TWO

CROSS-CULTURAL PRAGMATICS RESEARCH: EMPIRICAL STUDIES

4

'It's not my fault!': Japanese and English Responses to Unfounded Accusations

Noriko Tanaka, Helen Spencer-Oatey and Ellen Cray

4.1 Introduction

It was 1986, and I (Noriko Tanaka) was in Canberra, experiencing my first long stay abroad. I had bought a desk lamp but, when I got back to my apartment, I found that it was broken. I returned to the store to exchange it, and the person at the desk simply said, 'I see. Do you want to exchange it?' I was shocked and felt insulted, because in Japan the person at the store would apologize profusely in such a situation. Later, an Australian told me that Australian people tend to regard it as the customer's fault, because the customer did not notice it was broken. I felt that this idea of 'customer responsibility' contrasted sharply with the Japanese belief that 'customers are gods'. Although I could understand that shop assistants cannot be held responsible for manufacturing defects, I felt that Japanese people would not *feel* this way, because their apologies are not only linked to a sense of personal responsibility, but also to a desire for a harmonious atmosphere.

On another occasion, an Australian student drove into the car of one of my Japanese friends, causing some minor damage. The next day, my friend went to the Australian's house to discuss compensation, but she was not in. Although her parents were there, they did not express any apology for what their daughter had done. My Japanese friend was shocked and offended at their behaviour, feeling that Japanese parents would have apologized in that situation, and that the Australian parents were impolite and even insulting. However, discussing the incident with some Australian friends, I was told that the Australian parents' attitude was acceptable, because their daughter was an adult.

Incidents such as these point to possible cultural differences in so-called 'polite' behaviour, and at the same time highlight the tendency for people to react emotionally to unexpected behaviour (see Chapter 7). If such incidents occur in an intercultural encounter, people may attribute them to 'cultural differences', especially if they offer support for previously held stereotypes. This chapter explores such issues with respect to apologizing behaviour in Japanese and English.

4.2 Cross-cultural perspectives on apologies

People in most cultures would probably agree that an apology is needed when an offence or violation of social norms has taken place. However, there may be differing opinions as to when we should apologize (what situations call for an apology), and how we should apologize (what semantic components are necessary for an adequate apology in a given context).

4.2.1 Apologies in Japanese and English: stereotypical conceptions

It seems that both Japanese and Westerners hold similar stereotypical conceptions of apologizing behaviour in each other's cultures; namely, that Japanese apologize more frequently than native speakers of English, and that an apology in Japanese does not necessarily mean that the person is acknowledging a fault. Consider, for example, the following extracts from the English-speaking media:

> (ABC News broadcaster reporting on a Japanese ice-skater who fell at the Olympics) 'I am sorry, I made a mistake,' she said. No one questioned her sincerity, but apologies are almost automatic in Japan; every day, everywhere, everyone here says they are sorry. Apologizing is so much a part of Japanese culture that foreign executives who want to do business here now go to school to learn the techniques. But the instructor Eiichi Shiraishi admits saying you are sorry does not mean you have done something wrong. < *shazai no imi de tsukau baai mo arimasu keredomo* > [video-taped clip of Shiraishi speaking; interrupted before the utterance was completed; $there are some occasions we use it as an apology but we also$, Tanaka's translation]. [Broadcaster continues] I believe that in most cases the phrase 'I'm sorry' or 'sumimasen' is often

used to be diplomatic. People here don't always mean that they are truly sorry, which brings up the question of the sincerity of Japan's recent apologies. Was Prime Minister Miyazawa really sorry when he apologized for questioning Americans' work ethic? A month ago, Japanese Prime Minister Miyazawa visited South Korea and said he was sorry that Korean women had been forced to provide sex for Japanese soldiers during World War II, but today the Japanese Foreign Ministry said there would be no compensation at all for those women. (ABC News, shown on *World News Tonight*, broadcast by NHK Tokyo, 20 February 1992)

While other war crimes have, to varying degrees, been laid to rest, Japan's burn on, fuelled by the country's seeming inability to issue an unambivalent apology. This is peculiar coming from a country which thrives on saying sorry. 'In daily life the Japanese apologise every other sentence,' says Richard Bowring, Professor of Japanese at Cambridge University. 'They do it 50 times a minute – it's the way they oil society.' (Edward Pilkington, *Guardian*, 15 August 1995)

In fact, it is all too easy to say sorry in Japanese. The language, perhaps more than any other, has many forms of apology which present a bewildering pattern of complexity to anyone unfamiliar with Japan's culture. (*The Times*, 16 August 1995)

Japanese writers also seem to acknowledge such differences. Naotsuka (1980), for example, describes American apologizing behaviour (in comparison with Japanese) as follows:

'I am sorry' – guilty – take responsibility – compensation. Such a system prevents American people from saying 'sorry' as Japanese do. One attacks the other furiously. If not, the other takes advantage of his/her weakness. Being attacked, counterattack. That's their way. (Naotsuka 1980: 57, translated by Tanaka)

Sugimoto (1998: 254) compared the norms of apology as depicted in US American and Japanese etiquette books and manuals and argues as follows:

Etiquette books suggest that Japanese are expected to apologize for actions of a far greater number of people than are U.S. Americans. In U.S. American conduct manuals, people apologize only for their own mistakes, with the exception of women's apologizing for the mishaps of their spouses, young children or pets.... By contrast, in Japanese conduct manuals, the readers are told to apologize for offenses committed by a greater range of people beyond themselves. In addition to examples of women's apologizing for the mishaps of their husbands . . ., children . . ., and pets . . ., Japanese conduct manuals contain numerous examples of people apologizing for others' misconduct such as: (a) parents' apology for offenses committed by their adult children, in situations such as a car accident . . . or not keeping in touch with a former school teacher . . .; (b) matchmakers' apology to one party for the delay in reply by the other party or for their rejection of the match . . . ; and (c) apology for recommendees' misconduct by those who recommended them for employment, when the recommendees quit the job or embezzled the company money. . .

However, as Sugimoto (1998: 251) points out, it cannot be inferred that people actually apologize according to the norms depicted in etiquette literature; rather, they are better seen as behavioural ideals for a dominant segment of the population. To find out how people actually apologize, we need to turn to linguistic studies.

4.2.2 Linguistic studies of Japanese and English apologies

A number of linguistic studies have explored cultural differences in apologizing behaviour: for example, Cohen and Olshtain (1981), Olshtain (1989), and Vollmer and Olshtain (1989). A range of semantic components for performing apologies have been identified (see Table 2.2), and some differences in frequency of use of the various components have also been found. Several studies have focused on Japanese and English apologies (e.g. Barnlund and Yoshioka 1990; Tanaka 1991; Kotani 1997) and have found a number of differences between Japanese and English apologies.

Barnlund and Yoshioka (1990) devised a questionnaire containing 12 scenarios describing offences of varying degrees of severity (e.g. having an accident in a borrowed car and causing minor damage; having an accident in a borrowed car and seriously injuring someone). For each scenario, respondents were asked to select their preferred way of handling the situation from the following 12 options: not say or do anything, explain the situation, apologize ambiguously, apologize non-verbally, casually say 'sorry', act helpless, say directly 'I am very sorry', write a letter of apology, apologize directly several ways and several times, offer to do something for the person, leave or resign a position, commit suicide. The questionnaire was completed by120 Japanese university students and 120 American university students, and the researchers found both similarities and differences in the responses. For both groups, the most frequent overall choice was 'say directly "I am very sorry"' (28.7 per cent for the Japanese and 23.3 per cent for the Americans). For the Americans, though, the second most frequent overall choice was 'explain the situation' (21.5 per cent for the Americans, 12.2 per cent for the Japanese), whereas for the Japanese it was 'do something for the other person' (21.1 per cent for the Japanese, 15.3 per cent for the Americans). On the basis of these questionnaire results and accompanying interview data, the authors claim 'the results indicate that Americans seem less comfortable in giving and receiving apologies and tend to prefer less direct and extreme forms of apologizing. The tendency to explain failure rather than admit to it may strike more deeply into the American psyche than it appears to do' (Barnlund and Yoshioka 1990: 204).

Tanaka (1991) used a production questionnaire (see Chapter 15) to explore apologies in Japanese and Australian English (10 university students for each). She found that participant relations (social distance and relative power) had a greater effect on Japanese apologizing behaviour than on English; and she also found that the Japanese respondents had a greater tendency to apologize for offences caused by other family members than Australian respondents did.

Kotani (1997) used in-depth interviews to explore Japanese university students' experiences of apologizing behaviour in the United States. She interviewed 15 Japanese students, and found that they did not consider it appropriate to offer lengthy explanations in apologies, irrespective of whether the person was at fault or not. They also tended to expect their apologies to be reciprocated or denied by others, rather than be accepted as an admission of responsibility. It would be interesting to carry out a similar study with American students.

All of these studies have identified some differences in apologizing behaviour in Japanese and English. However, some of them have research procedure weaknesses (e.g. Barnlund and Yoshioka (1990) only allowed respondents to choose one option when in reality people might use more than one, and Tanaka (1991) only used a very small number of respondents). So there is clearly a need for much more empirical research in this area. This study is an attempt to add to our understanding of apologizing behaviour in Japanese, British English and Canadian English, focusing on the effect of 'personal fault'. We decided to focus on this factor since little linguistic research has been done on this to date, and since the stereotype of Japanese and

Western apologizing behaviour suggests that Japanese are more willing to apologize when they are not at fault than Westerners are.

4.3 Research procedure

A production questionnaire with accompanying rating scales (see the Appendix to this chapter) was used to explore the issue. This enabled us to obtain comparable data in Japan, Britain, and Canada. Naturally we cannot be sure that people's responses in authentic situations would necessarily be the same as those given in the questionnaire. Nevertheless, a questionnaire of this kind can act as a useful starting point for further more authentic research, and, as Beebe and Cummings (1996; see Chapter 15 of this book) found, can model the 'canonical shape' of authentic responses.

4.3.1 Design of the questionnaire

The questionnaire comprised eight scenarios, all of which contained a similar complaint against the respondent. Since we were interested in finding out whether people apologize in situations where 'guilt' and 'responsibility' are in doubt, we decided to omit scenarios in which the accused person is clearly responsible for the offence. So for half of the scenarios, responsibility for the offence lay mainly with the person who was making the complaint (henceforth, CP scenarios); for the other half, responsibility for the offence lay mainly with a third party or with external circumstances (henceforth, EC scenarios). This resulted in four pairs of scenarios, in which the offence was kept constant (a late arrival of 30 minutes), but the participant relations were varied across the pairs. The order in which the scenarios were presented was randomized. The research design is shown in Table 4.1. (See the Appendix for the exact scenarios used.)

For the first two pairs, the complaint was against the respondent personally (the student and the friend respectively); for the second two pairs, the complaint was against a 'relevant party' to the respondent (the respondent's employing company and the respondent's father respectively). We hoped in this way to probe people's sense of corporate (non-)responsibility, as well as personal (non-)responsibility.

Respondents were asked to respond to a first-pair prompt by writing the exact words they thought they would use in reply. In addition, they were asked to provide some contextual assessments of the scenarios: how annoying they thought the problem was for the person complaining; how far they felt responsible for the problem occurring; and how important they felt it was to placate the person complaining. These were included so that we could check whether

Table 4.1 Design of the questionnaire scenarios

	Complaining Person mainly responsible for the problem (CP Scenarios)	Third Party/External Circumstances mainly responsible for the problem (EC Scenarios)
Scenario 5 [Complaining] Lecturer – [Responding] Student	✓	
Scenario 3 [Complaining] Lecturer – [Responding] Student		✓
Scenario 2 [Complaining] Friend – [Responding] Friend	✓	
Scenario 8 [Complaining] Friend – [Responding] Friend		✓
Scenario 4 [Complaining] Customer – [Responding] Company Employee	✓	
Scenario 7 [Complaining] Customer – [Responding] Company Employee		✓
Scenario 1 [Complaining] Father's Boss – [Responding] Son/Daughter	✓	
Scenario 6 [Complaining] Father's Boss – [Responding] Son/Daughter		✓

the different groups of respondents perceived the scenarios in similar ways. Three 5-point Likert-type rating scales were thus listed under each scenario, and respondents were asked to circle the numbers on these scales that corresponded to their evaluations.

Japanese and English versions of the questionnaire were produced using backtranslation and the decentring process suggested by Brislin (1976) (see Chapter 14). This was to ensure that the scenarios and the rating scales were not only equivalent in meaning for speakers of Japanese, British English and Canadian English, but also culturally appropriate for them all.

4.3.2 The respondents

The questionnaires were completed by undergraduate university students in Japan, Britain and Canada.[1] They were distributed in class, and filled in immediately. In Britain and Canada, only students who identified their main home language as English as well as their nationality as British or Canadian respectively were included in the sample. The numbers of students who completed the questionnaires were as follows: 131 Japanese, 165 British, and 96 Canadian. There were slightly more male than female respondents in Japan and Britain (65 per cent and 54 per cent males respectively), and almost equal proportions in Canada (48 per cent males). In all three countries, 89 per cent or more of the respondents were aged 17–24.

4.4 Results

4.4.1 Contextual assessments

The three groups of respondents' mean ratings (and standard deviations) of the CP and EC scenarios (averaged across the four situations) are shown in Table 4.2.

As can be seen from Table 4.2, all three groups of respondents rated both the CP and EC scenarios as 'annoying' to the person complaining. There was a tendency for the Japanese respondents to rate them as slightly less annoying than the British and Canadian respondents did, and for both CP and EC scenarios, ANOVA tests showed this difference to be statistically significant (Annoying, CP: $F = 5.19$, df = 2,383, $p = 0.001$; Annoying, EC: $F = 7.21$, df = 2,362 $p = 0.006$). However, β^2 figures show that only 2.6 per cent and 3.8

Table 4.2 Mean ratings (and standard deviations) of contextual assessment factors in the scenarios

	Japanese	British	Canadian
'Annoying': CP	3.94 (.88)	4.09 (.57)	4.23 (.47)
'Annoying': EC	4.07 (1.00)	4.35 (.63)	4.41 (.47)
'Responsible': CP	1.99 (.61)	1.96 (.65)	1.89 (.58)
'Responsible': EC	2.42 (.66)	2.25 (.64)	2.44 (.65)
'Make less annoyed': CP	3.11 (.80)	3.84 (.74)	3.69 (.68)
'Make less annoyed': EC	3.71 (.80)	3.85 (.83)	4.02 (.68)

Note: Ratings are based on a 5-point Likert-type scale from 1 (*not at all annoying/responsible/important*) to 5 (*very annoying/responsible/important*)

per cent respectively of the variance is attributable to nationality, which suggests that the statistical differences are not very meaningful, and that on the whole all three nationality groups perceived the scenarios to be similarly annoying to the person complaining.

In terms of responsibility, all three groups of respondents rated themselves as 'not very responsible' for the problems described in the scenarios, although the mean ratings for EC scenarios were slightly higher than for CP scenarios (see Table 4.2). ANOVA tests showed that nationality had no statistically significant effect on the ratings of CP scenarios (Responsibility, CP: $F = 0.79$, df $= 2,382$, $p = 0.46$), but had a slight but non-meaningful effect on the ratings of EC scenarios (Responsibility, EC: $F = 3.36$, df $= 2,362$, $p = 0.04$, $\beta^2 = 0.018$). These findings thus confirm that all three groups of respondents regarded themselves as not being responsible for the problems that occurred, and that their perceptions were similar.

In terms of the importance of 'making the person less annoyed', all three groups of respondents rated this as 'important' for EC scenarios, with the Canadian respondents giving the highest ratings. An ANOVA test showed there to be a slightly significant difference in ratings across the nationality groups (Make less annoyed, EC: $F = 4.34$, df $= 2,361$, $p = 0.014$, $\beta^2 = .023$), but since only 2.3 per cent of the variance was attributable to nationality, this does not appear to be a meaningful difference. For the CP scenarios, British and Canadian respondents rated these as more important to 'make the person less annoyed' than the Japanese respondents did. An ANOVA test showed that nationality had a very statistically significant effect on these ratings (Make less annoyed, CP: $F = 35.29$, df $= 2,379$, $p < 0.001$, $\beta^2 = .157$), and that 15.7 per cent of the variance is attributable to nationality, suggesting that this is a fairly meaningful difference. Comparing the EC and CP scenario ratings for the importance of 'making the person less annoyed', there was a bigger drop in the ratings for the Japanese and Canadian respondents than for the British respondents. Paired-sample t-tests showed that 'source of responsibility' had a significant effect on both Japanese ($t = -9.15$, df $= 122$, $p < 0.0001$) and Canadian ($t = -5.27$, df $= 95$, $p < 0.001$) ratings of the importance of 'making the person less annoyed', but not for the British respondents ($t = -1.01$, df $= 139$, $p = 0.31$). This suggests that to the Japanese, and to a lesser extent the Canadians, the importance of placating the complainant depended on who was responsible for the offence. For the British the source of responsibility had no significant effect on the felt need to placate.

It seems, therefore, that all three groups of respondents had basically similar perceptions of the CP and EC scenarios in terms of 'annoyance' and 'personal responsibility'. They were also fairly similar for the EC scenarios in terms of 'importance of making the person less annoyed'. However, for the CP scenarios, the effect of nationality was greater, with Japanese respondents judging it to be significantly less important to placate the person than the British and Canadian respondents did.

4.4.2 Production responses

The production responses given by the three groups of respondents were analysed for the semantic components that they contained. The CCSARP coding scheme (Blum-Kulka *et al.* 1989) was used as the starting point for the analysis; however, we found that we needed to make some minor modifications to it, particularly in respect to the strategies *Taking on Responsibility* and *Explanation or Account*. It seemed that 'Responsibility' formed a continuum from 'clear acceptance of responsibility' at one end, through 'indeterminate responsibility' in the middle, to 'clear rejection of responsibility' at the other end. Sometimes, an explanation or account seemed to be neutral in terms of responsibility (e.g. Scenario 1, *He's gone for a health check*); but at other times it seemed to be a strategy for minimizing responsibility (e.g. Scenario 3, *I met another lecturer and I couldn't get away from him.*) So we decided not to use *Explanation or Account* as a separate category. Instead, we used 'Responsibility' as a main category, with three principal sub-categories: admission of responsibility, indeterminate responsibility, rejection of responsibility.[2] Many respondents used a number of strategies in relation to responsibility; however, for the purpose of this analysis, we looked at the overall thrust of the responsibility comment(s) and gave just one coding. If the respondent clearly admitted responsibility, we classified it as 'admission of responsibility'; if the respondent clearly rejected responsibility, such as by denying fault or referring to an agreement, we classified it as 'rejection of responsibility'; and if the respondent gave a more ambiguous response in terms of responsibility, such as by simply giving an explanation, by referring to some kind of misunderstanding, or by stating what was thought had been agreed, we classified it as 'indeterminate responsibility'. Sometimes it was difficult to categorize the responses in this way, but in most cases there was no problem.

For *Offer of Repair*, we broadened this category to include not only offers of repair or help, but all comments that functioned to 'manage the problem or offence' in some way; e.g. comments of reassurance, task-oriented remarks, and so on.

The following categories were thus used in this analysis:[3]

(1) IFID (Illocutionary Force Indicating Device), e.g.
- *I'm sorry for the misunderstanding.*
- *I apologize for being late.*
- *Mooshiwake gozaimasen.* $I apologize.$[4]
- *Okurete sumimasen.* $I'm sorry for being late.$
(2) Responsibility
  2.1 Admission of responsibility, e.g.
  - *I thought we agreed to meet at half two. I must have misunderstood.*
  - *I got caught up in a discussion with another prof. My fault completely.*
  - *Kochira no techigai desu.* $That's our fault.$
  - *Watashi no kikichigai deshita.* $I misunderstood.$
  2.2 Indeterminate responsibility, e.g.
  - *I heard him mention that he has his annual health check-up today, so I think he's still there.*
  - *That's strange sir. It says here that it was to be delivered tomorrow morning. There must have been some sort of misunderstanding.*
  - *Chichi wa kenkoo-shindan ni dekakete iruto omoimasu.* $I think my father went for the health check.$
  - *Ekimaette iu yakusoku ja nakattakke?* $Didn't we agree to meet in front of the station?$
  2.3 Rejection of responsibility, e.g.
  - *Last week I overheard him telling you that he had a doctor's appointment today.*
  - *Actually sir, you signed for the goods to be delivered tomorrow.*
  - *Yakusoku shita toori ekimae de matteta yo.* $I was waiting in front of the station as we had agreed.$
  - *Okurete masen'yo. Niji-han ni au yakusoku desukara.* $I'm not late. We agreed to meet at 2:30.$
  2.4 Other responsibility-related comment, e.g.
  - *I'll explain on the way.*
  - *I'm afraid I don't know.*
  - *Dokoe ittaka wakarimasen.* $I don't know where he is.$
(3) Manage problem, e.g.
  - *I'll take a message so that I can pass it on to him.* (Offer of help/repair)

- *Nanika wakarimashitara, renraku itashimasu.* $I'll let you know if I get some information.$ (Offer of help/repair)
- *I'll see if I can get them to deliver it this afternoon.* (Offer of help/repair)
- *Hirugohan ogorukara yurushite.* $I'll buy you a lunch, so forgive me.$ (Offer of help/repair)
- *We'll not be able to deliver the goods now until tomorrow.* (Refuse repair)
- *I'm sure he'll be there soon!* (Reassure)
- *Mamonaku tsuku to omoimasu.* $It will get there soon.$ (Reassure)
- *You can try and call him on his mobile.* (Make a suggestion)
- *Let's get going or we'll miss the concert.* (Task-oriented comment)
- *Tonikaku isogoo.* $Let's hurry anyway.$ (Task-oriented comment)

Table 4.3 shows the percentage of production responses that contained each of these strategies. For the main categories, IFID, Responsibility and Manage Problem, the figures represent the

Table 4.3 Percentages of production responses containing different types of semantic components

	Complaining Person mainly responsible for the problem (CP Scenarios)			Third Party/External Circumstances mainly responsible for the problem (EC Scenarios)		
	Japanese	British	Canadian	Japanese	British	Canadian
Total number of responses	521	642	384	514	584	384
Percentage of responses with						
IFID coding	**21.88**	**41.28**	**34.64**	**64.01**	**57.54**	**59.12**
Responsibility						
Admit	4.22	2.49	3.13	1.95	1.37	1.30
Indeterminate	51.25	47.51	57.29	90.08	88.01	91.15
Reject	33.78	37.85	32.55	0.78	4.80	3.91
Other	4.42	5.76	3.38	–	1.71	1.56
Percentage of responses with						
Responsibility coding	**93.67**	**93.61**	**96.35**	**92.80**	**95.89**	**97.92**
Manage Problem						
Refuse repair	0.77	0.93	0.52	–	–	0.78
Offer help/repair	4.41	13.24	19.01	2.53	5.48	10.68
Reassure	0.96	6.39	5.21	7.98	13.36	19.79
Suggest	4.22	1.56	0.52	8.17	0.86	0.52
Task-oriented	0.77	4.67	3.91	–	5.31	9.64
Percentage of responses with						
Manage Problem coding	**11.13**	**26.79**	**29.17**	**18.68**	**25.00**	**41.41**

percentage of responses that contained one or more phrases with these codings (i.e. in contrast with the percentage of responses that did not include any phrases with these codings).[5] The sub-categories of Responsibility and Manage Problem were analysed as mutually exclusive categories, as explained above.

As can be seen from Table 4.3, the responses produced by all three groups of respondents contained a very high percentage of 'Responsibility' comments; and for the CP scenarios, the proportion of responses that explicitly rejected responsibility (typically, by pointing out how the person who was complaining was to blame) was also very similar across the three nationality groups.

In terms of use of 'IFIDs', the percentages of responses containing at least one IFID was very similar across the three nationality groups for the EC scenarios, but showed a significant difference for the CP scenarios. Chi square tests confirmed that nationality had no significant effect for EC scenarios (χ^2 = 5.03, df = 2, $p >$ 0.05), but did have a significant effect for CP scenarios (χ^2 = 49.41, df = 2, $p < 0.001$). Looking at the use of IFIDs in CP scenarios compared with EC scenarios, it can be seen that for all three nationality groups the percentage of responses containing at least one IFID was lower for the CP scenarios than for the EC scenarios. However, the size of the drop varied across the three nationalities: it was smallest for the British respondents (16.26 per cent) and highest for the Japanese (42.13 per cent). This is broadly in line with the difference in the EC and CP 'Placate' ratings shown in Table 4.2.

With regard to 'Manage Problem', there were also some clear nationality differences. For the EC scenarios, they were much more frequent in the Canadian responses than in either the British or the Japanese responses, with the Japanese showing the lowest percentage frequency of use. For the CP scenarios, a similar pattern was found, although the gap between the British and Canadian percentage frequency of use was smaller than for the EC scenarios. Once again, chi square tests showed nationality to have a significant effect (EC scenarios: χ^2 = 59.60, df = 2, $p < 0.001$; CP scenarios: χ^2 = 55.73, df = 2, $p < 0.001$).

4.5 Discussion

These results do not fit in with either Western or Japanese conceptions of Japanese versus English apologizing behaviour. Overall, the Japanese did not apologize (in terms of use of IFIDs) significantly more frequently than the British or Canadian respondents, and when the person who was complaining was at fault, the Japanese respondents actually apologized very much *less* frequently than either the British or Canadian respondents. What, then, might explain such findings?

4.5.1 'Sumimasen' *versus* 'I'm sorry'

One possibility is that people's stereotypical conceptions of the apologizing behaviour of Japanese compared with that of English speakers are inaccurate. English-speakers might think that Japanese apologize more frequently than they really do because '*sumimasen*' is used so frequently. *Sumimasen* can be translated as 'I'm sorry' and be used for an apology; however, it can also be used for various other purposes. Ide (1998), for example, identifies seven different functions of *sumimasen*, after observing how it was used authentically in a clinic in Tokyo. She found that in addition to it being used to convey sincere apologies, *sumimasen* was also used to express thanks, to convey a mixture of thanks and apologies, as a preliminary to a request, as an attention-getter, as a leave-taking device, and more ritualistically (i.e. with little semantic content) as a device to confirm what someone has said or simply to acknowledge it. Ide (1998: 510) argues that *sumimasen* thus 'functions in both a "remedial" and a "supportive" manner in discourse, carrying pragmatic and ritualistic functions that extend beyond conveying the semantic meaning of regret or gratitude in actual discourse'. One possibility, therefore, is that people with only a superficial knowledge of Japanese and English think that *sumimasen* and 'I'm sorry' are equivalent. So when they hear Japanese use *sumimasen* much more frequently than they hear English-speakers use 'I'm sorry', they interpret this as indicating that Japanese apologize more frequently than English-speakers do.

4.5.2 The effect of situation

Another possible explanation for the findings is that people's conceptions of Japanese and English apologizing behaviour are accurate for certain types of situations, but not for others. For example, it could be that IFIDs are used more routinely in Japan than in Britain and Canada, and/or are used more frequently in situations where the person apologizing is personally at fault and the offence is more substantive. Such types of contexts were not included in this study, so it is possible that a different set of results would have emerged with scenarios that manipulated a different set of contextual features. Even in this study, there was a certain amount of variation from scenario to scenario. For instance, the Japanese respondents used IFIDs more frequently than the British and Canadian respondents did (86.72 per cent compared with 68.84 per cent and 65.63 per cent respectively) when responding to Scenario 7, where the customer complains and external circumstances are to blame. And they used them very much less frequently than the British and Canadian respondents did (12.31 per cent compared with 59.84 per cent and 61.46 per cent respectively) when responding to Scenario 5, where the lecturer complains but is in fact responsible for the misunderstanding. So it is clearly possible that a different set of scenarios might have yielded a different set of results. Nevertheless, this cannot explain why the variable 'source of responsibility' should have had a consistently much greater effect on the Japanese responses than on the British and Canadian responses, when according to the stereotype (that Japanese apologize more frequently when they are at fault than English-speakers do), the opposite should have emerged.

4.5.3 Representativeness of the respondents

A third possible explanation of the unexpected findings could be that the respondents were not truly representative of their respective national cultures. For example, Gudykunst and Nishida (in press; see also Chapter 14 in this book) argue that Japanese college students demonstrate high levels of individualism, and may in fact be more individualistic than American students. If this is the case, then they may not be representative of Japanese people in general, on which the stereotype is based. In keeping with this, Tanaka (1999) argues that Japanese traditional norms may be changing. She gathered production questionnaire data, using the same discourse completion scenarios, from Japanese students in 1986 and in 1997. Comparing the two sets of data, she found that the use of IFIDs was less frequent in 1997 than in 1986, especially for scenarios where the person complaining was at fault.

So it is possible that the stereotype of Japanese versus Western apologizing behaviour is derived from traditional Japanese norms, which university students do not necessarily subscribe to (and may decreasingly be subscribing to), but which many ordinary adult Japanese people still uphold.

4.5.4 The research procedure

A final possible explanation of the findings is that it is an artifact of the research procedure; in other words, that the responses given by the respondents do not reflect what they would really say in authentic situations. This is obviously a genuine concern, and as Kasper explains in Chapter 15, research has shown that production questionnaire data and authentic data differ in various respects. Nevertheless, she argues that production responses can indicate what contextual factors influence respondents' choices, and this suggests that even if the frequency of use of the various semantic components is different in real life from the percentage frequencies found in the questionnaire responses in this study, the effect of the variable 'source of responsibility' is likely to be similar.

4.6 Concluding comments

More research is clearly needed into Japanese and English apologizing behaviour. It would be interesting to collect data from a different sample of respondents (e.g. business people, or university staff) and, using a similar production questionnaire to the one in this study, to compare the results with the findings from this study. If feasible, it would also be particularly helpful to gather authentic data, paying particular attention to the variable 'source of responsibility'. Only then can we be clearer about the relative accuracy of Japanese and Western conceptions of apologizing behaviour in Japanese and English.

Discussion questions

1   Look again at the two incidents in Australia that Tanaka describes. How would you have felt in those circumstances? Would you have been offended as she and her friend were? Why/why not?

2   Look again at the news broadcast about the Japanese ice-skater who apologized for her sports performance.

2.1 Why were the Americans surprised that the figure skater (Midori Ito) apologized to the Japanese nation? Do you find it surprising? Why/why not?

2.2 Why does the broadcaster question the sincerity of Japanese apologies?

2.3 How might a Japanese person explain such language use?

3   Look again at the possible explanations given in section 4.5 for

the findings of this study. Which of them do you find more convincing? Give reasons for your choice(s).

4   Why do people from other countries sometimes feel that English speakers are insincere in their use of 'sorry' and/or 'thank you', and are such feelings justified? To what extent are these phrases used ritualistically (i.e. with little semantic content) in English?

5   A Chinese student studying in Britain was invited to a British home for dinner. As she got up to leave, the following conversation took place:

Chinese student: Sorry. I've caused you a lot of bother this evening.

British host: Bother? It's been no bother. What do you mean? I hope you've enjoyed yourself.

Chinese student: Yes, of course. But I've really given you trouble. I've taken up so much of your time.

British host: But we invited you to come ... we wanted you to come.

Chinese student: Next time you must come to my home and I'll cook you a Chinese meal.

5.1   How usual/unusual do you find this conversation and why?

5.2   Considering the notion of 'cost/benefit', in what ways are apologies and expressions of gratitude similar, and in what ways are they different?

Notes

1. We would like to thank the students at Meikai University, University of Luton and Carleton University for their cooperation in completing the questionnaire.
2. A few other responsibility-related comments occurred, such as *I'll tell you later*. These are classified as 'Other' in this analysis.
3. In addition, we coded the responses for use of address terms, and for expressions of concern. However, only a very small percentage of the responses contained such strategies, so the results of these additional codings are not reported here.
4. $ English text. $ = English translation.
5. If a response had two or more phrases with the same semantic coding (for example, if someone used two IFIDs in their response), this was only counted once in this analysis.

Appendix to Chapter 4

The scenarios and rating scales used in the production questionnaire are reproduced below.

English version

1. This morning your father went to a clinic for his annual medical health check (which his company provides for their employees). About a week ago, you overheard your father telling his boss about the date and time of the health check on the phone. However, mid-morning today, the telephone rings and it is your father's boss. He says in an annoyed tone:

Father's boss: *I'm phoning to ask where your father is. He's supposed to be here for our team meeting, and we've all been waiting for him for about 30 minutes. What's happened to him?*

[Please write the EXACT words you think you would say in response.]

You: ....

2. You arrange to go to a concert with a friend. As you clearly agreed, you wait for him in front of the train station, but after 30 minutes he still does not appear. You give up on him, and go into the station. You then find him at the ticket gate. It is still just possible to get to the concert in time. Your friend is cross with you and says in an annoyed tone:

Your friend: *You're 30 minutes late! What happened?*

3. You have a meeting with your lecturer at 2.00 p.m. As you are on your way, another lecturer stops you to talk about a serious problem with one of your assignments. Because of your discussion, you arrive 30 minutes late for your meeting. Your lecturer is cross with you and says in an annoyed tone:

Your lecturer: *You're 30 minutes late! We agreed to meet at 2 o'clock. What happened?*

4. You are working in the Customer Service section of a department store. The telephone rings, and a customer complains that his goods have not been delivered yet. The purchase form is in front of you, and you see that he signed for the goods to be delivered tomorrow morning. The customer says in an annoyed tone:

Customer: *I bought a table from your store yesterday. You were supposed to deliver it this morning, but it's 12.30 now, and it hasn't arrived. What has happened?*

5. You have a meeting with your lecturer at 2.30 p.m. You arrive there at exactly 2.30 p.m, but he is cross with you, saying you promised to be there at 2.00 p.m. Your lecturer says in an annoyed tone:
Your lecturer: *You're 30 minutes late! We agreed to meet at 2 o'clock. What happened?*

6. Your father left home for work at the normal time this morning. Afterwards, you happened to hear on the local radio that there was an accident on the line your father uses and the trains are running late. Later the telephone rings; it is your father's boss. He says in an annoyed tone:
Father's boss: *I'm phoning to ask where your father is. He's supposed to be here for our team meeting, and we've all been waiting for him for about 30 minutes. What's happened to him?*

7. You are working in the Customer Service section of a department store. The telephone rings, and a customer complains that his goods have not been delivered yet. You know that there was a traffic accident near your warehouse, and that the road from your warehouse was closed for several hours. The customer says in an annoyed tone:
Customer: *I bought a table from your store yesterday. You were supposed to deliver it this morning, but it's 12.30 now, and it hasn't arrived. What has happened?*

8. You arrange to go to a concert with a friend. You agree to meet at the ticket gate of the station near the concert hall, but you are 30 minutes late because there was an accident and your train was late. You find your friend still waiting at the ticket gate. It is still just possible to get to the concert in time. Your friend is cross with you and says in an annoyed tone:
Your friend: *You're 30 minutes late! What happened?*

For each scenario, respondents provided the following contextual ratings on Likert-type 5-point scales:

When [your father's boss] says to you, '. . . .', at this point (i.e. before you reply)
- How annoying do you think the problem is for [your father's boss]? (Not at all annoying – Very annoying)
- How far do you feel responsible for the problem occurring? (Not at all responsible – Very responsible)

● How important do you think it is to try and make [your father's boss] less annoyed? (Not at all important – Very important)

For each scenario, respondents were also given the opportunity to comment on their production responses and their ratings.

Japanese version

1　今朝、あなたの父は、（会社が従業員のために行っている）定期健康診断を受けに診療所に出かけました。一週間ほど前、あなたは父が電話で健康診断の日時を会社の上司に告げているのを聞いています。ところが、午前中にその上司から電話がかかってきました。彼は怒ったような口調で言います：

父の上司：お父さんはどちらにいらっしゃるか、伺いたくてお電話したんですが。実は、私達の部署の会議に出席なさることになっていて、皆もう３０分くらいお待ちしているんですよ。どうかされたんですか？

（答えとして言うだろうと思う言葉をそのまま書いてください。）

あなた：_____

2　友達とコンサートに行くことになりました。きちんと約束した通り、駅前で彼を待ちましたが、３０分たってもまだ現れません。あきらめて駅の中へ向かいます。その時、改札口の所にその友達が見えました。まだ開演には間に合う時間ですが、彼は怒ったような口調で言います：

友達：３０分も遅れるなんて！　いったいどうしたんだよ？

3　あなたは先生と2時に会う約束をしています。行く途中で、別の先生に呼び止められ、あなたの提出したレポートのひとつに大きな問題があると言われました。その話をしていたため、着いたときには、約束の時間を30分過ぎてしまいました。先生は怒ったような口調で言います：

先生：30分も遅れるなんて！　いったいどうしたんだい？

4　あなたはデパートの顧客サービス部門で働いています。ある男性客から電話があり、頼んだ品物がまだ届かないと苦情を言われました。目の前にある「配達申込書」を見ると、その客は明日の朝に配達を指定しているのですが、彼は怒ったような口調で言います：

客：昨日おたくでテーブルを買って、今朝届けてもらうことになっていたのに、もう12時半ですよ。いったいどうなってるんですか。

5　あなたはある先生と2時半に会う約束をしました。2時半ちょうどにそこへ行ったのですが、先生はあなたが遅刻したと言うのです。先生は怒ったような口調で言います：

先生：30分も遅れるなんて！　いったいどうしたんだい？

6　今朝、あなたの父はいつもの時間に仕事に出かけました。その後ラジオを聞いていて、父の通勤路線で事故があり、電車が遅れているということを知りました。しばらくして、電話が鳴りました。父の上司からで、彼は怒ったような口調で言います：

父の上司：お父さんはどちらにいらっしゃるか、伺いたくてお電話したんですが。実は、私達の部署の会議に出席なさることになっていて、皆もう３０分くらいお待ちしているんですよ。どうかされたんですか？

7　あなたはデパートの顧客サービス部門で働いています。ある男性客から電話があり、頼んだ品物がまだ届かないと苦情を言われました。実は、倉庫の近くで交通事故があり、その道が数時間通行止めになっていたのです。客は怒ったような口調で言います：

客：昨日おたくでテーブルを買って、今朝届けてもらうことになっていたのに、もう１２時半ですよ。いったいどうなってるんですか。

8　友達とコンサートに行くことになりました。コンサートホール近くの駅の改札口で会う約束をしたのですが、事故のために電車が遅れ、３０分遅刻してしまいました。改札口の所に友達が待っています。まだ開演には間に合う時間ですが、彼は怒ったような口調で言います：

友達：３０分も遅れるなんて！　いったいどうしたんだよ？

それぞれのシナリオに対して回答者に下記の点について5段階で評価
してもらった。

[父の上司が、「お父さんはどちらにいらっしゃるか.....どうかされた
んですか?」]と言った時点で（つまりあなたがそれに対してまだ何も
言わない時点で）:
● この事態は、この[父の上司]にとって、腹立たしいことだと思いますか。
　　（全然腹立たしくない --- とても腹立たしい）
● この事態が発生したことについて、あなたには責任があると感じますか。
　　（全然責任はない --- とても責任がある）
● この[父の上司]をなだめたほうがいいと思いますか。
　　（全然思わない --- 強く思う）

それぞれのシナリオに対して、コメントがあれば書いてもらう欄を設
けた。

5

Responding to Compliments: British and Chinese Evaluative Judgements

Helen Spencer-Oatey, Patrick Ng and Li Dong[1]

5.1 Introduction

Compliments are usually intended to have a positive effect on interpersonal relations; as Holmes points out, they are typically 'social lubricants which "create or maintain rapport"' (1995: 118). However, if the compliment is interpreted negatively (for example, because the compliment is clearly untrue, because it implies envy or desire, or because it assumes an unwarranted degree of intimacy), the effect on interpersonal relations is naturally less positive. Similarly, a person's response to a compliment needs to be evaluated positively, if the overall effect of the interchange is to be positive.

Many authors have identified cultural differences in complimenting behaviour (e.g. Wolfson 1981, Barnlund and Araki 1985, Herbert 1989, Lewandowska-Tomaszczyk 1989, Chen 1993, Loh 1993, Ylänne-McEwen 1993). However, few studies have explored the ways in which culture may affect people's interpretations of complimenting behaviour. This chapter reports a preliminary study of British, Mainland Chinese and Hong Kong (henceforth, HK) Chinese evaluative judgements of compliment responses.

5.2 Compliment response strategies

5.2.1 Taxonomies of compliment response strategies

Pomerantz (1978), in her classic study of compliment responses, drew attention to the dilemma faced by complimentees: on the one hand, there is pressure to agree with the compliment; on the other hand, there is pressure to avoid self-praise. In other words, recipients of compliments face conflicting constraints: if they uphold the maxim of agreement, they may flout the maxim of modesty, yet if they uphold the maxim of modesty, they may flout the maxim of agreement (see Leech 1983 and Chapter 2 in this book). So complimentees have to find ways of resolving this conflict, and a wide range of compliment response strategies for handling it have been identified.

Pomerantz (1978) and Holmes (1995) both suggest that for English, this wide range of strategies can be usefully divided into three broad categories: (a) acceptance, (b) rejection/deflection, and (c) evasion/self-praise avoidance. Similarly, Ye (1995) uses three broad categories for compliment responses in Chinese: (a) acceptance, (b) acceptance with amendment, and (c) non-acceptance. These three taxonomies are reproduced and illustrated in Table 5.1.

As can be seen, the three taxonomies differ both in the number of strategies identified, and also in the detailed categorization of strategies. Nevertheless, there is considerable agreement among them, especially in terms of the broad threefold division of strategies.

5.2.2 Compliment responses in Chinese and English

According to English etiquette books, the 'best way' to respond to a compliment is to accept it (see, for example, Hunter 1994). And as Pomerantz (1978) explains, rejection of compliments is often regarded as a symptom of a problem, such as low self-esteem. Studies which have explored compliment responses in English have found that English speakers indeed only rarely reject or disagree with a compliment, and that acceptance is much more common, as the figures in Table 5.2 show. However, it can also be seen that the frequency of acceptance responses may vary somewhat among different English-speaking countries, and that other types of responses to compliments are clearly very common.[2]

In contrast to English, the 'best' response to compliments in Chinese is traditionally thought to be a rejection or denial. Ye (1995), for example, says that in Chinese, a denial is the routinized response

Table 5.1 Taxonomies of compliment response types in English (Pomerantz 1978 and Holmes 1995) and Mandarin Chinese (Ye 1995)

POMERANTZ (1978)	HOLMES (1995)	YE (1995)
1. ACCEPTANCE 1.1 Appreciation Token. e.g. A: *That's beautiful.* B: *Thank you.* 1.2 Agreement, e.g. A: *Oh it was just beautiful.* B: *Well thank you.*	**1. ACCEPT** 1.1 Appreciation/Agreement Token, e.g. *Thanks, yes* or smile 1.2 Agreeing Utterance, e.g. *I think it's lovely too.* 1.3 Downgrading/Qualifying Utterance, e.g. *It's not too bad, is it?* 1.4 Return Compliment, e.g. *You're looking good too.*	**1. ACCEPTANCE** 1.1 Appreciation Token, e.g. 谢谢 $Thanks$ 1.2 Agreement, e.g. 我也挺喜欢的 $I like it too$ 1.3 Pleasure, e.g. 我听了真高兴 $I am very happy to hear that$ 1.4 Smile
2. SELF-PRAISE AVOIDANCE 2.1 Praise Downgrade 2.1.1 Downgraded Agreement, e.g. A: *That's beautiful* B: *Isn't it pretty?* 2.1.2 Disagreement, e.g. A. *Good shot.* B. *Not very solid though.* 2.2 Referent Shifts 2.2.1 Reassignment, e.g. A. *You're a good rower, Honey.* B. *These are very easy to row. Very light.* 2.2.2 Return Compliment, e.g. A. *Ya' sound really nice.* B. *Yeah, you soun' real good too.*	**2. DEFLECT/EVADE** 2.1 Shift Credit, e.g. *My mother knitted it.* 2.2 Informative Comment, e.g. *I bought it at Vibrant Knits place.* 2.3 Ignore, e.g. *It's time we were leaving, isn't it?* 2.4 Legitimate Evasion (Context needed to illustrate) 2.5 Request Reassurance/Repetition, e.g. *Do you really think so?*	**2. ACCEPTANCE WITH AMENDMENT** 2.1 Return Compliment, e.g. 你也不错 $You are not bad, either$ 2.2 Downgrade, e.g. 马马虎虎 $Just so-so$ 2.3 Magnification, e.g. 你不看这是谁写的? $Don't you see who wrote that?$ 2.4 Request for Confirmation e.g. 是吗? 你真觉得不错? $Is it? Do you really think it's OK?$ 2.5 Comment, e.g. 朋友送的 $A friend gave it$ 2.6 Transfer (switch of focus), e.g. 你喜欢吃就多吃点儿 $Have more since you like it$
3. REJECTIONS 3.1 Disagreement, e.g. A. *You did a great job cleaning up the house.* B. *Well, I guess you haven't seen the kids' room.*	**3. REJECT** 3.1 Disagreeing Utterance, e.g. *I'm afraid I don't like it much.* 3.2 Question Accuracy, e.g. *Is beautiful the right word?* 3.3 Challenge Complimenter's Sincerity, e.g. *You don't really mean that.*	**3. NON-ACCEPTANCE** 3.1 Denial (of content), e.g. 不行, 不行 No, no 3.2 Delay (of paying of compliment), e.g. 吃了再说 $Don't comment until you've tasted it$ 3.3 Qualification (denial of quality), e.g. 差远了 $It's far from it$ 3.4 Idiom, e.g. 不好意思 $I'm embarrassed$ 3.5 Diverge (denial by focus switch), e.g. 别逗了 $Don't make fun of me$ 3.6 Avoidance (of responding to compliment content), e.g. 你太客气了 $You're being too polite$

Table 5.2 Frequencies of selected types of compliment responses in English

	Acceptance (%)	Rejection (%)
Holmes (1986) New Zealand English	28.52	5.81
Herbert (1989) American English	36.35	9.98
Chen (1993) American English	32.45	12.70
Ylänne-McEwen (1993) British English	43.00	1.00
Loh (1993) British English	56.00	8.50
Herbert (1989) South African English	76.26	0.00

Table 5.3 Frequencies of selected types of compliment responses in Chinese

	Acceptance (%)	Rejection (%)
Chen (1993) PRC students in China	1.03	50.70
Ye (1995) PRC students in China	20.20	7.80
Yuan (1996) PRC students in China[3]	59.82	27.68
Loh (1993) HK students in Britain	41.00	22.00

to a compliment. Studies that have explored compliment responses in Chinese have indeed nearly all found that rejections are much more common than in English but, as Table 5.3 shows, most studies also found acceptance responses to be relatively frequent.

5.2.3 Evaluating 'non-balanced' responses

Tables 5.2 and 5.3 suggest that 'other' types of responses to compliments (in other words, responses that are neither clear acceptances nor clear rejections) are common in both English and Chinese. This is presumably because they offer an acceptable balance between the pressures to agree and to be modest.

However, since there are differences in the stereotypical beliefs about how to respond to compliments in English and Chinese, and since some differences have been found in the compliment response patterns used in the two languages, what happens when people use a response strategy that seems to place greater emphasis on either 'agreement' or 'modesty'? This study investigated this issue, by exploring the following questions:

(1) When people respond to a compliment by using an acceptance strategy, it seems that they are placing greater emphasis on the agreement maxim than the modesty maxim.

- How then are they evaluated? Do people judge them to be conceited, especially if they explicitly agree with the compliment, rather than simply use an appreciation token like *thank you*? Or do they judge them to be appropriately sincere?
- Are there cultural differences in the ways in which British and Chinese evaluate such responses?

(2) When people respond to a compliment by using a rejection strategy, it could be argued that they are placing greater emphasis on the modesty maxim than the agreement maxim.

- How then are they evaluated? Do people judge them to be insincere and falsely modest, or do they judge them to be appropriately modest?
- Are there cultural differences in the ways in which British and Chinese evaluate such responses?

5.3 Research procedure

A questionnaire (see the Appendix to this chapter) was used to explore these questions, so that comparable data could be obtained in Britain, Mainland China and HK. Naturally, people's evaluations of compliment responses in real life are influenced by many non-verbal and vocalization features, which a written questionnaire cannot begin to probe. Nevertheless, a questionnaire of this kind can provide a useful starting point for further more authentic research.

5.3.1 Design of the questionnaire

The questionnaire comprised five scenarios, all of which contained a compliment on someone's successful performance/achievement, such as coming top in an examination. In all cases, the person who was complimented had clearly done well, so all of the compliments that were paid appeared to be sincere. The relationship between the complimenter and complimentee varied in power and distance (teacher–student, close friends, mother–son, strangers, unfamiliar peers) across the five scenarios, in order to check for the influence of these variables.

For each scenario, five different responses were listed: two acceptance responses, two rejection responses, and one deflection response. For the acceptance responses, one was the British stereotypical rejoinder *thank you*, and the other was an explicit agreement with the compliment, such as *Yes, I'm really pleased with the mark*. For the rejection responses, one was the Chinese stereotypical rejoinder *no, you're flattering me* (不你过奖了 *bu, ni guo jiang le*), and the other was an explicit denial of the compliment, such as *no, I did badly*. Each scenario also included one other type of response, which seemed more like a deflection response. This was included primarily to add variety. The order in which the different types of responses were presented in each scenario was randomized.

Respondents were asked to evaluate each of the responses in terms of appropriateness, conceit, and impression conveyed (favourable/bad). Three 5-point Likert-type rating scales were listed under each compliment response, and respondents were asked to circle the numbers on these scales that corresponded to their reactions to that response. For each scenario, respondents were also asked to add some explanatory comments, if they had rated any of the responses negatively (circling numbers 1 or 2) in terms of the impression it conveyed.

Chinese and English versions of the questionnaire were produced through the collaborative efforts of six bilingual speakers, who carefully checked the developing versions of the questionnaire for equivalence of meaning. Using the decentring process suggested by Brislin (1976) (see Chapter 14), the scenarios and the responses were modified, until all parties (British, HK and Mainland Chinese) had agreed on Chinese and English versions that were both acceptable and equivalent in meaning.[4] The Chinese version of the questionnaire to be used in mainland China was printed in simplified characters; the Chinese version of the questionnaire to be used in HK was printed in traditional characters.

5.3.2 *The respondents*

The questionnaires were completed by university students in Britain, HK and Mainland China. They were distributed during breaks in class, and filled in immediately. In Britain, only students who identified their main home language as English as well as their nationality as British were included in the sample. In HK, only students who had been brought up in HK and were ethnic Chinese were included in the sample. The numbers of students who completed the questionnaires were as follows: 172 British, 168 Mainland Chinese (67 in Guilin and 101 in Shanghai), and 158 HK Chinese. There were slightly more female respondents than male in all three regions (ranging from 54 per cent in Mainland China to 63 per cent in HK).

5.4 Evaluations of acceptance responses

5.4.1 Quantitative results

As explained in section 5.3.1, respondents evaluated each of the compliment responses for appropriateness, conceit, and impression conveyed (favourable/bad). The mean judgements (and standard deviations) on each of these scales for the acceptance responses, averaged across the five situations, are given in Table 5.4. Analysis of variance results showing the effect of nationality on the ratings of the acceptance responses are given in Table 5.5.

As can be seen from the figures in Table 5.4, all of the groups of respondents evaluated the acceptance responses fairly positively.

Table 5.4 Mean evaluations (and standard deviations) of acceptance compliment responses

	British	Mainland Chinese	Hong Kong Chinese
'Agree': appropriateness	3.83 (.59)	3.60 (.62)	3.55 (.61)
'Agree': conceit	3.44 (.65)	3.23 (.72)	3.24 (.63)
'Agree': impression	3.68 (.55)	3.53 (.66)	3.47 (.59)
Acceptance rejoinder: appropriateness	4.03 (.69)	4.15 (.56)	4.05 (.64)
Acceptance rejoinder: conceit	3.89 (.74)	3.76 (.69)	3.94 (.70)
Acceptance rejoinder: impression	3.96 (.67)	4.09 (.58)	4.03 (.63)

Note: Ratings based on a 5-point Likert-type scale from 1 (*not at all appropriate/very conceited/gives a very bad impression*) to 5 (*very appropriate/not at all conceited/gives a favourable impression*)

Table 5.5 Analysis of variance results showing the effect of nationality on the ratings of the acceptance responses

	F	df	p	β^2
'Agree': appropriateness	9.63	2,469	< .001*	.04
'Agree': conceit	4.85	2,468	.008*	.02
'Agree': impression	5.13	2,468	.006*	.02
Acceptance rejoinder: appropriateness	1.75	2,473	.175	.01
Acceptance rejoinder: conceit	2.80	2,471	.062	.01
Acceptance rejoinder: impression	1.75	2,471	.175	.01

* Significant at the 95% level

Both the agreement responses and the acceptance rejoinder (hence-forth, AR) *thank you* were judged to be appropriate responses. They were not evaluated as conceited, and they were judged as conveying a fairly favourable impression. The analysis of variance results shows that nationality did not have a significant effect on people's judgements of *thank you* responses.

For the agreement responses, however, there was a tendency for the British respondents to evaluate them slightly more positively than the HK and Mainland Chinese respondents. And according to the analysis of variance results, this difference is statistically significant. On the other hand, the beta[2] figures show that only 2 to 4 per cent of the variance is attributable to nationality, which suggests that the statistical difference is not very meaningful.

5.4.2 *Qualitative results*

Explanatory comments were added by 302 respondents (89 British, 138 Mainland Chinese and 75 HK Chinese) on their questionnaires. Of these, 98 people (18 British, 56 Mainland Chinese and 24 HK Chinese) made comments on one or more of the agreement responses, and 22 people (4 British, 15 Mainland Chinese and 3 HK Chinese) made comments on one or more of the AR responses.

In keeping with the positive ratings of the AR responses, there were only 30 comments (6 British, 20 Mainland Chinese and 4 HK Chinese) on the negative aspects of saying *thank you*. The most frequent criticism (made by respondents from each of the three groups) was that *thank you* showed conceit, and/or that it showed a lack of involvement because of the brevity of the response.

There were 157 comments altogether (25 British, 88 Mainland Chinese, and 44 HK Chinese) on the agreement responses, indicating that agreement responses are more problematic than acceptance rejoinders. As expected, the most frequent criticism was that they conveyed too much conceit or boasting; for example:

British: (1) *because he sounds like a smug bighead*
Mainland Chinese: (2) 太锋芒毕露 $showing off one's abilities too much$
HK Chinese: (3) 太自大 $too arrogant$

There were 101 comments like this (14 British, 56 Mainland Chinese and 31 HK Chinese), showing that all three groups of respondents are concerned about conceit, but in line with the quantitative data, suggesting that the Mainland and HK Chinese respondents perceived the agreement responses as conveying slightly more conceit than the British respondents did.

For the agreement responses, the other main concern, which again was shown by respondents from all three groups, was about complacency/over-confidence, sometimes with a suggestion that it was unfounded. For example, there were 31 comments (7 British, 16 Mainland Chinese and 8 HK Chinese) as follows:

British: (4) *too self assured*
Mainland Chinese: (5) 过于骄傲，给人感到虚有声势，
                          长期看来不可能做常胜将军 $too conceited,
                          sounds like bluffing; in the long run it's
                          impossible always to be number one$
HK Chinese: (6) 过分自满 $too complacent$

5.5 Evaluations of rejection responses

5.5.1 Quantitative results

Respondents also evaluated each of the 'rejection' compliment responses for appropriateness, conceit, and impression conveyed (favourable/bad). The mean judgements (and standard deviations) of these responses, averaged across the five situations, for each of the scales, are given in Table 5.6. Analysis of variance results showing the effect of nationality on the ratings of the acceptance responses are given in Table 5.7. As can be seen, nationality had a much greater

Table 5.6 Mean evaluations (and standard deviations) of rejection compliment responses

	British	Mainland Chinese	Hong Kong Chinese
'Disagree': appropriateness	2.32 (.62)	2.17 (.63)	2.97 (.70)
'Disagree': conceit	3.06 (.89)	3.21 (.87)	3.50 (.64)
'Disagree': impression	2.66 (.61)	2.36 (.63)	3.04 (.64)
Rejection rejoinder: appropriateness	2.61 (.77)	3.09 (.73)	3.98 (.66)
Rejection rejoinder: conceit	2.89 (.85)	3.47 (.69)	3.99 (.68)
Rejection rejoinder: impression	2.71 (.71)	3.18 (.71)	3.94 (.67)

Note: Ratings based on a 5-point Likert-type scale from 1 (*not at all appropriate/very conceited/gives a very bad impression*) to 5 (*very appropriate/not at all conceited/gives a favourable impression*)

Table 5.7 Analysis of variance results showing the effect of nationality on the ratings of the rejection responses

	F	df		p	β^2
'Disagree': appropriateness	68.73	2	473	< .001*	.23
'Disagree': conceit	11.53	2	465	< .001*	.05
'Disagree': impression	46.09	2	466	< .001*	.17
Rejection rejoinder: appropriateness	144.67	2	471	< .001*	.38
Rejection rejoinder: conceit	84.65	2	468	< .001*	.27
Rejection rejoinder: impression	123.67	2	458	< .001*	.35

* Significant at the 95% level

effect on people's evaluations of the 'rejection' compliment responses than the 'acceptance' compliment responses.

For the 'disagreement' responses, British and Mainland Chinese respondents judged them to be somewhat inappropriate, whereas the HK respondents had more neutral opinions. All three groups evaluated them neutrally in terms of conceit, but all three groups differed in their judgements of the impression conveyed by 'disagreement' responses. Both the Mainland Chinese and the British felt they conveyed rather negative impressions (with the Mainland Chinese judging the impression to be very significantly more negative than the British, according to further tests), whereas the HK Chinese evaluated the 'disagreement' responses neutrally in terms of impression conveyed. The analysis of variance results show that these nationality differences are statistically very significant, and the beta^2 figures suggest that nationality had a fairly meaningful effect on the respondents' evaluations of 'disagreement' compliment responses: for appropriateness, 23 per cent of the variance is attributable to nationality, and for impression, the figure is 17 per cent.

For the 'rejection rejoinder' (henceforth, RR) responses, there was even more variation among the three groups of respondents. The British respondents judged them somewhat negatively on all three scales; the Mainland Chinese respondents judged them fairly neutrally on all three scales; and the HK Chinese judged them fairly positively on all three scales.[5] The analysis of variance results show that these differences are statistically very significant, and the beta^2 figures indicate that the differences are meaningful: for acceptability, 38 per cent of the variance is attributable to nationality; for conceit, 27 per cent of the variance is attributable to nationality, and for impression, the figure is 35 per cent.

5.5.2 Qualitative results

Comments on one or more of the 'disagreement' responses were made by 243 respondents (60 British, 129 Mainland Chinese, and 54 HK Chinese), and 115 respondents (56 British, 49 Mainland Chinese and 10 HK Chinese) made comments on one or more of the RR responses.

For each of the three groups of respondents, the 'disagreement' responses attracted the largest number of comments. There were 580 comments altogether: 121 made by the British, 349 made by the Mainland Chinese, and 110 made by the HK Chinese. However, unlike the comments on the acceptance responses, which showed a basically similar pattern of concerns across the three groups, there were considerable differences between the British and the Chinese comments.

Of the British comments, 40 drew attention to the inaccuracy of the 'disagreement' responses, making remarks such as the following:

British: (7) *He thought it went well so he should admit it.*

                 (8) *He knows he did well – why say no?*

As comment (8) indicates, some of the British seemed to be struggling to explain why someone should disagree under such circumstances. For example, another respondent wrote:

British: (9) *John already thought it went well so why was he saying it was no good? He was being complimented, why was he so adamant it was no good?*

Many of the other British comments were attempts to explain such seemingly strange responses. For example, 36 comments explained it in confidence terms: that John was psychologically unable to accept the compliment, for example because he lacked confidence, had low self-esteem, underestimated his abilities, or was just embarrassed:

British: (10) *He did play well so why say he didn't? Lack of self-confidence.*

                 (11) *John should try to take a little credit. He needs to have higher self-esteem perhaps.*

Another interpretation was that the disagreement was strategic in some way; for example, that it was an attempt to gain further compliments. For instance, there were 12 comments as follows:

British: (12) *John knows the food was good, he is just fishing for more compliments.*

Others interpreted the 'disagreement' responses as showing conceit:

British:
(13) *John knows he did well, and so the fellow student would find him conceited.*
(14) *Showing off by thinking he should have done better when he did as well as he could.*

There were 10 comments that referred to the negative implications of a 'disagreement' response for the person giving the compliment and/or for related others:

British:
(15) *basically telling his friend he doesn't know what he is talking about*
(16) *undermines other people in class*

Like the British respondents, both the Mainland and the HK Chinese respondents commented on the inaccuracy or untruthfulness of the 'disagreement' responses: there were 74 Mainland Chinese comments on this, and 27 HK Chinese comments. However, in contrast to the British, they had no apparent difficulty in understanding why such responses might be used, and clearly associated them with modesty issues. There were 120 Mainland and 29 HK Chinese comments that the 'disagreement' responses were too modest; for example:

Mainland Chinese:
(17) 过分的谦虚等于骄傲 $Excessive modesty equals conceit.$
(18) 在老师面前表现得过分谦虚有虚伪感 $Behaving too modestly in front of the teacher seems insincere.$

HK Chinese:
(19) 无需在亲人前自谦 $There's no need to denigrate yourself in front of people who are close to you.$

As can be seen from the comments above, excessive modesty was associated with falseness/insincerity and with conceit. There were 117 Mainland and 35 HK Chinese comments that the 'disagreement' responses were insincere or false, and there were 48 Mainland and 4 HK Chinese comments that they showed conceit.

The above comments also show that appearing modest is very dependent on participant relations, especially in Mainland China. There were 64 Mainland and 18 HK Chinese comments that referred to role relations in evaluating the 'disagreement' responses. Some people commented that 'disagreement' responses were too formal or polite for the context (there were 15 Mainland Chinese comments like this), or that they seemed too cold or distant (there were 29 Mainland and 10 HK Chinese comments like this); for example:

Mainland Chinese: (20) 对好友的恭维过于谦虚有生疏感 $If one's too modest about a good friend's compliment, it seems too distant.$

HK Chinese: (21) 我认为面对自己的母亲答案应该忠肯和直率，不需太客气 $I think one should be honest and straightforward in replying to one's mother; there's no need to sound too polite.$

Compared with the British respondents, far fewer of the Chinese respondents linked a 'disagreement' response with confidence issues, although some made this connection: there were 14 Mainland and 2 HK Chinese comments that referred to lack of confidence or low self-esteem.

In terms of the negative implications of a 'disagreement' response for the person giving the compliment and/or for related others, the Mainland and HK Chinese, like the British respondents, made a few comments. There were 17 Mainland and 8 HK Chinese comments that referred to this, arguing that a 'disagreement' response could suggest poor judgement, could put others down, could make others feel uncomfortable, or could imply disrespect; for example:

Mainland Chinese: (22) 这个回答会打击祝贺他的人的兴致和好意 $This response could attack the kind intent and interest of the person paying the compliment.$

(23) 看似李明的回答很谦虚，但在他的回答中隐含了我的足球 踢得不好，你说我踢得好，你的眼光可不怎么样 $It seems as though Li Ming's response is very modest, but his response implies 'I played badly, but you said I played well, so your judgement can't be very good'.$

HK Chinese: (24) 令老师尴尬 $makes the teacher embarrassed$

For the RR responses, the number of comments made by the different groups of respondents reflected the differences in the mean evaluations shown in Table 5.6: the British respondents made 108 comments, the Mainland Chinese made 75, and the HK Chinese made 12.

For the British respondents, many of the comments were similar to those made for the disagreement responses: people drew attention to the inaccuracy or untruthfulness of the rejection, and once again tried to explain it either in terms of confidence or in terms of ulterior motive. For example, 19 British comments referred to psychological factors associated with lack of confidence:

British: (25) *embarrassed by good comment*
                  (26) *response shows lack of self-confidence*

And 12 British comments referred to an ulterior motive:

British: (27) *saying flattering is wanting more said on the
                  subject*
                  (28) *Why should a teacher (authority) flatter –
                  they wouldn't. Therefore shows some conceit
                  and appears to be pushing for more approval.*

As the last comment indicates, some British respondents interpreted RR responses as showing conceit; in fact, there were 31 comments to that effect.

In terms of the negative implications of an RR response for the person giving the compliment and/or for related others, the British made 12 comments, covering a similar range of issues to those mentioned in relation to the disagreement responses; for example:

British: (29) *seems to make the other person seem that they
                  are lying*
                  (30) *Because he shouldn't accuse his close friend of
                  sucking up to him – the friend would say the
                  truth and he should believe it.*

In great contrast to the British evaluations, the HK respondents made very few negative comments. It seems that the only slight reservations that the HK respondents had about this response was its appropriateness for the context. Three comments said that the RR response was too distant or 'polite' for the context, and one evaluated it as too modest and four as insincere or false. The Mainland Chinese, on the other hand, were much more concerned about these contextual factors. There were 23 comments that the RR response was too distant or 'polite'. There were also 10 comments that it was too modest, and 21 comments that it sounded insincere or false.

None of the HK respondents interpreted RR responses as having any kind of negative implications for the person giving the compliment or for related others, and there were only 3 Mainland Chinese comments about this.

5.6 Discussion

5.6.1 The Modesty Maxim

A number of authors (e.g. Gu 1990, Chen 1993) have stressed the importance of modesty in Chinese; Gu (1990: 238–9), for example, referring to Confucian philosophy, explains that modesty is one of four essential elements of the Chinese concept of *limao* or 'politeness'. And Leech (1983: 137) argues that in Japanese society the Modesty Maxim seems to be more powerful than it usually is in English-speaking societies. To what extent, then, do the results of this study support these claims?

Leech (1983) (see Chapter 2) conceptualizes the Modesty Maxim as having two components: minimization of self-praise, and maximization of self-dispraise. In discussing the Modesty Maxim, however, most authors (including Leech himself) seem to focus on the second element. Yet the first element, the avoidance of appearing conceited, is clearly an important component. Judging from the comments reported above, all three groups of respondents explicitly identified conceit as a negative and unacceptable trait, implying that the first component of the Modesty Maxim is of equal importance in these three sociocultural groups. What linguistic behaviour, though, tends to give rise to judgements of 'conceit'?

Perhaps somewhat surprisingly, none of the groups of respondents evaluated any of the acceptance responses as conveying conceit. The figures given in Tables 5.4 and 5.5 show that even though the three groups differed slightly in their evaluations, the majority of each group judged them to be acceptable in terms of conceit. Conversely, the British evaluated the RR response (which is typically regarded as a strategy for conveying modesty) as tending towards conceit. For this particular RR response, however, this may be partly due to the lack of precise translation equivalence between *ni guo jiang le* and *you're flattering me*. As comment (28) suggests, the word 'flatter' in English has negative connotations, and is often associated with over-praising someone in order to achieve some ulterior aim. This implies that the complimentee has control of something that is desirable to the other person, and so by using such a phrase the complimentee is showing conceit by claiming power she or he does not really have. Nevertheless, even though *ni guo jiang le* does not have such implications (at least not traditionally), the comments reported in section 5.5.2 show that 'disagreement' responses were evaluated as conceited by a fair number of Mainland Chinese, arguing that excessive modesty is equivalent to conceit. Clearly, then, it is too simplistic to regard acceptance strategies as being closely linked with conceit, and rejection strategies as being closely linked with modesty.

If we turn to the second component of Leech's (1983) Modesty Maxim, the maximization of dispraise of self, a different picture emerges. The vast majority of the British respondents did not associate the self-denigration of the rejection responses with modesty at all: only three people mentioned it. They associated it either with a lack of confidence or with an attempt to fish for more compliments. In contrast, though, the vast majority of the Mainland and HK Chinese respondents linked the two. This suggests that the second component of the Modesty Maxim is very much more weakly adhered to in Britain than in China. However, once again we need to consider the strategies used for implementing this component of the strategy. Leech's wording, 'maximize dispraise of self', implies that the more one dispraises oneself, the more one upholds the Modesty Maxim. Yet the Chinese comments (especially the Mainland Chinese comments) show clearly that excessive modesty seems false and insincere, and is interpreted as conveying conceit rather than modesty. However, what counts as an appropriate degree of modesty, and what counts as an excessive degree of modesty, is clearly socially determined. With regard to HK and Mainland China, it seems that a smaller degree of self-denigration is tolerated among Mainland Chinese students than among HK students. Why this should be so is unclear. Further research is obviously needed, first to check the reliability of the finding and, if it is confirmed, to explore some possible explanations.

5.6.2 The Agreement Maxim

Both Pomerantz (1978) and Leech (1983) draw attention to the potential conflict between the Modesty Maxim and the Agreement Maxim. Disagreements are typically associated with threats to another person's face (Brown and Levinson 1987), so from this perspective, when people respond to a compliment, they have to balance the following: on the one hand, upholding the other person's face by agreeing with them, and on the other hand, avoiding the risk of negative evaluation by others by appearing conceited.

The comments reported in section 5.5 indicate that, for each of the three groups of respondents, only a relatively small number expressed concern over the effect of a rejection response on the other person's feelings. Certainly a few mentioned it, but not very many. This suggests that the Agreement Maxim is not a very powerful influence on people's choices of compliment response strategies, certainly compared with the Modesty Maxim. This is in keeping with Leech's (1983) own comment that there is less evidence for the Agreement Maxim than for the Modesty Maxim.

However, another perspective is to judge the use of agreement/ disagreement strategies, not in relation to the other person's face, but in relation to the complimentee's face. If someone responds to a compliment with a rejection response, not only may it be threatening to the other person's face, but it is also potentially threatening to the respondent's own face and thus to be avoided. This seems to have been the interpretation given by a fair number of the British respondents in this study. As reported in section 5.5, quite a lot of them interpreted the rejection responses as conveying a lack of confidence, an inability to accept a compliment, and so on. This is the interpretation that Pomerantz (1978) gives to the use of disagreement. However, because of the strong influence of the self-denigration component of the Modesty Maxim among Chinese respondents, this was not a common interpretation among those respondents.

5.7 Concluding comments

All of the scenarios used in the study made it clear that the complimentee had done genuinely well, and that he was convinced of this himself. Needless to say, there are numerous occasions when this is not the case. Clearly, the findings from this study cannot be assumed to apply to other types of complimenting situations without further research.

Further research is also needed on what types of strategies are regarded as appropriate compliment responses in different contexts and for different sociocultural groups. For example, it would be interesting to know whether the self-denigration component of the Modesty Maxim only applies to distant relationships, or whether there are different strategies for upholding it in different types of relationships. There is clearly much more work that needs to be done.

Discussion questions

1 Jonathan is a teacher in an adult school class in the United States. After class, he speaks to Anh, one of his students who is from Vietnam:

J: Anh, your English is improving. I am pleased with your work.

A: Oh no, my English is not very good. (*looking down*)

J: Why do you say that, Anh? You're doing very well in class.

A: No, I am not a good student.

J: Anh, you're *making progress* in this class. You should be proud of your English.

A: No, it's not true. You are a good teacher, but I am not a good student.

Jonathan is surprised by her response and wonders why she thinks her English is so bad. He doesn't know what to say and wonders if he should stop giving her compliments.

1.1 Why is Jonathan confused/surprised by Anh's responses?

1.2 Should he stop complimenting her?

1.3 What different norms do the two speakers seem to hold regarding complimenting?

(Based on Levine *et al.* 1987: 17)

2 An American woman received a letter from a Japanese friend who had just got married. The Japanese woman wrote in her letter, 'My husband is not very handsome. Your husband is much more handsome than mine.' The American woman was very surprised by what her friend wrote.

2.1 Why do you think the American woman was surprised?

2.2 Why do you think the Japanese woman wrote, 'My husband is not very handsome'?

(Based on Levine *et al.* 1987: 23)

3 Consider your own complimenting behaviour:

3.1 How often do you pay compliments, and to whom?

3.2 What do you most frequently pay people compliments about?

3.3 Why do you pay compliments? Do your compliments always reflect your genuine opinion? Why/why not?

4 How does complimenting behaviour fit in with the conceptualization of face given in Chapter 2?

5 Look at the questionnaire used in this study. For each scenario, consider:

5.1 Would you have complimented the person in this situation?

5.2 Would you have used a different wording for the compliment? Why/why not?

5.3 How would you evaluate each of the compliment responses, and why?

5.4 How do you think you would have responded in these circumstances?

Notes

1. The authors would like to thank Liu Shaozhong, Xing Jianyu and Harry Wang for helping in the translation and decentring process of the development of the Chinese and English versions of the questionnaire, and Kang Qing and Liao Fengrong for administering the questionnaires in China.

2. Since each study uses slightly different categorizations of sub-categories, we have made some classification adjustments for comparative purposes. 'Acceptance' includes only the strategies *appreciation token* and *agreement*; 'Rejection' includes clear non-acceptances, such as *disagreement* or *queries of accuracy*.

3. Unlike the other studies, Yuan's (1996) figures do not reflect mutually exclusive categories, but rather show the percentage of responses that included this semantic component.

4. The following minor differences were deliberate: Chinese names were used in the Chinese version, and the tourist in scenario 4 spoke English rather than French.

5. Further tests showed that on all three scales, there was a very significant difference in the ratings of each of the pairs of countries ($p < .001$ in all cases).

Appendix to Chapter 5: The scenarios

1. John has just found out that he came top in an examination, after working really hard for it. After class, his teacher calls him over:

Teacher:		Congratulations, John! You did very well.
John:	(1)	No, no, I did badly.
John:	(2)	I was lucky with the questions, I guess.
John:	(3)	Yes, I'm really pleased with the mark.
John:	(4)	Thank you.
John:	(5)	No, you're flattering me!

2. John has just given a presentation to his class, which he feels went quite well. As he is leaving, one of his close friends, Peter, comes up:

Friend:		That was great, John. Your talk was really interesting!
John:	(1)	Thanks. Your presentation was excellent too.
John:	(2)	Yes, I thought it went quite well myself.
John:	(3)	No, you're flattering me!
John:	(4)	No, no, it was no good.
John:	(5)	Thanks.

3. John has just cooked an elaborate dinner for some family friends, and is pleased with how the dishes tasted. After they have gone, his mother says:

Mother:		Well done, John! The food tasted lovely.
John:	(1)	No, no, it was no good.
John:	(2)	Thanks.
John:	(3)	Do you really think so, mum?
John:	(4)	No, you're flattering me!
John:	(5)	Yes, the dishes turned out well, didn't they.

4. John is studying for a degree in French. One day as he is walking through the town, a French tourist asks him for directions. He answers him fluently, and afterwards the tourist comments:

Tourist:		You speak excellent French!
John:	(1)	No, far from it. I'm just a beginner.
John:	(2)	I'm studying it at university actually.
John:	(3)	Thank you.
John:	(4)	No, you're flattering me!
John:	(5)	I'm glad you think so!

5. John has just played in a university football match and scored a winning goal. Afterwards, a fellow student whom he knows slightly says:

Fellow student: Congratulations! You played brilliantly!
John: (1) Thanks. I felt in good form today.
John: (2) No, you're flattering me!
John: (3) Thanks.
John: (4) Not really, it was a team effort.
John: (5) No, no I didn't play well.

For each scenario, respondents rated each of John's responses on the following Likert-type 5-point scales:

Not at all Appropriate (1)   Very Appropriate (5)
Very Conceited (1)   Not at all Conceited (5)
Gives a very bad Impression (1) Gives a favourable Impression (5)

For each scenario, respondents were also asked to explain some of their ratings:

If you think any of John's responses give a bad impression (i.e. you have circled 1 or 2 on any of the 'impression' scales), please explain why.

Chinese version

1. 李明刚知道，经过刻苦学习, 他在考试中考得第一名。下课后, 老师叫他。

老 师: 李明, 恭喜您! 您考得很好!

1. 李 明: 不,不,考得不好。

2. 李 明: 我想这回我是走运罢了。

3. 李 明: 是的, 我对这次的分数很满意。

4. 李 明: 谢 谢。

5. 李 明: 不，您过奖了。

2. 李 明 刚向同学们做了一次演讲,他自我感觉还不错。临走时,他的好友

   王洪走过来:

   王洪: 太棒了,李明!你讲得很有趣!

   1. 李 明: 你的演说也很成功呀。

   2. 李明: 对,我也感到效果不错。

   3. 李明: 不,你过奖了。

   4. 李明: 不,不,讲得不好。

   5. 李明: 谢谢。

3. 李明为来他家里的朋友做了一顿精致的晚餐,自已也感到每道菜都色

   香味美。等客人走后,他的母亲说:

   母亲: 干得好,明明。今天的菜很好吃!

   1. 李明: 不,不,不太好。

   2. 李明: 谢谢。

   3. 李明: 妈,真的吗?

   4. 李明: 不,你过奖了。

   5. 李明: 对,味道还不错,是不是?

4. 李明在攻读英语专业。 一天,他上街时,一位英国旅客向他问路。李明

   很流利地回答了他的问题,于是,那位英国旅客说:

   旅客: 您的英语好极了!

   1. 李明: 不,还差远咧。 我刚开始学。

   2. 李明: 我在大学念的就是英语。

   3. 李明: 谢谢。

   4. 李明: 不,您过奖了。

   5. 李明: 您这么看我很高兴。

5. 李明刚参加了一场学生足球赛, 而且比赛中踢进了致胜的一球。 一

位不很熟悉的同学向他说:

同学: 恭贺您, 踢得真好!

1. 李明: **谢谢, 我今天状态不错。**

2. 李明: **不, 您过奖了。**

3. 李明: **谢谢。**

4. 李明: **不是嘛, 是全队的功劳。**

5. 李明: **不,不, 踢得不好。**

答卷人对 李明在每一情景中的各种回答按 Likert 式5分级制进行打分 :

很不得体 (1)　　　　　很得体 (5)

很骄傲 (1)　　　　　毫不骄傲 (5)

给以很不好的印象 (1)　　给以良好的印象 (5)

问卷同时要求答卷人对每一情景中的某些打分情况加以解释/进行说明:

如果您认为李明的某回答给以不好的印象 (譬如您在任何一组印象级别

号中圈了 1 或 2), 请您说明

6

Telephone Conversations in Greek and German: Attending to the Relationship Aspect of Communication

Theodossia-Soula Pavlidou

6.1 Introduction

Telephone communication has become an indispensable element of everyday life. Due to the lack of visual information, at least in the normal use of this medium, linguistic information is foregrounded, and the role of pragmatic aspects of language becomes more critical. Thus, telephone conversation is a challenge to anybody learning a foreign language and remains a sensitive area in intercultural encounters, even for those who have mastered the basics of a foreign language and culture. Let me illustrate this with an example from a German–Greek encounter. Recently, I (Greek) was working at home when the telephone rang; Elena, my daughter (Greek–German), also working in her room, and I both picked up the phone simultaneously, to find out that it was a close relative (German) who wanted to speak to my husband (German):[1]

{telephone rings}

Soula   {in Greek} [*Ne?*]
                               $Yes?$

Elena   {in Greek} [*Ne?*]
                               $Yes?$

{the rest of the conversation is in German}

Bärbel   *Ja, hier ist Barbara. Kann ich bitte den Wolfgang sprechen?*
          $Yes, this is Barbara speaking. Can I talk to Wolfgang
          please?$

Soula   {short hesitation, because of uncertainty as to which
          Barbara it is – we usually use the diminutive 'Bärbel' for this
          relative – and then a bit annoyed that she passes over Elena
          and me}
          *Ja, Bärbel, aber du kannst erst mal Elena und mir guten Tag
          [sagen.]*
          $Yes, Bärbel, but you can say hello to Elena and me first.$

Elena   [{hangs up}]

Bärbel   *Ja, natürlich. Ich habe erst mal gar nix verstanden [...]*
          $Yes, of course. I did not understand a thing in the
          beginning [...]$
          {although Bärbel does not speak Greek, she had hoped to at
          least understand the name, which she expected to hear in
          the very first answering turn}

The example above is one of the numerous instances indicating, if
not a cultural clash, at least a temporary cultural dissonance. It
illustrates the different expectations/orientations with which Greeks
and Germans enter the conversational space of a telephone call: the
former would expect to get some attention as partners in the
conversation, before taking care of the reason for calling, the latter
would expect not to be held on the phone unduly long, i.e. beyond
what it basically takes to handle the reason for the call. Both mean
well, but *in different ways*.

Linguistic research on telephone conversation bears the distinct
mark of conversation analysis, through which certain universal
features of the structure of telephone calls have been established
(e.g. Schegloff 1972, Schegloff and Sacks 1973, Schegloff 1994).
Cultural variation has also been hypothesized (e.g. Clark and French
1981) and indeed been observed (e.g. Godard 1977, Sifianou 1989,
Pavlidou 1994). In this chapter, I would like to argue that this
variation has to do mainly with the different norms pertaining to the
relationship aspect of communication in different cultures and,
consequently, with the different ways the relationship aspect of
communication is attended to.

Telephone calls most commonly have a tripartite structure: an
opening section, a middle section in which the main topic, i.e. the
reason for the call,[2] is exposed, and a closing section. The lion's share
of the literature on telephone conversation (from the seminal studies

of conversation analysts up to the most recent cross-cultural approaches) is concerned with the opening part (see e.g. Hopper 1992); studies on the closing part of telephone calls are still quite rare (e.g. Button 1987, 1990). In the following, I draw on my earlier work on the opening and closing sections of telephone conversations in Greek and German (e.g. Pavlidou 1991, 1994, 1997, 1998a). Focusing mainly on the use of phatic utterances and patterns of repetition, I want to show that participants handle organizational problems in ways which reflect culture-specific preferences for attending to the relationship aspect of communication.

My focus on the opening and closing sections of telephone calls is by no means intended to imply that I consider the relationship aspect of communication to be important or relevant only in these phases of the call; on the contrary, I am convinced that rapport issues never cease to be significant throughout any encounter (e.g. Pavlidou 1995, 1998b). However, the opening and closing sections of a telephone conversation pose some interesting interactional problems for the participants, such as how to counteract a possible intrusion through the telephone call, how to terminate the call without causing any bad feelings, and so on. It is in this sense that Laver (1975: 217) talks of the opening and closing phases of a conversation as 'the psychologically crucial margins of interaction'.

6.2 Telephone openings

6.2.1 The data sample

My analysis of telephone openings is based on a sample of 120 Greek and 62 German telephone calls (Pavlidou 1994). All calls were initiated and tape-recorded by young adults with a university degree, the Greek calls by five women and two men and the German calls by two women and three men. None of the calls was a 'first call'; in other words, the callers all phoned people they already knew. The underlying assumption for this was that, contrary to other settings, phatic utterances (which were an important focus of my research) are not used among complete strangers in the opening part of a telephone conversation. The calls were made for both social and practical reasons, and were made to people with varying degrees of closeness to the caller. The callers were instructed to erase any part of a call, or even whole calls, which they did not want other people to hear, and they were allowed to decide how best to tell the other participant about the recording.

6.2.2 General structure of telephone openings

In the opening section of a telephone call, the physical channel has to be opened and the acoustic contact between the partners has to be established. Moreover, it must be clarified whether the person answering the phone is the one the caller wishes to talk to, before the caller can proceed to the reason for calling.

The first step, i.e. the establishing of physical contact, is achieved with a summons–answer sequence, as Schegloff (1972) calls it: the ringing of the telephone functions as a summons to which the person picking up the phone responds, e.g. by saying 'Hello?'. After this very first adjacency pair, sequences of identification (self- and other-identification, either by name or telephone number), greeting and counter-greeting usually follow. Sometimes, when caller and called already know each other, ritual inquiries like 'How are you?' may appear before the partners proceed to the main section of the call. In other words, the opening section of a telephone call comprises a number of basic or constitutive sequences, which, however, may vary in their realization from context to context (cf. e.g. workplace versus home setting, business call versus private call, etc.) and from culture to culture.

6.2.3 Greek openings – German openings

6.2.3.1 Some basic features

Due to space limitations, in this section I can only point out some very general features of Greek and German telephone calls.[3] I would like to start by giving two examples of openings, a Greek one and a German one.

Example 1: A Greek opening

{A (Sofia, female, 26 years old) and B (Lia, female, 28 years old) are friends; A calls B to tell her about a lecture they wanted to go to, but after that they move on to another topic}

1   B   *Oriste.*
           $Yes, please.$
2   A   *Ja su LIA.*
           $Hello LIA.$
3   B   *Ja su SOFIA.*
           $Hello SOPHIA.$
4   A   *Ti jinete?*
           $How are you doing?$

5   B   *Kala. Ti na jini? Isiçia. ESI ti kanis.*
              $Fine. Nothing special. Everything is quiet. How are YOU.$

6   A   *Ka:la: c eγo.*
              $I am fine, too.$

7   B   *Mm.*
              $Hm.$

8   A   *θimi:θi:ka: telika ti mu e:le:je:s oti iθeles na su po: . [. . .]*
              $I finally reme:mbe:red what you to:ld me that you wanted me to te:ll you. [. . .]$

Example 2: A German opening[4]

{A (male, 28 years old) and B (female, 27 years old) are friends; A calls B in order to thank her for sending him some English workbooks, but after that they move on to other topics}
{telephone rings}

1   B   *B {name}*

2   A   *Tach, B hier is A.*
              $Hello B, this is A {name} speaking.$

3   B   *Ah, hallo A!*
              $Oh, hi A!$

4   A   *Ich wollt mich nur für die Hefte bedanken!*
              $I just wanted to thank you for the pamphlets!$

As indicated in the examples above, both Greeks and Germans perceive the ringing of the telephone as a summons to which they respond by picking up the receiver and taking the first turn in the conversation. Greeks usually answer the phone with utterances like *ne* ('yes'), *lejete* (say-IMPERATIVE), *embros* ('go ahead'), *malista* ('yes'), or as in the example above, with *oriste* ('yes, please', literally order-IMPERATIVE). Although Germans may sometimes also take the first turn in a similar manner and answer with, for example, *Ja bitte* ('Yes please') or *Hallo* ('hello'), it is more typical in German telephone calls for the answerer to take the first turn, as in the example above, and identify himself/herself, usually by saying his/her last name. This is then followed by the caller's self-identification, either by last or first name or both, commonly in combination with an appropriate greeting formula depending on the relationship and the time of the day.

In Greek telephone calls, on the other hand, self-identification, especially on the answerer's part, indicates a workplace setting and foregrounds the speaker's orientation to an efficient completion of the call (as is common, for example, in business or institutional contexts);

otherwise, Greeks when talking to friends or relatives seem to prefer covert-identification, in other words, via voice-samples, as in Example 1.[5] Greetings may be interchanged, too, as is the case in turns 2–3 of the Greek example: *ja su* ('hello', literally 'health to you-T-form') or simply *ja* (literally 'health') is the most common informal greeting formula, used also for terminating the call, especially the variant *ja xara* (literally 'health joy').[6]

6.2.3.2 The use of phatic talk in Greek and German openings

The term 'phatic' was first used in linguistics in connection with the term 'communion'. The phrase 'phatic communion' was introduced by the anthropologist Malinowski (1966: 315) to describe 'a type of speech in which ties of union are created by a mere exchange of words'. As Haberland (1996: 164) emphasizes, for Malinowski (1966: 313, 316), the main contrast is between 'communion' and 'communication':

> A mere phrase of politeness, in use as much among savage tribes as in a European drawing-room, fulfils a function to which the meaning of its words is almost completely irrelevant. Inquiries about health, comments on weather, affirmations of some supremely obvious state of things – *all such are exchanged not in order to inform, not in this case to connect people in action, certainly not in order to express any thought.* ... [They serve] to establish bonds of personal union between people brought together by the mere need of companionship. (emphasis added)

In other words, the salience of propositional/descriptive/cognitive meaning or information content is minimized in phatic communion, while the relational aspect is positively maximized. Or, as J. Coupland *et al.* (1992: 214ff) very aptly put it, phatic communion can be associated with certain priorities in talk, i.e. a minimal commitment to open disclosure, seriousness, factuality, etc. and a foregrounding of positive relational goals.

Using the data set described above, I compared the use of phatic talk in the Greek and German telephone calls, focusing on the section which follows the initial answering, identification and greeting, and which precedes the mention of the reason for calling. The following utterances/features were regarded as phatic:

- ritual questions, e.g. *How are you?*
- comments on lack of contact, e.g. *We haven't met for ages.*
- ritual expression of wishes, e.g. *Happy Birthday!*
- apologies for the intrusion, e.g. *I hope I didn't wake you up.*

- comments on the connection, e.g. *This line is very poor*.
- the joking use of the V-form among intimates, e.g. *Ti kanete ciria mu?* $What are you [V-form] doing my lady?$
- the use of phatic particles, e.g. *Na? Hast du noch Gäste?* $PARTICLE? Have you still got guests?$

Counting the number of telephone calls that had one or more of these phatic utterances, I found that more than two-thirds of the Greek telephone calls contained them, but only just over one-third of the German calls did so (see Table 6.1). To explain this result, one might hypothesize that phatic talk is more readily deployed when people call each other primarily for social rather than transactional purposes; so if Greeks reach more readily for the telephone just to chat or to arrange to meet, this might in turn explain the greater use of phatic talk in Greek openings. Although there is some evidence to support this (both Germans and Greeks used more phatic talk in social calls than in transactional calls), there is no statistically significant difference in the proportion of social and transactional phone calls in the two data sets: both Greeks and Germans made more transactional telephone calls than social calls (see Table 6.2). Moreover, Greeks still used more phatic sequences in both types of calls than Germans, and the difference was particularly marked for the transactional calls (see Table 6.3).

Another way of explaining the findings shown in Table 6.1 would be by means of Brown and Levinson's (1987) politeness theory: if the

Table 6.1 Frequency of use of phatic talk in Greek and German telephone openings

	Conversations with phatic talk	Conversations without phatic talk	Total
Greek	85 (70.83%)	35 (29.17%)	120
German	23 (37.10%)	39 (62.90%)	62

$df = 1$, $\chi^2 = 17.91$, $p < 0.001$

Table 6.2 Distribution of reason for calling by nationality

	Social reason	Practical reason	Total
Greek calls	38 (31.67%)	82 (68.33%)	120
German calls	15 (24.19%)	47 (75.81%)	62

$df = 1$, $\chi^2 = 0.77$, $p < 0.500$

Table 6.3 Distribution of phatic utterances according to reason for calling

	Social reason		Practical reason		Total
	with phatic talk	without phatic talk	with phatic talk	without phatic talk	
Greek calls	34 (89.47%)	4 (10.53%)	51 (62.20%)	31 (37.80%)	120
German calls	9 (60%)	6 (40%)	14 (29.79%)	33 (70.21%)	62

$df = 1$, $\chi^2 = 3.25$, $p < 0.100$

caller wants something from the person called (which would constitute a face-threatening act to that person), then the caller seeks to mitigate the threat by using phatic talk, i.e. a positive politeness device. Along this line, the Greeks in the sample could be hypothesized to have used more phatic utterances because they made more face-threatening calls than the Germans. But if we investigate, for example the connection between use of phatic talk and the beneficiary of the call in transactional calls, we find that Greeks deploy phatic talk to a great extent even when they are not themselves (at least not exclusively) the beneficiary of the call.

As for the connection between the type of relationship and phatic talk in transactional calls, although the results are not statistically significant, in both the Greek and the German samples the most extensive use of phatic utterances occurs in relationships that are neither very formal nor too personal; however, the percentage is almost twice as high in the Greek openings in comparison to the German openings, as indicated in Tables 6.4 and 6.5.

Table 6.4 Use of phatic talk in Greek telephone openings according to the relationship of the participants (transactional calls only)

Relationship	Calls with phatic talk	Calls without phatic talk	Total
Personal	16 (53.33%)	14 (46.67%)	30
Familiar	28 (73.68%)	10 (26.32%)	38
Formal	7 (50.00%)	7 (50.00%)	14
			82

$df = 1$, $\chi^2 = 4.07$, $p < 0.200$

Table 6.5 Use of phatic talk in German telephone openings according to the relationship of the participants (transactional calls only)

Relationship	Calls with phatic talk	Calls without phatic talk	Total
Personal	3 (27.28%)	8 (72.73%)	11
Familiar	10 (43.48%)	13 (56.52%)	23
Formal	1 (7.69%)	12 (92.31%)	13
			47

$df = 1$, $\chi^2 = 5.19$, $p < 0.100$

6.2.4 Discussion

The findings reported above suggest that, at least sometimes, there are some differences in what Germans and Greeks consider to be appropriate ways of opening a telephone conversation: Greeks seem to prefer an exchange of phatic utterances before coming to the reason for calling, whereas Germans opt for a more direct path to the main section of the call.[7] While this difference can lead to cultural clashes and misunderstandings in Greek–German encounters, it can definitely not be explained away by saying either that Greeks are very considerate and Germans impolite, or vice versa (see section 6.4 for further discussion).

6.3 Telephone closings

6.3.1 The data sample

My analysis of telephone closings is based on a sample of 45 Greek and 27 German telephone calls made between relatives or friends. They are mainly a subset of the sample used for analysing telephone openings. However, fifteen of the German calls belong to the Brons-Albert (1984) corpus, and a further two are from the so-called Freiburger Korpus (TSG 1975). The full data sample used for telephone openings could not be used, either because the closings had not been recorded or because poor sound quality (especially of the German calls) made a detailed analysis impossible.

6.3.2 General structure

Every telephone call ends unequivocally when the telephone is hung up, i.e. when the physical channel is interrupted. But in order to reach that point, the partners have to make clear that nothing else is left to be said and then proceed to signalling the end of the call (Schegloff and Sacks 1973: 299ff). The first is conversationally achieved by a pre-closing (an offer to close the conversation) which, if accepted by the other, allows the partners to take the last conversational step, i.e. the terminal sequence, usually comprising an exchange of *goodbyes*. However, as there are no linguistic means, at least in English, which exclusively serve as pre-closings, the first closing turn (the pre-closing) has to be placed after a topic (the last topic) has been closed down (Schegloff and Sacks 1973: 305). So the 'archetype closing', as Button (1987: 102) calls it, looks like the following (if preceded by a sequence in which one partner offers to close down the topic and the other accepts to do so, e.g. A: *Okay?* B: *All right.*, cf. Schegloff and Sacks 1973: 306):

A: *We-ell.*   (offers to close; first close component)
B: *O.K.*   (accepts the offer; second close component)
A: *Goodbye.*   (first terminal utterance)
B: *See you.*   (reciprocates; second terminal utterance)
{telephone is hung up}

However, other sequences like thanking for the call, giving regards to somebody both partners know, exchanging wishes, and so on, may also be included in this last section of the call, in which conversationalists 'take leave' (cf. Clark and French 1981) of each other.

6.3.3 Greek closings – German closings

6.3.3.1 Some basic features

Again in this section I can only limit myself to some general features of Greek and German closings and refer the reader to the relevant literature for more information.[8] Let me start with two examples of closings, one in Greek and the other in German.

Example 3: A Greek closing

{A (female, 26 years old) calls B (male, 31 years old), a friend, to finalize the meeting point and time with other friends}

1   B   *Ne. Stasi Aristotelus stin Tsimiski.*
        $Yes. At the Aristotelous bus stop on Tsimiski street.$

2   A   *E: endaksi. Orea. Ipe θa pari se mena i Zoi, e: θa ime eðo PANO eγo.*
        $Eh, all right. Fine. Zoe said she'll call me, eh, I'll be here UPSTAIRS.$

3   B   *Endaksi. Ejine.*
        $All right. Done.$

4   A   *Mm. Afta.*
        $Mm. That was it.$

5   B   *Ocei. θa peraso na se pa:ro: pço noris fisika=*
        $Okay, I'll pick you up earlier of course$

[...] {brief moving out of closing}

10 B   *Ocei?=*
        $Okay?$

11 A   *=Ejine, ne.=*
        $Done, yes.$

12 B   *=Ejine. A[de.]*
        $Done. ADE.$

13 A   *[A:]de ja.*
            $ADE bye.$

14 B   *Jaxara, ja.*
        $Byebye, bye.$

{telephone is hung up}

Example 4: A German closing

{A (female, 26 years old) calls an old friend B (female, 27 years old), whom she had not seen for a long time – and whom she met again only recently – to invite her to a party}

1   A   *Gut. Dann sehen wir uns erstmal an diesem besagten Samstag.*
        $Good. We'll see then each other on this very Saturday.$

2   B   *An diesem besagten. Okay.*
        $On this very Saturday. Okay.$

3   A   *Gut?*
        $Good?$

4   B   *Jo, bis dann.*
        $Yap, till then.$

5   A   *Bis dann. Tschüs.*
        $Till then. Bye.$

6   B   *Tschüs.*
        $Bye.$
{telephone is hung up}

As shown in Examples 3 and 4, both closings end with equivalents of *goodbye* exchanges (this is also generally the case). In German the parting formula *tschüs* (cf. Example 4, turns 5–6) or its variations (the diminutive *tschüschen* or variants like *tschö*, *tschöho*, etc.) – some of which are dialect variants – are very commonly used in informal calls. More formal is the formula *auf Wiederhören*, which according to Werlen (1984: 257) has been formed specially for telephone communication in analogy to *auf Wiedersehen*; at the same time, however, these two formulae capture an aspect which seems to be quite important in the closing section of German telephone calls: a reference to future contact. In more informal calls, conventional phrases like *bis dann* ('till then') or *bis zum nächsten mal* ('until next time') can be used, either to refer to a specific future contact (as in Example 4, turns 4–5) or as a vague reference to future contact, that is, even when no specific arrangements have been made to meet (see Pavlidou 1997).

In Greek terminal exchanges, we find once again the formula *ja* ('bye', literally 'health') and its variations *ja su* (literally 'health to you-T-form') and especially *ja xara* (literally 'health joy'), as in Example 3, turn 14. The fact that this formula can be used both in openings and closings, or more generally, both when meeting and parting, is indicative of the little, if any, lexical import that it carries. In addition, there are other expressions used among familiars when parting, like *fiλa* (literally 'kisses'), and *filaca* (literally kisses-DIMINUTIVE), which shows liking and affection. Other informal parting formulae, used especially by younger people, include foreign expressions like *tsao* ('ciao') and *bai* ('bye').

Turning now to pre-closings, the German items used in this function include *also* ('so then'), *ja* ('yes'), *gut* ('good'), *okay* etc. (cf. also Werlen 1984: 255). Similarly, Greek closings are initiated with the discourse marker *lipon* ('well, so then') with falling intonation, or with expressions indicating agreement, most prominently *ejine* ('done'), *endaksi* ('all right'), and *ocei* ('okay'), but also *orea* ('nicely'), *kala* ('good') etc. Also, the particle *ade*, usually described as a hortative particle, is sometimes used as a pre-closing.

6.3.3.2 The use of repetition/redundancy in Greek and German closings

The 'archetype closing' presented in section 6.3.2 can be thought of as the skeleton around which the closing sections of both German and Greek telephone calls are organized. But especially in calls between familiars, 'varieties of closings' (Button 1990) are usually to be found. In such calls, as reported in Pavlidou (1997, 1998a), differentiation between Greek and German closings can be observed (e.g. a greater divergence from a dyadic structure and more repetition of agreement tokens in the Greek closings). In the following, I would like to focus on certain repetition phenomena in Greek and German closings.

Following Merritt (1994: 26), I use 'repetition' in a very general sense, covering 'all kinds of "happening again"'. But there is a very important qualification to this: there is a kind of repetition which is structurally required for the organization of conversation, as opposed to repetition that goes beyond the minimal structural necessities. For example, if somebody greets you or bids you farewell, you normally reciprocate this, e.g.

A: *Hello.*
B: *Hello.*

or

A: *Goodbye.*
B: *Goodbye.*

Taking into account the constituent sequences of the opening and closing sections of a telephone call, I consider this kind of repetition to be *conversationally required* or at least expected. On the other hand, if you respond to somebody's *Goodbye* with *Ciao, byebye* this utterance is redundant[9] as far as structural requirements are concerned, since from the organizational point of view either *ciao* or *byebye* would have been sufficient.

The analysis of my data sample suggests that Greek closings exhibit a greater degree of redundancy with respect to elements that are structurally required, i.e. terminal exchanges and closing components, than German closings. For example, in the last turn of example (3), there are two parting formulae, although one would have sufficed. In most of the German calls I have examined, the terminal exchanges consist basically of two short turns (like turn 6 in Example 4). It is rare for such formulae to be repeated within the same turn, or within an extension of such exchanges over more than two turns, as occurs in the following Greek example (turns 4–6):

Example 5
{same as in example (1): A (female, 26 years old) and B (female, 28 years old) are friends; A calls B to tell her about a lecture they wanted to go to, but after that they move on to another topic}

1 A *Ax kala* {hurriedly}. *Lipon. Klino ne?*
      $Ah, good {hurriedly}. So, then. I am hanging up, O.K.?$

2 B *Ejine. Ade, par esi kampa mera etsi?*
      $Done. ADE, you call me sometime, O.K.?$

3 A *Endaksi. Ne.* =
      $All right. Yes.$

4 B = *Ade tsao.*
      $ADE, ciao.$

5 A *Ade, ja, ja.*
      $ADE, bye, bye.$

6 B *Ade, ja, ja.*
      $ADE, bye, bye.$

{telephone is hung up}

Example 5 is interesting in other respects, as well:[10] it demonstrates repetition of an element, the particle *ade*, which is hardly structurally required. As mentioned in section 6.3.3.1, *ade* can be employed as a pre-closing, in which case it could be considered structurally necessary. But this is not the case in Example 5, turns 2, 4, 5 and 6 (nor in Example 3, turns 12–13). In fact, this particle indicates the speaker's orientation towards terminating the call and shows a desire for mutual consensus on this; it turns out to be an almost indispensable element of telephone closings among familiars (see e.g. Pavlidou 1998a).

Similarly, in the German closings we find repetition of the particle *ne*. This particle is derived from the modal adverb *nicht* ('not'); it functions as a tag-question with which the speaker seeks to keep the addressee involved in the conversation, or even get his/her confirmation,[11] and of course it does not play any constitutive role in the closing section. The following example[12] shows multiple recurrence of the particle *ne*:

Example 6
{A (female, 25 years old) and B (male, 30 years old) are relatives; B called to say that his pregnant wife does not feel very well, and so they will not be coming to A's party}

1   A   [...] *das kommt auf/ ein oder zwei mehr überhaupt nich an.*
          $[...] it makes really no difference if it is one or two persons more.$

2   B   *Ja, aber wenn die schon nachmittags sacht, daß et ihr nich gut is .. Also, wie gesagt, ne, falls . wider Erwarten . doch klappt, dann ruf ich vorher noch kurz an, ne.*
          $Yes, but if she says already in the afternoon, that she does not feel good .. So, as I said, NE, in case that. against our expectation. it does work, I will give you a ring before we come, NE.$

3   A   *Hm. Bis dann, ne.*
          $Hm. Till then, NE.$

4   B   *Bis dann! Tschö, A.*
          $Till then! Bye, A.$

5   A   *Tschö.*
          $Bye.$

{telephone is hung up}

Example 6 also exhibits repetition of the formula *bis dann* in turns 3–4. Although it is frequently the case that such a formulaic expression is reciprocated (cf. also *mach's gut* ('Take care'), *Grüss den Jürgen* ('Give my regards to Jürgen') etc.), reciprocation is not in the same sense constitutive for closing as, for example, the parting formula in the terminal exchange. Moreover, it is interesting that formulae or expressions referring to future contact are more frequently repeated than, for example, *mach's gut*.

6.3.4 Discussion

An obvious consequence of the redundancy discussed above is the greater length of the telephone closing. As already mentioned, on the whole, Greek closings exhibit a greater degree of redundancy in the use of elements that are constitutive for the closing section of the telephone call (i.e. agreement tokens and parting formulae); and this means that Greek closings can be expected to be longer than the German ones. This would imply that there is a tendency for the partners to cling together in Greek closings. Moreover, the extended use of *ade* emphasizes the locally negotiated mutuality of the decision to terminate the call. In the German closings this mutuality of the partners' decision to close the call is negotiated by means of tag particles like *ne*, which implicitly invoke already existing common ground. Moreover, repetition of expressions like *bis dann*, which project the relationship into the future, suggest that Germans build up on the past of their relationship and invest in its future, whereas Greeks invest in the *hic et nunc* of their relationship.

6.4 Phatic communion and the relationship aspect of communication

In the previous sections, we examined a number of differences between openings and closings in Greek and German telephone calls. We saw, for example, that Greeks prefer an exchange of phatic utterances before coming to the reason for calling, whereas Germans opt for a more direct path to the main section of the call. In addition, Greek closings exhibit a greater degree of redundancy in the use of elements that are constitutive for the closing section of the telephone call. However, a word of caution is needed here: in cross-cultural studies there is not infrequently a tendency to rush into sweeping generalizations. It is important, therefore, to stress once more that the rapport management features which differentiate Greek and German openings or closings are not exclusive to either Greek or German conversations. In other words, there are Greek telephone calls with the 'German' characteristics, and vice versa. The findings reported here suggest that Greek and German conversationalists display different preferences for the ways in which they organize the openings and closings of their telephone calls; such preferences may be contingent on specific constellations of parameters whose importance will be revealed only under more subtle contextual considerations and in which cultural differentiation plays only a small part. So in this sense it is better to conceptualize findings like mine as motivated hypotheses for further research.

All in all, taking into account what the constitutive components of openings and closings are according to conversation analysts, we can say that Greek openings/closings differ from their German counterparts not so much in the basics of conversational organization as in the interactional surplus they contain. However, this should not be understood as implying that in German telephone calls there is no interactional work, since interactional work is involved even in openings or closings which comprise just the basic sequences. This becomes obvious if any of these sequences are omitted. For example, if you just pick up the phone without saying *Hello?*, although the physical channel is open, contact has not been established and the conversation cannot begin in the expected way. Alternatively, if you terminate a call by just hanging up, or even by simply saying

Goodbye, without having properly initiated the closing section, you may unwittingly put your relationship with your telephone partner into jeopardy. What I maintain, then, is that the account of telephone openings and closings given by conversation analysts captures the interactionally necessary work for the conversation to start and end smoothly, and accordingly, it reflects a minimally required attendance to the relationship aspect of communication. However, this approach cannot account for the observed differences between Greek and German telephone calls, i.e. the interactional surplus. Any attempt to explain the differences has to be augmented by a framework which explicitly involves interactional considerations such as Brown and Levinson's (1987) and Laver's (1975, 1981). Since I have discussed elsewhere (Pavlidou 1994) the difficulties that arise in applying Brown and Levinson's framework to my findings, I will focus here on Laver's approach, for two reasons: (a) he is explicitly concerned with the initial and closing phases of conversation which he calls 'transitional' (e.g. Laver 1975: 218), because the former leads from non-interaction to interaction and the latter 'from full interaction to departure'; (b) he focuses on the functions of phatic communion in these phases.

After an insightful analysis, Laver (1975: 236) comes to the conclusion that the functions of phatic communion 'in the crucial marginal phases of encounters when their [the participants'] psychological comfort is most at risk' are 'to establish and consolidate the interpersonal relationship between the two participants' and to ease 'the transitions to and from interaction'; or, putting the two functions together, phatic communion serves 'to facilitate the management of interpersonal relationships'. Laver's proposal is certainly helpful for interpreting my findings on Greek and German openings/closings, but only locally or partially. For example, as I have argued elsewhere using Laver's framework, in the German closings the emphasis is on the 'consolidation of the relationship', whereas Greek closings are organized toward a 'cooperative parting' (Pavlidou 1997: 216). However, an overall synthesis would be difficult to achieve for the following reasons (*inter alia*).

Firstly, Laver's (and others') conception of phatic communion as 'applying to choices from a limited set of stereotyped phrases of greeting, parting, commonplace remarks about the weather, and small talk' (Laver 1975: 218) leads to a static understanding of a very important phenomenon.[13] As the study of the opening sections of calls shows, other means such as particles like the German *Na?*, playful use of V-form, and the repetition of a simple greeting formula also have a phatic function. Secondly, Laver's analysis suggests, at least implicitly, that phatic communion is the only (verbal) means available for facilitating the management of interpersonal relationships. However, other means can achieve the same ends; for example, elaboration of the mutuality of the partners' decision to terminate the call (cf. Pavlidou 1998a: 92) or the playful use of the V-form (cf. Pavlidou 1994: 501). In other words, although it is very important to recognize the significance of phatic communion and to give it a proper place in a theory of communication, it would be wrong either not to acknowledge that other means can facilitate the management of interpersonal relationships, or to conflate such means with phatic communion.[14]

In other words, I take phatic communion to be just one way of attending to the relationship aspect of communication. However, one can attend to the relationship aspect of communication not only by doing something (i.e. interactional work), but also by not doing something, which brings me back to my results. The 'Greek' way may be to exhibit an interactional surplus and build the relationship through small talk, but the 'German' way may be to refrain from keeping the partner on the phone for too long and letting them know pretty soon the reason for calling. In other words, both styles may pay equally good, though different, services to the relationship aspect of communication. What I am claiming then is that there are numerous ways of attending to the relationship aspect of communication: e.g. phatic communion, redundancy, negative politeness, talk about the relationship itself, and also strategies of directness which may result in the omission of all of the previous strategies. Which way is opted for presumably depends not only on the phase of the conversation, but also on cultural factors.

Discussion questions

1   In your country/language, how are the opening and closing sections of telephone conversations between acquaintances usually managed (e.g. who speaks first, how is recognition accomplished, how fast do you get to the reason for calling, which linguistic items can function as pre-closings, etc.)? Do the characteristics seem more similar to the Greek or the German conversations described here?

2   In your country, what types of comments or topics are considered 'safe', and suitable for phatic talk with people you do not know well? How comfortable would you feel using each of the phrases below to a casual acquaintance you met in a corridor at

university/work, and why? What other phrases might you be likely to use in this context?

a) *How are things?*
b) *Have you had lunch?*
c) *Where are you going?*
d) *It's really cold today, isn't it?*
e) *How's life?*

3   Try to explain the differences reported here between the German and Greek ways of attending to the relationship aspect of communication using Spencer-Oatey's rapport management concepts of equity and association rights (see Chapter 2). How satisfactory is this framework?

Notes

1. The Greek examples are presented in a phonetic transliteration (as close to IPA as possible), using however capital letters to indicate the beginning of a sentence or a name; stress is not marked. In translating the Greek and German excerpts into English, I tried to give an approximate English equivalent without losing totally the original linguistic form; conversational particles in Greek or German which have no exact equivalent in English are left untranslated; they appear in capitals in the English translation of the excerpt. Brackets enclosing three dots, i.e. [...] mean that part of a turn, or turn sequence, has been left out.
    $ English text. $ = English translation.

2. Of course, not every telephone call is motivated by a practical or transactional reason, as we shall see below; there are also calls which are made 'just to hear how you're doing', 'just to talk'. In my view, these are equally legitimate 'reasons' for calling, serving primarily social rather than transactional purposes.

3. For more information on German openings cf. e.g. Henne and Rehbock 1979, Berens 1981, Brinker and Sager 1989, Liefländer-Koistinen and Neuendorff 1991; on Greek openings cf. Sifianou 1989, Bakakou-Orfanou 1990, and Pavlidou 1991, 1994, 1995.

4. This opening is taken from the telephone call number 22 in the Brons-Albert corpus (Brons-Albert 1984); the original transcription is retained. No information is given as to whether 'B' and 'A' are last or first names; presumably, 'B' is a last name in the first line, but a first name in the second line, since friends in Germany (who also use the T-form, as becomes clear later on in the call) would not address each other with their last names.

5. An important element in these very first turns of telephone calls among familiars is *ela* (literally: come-IMPERATIVE) which may appear in

almost every turn of the opening section with various phatic functions: from showing that the physical channel has been established up to signalling recognition of the interlocutor (cf. Pavlidou 1995, 1998b).

6. Another variant, used among strangers or when the addressee is older than the speaker, has a higher status etc., is *ja sas* (literally 'health to you-V-form'). Other greeting formulae, like *kalimera* (literally 'good day'), *kalispera* (literally 'good evening'), *çerete* (literally 'rejoice'-IMPERATIVE), may be used as well, but they can be understood as more formal.

7. Other studies e.g. Liefländer-Koistinen and Neuendorff 1991, House and Kasper 1981, Byrnes 1986, also provide some evidence in support of this conclusion.

8. For German closings, cf. Henne and Rehbock 1979, Werlen 1984, Brinker and Sager 1989, Liefländer-Koistinen and Neuendorff 1991; for Greek closings, cf. Pavlidou 1997, 1998a, 1998c.

9. I owe this coinage to Sue Ervin-Tripp (personal communication, Berkeley, summer 1997).

10. It also shows repetition of markers of agreement (turn 3: *Endaksi. Ne.* $All right. Yes.$) which is not necessary from the organizational point of view.

11. There are other particles like this in German (e.g. *nö, ge, gell, wa*) with similar function, but usually with more restricted use according to the geographical-dialectal origin of the speaker.

12. This closing comes from telephone call number 20 in the Brons-Albert corpus (Brons-Albert 1984); it is presented here in the original transcription.

13. Cf. also Coupland *et al.*'s (1992) arguments for a dynamic understanding of phatic communion.

14. It would be equally wrong to subsume any non-propositional aspect of interaction under the term 'phatic' and thus miss the important elements that the term stands for (see section 6.2.3.2). More on this in Pavlidou 1998b.

Suggestions for Further Reading for Part Two

Cross-Cultural Empirical Studies involving Native Speakers

Aukrust, V.G. and Snow, C.E. (1998) Narratives and explanations during mealtime conversations in Norway and the U.S. *Language in Society*, 27: 221–46.

Bilbow, G. (1995) Requesting strategies in the cross-cultural business meeting. *Pragmatics*, 5(1): 45–55.

Blum-Kulka, S. and House, J. (1989) Cross-cultural and situational variation in requesting behavior. In S. Blum-Kulka, J. House and G. Kasper (eds), *Cross-Cultural Pragmatics: Requests and Apologies*. Norwood: Ablex, 123–54.

Bresnahan, M.J., Ohashi, R., Liu, W.Y., Nebashi, R. and Liao, C.-C. (1999) A comparison of response styles in Singapore and Taiwan. *Journal of Cross-Cultural Psychology*, 30(3): 342–58.

Clancy, P.M., Thompson, S.A., Suzuki, R. and Tao, H. (1996) The conversational use of reactive tokens in English, Japanese, and Mandarin. *Journal of Pragmatics*, 26: 355–87.

Eslamirasekh, Z. (1993) A cross-cultural comparison of the requestive speech act realization patterns in Persian and American English. In L.F. Bouton and Y. Kachru (eds), *Pragmatics and Language Learning*. Monograph Series, Vol. 4. Urbana-Champaign: Division of English as an International Language, University of Illinois at Urbana-Champaign, 85–103.

Goodwin, R., and Lee, I. (1994) Taboo topics among Chinese and English friends: a cross-cultural comparison. *Journal of Cross-Cultural Psychology*, 25(3): 325–38.

Hasegawa, T. and Gudykunst, W.B. (1998) Silence in Japan and the United States. *Journal of Cross-Cultural Psychology*, 29(5): 668–84.

Herbert, R.K. (1991) The sociology of compliment work: an ethnocontrastive study of Polish and English compliments. *Multilingua*, 10(4): 381–402. (A shortened version is reprinted in N. Coupland and A. Jaworski (eds), *Sociolinguistics: A Reader and Coursebook*. London: Macmillan, 487–500.)

Iwasaki, S. and Horie, P.I. (1998) The 'Northridge Earthquake' conversations: conversational patterns in Japanese and Thai and their cultural significance. *Discourse and Society*, 9(4): 501–29.

Nelson, G.L., Al-Batal, M. and Echols, E. (1996) Arabic and English compliment responses: potential for pragmatic failure. *Applied Linguistics*, 17(4): 411–32.

Olshtain, E. (1989) Apologies across languages. In S. Blum-Kulka, J. House and G. Kasper (eds), *Cross-Cultural Pragmatics: Requests and Apologies*. Norwood: Ablex, 155–73.

Pearson, V.M.S. and Stephan, W.G. (1998) Preferences for styles of negotiation: a comparison of Brazil and the U.S. *International Journal of Intercultural Relations*, 22(1): 67–83.

PART THREE

INTERCULTURAL DISCOURSE: ANALYTIC MODELS AND CONCEPTS

7

Understanding Misunderstanding: A Pragmatic-Discourse Approach to Analysing Mismanaged Rapport in Talk across Cultures

Juliane House

In this chapter I present a framework for analysing mismanaged rapport in talk across cultures which is exemplified by cases where speakers fail to successfully manage their interpersonal and interactional relationships. The structure of the chapter is as follows: by way of introducing the theme of the chapter I first briefly describe how the phenomenon of misunderstanding can arise from a variety of different sources. Second, I present a cognitive discourse processing model, which may be used to account in a systematic way for intercultural misunderstandings, and in particular for the role that emotive-affective factors play in discourse (mis)interpretation. Third, the operation of the model is demonstrated using examples from a corpus of everyday interactions between German and English native speakers triangulated by retrospective interview data. Since it transpires from the analyses of these data that cross-cultural differences in communicative preferences are responsible for causing misunderstandings and mismanaged rapport, the fourth and final part of the chapter presents results from a series of German and English contrastive discourse analyses in the form of a set of dimensions of cross-cultural differences that can serve as explanatory hypotheses for instances of mismanaged rapport in German–English intercultural discourse.

7.1 How misunderstanding comes about

Intercultural misunderstandings are complex phenomena, and there are many different and possibly interacting reasons why they occur in interactions between two (or more) interlocutors, including at least the following:

- inadequate perception (i.e. the hearer did not listen and/or hear properly);
- inappropriate comprehension to be located at various (and possibly interacting) linguistic levels;
- insufficient relevant knowledge of the world on the part of one or both interactants;
- uncooperativeness on the part of the hearer, who may have understood perfectly well what the speaker had tried to communicate but just intended to be 'awkward';
- production difficulties, i.e. while the hearer may have perceived and comprehended sufficiently well and may also have been cooperatively-minded, she or he is not able in the fast-moving discourse to assemble a response that is reasonably expected at this particular stage in the discourse.

Given this complexity, any attempt at describing and explaining misunderstanding – let alone defining it in any straightforward manner – must adopt what Halliday (1990) has called a 'transdisciplinary' approach, i.e. one that transgresses traditional disciplinary boundaries and eventually comes up with an eclectic model comprehensive and powerful enough to handle diverse cases of misunderstandings. In the past, however, misunderstandings were more often than not investigated in isolated fashion inside one particular research paradigm ignoring the cross-fertilization potential which a transdisciplinary venture can offer. As opposed to this isolationist trend, the following model is an attempt to incorporate and integrate a number of different approaches to 'understanding misunderstanding' such as discourse analysis, pragmatic theory, psycholinguistics and social psychology.

7.2 An integrative discourse comprehension and production model

The model assumes the existence of scripted behaviour imprinted in the human mind, and it postulates cognitive plans, frames and schemata – representations of repeated behavioural patterns which reduce cognitive work in humans. Such a model offers a fruitful way of approaching intercultural misunderstanding because it integrates in a systematic way different insightful perspectives. Norms and conventions as well as behavioural tendencies must have cognitive substrates, and the interpretation of contextualized, situated meanings and misunderstandings can also be related to underlying cognitive processing mechanisms. The model can therefore be described as a cognitive discourse processing model. It is based on Edmondson's (1987, 1989) discourse comprehension and production model, and the version presented in what follows is a revised form of the adaptation of Edmondson's model presented in House (1993).

The model operates on two 'levels': a conceptual and a linguistic level, with the latter providing for the decoding of the linguistic input and the encoding of the output. These 'levels' must be conceived as being networked in a complex fashion, more complex, in fact, than any diagrammatic display (such as that in Figure 7.1) is able to reveal. In the light of more recent work on the important role of emotive-affective factors in discourse comprehension and production and in particular in the perception of, and reaction to, intercultural misunderstanding, the model presented in House (1993) is revised here to take account of the fact that emotional reactions frequently accompany both revealed and hidden intercultural misunderstandings. In House (1996a), for instance, I have shown that an emotional reaction is often the major factor responsible for a deterioration of rapport and for the mutual attribution of negative personal traits which, in turn, effectively prevent any recognition of real differences in cultural values and norms. Ochs (1989), Besnier (1990), Bloch (1996), Caffi and Janney (1994) and Niemeyer and Dirven (1997), among others, as well as an increasing number of neuropsycho-linguistic studies (cf. e.g. Miall 1995, Ledoux 1996), have pointed to the importance and, indeed, temporal priority of emotional reactions in the limbic system before 'higher' cognitive 'construction-integration' can take place. It is on the basis of findings such as these, which clearly point to the crucial determinative nature of emotive phenomena, and indeed the inseparability of emotive and cognitive processes, that the revised discourse comprehension and production model has been set up.

Briefly, the operation of this model can be characterized as follows. First of all, in order to allow for the impact of emotionally determined discourse production and comprehension, one needs to:

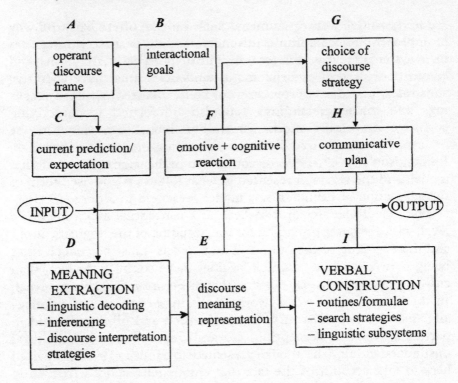

Figure 7.1 Schematic discourse processing model
Source: Adapted from S. Blum-Kulka and J. House, *Interlanguage Pragmatics*, Oxford University Press

(1) assume an awareness of self and other on the part of the system user, and
(2) posit some sort of 'system equilibrium index', which indicates the level of emotional involvement or disengagement; in other words, the type and nature of a language user's emotive stance.

Both awareness and equilibrium index have an impact on the entire system. Since they cannot be pinpointed or located at any single 'place' in the system, they are 'anywhere elements'.

Second, the individual 'boxes' (see Figure 7.1) of the model function and interact as described below. In Box A, a copy of the relevant stored situational constellation or schema is made and 'filled in' by knowledge derived from the current discourse situation. The result is a complex of both conceptual and linguistic representations making up the Operant Discourse Frame. Note that the term 'frame' (cf. Goffman 1986, Tannen 1979) is here used as distinct from 'schema', the latter being seen as providing the skeleton to be fleshed out in the ongoing discourse. In other words, a 'generalized' schema is built up into a particular discourse frame. In the ongoing discourse, however, it is always possible to call up alternative discourse schemata with the revision and reactivation of operant discourse frames leading to co-existent discourse frames (cf. the notion of 'co-existent discourse worlds' in Edmondson 1981).

The representations in Box A allow, then, both of prospective anticipation and of retrospective adjustment or re-interpretation. Typically, the following elements are contained in a currently activated discourse frame:

(1) knowledge of the currently relevant interactional move constellation;
(2) knowledge concerning the currently relevant discourse topic;
(3) a broad representation of the discourse outcomes arrived at so far in the ongoing interaction, and the relevance of (1) and (2) to these, where appropriate, with the scope of such representations being affected by memory span, attention and emotive arousal;
(4) a (partly or wholly) linguistic representation of the content and import of the preceding relevant last turn, and here especially its rhematic content, which is held in working memory and can be accessed from the currently activated frame.

Speaking in terms of the pragmatic theory approach to misunderstanding (cf. e.g. Dascal 1985, Blum-Kulka and Weizman 1988), it is clearly the level of propositional meaning which is captured here.

The relevant situational and interpersonal knowledge represented in box A would typically also include many of the aspects described by Spencer-Oatey in Chapter 2 in connection with the variables influencing rapport management strategies. Concretely, box A features knowledge of culturally variable norms such as at least the following four:

(1) contextual assessment norms, such as culturally determined conceptions of role relationships and the concomitant degrees of power and familiarity, rights and obligations;
(2) sociopragmatic and pragmalinguistic conventions governing rapport management, such as preference or dispreference for overt expression of criticism or for using particular routine formulae in certain discourse phases (see the examples in section 7.3 below);
(3) underlying cultural values and communicative styles, which differ across cultures (see the empirically established dimensions

along which German and Anglophone speakers differ, described in section 7.4 below);

(4) rapport management devices, such as German and English means of indexing deference, politeness or distance via the *Du* and *Sie* distinction in German, and the quasi-equivalent use of first names in conjunction with other means of distancing or de-distancing in English.

In intercultural encounters, representations of the above four (and possibly more) aspects vary individually and culturally, and this variation may lead to interactants' mutual misinterpretation of their intentions and behaviour.

Box B represents the speaker's main goal plus any evolving subgoals for the ongoing encounter. Just as Box A is made up of two elements – the basic schemata for interpretation and production on the one hand, and the accruing knowledge gained from the context on the other hand – so Box B is also made up of an interaction between choices of interactional and illocutionary options (see Edmondson 1981 and 1987 for further details on this fundamental distinction between interactional and illocutionary moves). Interactional options concern whether the speaker will take a positive ('satisfying') or a negative ('countering or 'contra-ing') stance to the interlocutor's preceding or current discourse move, while illocutionary options concern the type of speech act (e.g. a request, an apology, a complaint) which is culturally appropriate to this purpose. In distinguishing between interactional and illocutionary categories, the system becomes highly efficient in that the categories of illocutionary acts can be economically restricted. Further, by including in Box B interactional moves and their combinatorial potential, a knowledge store is derived which may also be employed in non-verbal modes of interaction.

Integrating the distinctions made by pragmatic theorists such as Searle (1983) and Blum-Kulka and Weizman (1988), we can here further include two types of goals for the evolving interaction: an 'individual-I-point' (the 'speaker meaning') and a 'collective-we-direction', a sort of 'drift' in which the discourse is jointly propelled.

Box C marks the result of ongoing processing, where a more or less specific type of input is expected.

Box D refers to the process of extracting a 'discourse meaning' involving complex subsystems of linguistic decoding, discourse interpretation strategies, inferencing procedures and politeness considerations. It incorporates concepts and distinctions elaborated in work on intercultural miscommunication such as, for instance, Gumperz' (1982a, 1982b, 1992a) work on participants' misusing 'contextualization cues' or Lakoff's (1990) concern with differing communicative styles.

Box E marks the outcome of the comprehension/interpretation processes in D in the form of a tentative discourse meaning for the current input.

Box F is a critical one in the current version of the model: here the interpreted input leads inititially to a non-linguistic, emotive-cognitive 'gut reaction'. It is this central part of the model which, together with the system's emotion-related 'anywhere elements', takes cognizance of the role of emotion in discourse comprehension and production. In line with recent discourse theories such as the one proposed by Jaszczolt (1996), who makes the important (and obvious) point that emotions tend to severely interfere with discourse interpretations, this model thus also explicitly accounts for the crucial role of human emotive reactions in discourse processing and behaviour. We may hypothesize that 'interfering' emotions tend to be exacerbated in the process of intercultural communication because intercultural communication involves interactants who may habitually use different, culture-specific communicative styles which are often not recognized as such but rather are ascribed to their interlocutors' personal deficiencies and oddities – an ascription which effectively mars interpersonal relationships and rapport.

The determinants of the response in Box F are to a substantial degree personality-based – they depend on a person's ability for interpersonal adaptation in the ongoing interaction (cf. Burgoon et al. (1995) and the degree to which there is 'permeability of ego-boundaries'). The concept of 'ego-flexibility' (Guiora et al. 1975) was operationalized as a speaker's ability to empathize with the thoughts and feelings of others, and to identify with the other's expectations and assumptions. Other personality traits impacting on a speaker's reaction in accordance with, or in violation of, expectation norms include cognitive flexibility, extroversion and introversion, risk-taking, and tolerance of ambiguity. Many of these factors have recently been subsumed under the psychological construct of 'ego boundaries' (Ehrman 1993). Ehrman (1993: 331) defines this concept as

(1) the ability to take in new information;
(2) the ability to hold contradictory or incomplete information without either rejecting one of the contradictory elements or coming to premature closure on an incomplete schema;

(3) the ability to adopt one's existing cognitive, affective, and social schemata in the light of the new information or experience.

This is also relevant for Box F since this box is characterized as 'emotive + cognitive reaction'.

Edmondson (1989: 290) posits some 'reactive formatives' which further concretize what is captured under the (non-linguistic) gut reaction to the current communicative situation in which a speaker finds himself or herself. These 'formatives' include the following aspects:

- affective weight of the current discourse topic or preceding discourse contribution (e.g. balancing speaker and hearer interests)
- evocative associations as when a preceding turn triggers recollection from episodic memory
- degree of importance attached by the speaker to his/her own face in the ongoing interaction
- the result of cognitive-intellectual processes evaluating the propositional content of a preceding turn
- role relationship (power and intimacy) between interactants

To elucidate the notion of 'reactive formative', Edmondson (1989: 290–1) gives the example of a speaker producing the utterance 'You're late', which is interpreted in the ongoing discourse by the hearer as accusatory in tone. Here the system might, on the basis of some of the reactive formatives, derive an ensuing move by answering questions such as:

- Am I in fact late?
- Is my interlocutor in a social position to comment on my time of arrival in this way?
- Do I care what this person thinks of me?
- Is punctuality something I value highly in others?
- Are there good reasons why my arrival occurred just now, and not earlier?
- Have I met with such criticism before? How did I successfully handle it on previous occasions?

Given such reactive formatives, the speaker has the options of 'ignoring' the utterance 'You're late' or proceeding to plan an utterance that is (on the surface) non-coherent; alternatively, she/he may feel insulted and wish to complain about the accusation and justify him/herself, or may opt for an apology, etc.

Box G: here the speaker may reconsider the 'gut' decisions made in F (which may not have surfaced to consciousness) and strategically manipulate them. The speaker may for instance choose to enact an intervening move which leads to looping inside the system, or may decide to 'prepare the ground' for a felt reaction in anticipation of the hearer's next move. Thus the speaker in G resorts to strategic knowledge as a basis for choosing interactional strategies (i.e. supportive moves, such as grounders) in order either to disguise the emotional gut reaction in F (if, for instance, this reaction is assessed as being potentially face-threatening to the interlocutor) or to reveal an emotive reaction – for instance to show irritation openly and forcefully, or to express pleasure over a compliment. Speakers at this stage of the system may become aware of their own and their interactant's emotional state and also regain their emotional equilibrium. They may, as a further option, decide to strategically stall, i.e. delay any reaction.

This box then may be likened to some sort of 'filter' which serves to modify, mitigate or intensify illocutionary options under the constraints of perceived social norms and conventions and in view of anticipated potentially face-threatening reactions of the interlocutor, which themselves serve to continually adjust initial responses. Using strategic interactional knowledge will therefore commonly involve looping in the system. In the above example ('You're late') a gut reaction of exasperation may, for instance, be modified by considerations of politeness leading to the suppression of the initial intuitive reaction and to the production of a more strategically adequate discourse move.

In Box H we have arrived at a prelinguistic communicative plan, and finally at Box I this communicative plan is transformed into linguistic representations on the basis of a complex of linguistic resources, search strategies, prepacked chunks such as discourse lubricants (gambits), and routine formulae.

Clearly, this model is not to be taken as depicting a straightforward linear-processing procedure, although the pathway mapped in Figure 7.1 and the labelling used here for expository purposes may well suggest that. Rather, the 'boxes' are interrelated in network fashion, and the whole system operates in parallel and simultaneously, i.e. various nodes, items and paths become activated at the same time. The model also allows for a number of short-cuts, which cannot be elaborated here (but see Edmondson 1989 and House 1993).

In the following section I wish to demonstrate the model's operation using two short excerpts from a corpus of authentic intercultural discourse.

7.3 Two cases of mismanaged rapport in intercultural interaction

The data presented here are taken from a corpus of authentic interactions between German and Anglophone native speakers. Participants (all between 20 and 28 years of age) are American university students spending a year at Hamburg university and their native German friends (also university students). The students audio-recorded themselves interacting in everyday situations, and these interactions were triangulated by retrospective comments elicited in narrative interviews with both interactants.

Data Extract 1: The Rice Episode

Brian, an American student spending a year in Germany, has cooked a meal for Andi, a German friend, who has recently helped him with his German seminar paper. Andi has just arrived.

01 Brian: *hallo Andi wie geht's?*
02 Andi: *ja prima oh prima doch ja;*
03 Brian: *so (.) es is alles fertig jetzt (.) ich hoffe es schmeckt dir gut (0.3) ich hab es selber gekocht [soweil]*
04 Andi: *[ja prima]*
05 Brian: *ißt man bei uns im Süden*
06 Andi: *{in a loud voice} aber das is ja so VIEL das is ja VIEL ZU VIEL Reis*
07 Brian: *das MACHT doch nichts (0.1) ich hab es ja bezahlt (.) und ich hab dich EINgeladen (.) [du hast]*
08 Andi: *[nein das] MACHT DOCH was DOCH DOCH denk doch an die armen vielen hungernden Menschen die sowas gern essen würden [also ich]*
09 Brian: *[ich ich] glaube ich (0.1) ich [finde]*
10 Andi: *[ich finde] man sollte in dieser gemeinsamen Welt in der wir alle doch leben (0.2) der Welt in der wir alle so UNgleich mit materiellen Gütern ausgestattet sind sollten wir uns zumindest in kleinem aßstab bemühen keine Verschwendung keine unnütze Ver[schwendung]*
11 Brian: *[also Andi] ich bin nicht ich (0.2) [glaube nicht]*
12 Andi: *[keine Ver]schwendung zu produzieren und immer in unserem Bewußtsein daran zu denken daß wir in der reichen westlichen Welt ... {monologue continues for 1½ minutes}*

01	Brian:	hallo Andi how are you?

01 Brian: hallo Andi how are you?
02 Andi: yeah fine oh fine really yeah;
03 Brian: so (.) everything's ready now (.) I hope you like it (0.3) I have cooked it myself [so because]
04 Andi: [yeah fine]
05 Brian: that's what we eat in the South
06 Andi: {in a loud voice} but that's so much that is FAR TOO MUCH rice
07 Brian: that doesn't MATTER (0.1) I have paid for it (.) and I have INVITED you (.) [you have]
08 Andi: [no it] DOES matter it DOES it DOES think of the many poor people who go hungry and would like to eat something like that
        [well I]
09 Brian: [I I] believe I (0.1) I [find]
10 Andi: [I find] one should in this common world in which we do all live (0.2) the world in which we are all endowed with material goods so UNequally we should at least on a small scale try to produce no waste no useless [waste]
11 Brian: [well Andi] I am not I (0.2) [don't believe]
12 Andi: produce [no waste] and always in our consciousness think that we in the rich western world ...
        {monologue continues for 1½ minutes}

In the retrospective interview which I conducted with each interactant, Brian said that in his role as host he felt unpleasantly 'talked at' by his friend, who in his view acted like a 'know-all' teacher figure. He was disappointed that his friend did nothing to keep a 'real conversation' going, and he felt overrun by the monologue. In fact he said he often felt in interactions with German friends that they did not want to, or were unable to, engage in any sort of small talk. He said it did not really surprise him that there wasn't even a word in German for 'small talk'. He had got the impression that it often happened in German conversations that the topic was more important than the human beings discussing it, and that discussions therefore often turned out to be serious, 'deep' and controversial. He thought there was often some sort of pressure to talk about something important and weighty, 'even' with students. In social talk, such as Data Extract 1, or in informal meetings or everyday conversations, Americans would prefer to 'engage in collaborative, connected and communicative talk wishing to establish common ground as a talking procedure. The German line of talk was more to separate oneself from one's interlocutor as one gets "sucked up" by the theme of the conversation.'

It is interesting to note that Brian seems to have a good intuitive understanding of the differences in German and American communicative norms but that, nevertheless, in the concrete performance of this conversation, he was both unaware of these differences, and unable to apply this knowledge to increase 'understanding' and retain his emotional equilibrium. Rather he let himself be overcome by a sense of misunderstanding, he felt sad and disappointed and in his own words 'took a dislike' to Andi, to whom he imputed inconsiderateness and 'selfishness' – and this despite the fact that this same Andi had 'selflessly' helped him before with his German essays.

Andi, the German interlocutor, said in the retrospective interview that he thought they had reflected well on the problems of the so-called 'Third World' and on the way structural problems in the economies of the developing countries might be resolved. He said he was often surprised that Americans had a different outlook on the resources available in different countries and that this kind of 'overly generous' handling of the resources was also reflected in their often rather irresponsible behaviour vis-à-vis food and possessions. He was surprised that Brian had said so little and suspected that he was not interested in the topic.

What precisely happened in this intercultural encounter, and how can we explain what happened with reference to the discourse processing model presented above? Clearly Data Extract 1 is a case of 'cross-talk', of misunderstanding emerging because of different communicative styles. The monologous and monothematic nature of the discourse is marked. In Edmondson and House's (1981) terms, Andi makes ample use of the supportive move type 'expander' in order to keep a particular topic in play. As a result of this, one gets the impression that one participant (Andi) is clearly 'hogging' the topic, and overruns the other's (Brian's) two attempts (see turns 9 and 11) to gain the floor. Andi's non-reciprocity (turn 2) of Brian's 'how-are-you' move (turn 1), and the non-concatenation of turns 5 and 6 are also marked. The move in turn 5 is clearly characteristic of a conversational opening phase or of phatic talk in general, which would conventionally (in Anglophone talk) be coupled with either a follow-up request for information or another remark which thematically links turn 6 with turn 5, opening up a chain of sequentially relevant moves as contiguous replies. By contrast, what happens in turn 6 is an abrupt topic switch in the form of a complaint, followed by a directive in turn 8, with both these speech acts being produced at high levels of directness (for further discussion and explanation of the notion of directness, see House 1979, House and Kasper 1981, and Blum-Kulka, House and Kasper 1989; see also Chapters 2 and 3 in this book).

With regard to the discourse processing model presented in Figure 7.1, we can first of all state that the misunderstanding revealed in the retrospective interview is clearly conceptually-based. It seems to result from differences in the pragmatic knowledge base and the interactional goals (Boxes A, B and G). Andi and Brian have different conceptions of what communicative conventions hold in a conversational opening phase, of the topics appropriate for a dinner table conversation, and of the appropriateness of turn allocation and floor holding during a dinner table conversation. Andi's unexpected moves thus strike Brian as offensively self-oriented and as showing preoccupation with a particular topic which is relentlessly and monologically pursued. Further, we can interpret Andi's rejection of Brian's attempts to gain the floor as a short-cut in the processsing route: by ostensibly not listening to Brian, Andi jumps directly from his own interactional goal (Box B) to an immediate communicative plan (Box H) and its linguistic encoding, thus bypassing not only his interlocutor's real input but also any strategic considerations of his own. This creates, in Goffman's (1986) terms, an impression of 'non-alignment', since Andi often produces neither a response nor a reply, he simply initiates. The 'Individual I-Meaning' and the 'Collective We-Direction' (in the sense of Blum-Kulka and Weizman 1988) seem to be widely divergent in this stretch of talk.

The importance of emotional/affective factors come into play with Brian's feelings of being 'talked at', his disappointment, sadness and anger, all of which Brian attributed to Andi as a person, not to his culture-conditioned communicative style. The emotive-cognitive gut reaction (Box F) can be said to be negative for one of the conversationalists, with the 'system equilibrium index' indicating a strong disturbance of his equilibrium. As to the interactants' awareness of the existence and causes of the emotional 'disturbance' which result from the nature of the interaction in Data Extract 1, the retrospective comments clearly reveal that Andi lacks this awareness. It is only Brian who is acutely aware of his own emotional upset, but is unable to 'proceduralize' his (intuitive) knowledge of German and Anglophone interactional differences.

In Data Extract 2, which features a similar setting (dinner, two male students, student residence), the differences in German and Anglo-phone communicative orientations and preferences are again marked.

Data Extract 2: Mad Cow Disease

Norman, an American exchange student, and Hannes, a German student, live in the same student residence. Norman has cooked a meal for the two of them, and Hannes has just arrived in the kitchen.

01	Norman:	*hallo Hannes (0.1) schön dich zu sehn (0.2) wie gehts dir so?*
02	Hannes:	{*setzt sich*} *ach hallo Norman (.) och Mann ja also(0.2) wenn ich EHRLICH bin du (.) ich hab vielleicht n Hunger was hast dun geKOCHT ?(0.3) [riecht ja]*
03	Norman:	*[Spaghetti] (???) [etwas was ich]*
04	Hannes:	*[ja Klasse] also ja aber ja ich hoffes is nich Rind-Rind-fleisch die Sache [is ja]*
05	Norman:	*[ich ich] also ich hoffe du bist nicht enttäuscht ich hab SPAGHETTI gekocht und die Sauce dabei natürlich ich meine ich hab [nicht besonders]*
06	Hannes:	*[worauf ich] hinaus will ist ist also (.) das sollten wir WISSEN es ist aus Argentinien oder?*
07	Norman:	*ja (0.2) ich meine(.) weißt du (.) das kann und ist (.) also wahr[scheinlich]*
08	Hannes:	*[nein was] ich mein is also die Sache is doch DIE dass eben die Gefahren der Verseuchung und dass also (0.2) du hast ja sicher gelesen wie sie es machen die Exportverbote zu umgehn [und so]*
09	Norman:	*[hmm ich] (0.2) ich also [ja]*
10	Hannes:	*[ich] hab gelesn dass die Engländer ihr Rindfleisch in die irische Republik schmuggeln und also erm (0.2) nach Eire über die gruene Grenze und dann (.) die Sache is DIE* {*continues*}

{Norman is silent now}

01	Norman:	hallo Hannes (0.1) good to see you (0.2) how are things with you?
02	Hannes:	sits down} oh hallo Norman (.) oh man well (0.2) to tell the TRUTH (.) I am very very hungry what have you COOKED? (0.3) [smells]

03 Norman: [spaghetti] (???) [something I]
04 Hannes: [yeah great] so yeah but yeah I
        hope it's not beef the thing [is]
05 Norman: [I I] well I hope you
        are not disappointed I have cooked SPAGHETTI
        and the sauce with it of course I mean I have
        [not specially]
06 Hannes: [what I'm] getting at is is well (.) we should KNOW
        that it is from Argentina or?
07 Norman: yeah (0.2) I mean (.) you know (.) that can be and is
        (.) well pro[bable]
08 Hannes: [no what] I'm getting at is well the thing
        IS that the danger of food deterioration and that well
        (0.2) you have surely read how they go about getting
        round the ban on exports [and so]
09 Norman: [hmm I](0.2) I well [yes]
10 Hannes: [I] read
        that the British are smuggling their beef to the
        Republic of Ireland to well (0.2) erm Eire via the
        green border and then (.) the thing IS {continues}
{Norman is silent now}

In the retrospective interview Norman said that he did not
understand why his friend continued arguing when he had thought
that they would simply sit and eat together and make conversation.
He thought Hannes – whom he knows is a bit of an 'environmental
freak' – insisted 'a bit too much and too long' on pursuing 'his topic'.
He was acutely aware of the fact that he was 'pushed out of the
conversation', i.e. unable to contribute anything to it – mainly
because his opinion was never elicited. He thought the talk was odd
since they were, after all, not in a debating club, but at dinner, a social
occasion. He thought his friend became increasingly alienated from
him in the course of the talk: 'He acted like a stranger and I felt
strange too.' One might argue that – as in the situation in Data
Extract 1 – the American students' German interlanguage prevented
them from taking a more decisive part in the talk. But in the
retrospective interviews, such linguistic handicap was not identified
as an issue at all. And from my own (informal) assessment of Brian's
and Norman's competence in colloquial German (a language they
also studied as their major in their home university), they were
certainly sufficiently capable of holding their own in a dinner table
conversation.

Norman's emotional reaction to the conversational style pursued by his interactant is marked in that he expressly mentioned his feelings of 'strangeness' and alienation, to the point where he shut up completely. Hannes' retrospective comments revealed a rather more neutral assessment of the interaction with his friend Norman. He had not noticed that Norman was increasingly monosyllabic and in the end positively muted. Instead he remarked that he himself found it important to broach the topic of BSE and its hidden dangers. He seemed to have no awareness of the mismanaged rapport which characterized the interaction in the eyes of his interlocutor.

Note that in Hannes' turns there is a clear preference for gambits such as 'underscorers' which are clearly focused on the message itself (e.g. *die Sache is ja die* (the thing is) in turn 4; *worauf ich hinaus will* (what I'm getting at) in turn 6, and also *was ich mein … die Sache is* (what I'm getting at, the thing is) in turn 8. Further, as in Data Extract 1, we again notice the non-reciprocity of the 'how-are-you' move on the part of the German native speaker in turn 2.

In terms of the discourse processing model, we can first of all say that the interactants' level of awareness of the evolving interpersonal relationship varies greatly: while Hannes is not aware of the rapport deterioration, Norman is highly conscious of it. In the 'system equilibrium index' we can register a marked imbalance, to the point where one of the interlocutors is effectively silenced. We can again explain this interactional trouble by reference to differences in relevant knowledge representations, interactional goals and choices of discourse strategies (Boxes A, B, G). Interactants' emotive-cognitive 'gut reaction' (Box F) also clearly diverges.

Indications of the differences in strategic, pragmatic knowledge can be seen in the following: the differential use of the 'polite' inquiry-after-other by Norman in turn 1, the non-reciprocal move by Hannes in turn 2, and Norman's employment of a 'disarmer' in turn 5, which is an interpersonally active (inherently polite) discourse strategy designed to make the other feel good (*Ich hoffe du bist nicht enttäuscht* – 'I hope you're not disappointed'). Note here that Hannes himself does not use any interpersonally active supportive moves, but rather resorts to ideationally focused discourse strategies such as expanders (expanding on the topic chosen) and topic introducers, e.g. in turn 6 *das sollten wir wissen* ('we should know that'). The fact that Hannes often does not seem to listen to what his interlocutor is saying – for instance in turns 6 and 8 – can be explained by a system short-cut, i.e. his shifting from his interactional goal (Box B) to a communicative plan (H), ignoring both the other's input and the possibility of modulating his own ouput strategically (Box G).

Taken together, the analyses of the two data extracts – which in fact are typical of many others in my data – show that mismanagement of rapport and conceptually-based misunderstandings occurred because of the differential weighting given to small talk by German as opposed to Anglophone speakers. This difference is manifest in a greater focus on the content of the talk by German speakers (evidenced in the use of certain gambits and discourse strategies, and a preference for a monothematic line of discourse) as opposed to a more developed 'etiquette of simulation' on the part of Anglophone speakers, evidenced for instance in the use of reciprocal routines such as the 'how-are-you' move, interpersonally active discourse strategies such as the disarmer, and a dialogic line of discourse.

Why should it be the case that the communicative preferences, interactional styles and expectancy norms revealed in the two data extracts differ in this way? Are the differences found in these two cases reducible to personal idiosyncrasies or are they indicative of more general cross-cultural differences in communicative styles and priorities? In the following section I will briefly try to give some tentative answers to these questions.

7.4 Understanding misunderstanding: some explanatory hypotheses

In order to attempt a 'deeper' explanation of the analytic findings described in the previous section, it may be interesting to look at the results of a series of contrastive German–English discourse analyses I have conducted over the past twenty years (for overviews see House 1996a, 1996b, 1998). The data collection methods in these studies are varied: they include open (non-prescriptive) dyadic role-plays often followed by retrospective interviews, discourse completion tasks combined with metapragmatic assessment tests, field notes, diary entries and interviews, as well as authentic interactions of the type presented in this chapter. Apart from oral data I have also undertaken contrastive pragmatic analyses of German and English written discourse and translations in a variety of different genres (House 1977, 1997). The discourse analyses of these different data sets are all based on the discourse model provided in Edmondson (1981) and on Edmondson and House's interactional grammar (1981) as well as the categorial scheme developed inside the Cross-Cultural Speech Act Realization Project (CCSARP) (Blum-Kulka et al. 1989).

The discourse phenomena investigated include opening and closing discourse phases, topic nomination, topic maintenance and change, discourse strategies, gambits and the execution of specific speech acts. From the individual results of all these analyses a consistent pattern has emerged. In a nutshell, German speakers tend to interact in many different situations in ways that can be described as more direct, more explicit, more self-referenced and more content-oriented. German speakers are also found to be less prone to resort to using verbal routines than Anglophone speakers. This pattern of cross-cultural differences can be displayed along five dimensions:

Orientation towards Content ——— Orientation towards Addressee
Orientation towards Self ——— Orientation towards Other
Directness ——— Indirectness
Explicitness ——— Implicitness
Ad hoc Formulation ——— Verbal Routines

The validity of these dimensions is supported by the results of other contrastive-pragmatic German–English studies, such as Byrnes (1986), Clyne (1987), Kotthoff (1989) and Watts (1989).

It is important, however, to emphasize that we are here not dealing with clear-cut dichotomies. Oppositions such as 'directness versus indirectness' represent different end-points of a continuum. In general, however, my analyses suggest that German subjects prefer the left-hand positions of these dimensions. Now if we relate the hypothesized dimensional preferences to the differences in interactional behaviour found in Data Extracts 1 and 2 above, we can see that the dimensions may serve as explanatory hypotheses for these findings. In other words, interactants' discourse behaviour in Data Extracts 1 and 2 may be explained with reference to the operation of different empirically established communicative preferences displayed as a set of dimensions of cross-cultural differences.

7.5 Conclusion

Rather than trying to examine mismanaged rapport in talk across cultures inside one single research paradigm – a procedure inherently unsuitable given the complexity of the object to be investigated – I have suggested in this chapter that basing one's analysis of intercultural talk on a cognitive discourse processing model, which integrates different approaches in a transdisciplinary manner, may be a more fruitful way of trying to understand intercultural misunderstanding and mismanaged rapport.

On the basis of the explanatory framework provided by this model, authentic intercultural data triangulated with interactants' subjective interpretations were analysed, and the hypothesis was put forward that the results of relevant contrastive pragmatic analyses can help explain why misunderstanding occurs and why some misunderstandings result in mismanaged rapport. It was suggested that a set of empirically derived dimensions of cultural differences may be taken as guidelines to understanding some of the underlying reasons for the often emotionally charged nature of interpersonal relations in intercultural talk.

What we need in the future is continued transdisciplinary work on the development and refinement of cognitive discourse processing models as well as more large-scale cross-cultural and intercultural pragmatic research, using many different language pairs and relying on a multi-method approach to data elicitation, as well as on triangulation of the discourse analyses with interactants' own voices.

Discussion questions

1   Look again at the data extracts.

1.1 Suppose you were invited to dinner under those circumstances. Would you have acted as the German students did? Why/why not?

1.2 Suppose you were the host under those circumstances. Would you have reacted as the American students did? Why/why not?

2   Think about informal dinner conversations between hosts and guests in your own country.

2.1 During the first few minutes after the guest's arrival, how important is it for both parties to engage in small talk? Are there any routine phrases or common topics that are used for this?

2.2 Are there any conversation topics that *should* be brought up during the event (e.g. comments on the food)? Are there any conversation topics that are best avoided? To what extent do contextual factors, such as the relationship between the participants, affect the choice of conversation topics?

2.3 Consider turn-taking during informal dinner conversations. Are the turns usually fairly equally distributed or is it common for one person to have extended turns? Is it usual for participants to overlap their turns, or do they normally wait until the other person has finished? How comfortable/uncomfortable do people feel when there is silence?

If you are working with people from other countries, compare and discuss your answers.

3   Using the information you've put forward in question 2, try to write some simple scripts (see Chapter 3) for 'topic choice' and/ or 'turn-taking' in informal dinner conversations in your country.

4   Look again at Brian's and Norman's reactions. Use the rapport-management concepts of 'face' and 'sociality rights' (see Chapter 2) to try to explain why they felt as they did.

5   How does the concept of 'culture as communicative style' fit in with the concepts used in Chapter 3 to unpackage culture?

6   Is the notion of intracultural variation compatible with the claim that there are dimensions of communicative style on which cultures differ? Why/why not? (You may wish to refer to Chapter 3 and Chapter 14.)

Suggestions for further reading

Aston, G. (1988) *Learning Comity: An Approach to the Description and Pedagogy of Interactional Speech.* Bologna: University Press.

Hellinger, M. and Ammon, U. (eds) (1996) *Contrastive Sociolinguistics.* Berlin: Mouton de Gruyter.

House, J., Kasper, G. and Ross, S. (eds) (forthcoming) *Misunderstanding in Spoken Discourse.* London: Longman.

Thomas, J. (1995) *Meaning in Interaction: An Introduction to Pragmatics.* London: Longman.

8

Pragmatic Transfer in Intercultural Communication

Vladimir Žegarac and Martha C. Pennington

8.1 Introduction

Each chapter of this book touches, more or less directly, on the ways in which culture-specific aspects of communicative competence affect what goes on in situations of communication between people from different cultural backgrounds. An insight into pragmatic transfer (where by 'pragmatic transfer' we mean, roughly, the carryover of pragmatic knowledge from one culture to another) is important for a good understanding of intercultural communication. This chapter aims to provide the basis for understanding pragmatic transfer by focusing on the following questions:

1. What is pragmatic transfer?
2. How can pragmatic transfer be identified?
3. How can pragmatic transfer be investigated empirically?
4. How can pragmatic transfer be explained theoretically?
5. How does pragmatic transfer relate to second language acquisition?

Each of these questions raises a range of issues, only some of which can be considered here. Our main aim is to provide the reader with a good vantage point for further independent investigation of pragmatic transfer in the context of intercultural communication.

There are two types of approach to pragmatics: the social and the cognitive. These two approaches lead to different outcomes: social pragmatics provides descriptions of communicative behaviour, whereas cognitive pragmatics explains how this behaviour is made possible by specific cognitive mechanisms (cf. Blakemore 1992: 47). Despite occasional claims to the contrary, the two approaches are not intrinsically incompatible. Some (if not most) issues relating to verbal communication can only be studied successfully from both points of view. Pragmatic transfer is a case in point. It is a cognitive phenomenon by definition, because it concerns some aspects of human knowledge, but it must also be studied descriptively from a social point of view, because the observation and analysis of communicative behaviour (whether based on naturally occurring or experimentally elicited data) present by far the most important source of evidence for pragmatic transfer. In particular, the discussion of the fourth question ('How can pragmatic transfer be explained theoretically?') explores the possibility of reconciling and combining the insights from social pragmatics (especially Brown and Levinson's (1987) work on face) with the cognitive approach of Sperber and Wilson's (1986/1995) relevance theory.

8.2 What is pragmatic transfer?

The term 'transfer' is generally used to refer to the systematic influences of existing knowledge on the acquisition of new knowledge. People usually approach a new problem or situation with an existing mental set: a frame of mind involving an existing disposition to think of a problem or a situation in a particular way (see Sternberg 1995: 342–5; Holyoak and Thagard 1995). Mental sets are largely determined by culture-specific knowledge. Therefore, communication between individuals from different cultural backgrounds may be influenced by their different mental sets. For example, in some cultures an offer of coffee after a meal is generally recognized as a polite way to indicate to the guests that they ought to leave soon if they do not wish to outstay their welcome. In other cultures, an offer of coffee on a similar occasion is just an act of the host's kindness (or even an invitation to the guests to stay a little longer than they had intended).

If interactants from different cultural backgrounds are unaware of the differences in their respective mental sets, misunderstandings are likely to occur. Misunderstandings of this sort involve the carryover of culture-specific knowledge from a situation of intracultural communication to a situation of intercultural communication. In psychology, the term 'transfer' refers to any carryover of knowledge or skills from one problem situation to another. In the offer-of-coffee example, we assume that the transfer in question is pragmatic for the following reasons. The problem has to do with the way in which an offer of coffee is typically understood in the context of a particular type of situation: roughly, guests having a meal at a friend's home. A communication problem is at stake: to figure out what is the intended implicit import of the offer of coffee; and the difficulty does not lie with the linguistic meaning of the words used. (If it did, the transfer would be linguistic/semantic, rather than pragmatic.) To conclude: this example points to the reasons for studying pragmatic transfer, e.g. transfer may lead to miscommunication; it gives some indications about the possible approaches, e.g. pragmatic transfer is close to the psychological notion of transfer as a factor in general problem solving; and it provides a good basis for a fairly adequate definition of the term 'pragmatic transfer':

> Pragmatic transfer is the transfer of pragmatic knowledge in situations of intercultural communication.

This definition is rather more complex than it may seem at first sight, because some of its elements are not entirely well understood. For instance, there is no universal agreement among researchers on answers to questions like the following: What is pragmatic knowledge? How is it stored and put to use? What is the relation between pragmatic knowledge and linguistic knowledge? and many others. Studies of pragmatic transfer are partly guided by views on these issues, but they also provide valuable input for assessing the validity of such views. Fortunately, the starting point for investigating pragmatic transfer – the identification of situations in which transfer has occurred – does not depend on a great number of theoretically contentious premises.

Although it is customary to study pragmatic transfer in the context of second language acquisition, this is by no means necessary: as the offer-of-coffee example shows, pragmatic transfer is relatively independent of language because pragmatic knowledge is distinct from, although it interfaces with, linguistic knowledge. To give another illustration, Chapter 12 discusses the difficulties that East Germans have in job interviews conducted by prospective West German employers. The following is a slightly adapted version of a typical exchange in English translation (see Chapter 12, Example 6, for a detailed transcription of the German text):

| Interviewer: | And with your boss? Did you ever have well any argument? No? |
| Applicant: | Never. |

> Interviewer: Because you got on with him so well?
>
> Applicant: No, that's got nothing to do with it. I'm respectful.

From the point of view of the East German applicant, being respectful is a very desirable quality. The pragmatic (i.e. communicative) competence of the applicant which has been shaped by life in East Germany is transferred to a situation in which successful impression management presupposes a set of cultural values which the applicant is blissfully unaware of. This is an example of pragmatic transfer within a single language.

8.3 How can pragmatic transfer be identified?

There is no fail-safe procedure for establishing that an act of communication is influenced by pragmatic transfer. However, the assumption that this type of transfer is involved may be supported by observations which focus on the communicative behaviour of learners in their first language (L1) and second language (L2), in comparison to the linguistic behaviour of native speakers of the second language. This is easiest to explain by using an example, such as responses to compliments. People from different cultures often respond to compliments in systematically different ways. Let us assume that in a particular situational context, speakers of a particular language X (LX) accept compliments without showing modesty. In such cases a speaker might accept a compliment such as 'You did a really good job' with a simple expression of 'Thanks', i.e. without expressing any reservations about the validity or the importance of the compliment. Let us assume further that in the same type of situation, native speakers of another language Y (LY) typically accept compliments, but play down (and are culturally expected to play down) their importance. It seems reasonable to assume that native speakers of LY who are learning LX may respond to compliments in LX in the same way as they would in LY. For example, they might respond to the compliment 'You did a really good job' with an expression of modesty (e.g. 'You are too generous'). If this happens, we have fairly good grounds for assuming that native speakers of LY have carried over some pragmatic knowledge associated with the culture of LY to the performance of compliment responses in LX. In other words, they have carried over the L1 cultural knowledge that an expression of modesty is an appropriate response to a compliment, where in fact an acceptance/agreement response is more usual. This is a case of so-called negative pragmatic transfer, because the L2 learner has mistakenly generalized from pragmatic knowledge of L1 to an L2 setting. Negative transfer may, but need not, lead to miscommunication. This type of transfer is called negative, not because of its adverse effect on communicative success, but because it involves an unwarranted generalization from L1 pragmatic knowledge to a communicative situation in L2. Negative pragmatic transfer thus leads to imperfect pragmatic competence in L2, but imperfect pragmatic competence does not necessarily cause communicative failure. For example, if native speakers of L2 realize that a non-native speaker's pragmatic knowledge of L2 is (or is likely to be) imperfect, they may make allowances (e.g. they might assume something like: *the non-native speaker is not being rude, he simply does not know that this type of answer is not appropriate in our culture*).

Just as negative transfer does not always lead to miscommunication, positive transfer does not always enhance the chances of communicative success. In some circumstances, the realization that the L2 learner is behaving like a native speaker may seem more important than what they are trying to communicate. For instance, if the L2 learner responds to compliments in the culturally appropriate way, while their L2 pragmatic competence is evidently flawed in many other respects, their appropriate communicative behaviour may be unexpected and so may be perceived as puzzling and mildly amusing. Instead of paying attention to the speaker's informative intention, the addressees may wonder about the peculiar correctness of the learner's use of L2. So positive transfer does not guarantee communicative success. This type of transfer is generally more difficult to identify than negative transfer, because the evidence for it is less direct. For example, let us assume that in both L1 and L2 compliments can be accepted with the same degree of modesty. This indicates that some aspect of a learner's L1 pragmatic knowledge is relevant to performance in L2. So if the L2 learner uses an expression of modesty in accepting compliments in L2 in roughly the same way as in L1, it is reasonable to assume that the learner's knowledge about communicating in L1 has contributed to their ability to communicate in L2.

8.4 How can pragmatic transfer be investigated empirically?

Like all empirical research, investigations of pragmatic transfer based on the analysis of data must take into account a wide range of factors.

These studies fall into two broad categories: quantitative and qualitative. Quantitative studies involve the collection of data from a considerable number of speakers. These data are then analysed statistically, and the emerging patterns of findings are interpreted. Qualitative studies focus on the meticulous description and explanation of a sample of naturally occurring data from a small number of individuals, sometimes only one. They aim at explaining a particular aspect of one, or perhaps several, situations of communication. The best way to find out about quantitative and qualitative studies of pragmatic transfer is to read some articles based on such research, and to try to design and carry out some small-scale projects. Here, a brief overview of two studies of pragmatic transfer is given in order to highlight some important aspects of such studies (see Chapter 15, and the remarks on 'emic' and 'etic' approaches to cross-cultural research in Chapter 14).

8.4.1 A quantitative study of pragmatic transfer: Yoon (1991)

Responding to a compliment is an interesting type of speech act because the communicative situation in which it is performed presents the hearer with the following problem: to accept the compliment may be seen as lacking modesty; to reject the compliment may be seen as lacking appreciation for the speaker's opinions and values. From the social point of view, neither lack of modesty nor lack of respect for the interlocutor is desirable. That is why in many societies there are communicative strategies (i.e. set ways of communicating in a particular type of situation, in this case responding to a compliment) whose purpose is to avoid this conflict.

If the verbal strategies for responding to a compliment differ across cultures, then this cultural divergence can be expected to be the locus of pragmatic transfer. Yoon (1991) investigates this possibility by comparing the speech patterns of monolingual speakers of American English and Korean with those of bilingual Korean/English speakers, when responding to compliments. The study involved 35 native speakers of American English, 40 speakers of Korean residing in Korea, and 33 Korean/English bilingual speakers who had lived in the USA for at least sixteen years. Each group was asked to complete a questionnaire in their native language; in the case of the bilingual speakers, they completed one in each language. The questionnaire was in the form of a discourse completion task: *Write down quickly what you would say in the following situation:* ... (where the situation involved responding to a compliment made by a speaker of slightly higher status). Despite the reservations that are sometime   ressed in the literature (see Chapter 11), the discourse completion task is still considered a valuable tool in social pragmatics; and while it is wise to exercise caution in taking the validity of the findings for granted, this method should not be rejected out of hand (see Chapter 15).

The data obtained by Yoon arguably revealed not only the presence, but also the degree and the direction of bilingual transfer. First, significant differences between the responses of American English-speakers and Korean Korean-speakers were observed. American English-speakers' responses showed a significant preference for an agreement strategy, while Korean Korean-speakers showed a marked preference for a modesty strategy. Second, Korean/English bilinguals, in their responses in English, used an agreement strategy to a lesser extent than native American English-speakers, but to a greater extent than Korean Korean speakers. This finding suggests negative pragmatic transfer from Korean. Third, Korean/English bilinguals, in their responses in Korean, used a modesty strategy to a greater extent than American English-speakers, but to a lesser extent than Korean Korean-speakers. This finding suggests negative pragmatic transfer from American English to Korean for the bilingual speakers.

8.4.2 A qualitative study of pragmatic transfer: Tyler (1995)

Tyler (1995) points out that quantitative studies shed little light on the ways in which people who engage in communication draw upon their knowledge of their own culture. She presents a qualitative case study based on a videotaped verbal interaction between a native speaker of Korean and a native speaker of American English. The interactants engaged in communication without realizing that they had very different assumptions about their respective roles and statuses, and this led to miscommunication: each participant assumed that the other one was uncooperative. The study shows how intercultural miscommunication arises through negative pragmatic transfer.

Tyler analyses the videotape of an actual tutoring session. The tutor was a male Korean graduate in Computer and Information Science who had spent over two years in the USA. His English was reasonably good, and he had volunteered to give tutoring sessions in Computer Programming. The student was a female native speaker of American English taking an introductory computer programming course who needed help with a programming assignment: to write a computer program for keeping score in bowling. It is important to note that both interactants were motivated to do well: the Korean computer science graduate took part in the tutoring sessions in order to improve his English communication skills; the US native-speaker student needed help on an assignment, and failure to complete the assignment would have had an adverse effect on her final grade.

At the beginning of the interaction, the student asks if the teacher knows how to keep score in bowling. The tutor's response is: 'Yeah, approximately'. In fact he is very familiar with bowling, but the student interprets his response as an acknowledgement of his lack of knowledge of bowling. In the context (i.e. the set of background assumptions) readily available to the student, the hedge, 'approximately', seems relevant as an indication that the teacher is less than fully competent as a bowler (a useful study of hedges, or down-graders, is Itani 1996). The teacher is unaware of this. In the teacher's culture, the translation equivalent of 'approximately' ('com', literally 'a little') is conventionally used as a marker of modesty. In the light of his cultural background, the teacher perhaps assumes that it would be inappropriate to make an unqualified statement about his competence and, under the influence of his pragmatic knowledge of L1, opts for an expression which is inappropriate in L2. The initial misunderstanding between teacher and student leads on to pervasive miscommunication. For example, when the teacher accompanies his typing on the computer with loud comments like 'uhmm Open, spare, strike', the student thinks that the teacher is trying to work out for himself the meaning of these words, whereas the teacher is trying to help the student to learn a particular sequence of instructions. Assuming that the teacher lacks adequate knowledge of bowling, the student says: 'That has to do with the bowling game'. By stating the obvious, the student is taken to suggest that the tutor knows next to nothing about bowling. To make things worse, the student – who has previously admitted that her knowledge of bowling is limited – makes a number of incorrect assertions about the game, and challenges the teacher's views repeatedly. Given the scale of the misunderstanding, it is hardly surprising that the teacher finds the student uncoopera-tive and aggressive, while the student thinks that the teacher is confused and incompetent.

A description of what seems to go on during instances of (mis)communication like those considered here is only a first step towards explaining pragmatic transfer. The next, and most im-portant, step is to show how the carryover of pragmatic knowledge from one communicative situation to another can be accounted for in terms of pragmatic theory, whose primary aim is 'to describe the factors other than a knowledge of sentence meaning that affect the interpretation of utterances' (Wilson and Sperber 1986: 22).

8.5 Explaining pragmatic transfer

Good explanations of pragmatic transfer have both practical and theoretical implications: practical, because they can help us understand, solve, and anticipate problems in communication across cultures, and theoretical, because the possibility of explaining pragmatic transfer may provide evidence for or against the theoretical framework used in the analysis. This section provides a sketch for such a framework. First, some important questions that a pragmatic analysis needs to answer are considered. This is followed by an outline of a universal comprehension strategy which follows from a basic pragmatic principle. Finally, the way this strategy interacts with culture-dependent preferences or conventions for conducting communicative exchanges is examined.

8.5.1 Three questions for pragmatic analysis

Countless examples can be found to illustrate the gap between knowing what a sentence means and knowing what a particular speaker means by an utterance of that sentence on a given occasion. One of the goals of linguistics is to explain how meanings are assigned to words in context. The main goal of pragmatics is to explain how speakers use language (as well as non-verbal modes of expression) to convey information which goes beyond the meanings of the words used. In order to live up to this task, pragmatic theory needs to address three questions:

1. What did the speaker intend to say (i.e. to communicate directly)?
2. What did the speaker intend to *imply* (i.e. to communicate indirectly)?
3. What was the intended *context*?

(It should be noted that the term 'context' is used more broadly in social than in cognitive approaches to pragmatics. In social approaches 'context' is the total linguistic and non-linguistic background to an act of communication. In Sperber and Wilson's (1986/ 1995) cognitive approach, this term refers to the set of assumptions exploited in utterance interpretation.)

In deciding on the intended interpretation of the utterance, the addressee has to make some assumptions about these three questions. For example, the initial misunderstanding in Tyler's study occurs because the student did not realize what the tutor intended to say by the utterance: 'Yeah, approximately'. She thought that he was using the adverb as a way of limiting or hedging on the extent of his knowledge of bowling. But the tutor actually meant to say something like 'I know how to keep score in bowling'. By using the adverb 'approximately', he intended to indicate that he was observing a social convention about the need to show modesty, implying that he did not want to impose his authority on the student. The student was unaware of this. Due to her cultural background, the context in which the tutor intended her to interpret his utterance was not available to her: the English adverb 'approximately' is not conventionally used to indicate modesty. When the tutor said: 'uhmm Open, spare, strike', the student misinterpreted his attitude towards this utterance. She thought that he was treating these instructions as mere possibilities, hoping to remember or discover the correct procedure, whereas he considered them as factual information which the student ought to learn.

To sum up: the student's failure to work out what the tutor intended to say and what he intended to imply stemmed from the teacher's inability to anticipate in which context the student was likely to interpret the teacher's utterance. What let the tutor down was not his knowledge of the English language, but his knowledge about how this language is used. This pragmatic knowledge is organized in a particular way and it is applied in communication in accordance with some basic communicative principles and strategies.

8.5.2 Pragmatic competence and pragmatic transfer

A generally accepted model of pragmatic competence does not exist, but some important insights into human communication can be brought to bear on this subject. First, communication involves information processing, which is constrained by considerations of efficiency. Second, it involves reasoning based on the interpretation of communicative signals (gestures, utterances) in context. In particular, communication cannot be reduced to the hearer's or analyst's recovery of the linguistic meaning of the words. Third, the relation between types of signals and contexts in which they are processed may be conventionalized to a greater or lesser extent. Fourth, the culture-specific conventionalized aspects of interpretation build on certain universal dispositions for the formation of specific types of concepts in the social domain.

Points one and four are the bread and butter of cognitive pragmatics (e.g. Grice 1989; Sperber and Wilson's 1986/1995 relevance theory) and cognitive anthropology (see Sperber *et al.* 1995; Gumperz and Levinson 1996; Bloch 1998). Point two has been central to the many developments of Grice's (1989) ideas (e.g. Clark 1996; Levinson 1983; Sperber and Wilson 1986/1995). The third point has received more attention in empirical research within social pragmatics (a good overview is Schiffrin 1994) than within the cognitive approach of Sperber and Wilson (but see Sperber 1996; Žegarac 1998). It has also been studied extensively in psychology (Gibbs 1981, 1986) and in pragmatic theory and philosophy of language (see Morgan 1978; Bach and Harnish 1979/1982; Searle 1996).

8.5.2.1 Communicative efficiency: relevance

Good speakers manage to communicate a lot of information in a way which does not put more strain on the cognitive resources of their addressees than is necessary. In other words, the goal of communication is not merely to convey information, but to convey it economically. This observation underlies the most important communicative principle, the principle of communicative efficiency, or, more technically, the communicative principle of relevance. Relevance (especially the tendency to minimize the expenditure of processing effort) is the driving force behind pragmatic transfer. The more a new problem resembles old ones which have been solved successfully in the past, the easier it will be to solve the new problem. Since every communicative situation presents a new problem for the interlocutors, the more they can rely on their experience from previous exchanges, the easier the problem will be.

The Communicative Principle of Relevance
Every communicative signal (pointing gesture, utterance, etc.) communicates the following guarantee:
(a) the signal is worth processing (i.e. worth paying attention to), and
(b) the signal used is the most relevant one compatible with the speaker's abilities and preferences.
(A signal is relevant to the addressee to the extent that it communicates information which is worth having, and to the extent that it makes it easy for the addressee to figure out this information.)
(adapted from Sperber and Wilson 1995: 260–70)

It follows from the Communicative Principle of Relevance that in all genuine acts of verbal communication:

(i) the speaker should aim to produce an utterance which conveys the information s/he intends to communicate and makes it as easy as possible for the addressee to figure out the speaker's intended meaning, and

(ii) the addressee is entitled to expect the speaker's behaviour to be consistent with the communicative principle of relevance.

Hence, this principle provides the basis for the following comprehension strategy used in utterance interpretation:

Comprehension Strategy
Begin by processing an utterance in the initial context; if necessary, discard some contextual assumptions and replace them with others, until you arrive at an interpretation which is consistent with the Principle of Relevance (or until you accept that miscommunication has occurred).

In the process of interpretation, then, context selection is driven by the search for relevance. The Communicative Principle of Relevance explains how successful context selection is possible: the addressee starts off with an initial context, then adjusts it by discarding those contextual assumptions which seem irrelevant and by replacing them with others which seem relevant. In many cases of miscommunication involving negative pragmatic transfer, the speaker makes incorrect assumptions about the context in which the hearer is likely to interpret the utterance. The difficulties relating to context selection may lead to miscommunication when the following two conditions obtain: (a) the speaker's and the hearer's background knowledge from which the context for utterance interpretation is selected differ significantly, and (b) the speaker and the hearer are unaware of these differences.

Let us consider whether these observations on utterance understanding can provide the basis for an account of the miscommunication between the teacher and the student in Tyler's (1995) study (section 8.4.2). First, at the outset, the teacher and the student probably have different contextual assumptions about the respective roles of teacher and student in classroom interaction based on their different backgrounds. The student's context includes some assumptions to the effect that many aspects of the relationship are negotiable. By contrast, the teacher more probably assumes that in this type of situation his authority is taken for granted and cannot be questioned. Moreover, the teacher possibly mistakenly assumes that some semantic translation equivalents ('*com*' (Korean) / 'approximately' (English)) are also pragmatically equivalent. So it is very likely that the teacher and the student are both unaware of the fact that they do not share the same contextual knowledge (due to their different cultural backgrounds), and for this reason their exchange runs into difficulties. They cannot resolve those difficulties, because each fails to make appropriate adjustments to their initial context. Thus, the teacher's utterance 'Yeah, approximately' seems relevant to the student in one way (namely, as communicating an admission of his incompetence), while the teacher intends it to be relevant in a different way (namely, as a modest assertion of his competence).

8.5.2.2 Speaker's preferences, context selection, and sociocultural conventions

Tyler's example indicates the link between the problem of context selection, which is of central importance in cognitive accounts of utterance comprehension, and sociocultural conventions, which are the focus of social approaches to pragmatics. This link becomes particularly clear once the role of the speaker's preferences in utterance understanding is examined more closely. Consider the following exchange:

A: So, it's your birthday on Monday. And how old will you be?
B: Too old to want to talk about it.

A's question makes evident which information would be relevant to her (namely, fairly precise information about B's age). B's answer is evidently not optimally relevant to A, because it does not provide this information. Instead, B communicates her preference for not talking about her age. So, B's utterance is consistent with the Communicative Principle of Relevance, because it is the best (i.e. most relevant) answer available to B, given her preferences. Now, very often, the speaker's preferences reflect, not so much individual taste, disposition towards the hearer, values, mood, and so on, but rather social conventions about communication. Thus, depending on the setting in which the exchange takes place, B may well be indirectly reprimanding A for transgressing some social conventions about (not) asking personal questions (such as questions relating to age, income, etc.). But B's communicative intention will be fulfilled only if A is sufficiently aware of the social conventions that B has in mind to be able to access some assumptions about them, and to include those assumptions in the context for the interpretation.

Similarly, in the teacher–student exchange in Tyler's article, the teacher's utterance 'Yeah, approximately' seems relevant to the student in the immediately available context as the teacher's acknowledgement of his lack of knowledge of the game of bowling. The contextual assumptions about the appropriateness of the teacher conveying modesty are simply not available to the student: they are not part of her cultural background. It seems plausible to assume that, if such assumptions were available to her, the student might be able to work out (the possibility) that the teacher is being modest, even if she is not aware of a particular convention about using hedges to indicate modesty. For example, learners of English from many cultural backgrounds do not find it all that difficult to grasp that the expression 'I am afraid ...' is readily used to indicate the speaker's regret at not being able to make a contribution which is presumed highly desirable to the hearer. This understanding follows rather intuitively from (a) an awareness that, given the immediate context, the speaker could not be intending to communicate any significant degree of fear, and (b) a universal disposition of humans to attend to particular types of needs of their fellow humans, i.e. face needs. Hence, if the student had been aware that from the teacher's point of view, his affirmative answer should be accompanied by some indication of modesty, and that, in a teaching situation, his knowledge is presumed to be adequate, she might also have considered the possibility that the teacher had used the adverb 'approximately' as an indication of modesty.

A detailed account of what goes on in situations of intercultural communication must, however, do more than mention the speaker's preferences. It must answer the questions: 'Why do speakers have the preferences that they have?' and 'How are particular preferences related to particular aspects of the communicative situation?' Accommodation Theory (Giles and Coupland 1991; see also Chapter 9 of this book) brings together insights from several disciplines in an attempt to explain the types of preferences that are universally observed in communicative interaction between humans, and their culture-specific realizations. According to Accommodation Theory, the speaker's linguistic choices reflect two sorts of pressures: (a) the tendency to conform to the needs, abilities, interests, etc., of the addressees (i.e. the tendency to attend to the addressees' face), and (b) the tendency to use a speech style which reflects the speaker's individual and social identity (i.e. the tendency to maintain the speaker's own face).

Which of these two types of pressures is prevalent on a given occasion depends on the pressures presented by the particular communicative situation. For example, Yoon's (1991) study (see section 8.4.1) shows that the Korean/English bilinguals' use of agreement strategies in English and modesty strategies in Korean, which differ from both American English-speakers and Korean Korean-speakers respectively. This could easily be explained in terms of accommodation theory. On the one hand, the pressure to conform to the needs, abilities, interests, etc. of the addressees explains why Korean/English bilinguals tend to use the agreement strategy more when communicating in English than when communicating in Korean: they adjust their linguistic choices to the expectations of their American-born interlocutors. It also explains why they tend to use a modesty strategy more when they communicate in Korean than when they communicate in English: they adjust their linguistic choices to their native Korean addressees. On the other hand, the pressure to use a speech style which reflects the speaker's group identification or individual identity explains why the same group of speakers use the agreement strategy to a lesser extent than native American English-speakers: they wish to identify themselves as having an identity distinct from that of the Americans. It also explains why they use a modesty strategy to a lesser extent than native speakers of Korean based in Korea: having lived in the USA for at least sixteen years, they have acquired an identity distinct from that of Koreans who live in Korea. This account is interesting because it shows that what appears to be the result of 'negative' transfer is not always caused by ignorance or lack of proficiency in a second language, but may be motivated by social psychological pressures.

In Yoon's study, the communicative strategy adopted by the Korean/English bilingual speakers conforms to considerations of face in a fairly straightforward way. Other cases of pragmatic transfer are more complicated. Let us consider a conversation described in Chapter 10. German informal conversational style is characterized by socially accepted challenges of the interlocutor's views. In the conversation described, between two German and two Chinese students who were meeting for the first time, this strategy backfired. The Chinese students perceived their German interlocutors as rude, which is hardly surprising: disagreement with one's views is understood as a direct threat to face, unless some contextual assumptions which remove the force of threat are available. In this conversation, such assumptions were available only to the German students, who followed the conventional wisdom of their own culture that argumentative style makes for more interesting informal conversations, but not to their Chinese interlocutors, whose cultural background does not include such assumptions for this situation. Had the mutual context of the interlocutors included this assumption, the debate might have proceeded in a fairly confrontational manner without causing offence, in much the same way as academic debates often do.

It follows from this that the Chinese students should familiarize themselves with a particular convention, in the context of which the (offending) communicative behaviour of the German students would appear neither face-threatening nor rude. However, it is often claimed that knowledge without justification is not real knowledge. Pragmatic knowledge is no exception. A good grasp of particular communicative norms, strategies, etc., can be achieved only provided they are properly grounded in the learner's system of pragmatic knowledge. Thus, the Chinese students who wish to communicate competently in a German cultural setting need to grasp more than the convention that it is quite appropriate to adopt an argumentative style in informal conversations. They also need to have some idea of why such a convention is acceptable: to the Germans, it makes conversation more interesting and lively; it indicates that the interlocutors take each other's views seriously, and so on.

The examples of pragmatic transfer considered so far have to do with the effects of the carryover of pragmatic knowledge to communicative behaviour. It seems important to note that pragmatic transfer also affects the ways in which speakers belonging to one culture interpret the communicative behaviour of those from another. For example, Greek university students studying in Britain often perceive British people's use of expressions of gratitude as insincere (Spencer-Oatey, personal communication). Most British people categorically deny this allegation (though, of course, expressions of gratitude, such as 'thank you', as well as any other type of utterance for that matter, can be used insincerely). Why, then, do Greek students have this impression? It seems that the pragmatic competences of native speakers of Greek and of native speakers of English differ with respect to conventions about the circumstances in which expressions of gratitude are appropriately used. To be more precise, in English, an expression of gratitude, such as 'Thank you', is appropriate on almost any occasion in which the speaker could be described as being in the hearer's debt, no matter how small the debt might be. But the corresponding conventions about the use of the Greek language are somewhat different in that expressions of gratitude in Greek should be used only provided the action being thanked for presents a considerable imposition on the hearer (for a detailed discussion of politeness in Greek, see Sifianou 1992a). As a consequence, thanking a close friend for a small favour may easily seem odd and even impolite. If this is correct, English speakers appear insincere to Greek speakers, because the latter judge the former by their own standards for the use of expressions of gratitude. In other words, they interpret the verbal behaviour of British people in the context of Greek conventions concerning the level of gratitude required to be worth communicating. This is a case of pragmatic transfer from Greek to English, which in this instance manifests itself in the interpretation, rather than in the production, of communicative acts.

To conclude: utterance comprehension is driven by a principle of communicative efficiency (the Principle of Relevance) and it is constrained by the cognitive abilities of the interlocutors, in particular, the availability of the appropriate context for utterance interpretation. An important factor in context selection is the identification of the speaker's preferences. Some of these preferences follow in a more or less straightforward way from universal considerations of face and communicative efficiency, whereas others reflect the culture-specific conventions of communicative behaviour (or idiosyncratic characteristics of the speaker, which are not examined here). An important part of the speaker's task is to anticipate the set of contexts available to the addressee. An important part of the addressee's task is to figure out in which context the speaker intended the utterance to be processed. The intended context often includes some assumptions about the speaker's preferences which are rooted in sociocultural conventions of communication. These conventions relate to different aspects of the communication process.

8.6 Are there different types of pragmatic transfer?

Kasper (1992) proposes a framework for analysing pragmatic transfer which is based on Leech's (1983) distinction between pragmalinguistics and sociopragmatics. According to Leech, the term pragmalinguistics refers to 'the particular resources which a given language provides for conveying particular illocutions' (Leech 1983: 11), and Kasper (1992: 208) points out that it includes not only the resources used for conveying illocutionary meaning, but also the plethora of devices available for managing relationships. Sociopragmatics refers to the culturally-based principles or maxims that underlie interactants' performance and interpretation of linguistic action. These include both culturally-based assessments of the typical characteristics of a given communicative activity (e.g. typical degrees of distance and equality/inequality between participants, people's rights and obligations and so on) and culturally-influenced dynamic assessments of actual communicative events. Pragmatic transfer can occur in both aspects, so Kasper (1992) refers to pragmalinguistic transfer and sociopragmatic transfer.

Table 8.1 shows how the exchange between the tutor and the student from Tyler's (1995) study could be described in these terms. Recall that the student asked the teacher if he knew how to keep score in bowling and the teacher replied 'Yeah, approximately'. Miscommunication occurred because the teacher had used the adverb 'approximately' as a marker of modesty, but the student interpreted it as a hedge on the propositional content of the utterance.

It should be clear from this example that social knowledge about communication is conventionally associated with particular linguistic expressions. So the social bases of communication (i.e. sociopragmatic knowledge) and the conventionalized meaning of particular expressions of the language (i.e. pragmalinguistic knowledge) are closely interrelated; for example, it is part of the conventionalized meaning of the Korean word '*com*' that it is an expression of modesty. So as Kasper (1992: 210) points out, while the distinction between pragmalinguistic transfer and sociopragmatic transfer is a useful one, 'the fuzzy edges between the two pragmatic domains will be noticeable'.

8.7 Pragmatic transfer, pragmatic theory and second language acquisition

Three observations about pragmatic transfer seem particularly important from a theoretical point of view: (a) transfer of pragmatic knowledge is fundamentally different from transfer of linguistic knowledge; (b) the everyday, common-sense meaning of the term 'transfer' may be misleading because it is different from the meaning of 'transfer' as a technical term used in psychology and second language acquisition; and (c) 'transfer' may be a useful technical term, even if its theoretical content is unclear. In this section we examine these claims in more detail.

Table 8.1 Likely pragmatic perspectives of the interlocutors in Tyler's tutoring session

	The situation from the teacher's point of view	The situation from the student's point of view
SOCIOPRAGMATICS		
Characteristics of the *type* of situational setting	• The teacher has higher status than students and the general pattern of teacher–student relationship is non-negotiable. • In classroom interactions, the teacher's knowledge is presumed (by both teacher and student) to be adequate, and superior to the student's knowledge. • Assertiveness on the teacher's part in a teaching context may intimidate the student. • All decisions relating to the teaching process are the teacher's responsibility.	• The teacher has higher status than students, but this does not entail that the pattern of the relationship is non-negotiable. • In classroom interactions, the details of the teacher–student role relationship are negotiated, taking into account the relevant competencies of both teacher and student.
Characteristics of the *actual* situational setting	• The primary aim of the tutoring session is to help the student with a computer programming assignment. • The teacher's expertise in all relevant aspects of the task (i.e. computer programming and bowling) is presumed by both teacher and student. • The secondary aim of the session is to help the tutor develop his teaching skills in English.	• The aim of the tutoring session is to get some help with her computer programming assignment. • The teacher's knowledge of computer programming (but not his knowledge of bowling) can be presumed. •The student is entitled to help the teacher in his understanding of bowling.
PRAGMALINGUISTICS		
Markers of illocutionary force	• 'Yeah' indicates assertion.	• 'Yeah' indicates assertion.
Politeness indicators	• '*Com*' is a politeness indicator of modesty in Korean. • 'Approximately' is a politeness indicator of modesty in English.	• 'Approximately' is a hedge on the propositional content of the utterance.

8.7.1 Pragmatic transfer and second language acquisition

Pragmatic transfer is often thought of as falling in the domain of second language acquisition (cf. Kasper 1992). In this section we want to consider some possible reasons for this view.

The notion of 'language transfer' was originally developed in applied linguistics, and it still holds a central place there. Knowledge of the mother tongue (or another language) is said to be transferred to the subsequent learning of another language. Thus, according to Lado (1957: 2):

> individuals tend to transfer the forms and meanings, and the distribution of forms and meanings of their native language and culture to the foreign language and culture, both productively when attempting to speak the language and receptively when attempting to grasp and *understand the language* ... (emphasis added)

Transfer is generally seen as a process that makes links between a source language (L1), i.e. one that a speaker has already acquired, and a target language (L2), i.e. one that a learner is attempting to learn (cf. Odlin 1989: 27). The quote from Lado (1957) above may be taken to imply that pragmatic transfer is a subtype of language transfer. This construal of Lado's observation is based on the underlying assumption that communicative success is primarily dependent on language understanding: the speaker or writer encodes certain meanings into a linguistic signal, and the listener or reader decodes the signal, thus retrieving the intended message (where encoding and decoding are processes which effect the automatic pairing of messages with signals and signals with messages, respectively). Such an approach to verbal communication entails a dubious theoretical commitment, namely the assumption that pragmatic competence is a subpart of linguistic competence. In this view, the grammatical system of a language incorporates not only phonology (the sound system of language), syntactic rules (the rules of phrase and sentence structure), and semantics (the system of meaning), but also pragmatics (the rules and principles of verbal understanding). However, this view is seriously flawed. In addition to the grammar of a language, the learner acquires competence about (a) when (not) to speak, (b) what to talk about in a particular type of situation, (c) when and where it is appropriate to talk about a particular topic, (d) in what manner the conversation should be conducted, and so on. As Hudson (1980: 220) points out:

If communicative competence is to cover all these types of ability underlying successful speech, it must include at least the whole of 'linguistic competence' plus the whole of the amorphous range of facts included under 'pragmatics' (the rules for using linguistic items in context); and it must also make close contact with 'attitudes, values and motivations' [Hymes 1971], with which linguistics generally has had little to do, even in discussions of pragmatics.

Hudson's observation that language acquisition should be seen as part of the acquisition of communicative competence is quite compelling. However, if this is the case, then it is difficult to maintain the view that pragmatic transfer falls strictly within the domain of second language acquisition.

8.7.2 Is 'pragmatic transfer' a useful term?

Pragmatic transfer occurs in a particular type of problem-solving behaviour: communication. This observation points to some possible criticisms of the term. For instance, since all communication situations present problems, and pragmatic transfer may occur among speakers of the same language, whose cultural backgrounds are similar in many respects (see Chapter 12), it seems reasonable to wonder whether the term pragmatic transfer should figure at all in analyses of intercultural communication. Would it not be better simply to explain intercultural and intracultural communication in the same way, without invoking any notion of transfer?

In fact, it seems more plausible to argue that a shift in the opposite direction is desirable, and to use the term 'pragmatic transfer' to include situations of both intracultural and intercultural communication. Typical communicative problems are rather different from typical problems of language acquisition, because pragmatic knowledge is neither organized nor put to use in the same way as linguistic knowledge. The term 'language transfer' seems more appropriate if restricted to the acquisition of (the grammar of) L2, because: (a) L1 and L2 present self-contained systems of knowledge (which may be isomorphic to a greater or lesser extent); and (b) the knowledge systems involved in linguistic transfer are not amenable to introspection. In contrast to language transfer, pragmatic transfer is pertinent to all situations of communication in which new communicative problems are solved by greater or lesser reliance on existing knowledge.

The independence of, as well as the differences between, linguistic knowledge and pragmatic knowledge suggest that pragmatic transfer should not be seen as inherently linked to language acquisition. Many observations made earlier in this chapter about pragmatic conventions (e.g. in the USA, teacher–student interaction is negotiable from a position of equality; a confrontational, argumentative style is considered to lend interest to informal conversations in German) are amenable to conscious introspection, unlike the rules of grammar. Consider the following sentences:

(1) Je crois avoir expliqué ce problème.
(2) *I believe to have explained this problem.

Introspection does not give us access to the rules of French grammar which make (1) grammatical in French, or to the rules of English which make (2) ungrammatical in English. So the knowledge of social norms of communication differs from linguistic knowledge in two important respects. Linguistic knowledge is a self-contained system dedicated to the production and recognition of grammatical patterns, whereas the social conventions of communication interact fairly freely with the rest of our general knowledge (about people, situations, surroundings, etc.). This is illustrated by the fact that sentence (2) is felt to be ungrammatical in any context of situation (although it may be judged acceptable if used by a foreigner), while the appropriateness of particular types of communicative act is highly context-sensitive: unlike the rules of grammar, the rules for the use of expressions of modesty, gratitude, etc. must make reference to the context of situation (see Chapter 3). For example, a direct request for action such as 'Give me some ice! Quickly!' will be perfectly appropriate in some circumstances (e.g. following an accident, when what matters most is to stop the swelling of the injured person's ankle), and very inappropriate in others (e.g. when ordering drinks in a pub).

Hence one might argue that it makes more sense to talk about the transfer of linguistic knowledge from L1 to L2, than to link pragmatic transfer to distinct languages and cultures. In the case of language transfer, a self-contained system of knowledge, i.e. the grammar of L1, affects the acquisition of another self-contained system of knowledge, i.e. the grammar of L2. What goes on in the development of the ability to behave in situations of (intercultural) communication is rather different. Given that pragmatic knowledge is relatively independent of linguistic knowledge, there is no reason why pragmatic transfer would not occur in a linguistically homogeneous but culturally heterogeneous community, and since, unlike linguistic knowledge (i.e. the knowledge of grammar), pragmatic competence is not a self-contained system of knowledge, there is no reason to restrict the term 'transfer' to the description of communication problems across linguistic boundaries.

A few points should perhaps be clarified. First, we are not claiming that pragmatic knowledge is generally used in a reflective, self-conscious manner. In spontaneous communication, people rely on routinized, almost automatized, decision-making, in much the same way as competent car-drivers spontaneously execute sequences of coordinated actions without rehearsing them consciously. The important point is that pragmatic knowledge is largely amenable to introspection and can be used reflectively when the need arises. Second, although pragmatic knowledge is an integral part of the knowledge used in interpreting human behaviour, people's knowledge about how particular aspects of communicative interaction are conducted does not consist of individually listed assumptions, but seems to be organized in various formats, such as schemas, frames and scripts (see Tyler's (1995) article for an attempt to use these categories in explaining data on pragmatic transfer; for discussions of these terms in cognitive psychology see Ringland and Duce (1988); see also Chapters 3 and 7). But however these chunks of knowledge related to different kinds of situations are stored and retrieved, pragmatic knowledge interacts fairly freely with general knowledge. Third, if, as we have claimed, (a) pragmatic knowledge is not insulated, as it were, from the general belief system of the interactants, and (b) the interpretation of human communicative behaviour is a special case of the interpretation of behaviour in general (see Chapter 3), then (c) the term 'pragmatic transfer' seems devoid of proper theoretical content: the notion of pragmatic transfer can be reduced to the general notion of knowledge transfer in psychology. This observation may well be valid, but there may still be a good case for using 'pragmatic transfer' as a technical term: it brings together, for the purpose of description and analysis, a range of different factors specifically involved in communication within one culture, and helps us to understand their importance in communication within that culture as well as across cultural boundaries.

A further objection to the term 'pragmatic transfer' (and to the term 'transfer' in general) might be that it is used in describing processes of communication in which nothing really transfers or changes place. For example, when someone wants to transfer a sum of money, say £1364, from one account to another, transfer can be said to have been effected only provided the sum of £1364 has been debited from the first account and credited to the second. Nothing of this sort seems to happen in the transfer of (pragmatic or linguistic) knowledge. The best reply to this remark is that the meaning of 'transfer' as a technical term is different from the everyday, common-sense, meaning of this word. The term 'pragmatic transfer' is probably best thought of as referring to the projection of existing knowledge to new situations of communication. Another interesting difference between the technical and the everyday use of the word 'transfer' is that the reliance on existing pragmatic knowledge in solving new communication problems leads to modifications of that knowledge. The (lack of) analogy with the transfer of money is illustrative again. Thus, the assertion that a sum of £1364 has been transferred from one account to another would not be justified if £1364 was the sum taken from the first account, and £635 the sum paid into the second account. However, in order to assume that pragmatic transfer has taken place, it is sufficient for existing pragmatic knowledge to play some role, i.e. to be exploited to some extent, in solving a new communication problem.

To conclude: there is an important distinction between the knowledge of the meaning of a word or larger expression (i.e. its linguistic meaning) and the knowledge about how that word or expression is used. Therefore, the view that pragmatic transfer is a type of language transfer is unfounded. Pragmatic transfer is best seen as a special case of general knowledge transfer (in the sense in which this term is used in psychology). What makes it special is that it involves a particular type of knowledge, pragmatic knowledge, and what makes it a case of general knowledge transfer is the fact that pragmatic knowledge interacts freely with general knowledge (and is, in this sense, an integral part of general knowledge).

Discussion questions

1   *Culture and the perception of situations*
    Chapter 12 considers the verbal behaviour of job applicants from East and West Germany in job interviews held in a West German setting. Look at two of the data extracts given there: Example 4, which is an exchange between an interviewer and an East German applicant, and Example 5, which is an exchange between an interviewer and a West German applicant (see section 12.5.2).

1.1 Read these two exchanges carefully. Write a summary of the differences between the East German and the West German applicants' responses to the interviewer's questions.

1.2 Does one of the applicants seem to respond 'better' than the other? If so, does negative pragmatic transfer seem to play a role in the poorer performance of one of the applicants? Discuss.

2 *Communication strategies and pragmatic transfer*
Chapter 11 considers an exchange between co-workers, one Japanese and one American, who are reviewing some advertisements. Misunderstanding occurs because the American co-worker does not realize how strongly his Japanese colleague disagrees with his view. (See Chapter 11, section 11.4, Extract 1.) The American employee is not aware that his Japanese superior is using particular strategies to communicate disagreement, and that miscommunication thus occurs.

2.1 Discuss (briefly) the relation between the hearer's knowledge of particular culture-specific communication strategies and his ability to interpret correctly communicative acts which employ these strategies.

2.2 How can pragmatic transfer make it easier or more difficult for members of one culture to learn the communicative strategies of another? Discuss with reference to examples (both from your own experience and from the literature).

3 *Creating rules of thumb for intercultural communication*
Some suggestions for communicating with people in specific groups can be discovered by paying attention to speakers' communication patterns or by reading about those patterns in a collection such as this one. For example, based on the discussion here, the following 'rules of thumb' for communicating with Germans, Chinese, and North Americans can be given:

When speaking to a German
    ... do not hesitate to state your opinion directly and to disagree openly.
When speaking to a Chinese
    ... be careful not to express direct disagreement.
When speaking to a North American
    ... do not be too modest about your abilities or accomplishments.

3.1 Using information provided in this book or using your own experiences, expand these lists; i.e. try to go beyond the simple prescriptions shown in the three examples above.

3.2 Consider the value as well as the limitations of teaching 'rules of thumb' like the ones shown above when teaching pragmatic transfer and intercultural communication.

Suggestions for further reading

Blakemore, D. (1992) *Understanding Utterances: An Introduction to Pragmatics*. Oxford: Blackwell.

Kasper, G. (1992) Pragmatic transfer. *Second Language Research*, 8(3): 203–31.

Odlin, T. (1989) *Language Transfer*. Cambridge: Cambridge University Press.

Wilson, D. (1994) Relevance and understanding. In G. Brown, K. Malmkjaer and A. Pollitt (eds), *Language and Understanding*. Oxford: Oxford University Press, 35–58.

9

Accommodation Theory: A Conceptual Resource for Intercultural Sociolinguistics

Virpi Ylänne-McEwen and Nikolas Coupland

9.1 Introduction

The central insight behind the concept of communicative accommodation is rather simple – no doubt deceptively so. It is that speakers are motivated to reduce linguistic or communicative differences between themselves and their speaking partners under specifiable circumstances, principally when they want to be approved of and when they want their communication to be more effective. Correspondingly, speakers will be motivated to resist 'accommodating', and will even accentuate differences between themselves and their listeners, when approval and effectiveness are less important to them, and when they want to symbolize and emphasize difference and distance.

Building on this central idea, a large and diverse body of theoretical and empirical research has been undertaken over more than twenty years, developing what is referred to nowadays as Communication Accommodation Theory (CAT). Our intention in this chapter is not to review or integrate all of this work. Indeed, this has been done in several articles and books fairly recently.[1] Instead, we intend to provide, firstly, an introduction to the central concepts and categories used in CAT research. We illustrate the sorts of social situations and social processes which these concepts and categories can help us describe and explain. Secondly, we consider the various ways in which Accommodation Theory can be related to cultural difference and to those situations which are often described as being 'inter-cultural'. A theory which deals with social and sociolinguistic similarities and differences, and with communicative effectiveness, obviously has a direct relevance to cultural diversity and to 'intercultural communication'. But thirdly, we want to raise some difficulties and dilemmas, not least to do with the central notion of 'inter-culturality' and how we categorize social groups and relationships between them. In the final part of the chapter we want to suggest that CAT, and in fact any systematic approach to communication and culture, needs to be wary of generalizing too freely about the cultural identities of speakers and about the impact of communication strategies. Our overall claim is that Accommodation Theory remains a rich and powerful model of how relationships between individuals and social groups are negotiated through language and discourse. But we also suggest that the theory needs to respond to large-scale social changes in how cultural groups organize themselves and in how people find meaning in cultural difference and interaction across cultural boundaries.

9.2 Central concepts of Accommodation Theory

The origins of Accommodation Theory are to be found in social psychology, and particularly in Howard Giles' studies of accent variation. Speech Accommodation Theory (so-called at that time because accent features are specifically speech variables) was formulated by Giles (1973) when he devised a model of 'accent mobility'. The model was a reaction against assumptions made by William Labov in his seminal studies of sociolinguistic variation (e.g. 1966) in New York City. Giles proposed that a speaker's choice of a prestigious or a non-prestigious speech style need not be the result of his or her social class position or the formality or the informality of the speaking context, as Labov's approach assumed. Rather, it could be mediated by 'interpersonal accommodation processes'. Giles pointed out that the interviewees in Labov's studies may well have been responding, consciously or subconsciously, to the interviewer's own speech style; that is, they may have been 'accommodating' linguistically. For example, they could have produced casual-sounding speech because the interviewer himself had shifted style and was using a less standard accent. Alternatively, they could have been differentiating themselves from a standard-sounding interviewer. In fact, Labov's results were reliable enough to make it unlikely that any general explanation could be given along these lines.

But Giles argued convincingly that the interpersonal dimension of language use was potentially of crucial importance. In general, speech modification could be viewed not so much as determined by the social context, and more as a speaker's dynamic and subjective response to the addressee. The degree of behavioural matching between speakers needed to be analysed, and linked to social psychological factors which could explain and predict it.

The positive matching process was called *convergence* – 'a strategy whereby individuals adapt to each other's communicative behaviours in terms of a wide range of linguistic/prosodic/non-verbal features' (Giles *et al.* 1991: 7). As the definition suggests, convergence can operate well beyond accent variables. Speech rate and patterns of pausing, utterance length, gestures, posture, smiling, gaze, and so on can all feature in acts of convergence between speakers. The basic metaphor here is one of parallel and non-parallel lines, as if speakers' trajectories can be modelled as getting closer or further apart as talk proceeds. Indeed, convergence can be almost literally demonstrated in these terms, if we are able to quantify relevant aspects of speakers' communicative behaviour relative to one another. Speakers can be shown to be converging if, for example, their measured rates of speech (perhaps measured in syllables per second) become more similar over time or, as Giles predicted, if their accents become more similar through shifts in the quality or frequency of particular features of their pronunciation.

Convergence has been established as a very robust sociolinguistic phenomenon. There is a general propensity for communicators to converge along salient dimensions of speech and non-verbal behaviour in cooperative social encounters. The psychological process at the heart of convergence and of 'being accommodative' is 'similarity attraction' (Byrne 1971). Speakers who want to cooperate and who want to be approved of will tend to converge. Correspondingly, when a speaker becomes more similar to a listener, it is generally more likely that the listener will in fact approve of him or her more strongly. These tendencies give Accommodation Theory some power to explain the *strategic* use of language codes and communication styles. Codes and styles do not merely co-vary with social groups and social situations. Rather, we can begin to see code- and style-choice as sociolinguistic strategies which individuals and groups will employ – again, whether consciously or sub-consciously – to achieve the social and relational results they want. Although goals may be consciously held, the sociolinguistic means through which they are fulfilled are beyond the speaker's full consciousness. The hallmark of CAT has always been its ability to link descriptions of language in use to an appreciation of speakers' and groups' social goals and motivations.[2]

Keeping to the metaphor of parallel and non-parallel trajectories, *maintenance* and *divergence* of codes and styles are the obvious further possibilities. Maintenance simply identifies the option of a speaker or a group *not* modifying their communication relative to addressees (cf. Spencer-Oatey's 'rapport-maintenance' option, discussed in Chapter 2). Divergence refers to 'the way in which speakers accentuate speech and non-verbal differences between themselves and others' (Giles *et al.* 1991: 8). In CAT's treatment, the motivations associated with maintenance and divergence are more particular than those attaching to convergence. Both are specifically group-level strategies, designed to symbolize non-engagement between social or cultural groups. For example, ethnic minority community members may deliberately maintain their language or dialect code in the company of majority community members, as a symbolic act of resistance. In such a situation, increased use of the minority variety (either in terms of frequency or in some qualitative sense – e.g. using a greater number of non-standard dialect features or selecting more extreme ones) can be defined as divergence.

In the next section we consider selected instances of convergence, maintenance and divergence from CAT research in multicultural settings. But before turning to these we need to introduce some of the many refinements which have allowed accommodation research to work with more subtle concepts than the basic ones we have introduced this far. Some of them relate to the relationship between cognitive orientations and communication features. Some relate to the communication levels and dimensions through which accom-modation strategies can be implemented in the course of face-to-face communication.

As an essentially social psychological theory, CAT has needed to distinguish carefully between linguistic and psychological conver-gence and divergence. A person's integrative orientation to others has been termed *psychological convergence*, whereas *psychological diver-gence* denotes a desire of commitment to achieve greater distance and distinctiveness (Thakerar *et al.* 1982). Although, as we have explained, an integrative psychological orientation is predictably realized through (often measurable) communicative convergence, cognitive and behavioural dimensions are in fact independent. Contextual factors may well intervene to prevent speakers realizing their convergent attitudes through their language. One obvious factor is a low facility in the requisite code or style – for example when a speaker does not command the symbolic resources to show his or her convergent intent in some particular communicative dimension. Another factor is the overriding effect of social norms, for example if a social situation imposes the use of a particular language code or register.[3] This basic distinction gives us good cause to avoid 'reading off' relational strategies directly from the evidence of language texts, without considering the potentially complex social psychology of the speaking situation.

CAT has also distinguished subjective and objective accommodation. *Subjective accommodation* refers to speakers' beliefs about whether they or their interlocutor are converging or diverging. *Objective convergence* or *divergence* is the result of direct observation or measurement by researchers. The issue here is again fundamental to a social psychological view of communication, where verifiable facts based on researchers' analyses of data may have less explanatory value than the perceptions and beliefs of actual participants. It is important to note that 'speakers do not converge to (or diverge from) the *actual* behaviour of others, but rather to what they *think* are the communicative behaviours of their conversational partners' (Gallois *et al.* 1988: 161). For example, in a study by Beebe (1981), Thai/Chinese bilinguals believed they were converging towards Chinese-influenced vowel variants when being interviewed by an ethnic Chinese Thai, although this shift was actually divergent from the vowel forms produced by the interviewer. The interviewees held a stereotype of the linguistic behaviour of the group to which they saw the interviewer as belonging. They reacted to what they believed and in fact *predicted* the interviewer's speech to be like, and did this on the basis of non-speech attributes such as appearance features. Young (1988) similarly writes that it is not interlocutor ethnicity alone that causes linguistic variation, but a collection of attributes (of which one is ethnicity) by which interlocutors assess their relative similarity to each other. (We return to problems in the definition of cultural groups in the final section.)

In the early days of CAT it was conventional to distinguish *upward* and *downward* speech modifications, where both convergence and divergence can be of either sort. Upward shifts are shifts towards a more prestigious or acrolectal variety, and downward shifts are towards a less prestigious or basilectal variety. Quantitative studies have also distinguished various extents of convergence and divergence, and cases where communication is modified only in certain modes of communication and not others (cf. Street 1982; Bilous and Krauss 1988).

Accommodation can be established to be either *symmetrical* or *asymmetrical*, depending on whether only one party or group (asymmetrical), or both (symmetrical), converges or diverges. This distinction can help capture the power dynamics of communication between social groups. For example, Mulac *et al.* (1988) found symmetrical convergence in mixed-sex dyads, in that both the female and the male participant converged more to the linguistic style of their out-group (other-sex) partner than they did in an in-group (same-sex) situation. Non-reciprocated convergence was illustrated in White's (1989) study of interactions between American and Japanese groups. Japanese speakers maintained the high level of backchannelling (supportive expressions such as 'mhm' and 'uh-huh') that had been observed in their within-culture situations when conversing with Americans. The American speakers, however, used significantly more backchannelling when speaking with Japanese partners than with other Americans, that is, they converged in the frequency of backchannelling behaviour whereas the Japanese speakers did not.

A lot of research attention has more recently been devoted to evaluative aspects of accommodation, and the concepts of *over-accommodation* and *under-accommodation* have become important (Coupland *et al.* 1988 and, e.g. Gallois *et al.* 1995). There are clearly limits on (what people judge to be) the normal applicability and extent of accommodative adaptation, so that styles of talk may come to be evaluated as over-accommodative or overadapted. In multi-cultural contexts, talk which transcends these bounds – difficult though it is to establish empirically – is likely to be felt to be patronizing and deindividuating (treating individuals as social or cultural prototypes rather than attending to their individual competences and needs). A predictable scenario is when a member of a majority language group, possibly with a convergent psychological orientation ('with the best of intentions'), oversimplifies their first-language code, assuming this is a necessary adjustment for any minority language listener to be able to understand. This is the sociolinguistic territory Ferguson (1975, 1996) labelled 'foreigner talk', which can be well explicated in terms of CAT (see below).

Under-accommodation is a concept which captures equally difficult and potentially conflictual orientations between groups, for example when members of one group resolutely refuse to recognize and adapt to the conventional patterns of usage or the genuine communicative needs of another. An obvious example would be when a bilingual speaker refuses to codeswitch into the language their addressee is more comfortable using, or failing to conform to local cultural norms for greetings and leave-takings. Here we see how CAT needs to attend to much more than the describable properties of talk itself in its immediate context. A judgement about over- or under-accommodation can only be made relative to the norms and expectations which speakers hold about communication, and relative to their judgements of speakers' and listeners' rights and obligations in particular situations. CAT assumes that understanding the social meaning of communicative acts requires a rich appreciation of communicative context, both local and global, as it is subjectively experienced. Of course, speakers' appreciation of their own contexts of communication is often incomplete; they may, for example, be unable to predict how hearers will judge their communication strategies. This means that accommodating can often be fraught with uncertainties and, for example, miscarried attempts at convergence. Communication Accommodation Theory therefore has considerable relevance to our understanding of miscommunication (Coupland *et al.* 1991b), particularly between social groups where normative expectations for talk are not fully shared. (We consider one instance in detail in the next section.)

Finally in this section, it is important for us to recognize how accommodation research has begun to engage with discourse analysis and pragmatics, in place of the rather mechanistic descriptions of speech and language variables that it dealt with in its early years. The early studies, and so the early development of the theory, depended on quantitative measures. Convergence and divergence were quantified as shifting values of measurable variables, such as phonological or dialect standardness and the frequency of use of specific language codes. Quantification was important in establishing the basic claims of the model, for example that linguistic convergence is regularly associated with perceived solidarity, and divergence with psychological dissociation. But it is clearly the case that 'being accommodative' is realized through a very wide range of discourse moves and strategies, and that these are fundamentally interactive in nature.

Arguing this case, Coupland *et al.* (1988; see also Coupland *et al.* 1991a) proposed a significant broadening of the scope of the concept of 'communicative accommodation'. This model is schematized in Figure 9.1. It acknowledges that participants are speaker/hearers who can monitor their own performance as well as use the feedback to anticipate the receiver's attributions and evaluations of that performance in order to adjust their accommodation strategies. Listeners can label the speakers' performance as accommodative,

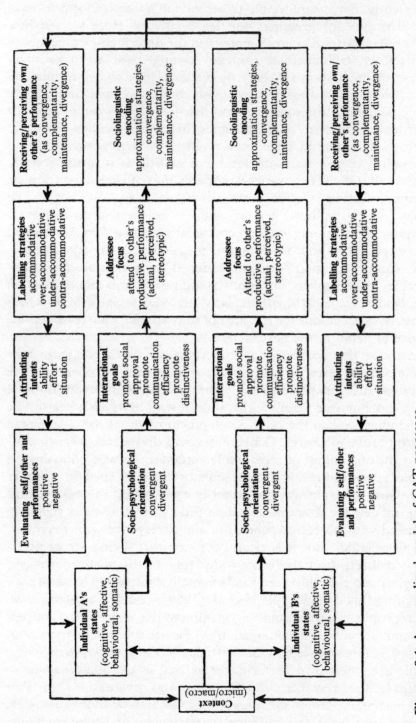

Figure 9.1 A generalized model of CAT processes
Source: Coupland *et al.* (1988) Accommodating the elderly: invoking and extending a theory. *Language in Society*, 17: 1–41. (figure is on p. 8)

over-accommodative, under-accommodative or contra-accommoda-
tive (conscious rendering of talk as non-accommodative) and, what is
more, the speakers themselves can predict that their own performance is subject to such labelling which may or may not match their
original intent. So although over-accommodation, for example, is an
evaluation made most saliently by the listener, the model acknowledges speakers' own perceptions of their behaviour and its
consequences. These kinds of attributional and evaluative processes
can create and alter situational and relational definitions. The model
also recognizes not only that micro-level contextual factors (such as
speakers' and listeners' goals and beliefs) play a part in accommodative processes, but that macro-level factors (such as those related to
the institutional roles and cultural identities of interlocutors) affect
the strategies used and their evaluations. An inter-ethnic encounter
in which one participant is in a gatekeeping position of some kind
would be a case in point (see, for example, Roberts *et al.* 1992, and
Chapter 12 of this book). Coupland *et al.* (1988) also suggest that the
effects of communication accommodation strategies may transcend
the boundaries of the immediate situation (in terms of psychological
states and communicative actions) and have longer-term consequences in, for example, a person's degree of life-satisfaction. The
Coupland *et al.* (1988) study focuses specifically on intergenerational
communication, but a case can equally be made regarding inter-
ethnic encounters. For example, repeated experiences of being a
recipient of foreigner talk, and evaluating such talk as inappropriate
and over-accommodative, may arouse hostile feelings in the recipient
and ultimately lead to avoidance of contact. The model represented in
Figure 9.1 does not make predictions of communicative outcomes.
Rather, unlike earlier work in accommodation linked to experimental
work (e.g. Thakerar *et al.* 1982), it helps clarify communicative
processes.

For handling discourse data, it has been useful to identify
accommodation which goes beyond approximation. Over and above
convergence, maintenance and divergence (labelled '*approximation*'
strategies), Coupland *et al.* (1988) identified three further broad
discursive dimensions in which accommodation can be interactionally achieved: *interpretability strategies*, where speakers modify the
complexity and comprehensibility of their talk, for example increasing clarity and explicitness; *discourse management strategies*, such as
being facilitative in the management of turn-taking and topic-
selection and attending to face-wants; and *interpersonal control
strategies*, allowing interlocutors discretion in the communicative

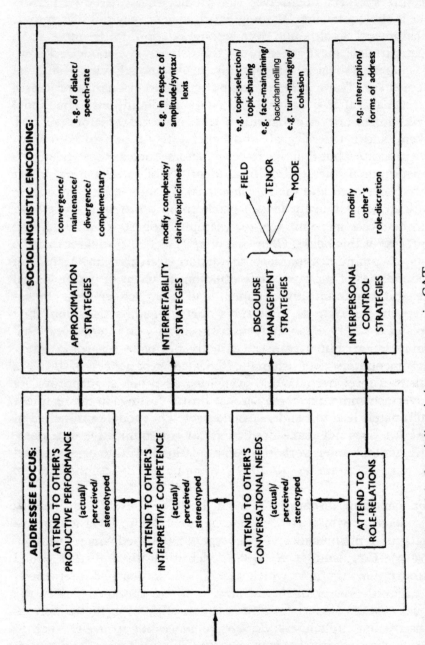

Figure 9.2 An extended model of sociolinguistics processes in CAT

Source: Coupland *et al.* Accommodating the elderly: invoking and extending a theory. *Language in Society*, 17: 1–41. (figure is on p. 28)

roles they adopt in face-to-face talk. These four general sets of options, under the general heading of 'discourse attuning', are summarized in Figure 9.2. The different attuning strategies ('socio-linguistic encoding') are tied to different kinds of addressee focus.

Firstly, approximation strategies arise from the speaker's focus on the interlocutor's actual productive communicative performance and degrees of similarity and difference. Secondly, interpretability strategies are linked to how the speaker perceives the other's ability to understand and deal with interaction, that is his/her receptive or interpretive competence. Foreigner talk can again be explained in this way. Ferguson originally introduced foreigner talk as an example of a 'simplified register', similar to 'baby talk', where the recipient's linguistic and cognitive abilities are perceived as somewhere below the optimal level for 'normal' fluency or syntactic complexity, for example. The CAT model explains such talk more precisely as an interactive phenomenon, for example showing how addressees' responses to foreigner talk can be *variable*, depending on normative expectations and on how the strategy is 'attributed' – what motive is ascribed to the speaker. Thirdly, discourse management strategies comprise a broad set relating to the listener's conversational needs (actual, perceived or stereotyped). A three-way classification is presented: *field* relates to the ideational/referential content construction (such as topic-selection or topic-sharing); *tenor* to the management of interpersonal positions, roles and faces (such as face-maintaining or backchannelling); *mode* to the procedural/textual dimensions that structure the interaction (such as turn-managing and cohesion) (for field, tenor and mode, see Gregory and Carroll 1978 and Halliday, e.g. 1973). Lastly, interpersonal control strategies are related to the focus on the role relations between the participants and are realized by specific forms of address, for example. The four categories presented in Figure 9.2 can and do overlap so that, for example, tenor as a discourse management strategy can be taken to subsume control, although there is also a separate category of interpersonal control strategies in the model. It is also important to point out, as presented in Figure 9.2, that a speaker may behave accommodatively without (e.g.) converging, for example by making his/her speech more intelligible in ways that are not matched by the hearer's behaviour. In this case, the speaker would be using an interpretability strategy. Accommodation, then, is a general term which subsumes approximation strategies such as convergence or divergence. This is also why terms such as over-accommodation (as opposed to over-convergence) are adopted.

As yet there have been only very few attempts to apply this more elaborate model of accommodation to sets of discourse data – and it is clearly a challenging task. The sheer range of possibilities in the selection and realization of speech acts, and in subtleties of sequencing and of interaction between speakers, in fact makes it unlikely that global quantitative measures of 'accommodativeness' can be made. On the other hand, such global assessments are routinely made by communicators themselves, and CAT has alerted us to the social impact of 'attuning' and 'counter-attuning' in social interaction. The challenge, we think, is worth taking up!

9.3 Accommodation research in multicultural settings: selected examples

We noted earlier that a good deal of accommodation research is concerned with group-level processes. To this extent it builds on a rich tradition of theoretical study in social psychology concerned with *intergroup communication*. We are unable to summarize this field of study here (see Giles and Coupland 1991 for a review). The central principles of intergroup theory were developed by Henri Tajfel (1974, 1978; see also Robinson 1996). A central observation is that individuals often interact with each other as representative members of social groups rather than actually as individuals, and that their communicative strategies are linked to these group orientations and to the potential gains and losses associated with them. Perhaps the strongest influence of this line of thinking on CAT is to be found in Giles and others' analyses of inter-group divergence, and the explicit link in this work with Ethnolinguistic Identity Theory (again see Giles and Coupland 1991; see also Giles and Johnson 1987). As we have seen, divergence is both motivated by and in many ways achieves a strong sense of in-group distinctiveness; it is one way of projecting a social and sometimes an ethnic identity through language. An individual's positive self-esteem is enhanced through the establishment of a distinct favourable social identity at the ethnic group level. Social identity is here viewed as a cognitive concept and is linguistically marked through a process of 'psycholinguistic distinctiveness'.

In this connection, it is not at all surprising that a lot of CAT research has been located in multicultural settings. These are settings where a sense of community or 'groupness' is often most marked, and where boundaries between groups, 'hard' or 'soft', permanent or shifting, are most salient in communication. Accommodation processes such as convergence and divergence are likely to be important means of marking intergroup alignments, and shifts of alignment over time. Also, 'long-term issues are of ... concern to researchers studying intercultural contact and adaptation by immigrants or sojourners, language rivalry, or situations of long-term intergroup contact (e.g. the impact of sexism or ageism)' (Gallois and Giles 1998: 146). Some recent versions of CAT indeed make a distinction between short- and long-term convergence (Gallois et al. 1995).

Many of the early CAT studies designed to test for links between linguistic convergence and relational effects were conducted in communities with acknowledged intergroup tensions. For example, Giles et al. (1973) established that a French-Canadian speaker (in a 'matched-guise' study, where the same speaker was recorded describing a picture in four different guises which reflected increasing degrees of effort in perceived accommodation: French, mixed French/English, fluent French-Canadian-accented English, and non-fluent French-Canadian-accented English) was rated most favourably by bilingual English-Canadian listeners when his speech was French-Canadian-accented and non-fluent. That is, he was approved of more strongly when he was seen to converge by making an effort to speak the language of the listeners. In addition, the English-Canadian subjects reciprocated the convergent accommodative strategies when given the chance in the experimental condition to communicate back to the French-Canadian man. It was suggested that 'the perception of accommodation from one speaker may be a salient cue as to whether integration and a strong desire for social approval should be features of the interaction for the other' (Giles et al. 1973: 187).

Correspondingly, divergent language shifts were shown to be particularly prominent in 'ethnically threatening' encounters, for example in Bourhis et al.'s (1979) study in Belgium of Flemish students' encounters with Francophone out-group speakers. Again in a language laboratory setting, Flemish students were asked to respond to a Francophone speaker's (trilingual in English, French and Flemish) questions first of an emotively-neutral nature, then of an ethnically-threatening one. It was found that when intergroup categorization was made explicit and the subjects were told that the Francophone speaker considered their ethnolinguistic aims illegitimate, and also when the respondents believed that they would be held responsible to the group (their fellow Flemish students) later for their individual replies, a shift into Flemish was made by almost all of the respondents.

Gal's (1978/1997) study of the linguistic repertoire of a bilingual community of Oberwart (Felsöör) in Austria detailed a further intriguing case of linguistic and psychological convergence and divergence behaviour. Traditionally, both Hungarian and German are spoken in this town with about a quarter of the population (in the 1970s) being bilingual. The two language codes carry very different symbolic statuses: Hungarian symbolizes peasant status and has very negative connotations, especially for young people, whereas German symbolizes modern non-agrarian lifestyles and has a more prestigious status. Gal found that 'as speaker's [sic] networks become less and less peasant they use H[ungarian] in fewer and fewer situations. And ... as time passes new generations use H[ungarian] in fewer and fewer situations regardless of the content of their social networks' (1997: 384). She also found striking differences in the language choice patterns of young women and men in particular in this community. Young women, when they diverge from peasant/agrarian female roles and work patterns, reject the use of Hungarian in preference for German, even if they have strong peasant social networks. Young men, especially those with strong peasant networks and who continue to work on the family farm, choose Hungarian in more interactions than young women and those with non-peasant networks. The young women's psychological divergence from the traditional peasant female identity has resulted in their rejection of that identity, in convergence to a more Austrian working lifestyle, and in the use of the German language in most situations. This in turn has had the general effect that more German is used in more interactions in the community. Young Oberwart women's marriage preferences also have had linguistic consequences in the community in another way: as they prefer to marry non-peasant men (another manifestation of the rejection of peasant identity), young peasant men, constituting precisely that small group most likely to be using Hungarian in various interactions, have been compelled to marry exogamously, finding wives from neighbouring monolingual German-speaking villages. The children of these marriages between bilingual Hungarian/German-speaking men and monolingual German-speaking women very rarely learn Hungarian, and so 'in an indirect way the present generation of young women is limiting the language possibilities of the next generation' (Gal 1978: 14).

Of course, convergence and divergence through the selection of a language code is the most obvious accommodation strategy in multilingual settings. The Gal example shows how multiple instances of divergence, while significant to individual speakers at the particular moments when they have to select a language code, can conspire to produce larger-scale patterns of language shift. But accommodation processes, and particularly the subjectivities of people's expectations, judgements and attributions, can work in much less obvious ways too.

An example of this is a recent study by Bailey (1997) of interactions between immigrant Korean shop-owners and sales assistants of small convenience stores in Los Angeles, USA, and their African-American customers. Such an encounter might open like this:

Extract 1

1	cashier:	hi {customer approaches counter} (0.2)
2	customer:	how's it going partner? euh
3		{cashier nods} (1.0)
4	customer:	you got them little bottles?
5	cashier:	(eh?) {customer's gaze falls on the little bottles} (3.5)
6	customer:	one seventy-fi:ve! {customer gazes at display of bottles} (2.0)
7	customer:	you've got no bourbon? (1.2)
8	cashier:	no: we don't have bourbon (1.0)
9	customer:	I'll get a beer then {customer talks to his nephew}
10	cashier:	two fifty {cashier rings up purchase and bags beer} (4.5)
11	customer:	I just moved in the area I talked to you the other day
12		you [remember me]?
13	cashier:	[oh yesterday] last night
14	customer:	yeah
15	cashier:	[(o:h yeah?)] {cashier smiles and nods}
16	customer:	[goddamn shit] [then you don't]
17	owner:	[new neighbour huh?]
		{customer turns halfway to the side towards the owner}
18	customer:	{loudly, smiling} then you don't KNOW me
19	cashier:	[(I know you)] {cashier gets change from the till}
20	customer:	[I want you to KNOW] me so when I walk in here
21		you'll know me I
22		smoke Winstons your son knows me
23	cashier:	[ye::ah]
24	customer:	[the yo]ung guy
25	cashier:	there you go {cashier proffers change}

(Bailey 1997: 345; transcription conventions very slightly modified. All participants are male)

In Extract 1, there are points where the African-American speaker is signalling solidarity (as he perceives it to be signalled) and, hence, the cashier and, later, the shop-owner have opportunities to match this behaviour. Solidarity signalling can be seen in line 2 by the use of *partner*. Also, in line 6, the customer's reference to the price of the drink can be seen as an assessment eliciting an evaluative response and agreement from the listener. Again in lines 11 and 12, the customer discloses personal information about himself and refers to the interactants' shared history through an earlier encounter, and in lines 16 and 18 he makes a joke. In lines 20–21, he expresses very explicitly his wish to 'be known' in the shop, that is to reduce interpersonal distance. To link what is happening here to Figure 9.2, it can be said that the customer is explicitly commenting on the social distance between himself and the others by particular tenor as a discourse management strategy. All the local strategies commented on above are responded to in a minimal way by the cashier and the shop-owner (lines 3, 13, 15 and 17), and, indeed, the cashier offers transactionally salient contributions in lines 8, 10 and 25, orienting to closing the encounter, rather than accommodating to the interpersonal stance of the customer.

The participants in these encounters were found to have very different concepts of the relationship between a customer and a storekeeper in that the storekeepers showed cultural preference for 'socially minimal' service encounters and reluctance to orient to intimacy with a stranger. The customers, on the other hand, often sought to establish more 'socially expanded' relationships by introducing personal topics, using humour and making assessments, for example. The shopkeepers did on occasions display attempts at convergence towards the customer's style (see discussion question 2 at the end of this chapter), for example by showing interest through asking questions, or smiling – but not sharing laughter – as a response to a joke. However, the degree of these shifts was minimal and the shopkeepers' different discourse management strategies (from the customers'), such as lack of backchannelling, was likely to be perceived as hostile. The customers' behaviour was in turn perceived as not very appropriate for increasing intimacy which, from the shopkeepers' point of view, would call for more silence and restraint. Bailey illustrates how the very different communicative norms and practices for displaying respect adopted by these two groups may be an important underlying cause for widely documented tensions and conflict: 'the relative restraint of immigrant Korean storekeepers... is perceived by many African Americans as a sign of racism, while the relatively personable involvement of African Americans is perceived by many storekeepers as disrespectful imposition' (Bailey 1997: 327).

Through this example we can see that a close analysis of the accommodative orientations of interactants is a valuable means of studying inter-ethnic tensions.

9.4 Cultural difference: some dilemmas

Recent developments in cultural studies and cultural theory seem to pose problems for CAT. They amount to a growing uncertainty about the definitions of culture, about the boundaries between cultural groups, and about how we should model the fundamental relationship between language and culture. It would be reasonable to say that Accommodation Theory, like most other established approaches to intergroup or 'intercultural' relations, has tended to trust the assumption that cultural groups generally have identifiable and meaningful boundaries. CAT has made this basic assumption in its research designs, in talking about 'French-Canadians', 'Welsh people', 'African-Americans' or 'Koreans', and in investigating their linguistic behaviours and their attitudes. The assumption is not that individuals will identify themselves unambiguously or consistently with such labels, but that the labels themselves 'make sense' – in social life and in social research.

But consider a different point of view, from a recent directory of key concepts in post-colonial studies:

> References to cultural diversity based on an assumption of 'pre-given cultural "contents" and customs' give rise to anodyne liberal notions of multiculturalism, cultural exchange or the culture of humanity ... cultural authority resides not in a series of fixed and determined diverse objects but in the process of how these objects come to be known and so come into being. (Ashcroft *et al.* 1998: 60)

The embedded quotation is from Homi Bhabha (1988), whose theoretical writings have challenged the conventional or 'modernist' academic approaches to cultural diversity. In Bhabha's (1994) view, cultural identity always shows indeterminacy and a struggle between alternatives — what he calls 'hybridity'. He argues that 'claims to inherent originality or purity of cultures are untenable' (1994: 20).

As Riggins (1997: 4) points out (in a very useful review and compilation of recent research on cultural 'otherness'), we have tended to make the assumption that social and cultural groups share similar characteristics. Yet many studies show that individuals' membership of social categories is indeed uncertain and emergent.

Riggins cites Stuart Hall's study of Afro-Caribbean identities and Hall's argument that self-identity should be conceptualized 'as a "production" which is never complete, always in process, and always constituted within, not outside representation' (Hall 1994: 392).

There is a strong flavour of social constructionism here, the argument that social realities are only fixed through discourse — through how we talk or write about them.[4] The 'critical' dimension of this stance is the argument that it is social elites who impose 'essentialist' definitions of cultural groups, and that they do this repressively, to perpetuate their own ideological values and priorities. Rampton's (1995, 1997) study of 'crossing' in the language of British urban adolescents, manifest in the use of Creole by adolescents of Anglo and Asian descent, the use of Panjabi by those of Anglo and African Caribbean descent, and the use of Indian English (stylized Asian English) by all three is worth citing in this context. The notion of crossing is a very useful perspective and challenges the essentialist assumption that a group uses 'its own' language variety. Crossing constitutes of course one set of accommodative options, even if not in an obvious sense convergent.

There are also echoes of postmodernist theory (e.g. Giddens 1991) in the argument that the world has moved on and that the old, structured certainties of class and ethnic self-definition have lapsed, in a welter of reflexive and hybrid identity options. As Giddens argues, the self in (what he calls) Late or High Modernity is an identity project, rather than one transmitted from a fixed and stable social structure. We are surrounded by media and other complex imagery which offer us multiple identities, which we take up and drop more as lifestyle projects than as essential determinants of who we are.

What are we to make of this orientation to the study of culture? How should we respond to it in research on cultural difference and language? Does it perhaps make the study of 'intercultural' relations and communication impossible, or even reprehensible, because it fixes the notion of 'cultural group' prematurely and in ways that do not reflect how cultural identity is nowadays lived and experienced? In our view, the first necessary response is to recognize the importance of the critical and constructionist argument for research on cultural difference and identity. In 1978, Edward Said first observed that there was in the West a persistent and structured view of peoples in Asia, the Far East and Africa that one could call 'Orientalism'. Said defined it as 'the corporate institution for dealing with the Orient – dealing with it by making statements about it, authorizing views on it, describing it, by teaching it, settling it, ruling over it: in short, Orientalism as a Western style for dominating, restructuring, and having authority over the Orient' (1978: 3; see also Karim 1997 on 'the Muslim other'). If Orientalism and similar colonial and post-colonial 'institutions' are defined partly by teaching them, then academic study and research are part of the process of perpetuating racial and cultural stereotypes. This is, in fact, a good example of why we can think of cultural perspectives themselves as discourses – as organized ways of thinking, speaking and writing about social groups. We do need to have a constant critical eye to our own studies, to make sure that the labels and categories we use, the questions we ask relating to them and the conclusions we draw, are not predetermined by dominant ideological values and priorities.

In accommodation research, for example, it would be naïve to assume that acts of linguistic accommodation by minorities to majorities – e.g. adopting the majority group's language code – are no more and no less than acts of psychological convergence. To take the case of Wales and the Welsh language, there have certainly been times in the community's history when this would have been the 'natural' assumption – meaning the assumption made by a culturally and numerically dominant English-speaking elite. Bilingual speakers' linguistic convergence to English may well have realized a form of aquiescence to, or even solidarity with, an emergent cultural norm – the norm of English language usage which developed rapidly in the mid and late nineteenth century, as industrialization rapidly increased and as recorded numbers of Welsh-speakers rapidly declined (Aitchison and Carter 1994). Correspondingly, divergence (a refusal to use English in Wales) could rightly be seen as a political act of resistance, grounded in an ideological view of Wales as an area of cultural conflict. But that interpretation of the same pattern of language use in the 1980s and 1990s would be much more controversial. In a sociolinguistic climate where the number of Welsh-speakers has stabilized and where policies of genuine bilingual parity are being actively promoted through schools and regionally devolved government (the Welsh National Assembly was formed in 1999), bilingual people's 'accommodation' in using English is less easily modelled as psychological convergence to an out-group majority norm. If it is convergence, it is as likely to be convergence to a rapidly spreading ideology of linguistic parity, with different and less adversarial political bases (cf. Williams 1987).

As regards the Postmodernist claim about complex and hybrid cultural identities, Wales is another relevant instance. It would be highly simplistic to assume, for example, that the half-million or so people in Wales who speak Welsh have a uniformly 'Welsh' cultural identity, while the two million or so who do not speak Welsh orient to 'English' identities. Current research is showing the highly complex and structured identities that, for example, young people in Wales recognize to be relevant to themselves and to their peers (see Garrett et al. 1999). Welsh teenagers identify radically different cultural profiles across the various Welsh regions. This includes variation along the subjective dimensions of 'Welshness', where they identify substantial differences between communities based on their reactions to the English-language pronunciation of typical regional speakers. The cultural politics of Welshness are therefore complex, but they are also shifting. The future of the Welsh language and, as a separate but related issue, the future of Wales as a culturally distinctive zone, largely lie in how young people select from various identity options and how they articulate their felt Welshness. It would indeed be a mistake to design studies of accommodation between groups of Welsh-speaking and English-speaking young people without acknowledging the detailed subjective profiles that they use to define their own and other people's Welshness.

Yet the main point here is that processes of cultural definition and identification are entirely researchable in their own right. It is through social psychological studies of subjective profiling that we can best confirm and fill out cultural theorists' claims about hybridity and lived cultural identities. Studies aiming to describe 'intercultural' communication should ideally be linked to studies of how individuals and social or cultural groups define themselves and others. In fact, this is precisely the agenda that Communication Accommodation Theory has established, aiming to locate the analysis of language within the analysis of social and cultural contexts, subjectively defined. (These relations are made explicit in Figure 9.1, above.)

The social constructionist argument is, in any case, that social and cultural reality is constituted in and through language. If this is to be more than a rather trite, universal and theoretical claim, then surely we need studies of *how* language constructs culture, in specific cases and contexts. Studying language and discourse in cultural settings offers us the best avenue to explore social construction, as situated social action. The perspective we adopt is, however, of crucial importance. We have to avoid reifying and 'essentializing' the groups we are concerned with. Being 'Welsh' or 'Iranian' or 'Malaysian', or for that matter 'European' or 'Asian', are clearly complex acts of attribution nowadays, especially in societies where these images and definitions are constantly reflected back at us – by politicians, by the media and indeed by academic research – in so many selective and edited forms. We might argue that this fluidity is a source of hope that the political and military consequences of extreme nationalism will gradually become less likely. Whether or not this is the case, language will continue to be the touchstone for cultural identificat-ion – either as a symbol in its own right or as the medium through which we 'deploy' and negotiate our identities. An important part of this negotiation is specified in the concepts we have introduced in this chapter – acts of communicative accommodation to or away from others, but also to or away from the cultural identities they are taken to represent.

Communication Accommodation Theory runs counter to an essentialist notion of culture. By resisting notions of cultural prototypes, it helps us understand the *local* context and the process of communication.

Discussion questions

1   Look back at Extract 1. Attempt (with others if possible) to outline the accommodative behaviour of the interactants in terms of Figures 9.1 and 9.2.
2   Do the same for Extract 2 below. How does the accommodative behaviour in this interaction differ from that in Extract 1? In what ways is it similar?

Extract 2
The interaction takes place in a shop between a Korean shop-owner, a Korean cashier and an African-American customer. The customer is a regular customer but has been away in Chicago for a month. The participants are all male and different from those in Extract 1.

(the customer enters store and goes to soda cooler)
1   customer: [hi]
2   owner: [how ar]e you? {customer takes soda towards cash register and motions towards displays} (7.5)
3   customer: wow you guys moved a lot of things around
4   cashier: hello: {stands up from where he was hidden behind the counter}
5   heh heh how are you? {cashier retrieves customer's alcohol and moves towards the till}
6   customer: what's going on man? {cashier gets up for customer's alcohol} (0.8)
7   customer: how've you been?

8	cashier:	sleeping
9	customer:	eh heh heh (1.8)
10	cashier:	that's it?
11	customer:	that:s it {cashier rings up purchases} (1.5)
12	customer:	I haven't seen you for a while
13	cashier:	he he where you been?
14	customer:	Chicago {cashier bags purchase}
15	cashier:	oh really?
16	customer:	[yeah]
17	cashier:	[how] long?
18	customer:	for about a MONTH (1.2)
19	cashier:	how's there
20	customer:	<u>CO:L</u>!
21	cashier:	[co:ld?]
22	customer:	[heh] heh heh heh
23	owner:	is Chicago cold?
24	customer:	u::h! {lateral headshakes} (1.4) man I got off the plane and walked out the airport I said 'OH shit' <u>HEH HEH HEH</u>
25	owner:	I thought it's gonna be nice spring season over there
26	customer:	well not now this about a month I been there I was
27		there for about a month but you know (.) damn {lateral headshakes}

{customer moves away from cash till towards owner} (1.4)

28	customer:	too co:l' I mean this was really cold
29	owner:	(they have snowy?) season there
30	customer:	I've known it to snow on Easter Sunday (.)

{15-second discussion, not clearly audible, in which the owner asks if there are mountains in Chicago, and the customer explains that there are not.}

31	customer:	see th- this- California weather almost never changes {spoken slowly and clearly as for a non-native
32		speaker} back there it's a
33		SEASONAL change you got fall winter spring
34	owner:	mm hm
35	customer:	you know but back there the weather sshhh {lateral headshake}
36	customer:	it's cold up until June I mean these guys like they –
37		wearing lon:g john:s from September until June
38	owner:	(it's hot season June?)
39	customer:	he-here it's hot but there it's {lateral headshake} (really?)

{customer moves towards exit}

40 owner: kay [see you later]
41 customer: [see you later] nice talking to you

(from Bailey 1997: 340–1. Transcription conventions slightly modified.)

3   In a study to examine intergroup relations (Bourhis and Giles
     1977), the following stimulus material was used: in a language
     laboratory setting, an RP accented English man said (on tape) to
     a group of adult Welsh learners of Welsh who had been asked to
     help in a survey on second language learning techniques:

> 'even in the boardrooms of some of your own education
> departments it is being said that "Welsh is dying, why can't
> you leave it alone? It is spoken by such a tiny proportion of
> people that it has one foot in the grave ... it is on the slippery
> slope of extinction" ... Now as I have already said, I believe,
> to be realistic, that the future of Welsh appears pretty dismal
> ... So could I have your opinion concerning the survival and
> status of the Welsh language in Wales?' (Bourhis and Giles
> 1977: 124–5)

In their replies to this question, the Welsh learners were found to
broaden their Welsh accents, compared with their answers to a
previous more emotionally neutral question. Some respondents
introduced Welsh words and phrases into their answers. One female
respondent paused for a while, then started to conjugate a socially
unacceptable verb into the microphone in Welsh.

3.1 How could the learners' responses be explained by Commu-
     nication Accommodation Theory?

3.2 How did the learners perceive the context?

Suggestions for further reading

Ashcroft, B., Griffiths, G. and Tiffin, H. (1998) *Key Concepts in Post-
Colonial Studies*. London: Routledge.

Coupland, N. (1995) Accommodation theory. In J. Verschueren, J.-O.
Östman and J. Blommaert (eds), *Handbook of Pragmatics Manual*.
International Pragmatics Association, 21–6.

Giles, H. and Coupland, N. (1991) *Language: Contexts and Consequences*.
Milton Keynes: Open University Press, chapter 3.

Giles, H., Coupland, J. and Coupland, N. (1991) *Contexts of Accommodation: Developments in Applied Sociolinguistics*. Cambridge: Cambridge
University Press, chapter 1.

Zuengler, J. (1991) Accommodation in native-nonnative interactions: going beyond the 'what' to the 'why' in second-language research. In H. Giles, J. Coupland and N. Coupland (eds), *Contexts of Accommodation: Developments in Applied Sociolinguistics*. Cambridge: Cambridge University Press, 223–44.

Notes

1. Overviews of Accommodation Theory include Coupland *et al.* 1988, Giles *et al.* 1991, Giles and Coupland 1991, Coupland 1995, and Niedzielski and Giles 1996. Section 9.2 draws, very selectively, from these sources.
2. The accommodation strategy of gaining approval and improving communication effectiveness through reducing linguistic differences is of course similar to Brown and Levinson's (1987) notion of positive politeness, and to Spencer-Oatey's concepts (see Chapter 2) of rapport-enhancement and rapport-maintenance orientations. CAT also shares its strategic orientation to communication with these other approaches. Later interpretations of 'accommodation' as a set of discourse-attuning options, which we consider below (cf. Coupland *et al.* 1988), bring all of these concepts even closer together. See also Jones *et al.* 1999 for a recent discussion of strategies and accommodation.
3. Ball *et al.* (1984) have studied the link between social norms and accommodation processes.
4. Wetherell (1996: 281) summarizes a social constructionist discourse analytic position thus:

   discourse is ... constitutive of both objects and people. Talk and writing are not merely about actions, events and situations, they are creative of those actions, events and situations ... In talking, people are constituting their social realities and collective cultures, manufacturing and constructing their lives, and are themselves manufactured as personalities and subjects in the process. Through this negotiation, the social world becomes populated with characters which are given certain attributes. Relationships become formulated as being of certain kinds, some forms of relating become defined as problematic and some as constructive and positive, and so on. Talk is not neutrally recording. Discourse comes to constitute social life as we know it.

PART FOUR

INTERCULTURAL DISCOURSE: EMPIRICAL STUDIES

10

Argumentation and Resulting Problems in the Negotiation of Rapport in a German–Chinese Conversation

Susanne Günthner

10.1 Introduction

This chapter deals with the question of how culturally-specific expectations of communicative situations and different conventions concerning communicative activities and genres can lead to difficulties in the interactive negotiation of meaning and the constitution of rapport. Thus, it is concerned with the way language is used to construct, maintain and confirm social relationships (cf. Chapter 2).

Based on an in-depth analysis of a conversation between Chinese and German students who were studying at a German university, I will show what the social consequences can be when interactants have diverging communicative expectations and use different strategies across various domains (discourse domain, participation domain and stylistic domain; cf. Chapter 2). The conversation is part of a larger corpus of audiotaped data which includes 25 conversations between German native speakers and Chinese speakers of German[1] and six conversations among Chinese native speakers (in Chinese). The analysis is based on methods of interpretative sociolinguistics and the theory of contextualization (Gumperz 1982a). Furthermore, I shall refer to ethnographic knowledge, as well as to the interpretations of the participants themselves, and of the Chinese and German informants to whom I presented parts of the audiotaped conversation in later meetings. The focus of the analysis is the organization of dissent sequences and the organization of arguments and counter-arguments. Conflict activities are of special interest to the analysis of rapport management, as they demand techniques of conversational cooperation as well as strategies of confrontation and thus require a combination of discursive methods such as signalling disagreement, coherence, giving accounts for one's arguments, defending one's position and doing 'facework'. Studies of argumentative sequences in intercultural settings not only draw attention to the fact that willingness to take part in argumentative and confrontational discourse can vary from one cultural group to another, but also that people from different cultural backgrounds may favour different ways of handling argumentative genres and activities (Naotsuka *et al.* 1981, Richards and Sukwiwat 1983, Günthner 1994).

10.2 Background to the conversation

The participants, two German students Doris and Andrea (both female) and two Chinese students Tan (female) and Yang (male), meet for tea. Tan and Yang, who both graduated from a university in China, were at the time of the conversation taking an MA course at a German university. The interaction came about for the following reasons: I had often talked to Doris about China, and she was very interested in knowing more about China and especially about the situation of women there. She asked me if I could introduce her to some Chinese students. As I knew that Tan would be very interested in meeting German students, I gave Doris her telephone number. So the two of them decided to 'meet for tea'. Both brought a friend along: Yang is a colleague of Tan and Andrea a friend of Doris.

After the conversation Tan evaluated the meeting as 'not bad', but commented that the Germans were quite 'direct', 'aggressive' and also 'rude, yes a bit offensive'. Doris mentioned that she and Andrea would not be interested in meeting the two Chinese students again as the conversation was 'just not interesting', 'the Chinese actually turned out to be boring conversationalists'. There were no further meetings between the four and the contact was broken off. What was the basis for these evaluations? The following analysis will look at the argumentative strategies used by the Chinese and German participants and will inquire into problems of rapport management in this interaction.[2]

The interaction begins with a small-talk period which accounts for the first 35 minutes. Tan serves tea and cakes, and Doris and Andrea ask about Yang's and Tan's situation in the student dormitory: how many foreign students live there, how many Chinese students, etc. Then they start talking about Chinese cuisine. Tan and Yang mention that they always cook for themselves, because they do not like the German food in the refectory. After that the topic switches from cooking and who does the cooking in China to the topic of 'women in China and Germany'. The German participants gradually initiate a very confrontational interactive frame. As this discussion is characterized by frequent use of disagreement sequences, the analysis will concentrate on the interactive management of disagreement, and demonstrate differences in the handling of verbal confrontation.

10.3 The interactive organization of dissent

Conversation analysts typically argue that agreements are preferred activities, and that disagreements are dispreferred activities which thus tend to be avoided or at least mitigated (Pomerantz 1984). This 'dispreference for direct disagreement' might be adequate for small-talk situations, but in argumentative sequences and confrontational discussions, disagreement is often produced in a very direct and unmitigated form (Günthner 1993, Kotthoff 1993). This direct, unmitigated use of dissent strategies even represents a constitutive feature for the construction of an argumentative sequence.

In my data, once an argumentative and confrontational frame is established, the German participants signal their dissent in such a way that the disagreement is focused and maximized.

10.3.1 Forms of dissent organization among the German participants

10.3.1.1 Dissent-formats
The term 'dissent-formats' refers to sequences where the speaker provides a (partial) repetition of the prior speaker's utterance and negates it or replaces parts of it with a contrasting element.[3] The substituted item is produced with emphatic stress and thus marked as an opposition to the replaced item:

YANG 6

8	Yang:	*das ist natürliche*
9	Andrea:	*das ist nicht NATÜRLICH.*
10		*sondern das ist eher tradiTIONELL.*

8	Yang:	this is natural
9	Andrea:	this is not NATURAL.
10		but it is actually tradiTIONAL.

Instead of mitigating the disagreement, Andrea organizes her utterance in a 'dissent-format' that consists of (i) contradiction by negation, (ii) correction by substitution, and (iii) prosodic marking of the contrastive elements 'NATURAL – tradiTIONAL'. In this way, she focuses on the polarity and highlights the dissent. Thus, she openly indicates a counter-position in an aggravated fashion without giving the prior speaker the chance to correct himself.

The dissent formats produced by the German participants show the following features:

(a) The utterance containing the disagreement repeats parts of the prior utterance and either negates it or substitutes central elements through contradictory devices.

(b) The correction of the problem item is highlighted by prosodic (contrastive stress), lexico-semantic (such as antonyms; opposing categories) and/or syntactic means of contrast (syntactic parallelism).

(c) The dissent is sequentially organized in a way that the speaker of the 'problem utterance' receives no possibility for self-correction.

YANG 31

6	Yang:	*ja so. wenn wenn diese Problem gelöst, dann natürlich (0.3)*
7		*die andere Problem ist leichter zu (0.3) [eh zu zu DISkutieren]*
8	Doris:	*[ne. eh ne. halt moment]*
9	Yang:	*eh zu VERSTEHEN. zu VERSTEHEN.*
10	Doris:	*ne. MOMENT. eh:m eh eh s'is für MICH kein Problem,*
11		*für mich is es KLAR*
12	Yang:	*ja.*
13	Doris:	*ehm FRAU UND MANN SIND NATÜRLICH GLEICH.*
14		*des is kein PROBLEM =*
15	Yang:	*=ja*
16	Tan:	*(hihihi)*
17	Doris:	*wenn DU allerdings sagst, eh::: die sind UN::gleich, NATÜRLICH UNGLEICH,*
18		*dann is es DEIN Problem, aber eh verstehst du,*
19		*des is nichts wo du drüber diskutieren kannst.*

6	Yang:	yes like this. when when this problem is solved, then of course (0.3)
7		it is easier to DIScuss (0.3) [the other problem]
8	Doris:	[no. eh no. wait a minute]
9	Yang:	eh to UNDERSTAND. to UNDERSTAND.

10 Doris: no. WAIT A MINUTE. eh:m eh eh for ME it's no
          problem,
11   for me it's CLEAR
12 Yang: yes.
13 Doris: ehm WOMEN AND MEN ARE NATURALLY
          EQUAL.
14   this is not a PROBLEM =
15 Yang: = yes
16 Tan: (hihihi)
17 Doris: however, if YOU say, eh::: they are NOT equal,
          NATURALLY UNEQUAL,
18   then it is YOUR problem, but eh you understand,
19   this is nothing you can discuss.

With the production of the clustered emphatic pre-elements 'no. eh no.',
Doris indicates her direct, unmitigated dissent. The function of these
dissent markers is to unequivocally signal disagreement and thus to
bracket the entire utterance as polar in relation to the preceding turn.[4]
Yang's repair (9) 'eh to UNDERSTAND. to UNDERSTAND.' is a
direct response to Doris' pre-elements. Doris then uses contrastive
elements and prosodic cues to mark emphasis and thus focuses on the
dissent and the polarity between her utterance and the prior speaker's:

you, your	–	my
problem	–	no problem
YOUR problem	–	for ME it's no problem
WOMEN AND MEN ARE NATURALLY EQUAL	–	They are NATURALLY UNEQUAL

The polarities are constructed by a change of deictic elements ('your'
– 'my'), by contrasting a referent with its negation ('problem' – 'no
problem'), and by confronting a lexical item with its antonym ('equal'
– 'unequal'). Instead of producing a simple negation 'no' as a sign of
disagreement, the German speakers thus make use of rhetorical
formats which take up the prior speaker's syntactic and lexical
framework, negate the statement or substitute a main element of the
utterance and thus highlight the polarity between the two turns.

10.3.1.2 Dissent-ties
A further strategy in the German participants' organization of dissent is
what I shall call 'dissent-tying'. The speaker latches her disagreeing
utterance to the prior turn and thus produces a syntactic and lexical
continuation of the preceding utterance. Instead of 'unisono'-tying (in

the sense of 'communicational dueting' (Falk 1979)), where the second speaker takes the floor to produce a continuation of the prior speaker's turn and thereby demonstrates concordance and camaraderie, here the second speaker ties her utterance to the prior one but then in continuing it demonstrates consequences which contradict the argumentative line of the first speaker. Tan states that in her generation housework is shared by husband and wife. It is the kind of work that just has to be 'done by one or other of them'. Andrea then ties her utterance – in the form of a sentence expansion to the right – with the pre-element 'yes' to the prior speaker's utterance (62).

YANG 5ff.

58	Tan:	*denn (0.2) es soll auch* =
59	Doris:	= (? ? ? ? [? ? ? ? ? ? ? ?)]
60	Tan:	[*ja von einem*] *von einem gemacht werden. JA*
61		*entweder der MANN ODER die FRAU*
62	Andrea:	*ja. und wenn der MANN keine Lust hat.*
63		*und die FRAU hat keine Lust*
64		*dann muß es die Frau machen.*

58	Tan:	then (0.2) it also should =
59	Doris:	= (? ? ? ? [? ? ? ? ? ? ?)]
60	Tan:	[yes be done] by one of them. YES
61		either by the HUSBAND OR the WIFE
62	Andrea:	yes. and when the HUSBAND doesn't feel like doing it
63		and the WIFE doesn't feel like doing it
64		then the wife has to do it.

Andrea builds up a contradiction to Tan's argument that husband and wife share the housework, by taking up her turn and expanding it with the clause-combining element 'and' in a counter-argumentative direction. In order to emphasize her point, she uses rhetorical means of building up contrasts by syntactic and lexical parallelism and prosodic marking of the contrast pair (HUSBAND–WIFE):

62	Andrea:	yes. and when the HUSBAND **doesn't feel like doing it**
63		and the WIFE **doesn't feel like doing it**
64		then the wife has to do it.

By the use of dissent-tying, Andrea at the same time achieves a 'probatio' and produces a 'refutatio': she supports her own argumentative line and tears down that of her opponent. The following transcript demonstrates the antagonistic use of 'duet'-formats.[5]

YANG 29

25	Yang:	*wenn wenn ich später von Arbeiten nach Hause ja komme*
26		*also = ich = (hihihi) = meine = wenn später = in =* *Zukunft = ja*
27		*und dann meine-meine (hihi) Frau (hihi) ist schon zu* HAUS
28		*und hat das Essen vorbereitet ja.*
29	Doris:	*und dann ist es so RICH:TIG GEMÜTLICH.*
30		*und DU SETZT dich in deinen SESSEL,*
31		*und SIE RACKERT sich ab. (-)*
32		*das glaub ich* [*dir gern*]
33	Andrea:	[(*hihihihi*)]
34	Doris:	*das finden alle MÄNNER* [*ganz TOLL*]
35	Andrea:	[*klar.*]'

25	Yang:	when when I later on come home from work yes
26		well = I = (hihihi) = mean = when later = in = the = future = yes
27		and then my' my (hihi) wife (hihi) is already at HOME
28		and has prepared dinner yes.
29	Doris:	and then it is REA:LLY COSY.
30		and YOU SIT in your chair,
31		and SHE SLAVES AWAY for you. (-)
32		well I do believe [that]
33	Andrea:	[(hihihihi)]
34	Doris:	all MEN think this is [just GREAT]
35	Andrea:	[of course.]

With the conjunction 'and' Doris ties her utterance to the prior one and continues to picture Yang's wishful thinking, by presenting more concrete details to illustrate and exaggerate his imagined scene:

30	and YOU SIT in your chair,
31	and SHE SLAVES AWAY for you. (-)

The rhetorical contrast between 'you sit in your chair' and 'she slaves away' is built up by the use of syntactic parallelism and semantic oppositions (sitting – slaving away). Thus, by formally continuing his sentence and exaggerating the picture described, Doris parodies Yang's utterance and exposes him as a typical member of the category 'men': 'all MEN think this is just GREAT'.

The strategy of dissent-tying reveals how participants in argumentative discourse try to build support for their own position by undermining the opponent's argument. It is an ideal rhetorical strategy to continue the opponent's logic of argumentation in an exaggerated way and thereby illustrate its untenable consequences.

10.3.1.3 Reported speech as a strategy of confrontation

A further technique of dissent used by the German speakers is the reproduction of the opponent's prior utterance in order to oppose it. Reported speech can vary from word-by-word reproductions of the actual utterances to total misrepresentations and distortions of the original wordings. Let me present a case where the speaker strategically distorts the original utterance. Yang argues that 'the women's problem' in China is not as severe as in Germany:

YANG 19

1	Yang:	*eh:m' ::: ich ich ich, ich muß muß muß sagen,*
2		*also in Deutschland die Frauenprobleme is'*
3		*eh' (-) also is eh STÄRKER als in Schina.*

1	Yang:	eh:m':::: I I I, I must must must say,
2		well in Germany the women's problem is'
3		eh' (-) well is eh is BIGGER than in China.

About eight minutes later Doris quotes this statement. The reported speech (69–70) demonstrates the strategic transformation of the original wordings:

YANG 24a

67	Doris:	*also [ich] VERSTEH eigentlich nich unbedingt*
68	Tan:	*[hm]*
69	Doris:	*WARUM du sagst eh in in Kina gibts kein Frauenproblem.*
70		*des Problem is eigentlich das gleiche bloß daß*
71		*(-) eh:m'daß es mehr verTUSCHT wird.*
72	Yang:	*<< p > keine so stark wie hier >*
73	Doris:	*JA WEIL DIE FRAUEN HIER BEWUSSTER SIND.*

67	Doris:	well [I] don't quite UNDERSTAND
68	Tan:	[hm]
69	Doris:	WHY you say that eh in in China there is no women's problem
70		the problem actually is the same it's just that
71		(-) eh:m' that it is HUSHED up much more.
72	Yang:	<< p > not as bad as here >
73	Doris:	YES BECAUSE WOMEN ARE MORE CONSCIOUS HERE.

The statement: 'in Germany the women's problem is' eh' (-) well is eh is BIGGER than in China' now becomes strategically transformed into: 'in China there is no women's problem'. Confronted with his distorted words, Yang corrects Doris' misrepresentation in a low voice: 'not as bad as here' (line 72). Shortly afterwards the conversation continues in the following way:

YANG 24b

7	Tan:	*und was denn nich gut?*
8	Andrea:	*ja ich denk, zum Beispiel*
9		*er sagt es gibt die Frauenprobleme nicht.*
10		*ich sage, es GIBT die Probleme.*
11		*aber die Frauen (-) tun nichts dagegen.*
12		*oder:' (-) oder denken nich [darüber na:ch]*
13	Doris:	*[es kommt nicht] an d'Öffentlichkeit=*
14	Andrea:	*= ja. oder sagens nich*

7	Tan:	and what is not good?
8	Andrea:	well I think, for example
9		he says there is no women's problem.
10		I say, there ARE problems.
11		but the women (-) don't do anything about it.
12		or:' (-) or they don't think [about them]
13	Doris:	[it is not] made a public issue=
14	Andrea:	= yes. or don't talk about them

The quoted speech (9) is again nowhere near a word-for-word reproduction of Yang's utterances (YANG 19: 1–3 and YANG 24a: 69) but plays a strategic role within the argumentative sequence: Yang, the present opponent, is now turned into a figure ('he') of Andrea's speech. Through the transformation of the original utterance, 'in Germany the women's problem is' eh' (-) well is eh is BIGGER than in China.' (YANG 19), into 'he says there is no women's problem.' (YANG 24b), Yang's original statement receives an illegitimate exaggeration, which provides the basis for Andrea's antithesis. This technique of distorting the quoted utterance of one's opponent by omitting his qualifications and reservations and thus simplifying and exaggerating his argument, is a strategic device suitable for building up an antagonistic counter-position and antithesis by maximizing contrasts.[6] Rhetorical means of contrast (lexical repetition, syntactic parallelism, contrasting of the two speaking subjects 'he' versus 'I' and prosodic marking) are used here again to underline the antagonism of the two opinions:

9   **he** says there is **no** women's problem.
10   **I** say, there **ARE** problems.

The trenchant formulations and simplifications organize the utterances in such a way that contrasts are built up and the rhetorical relation of thesis and antithesis is constructed.

The analysis of the strategies used by the German participants to signal dissent demonstrates that, once an argumentative or confrontational frame is established, they make use of highly aggravated forms of disagreement by employing dissent-formats, distorted quotations of the opponent's utterances and forms of building up contrasts. They not only state their disagreeing opinion but at the same time make use of the opponent's utterance in order to construct contrast and heighten the polarization. This leads to the question, what kind of techniques are used by the Chinese participants to signal dissent?

10.3.2 Forms of organizing dissent among the Chinese participants

A strategy continuously used by the Chinese participants is to temporarily signal formal consent and then in the following turn to indicate a discordant position without formally marking it as a disagreement. In order to analyse Yang's and Tan's strategies of disagreement, it is necessary to follow the question 'are there natural differences between women and men' over a longer sequence of talk. When Yang argues that there are 'natural differences between women and men', Doris asks for specification:

YANG 15
79 Yang: *das is also von der von der traditionell? oder politische?*
80   *(-) oder', die (nur?) eh die schon (-) von Natur aus*
81   *[(???)] so natürliche'*
82 Doris: *[ja] du glaubst es gibt eine NATÜRLICHE EINSCHRÄNKUNG?*
83   *(0.7)*
84 Yang: *ich glau:be (-) NICHT, aber ich (hi) ich muß sagen, es gibt. (1.0) ein bißchen.*
85 Doris: *wie meinst du das?*

79 Yang: this is from the traditional? or political?
80   (-) or' the (only?) eh the (-) by nature
81   [(???)] I mean natural'

82 Doris: [well] do you believe there is a NATURAL
LIMITATION?
83 (0.7)
84 Yang: I belie:ve (-) NOT, but I (hi) I must say, there is. (1.0)
a bit.
85 Doris: what do you mean by this?

Doris' question 'do you believe there is a NATURAL LIMITA-
TION?' (82) uses marked prosody (increase of volume and a rise of
the intonation contour) to contextualize her disagreeing position.
Yang answers by producing a hesitating agreement: 'I belie:ve (-)
NOT' (84). However, he then utters a disagreement, introduced with
'but': 'but I (hi) I must say, there is.' As no reaction follows (the
pause indicates the absence of a turn selection), Yang corrects his
utterance by toning it down: 'a bit'. After Doris asks him to provide
further explanations (85), the discussion on gender differences
continues, and she argumentatively provides counter-examples to
demonstrate that certain aspects of the life of women, which might on
the surface appear to be 'natural differences' (jobs of lower status,
caring for the children), do actually have social reasons (86ff.). Five
minutes later Doris refocuses on Yang's thesis about 'natural
differences' and asks him to restate his opinion:

YANG 17ff.
86 Doris: *des is kein natürlicher Unterschied in meinen [Augen]*
87 Yang: *[mhm ja] mhm*
88 Doris: *wo siehst DU denn die NATÜRLICHEN Unterschiede? (-)*
89 *weil du hast was von natürlichen Unterschieden*
gere [det]
90 Yang: *[viel]leicht*
91 *ich habe diese eh: (1.0) eh schwer zu sagen*
....

8 Doris: *[du] meinst rein körperlich, jetzt?*
9 Yang: *nein körperlich eh jetzt also*
10 Doris: *von der Kraft her? << p > oder wie meinst du? >*
11 Yang: *(nich klar?) zum Beispiel die also Polizei*
12 Doris: *POLIZEI?*
13 Yang: *KRIMINALpolizei. das ist nicht körperlich.*
14 Doris: *ne. das is NICH körperlich. das hat allerdings etwas damit*
zu tun',
15 *was für 'n Status Frauen in der Gesellschaft habn.*

16		*MÄNNER, werden in der Gesellschaft schon mal als Autoritätspersonen*
17		*dargestellt die MEHR zu sagen haben als FRAUEN.*
18	Yang:	*ja.*
19	Doris:	*und we- DANN wirds n' natürlich problematisch*
20		*wenn so'n UNgleiches Gesellschaftsbild da ist,*
21		*da dann dann is es auch schwierig auf einmal die FRAU in die gleiche Rolle*
22		*zu setzen wie der Mann (meist?) aber wenn normalerweise*
23		*der Mann und die Frau eine gleiche Rolle hätten*
24	Yang:	*ja.*
25	Doris:	*daß eh' wenn ne Frau was sagt, das GENAUSO (-) AUTORITÄT angesehen wird,*
26		*autoritär angesehen wie en Mann*
27	Yang:	*ja.*
28	Doris:	*dann wär das kein Problem.*
29		*des is ein GESELLSCHAFTLICHER Unterschied*
30		*und kein (-) NATÜRLICHER.*
31	Yang:	*ja(.hh)(hi)(.hh)*
32	Doris:	*ja. denk ich schon. also des is kein Unterschied.*
33		*was was vielleicht stimmen könnte*
34		*[oder was]*
35	Yang:	*[un und auch ein] eh eh ich meine auch*
36		*DENKWEISE von Frauen und von Männern*
37	Doris:	*versuch eh was fürn Unterschied*
38		*is [das?]*
39	Yang:	*[Denk]weise.*
40	Doris:	*was is das fürn Unterschied? (0.6)*
41	Doris:	*wie denken Frauen, [wie denken (???) Männer?]*
42	Yang:	*[(? ? ? ? ? ? ? ? ? ? ? ?)]*
43	Tan:	*[ich glaube das]*
44		*schon (-) auch (-) eh: wegen der Tra'dition wegen DIE Tradition = oder = so = was =*
45	Doris:	*also [ich]*
46	Yang:	*[viel]leicht wegen [die Tradition]*
47	Andrea:	*[also die] Frauen*
48	Andrea:	*können also die Frauen sind doch nich dümmer als die Männer.*
49	Yang:	*nein. (-) [das is richtig]*
50	Doris:	*[oder denken anders]*
51	Andrea:	*du meinst die denken mehr mit Ge[FÜHL oder]*
52	Yang:	*[ich glaube eh]*

53	Yang:	*manchmal in in eine bestimmte Bereich ja besser als die Männer.*
54		*und die MÄNNER arbeiten in eine bestimmte Bereichen*
55		*besser als [d'] Frauen*
56	Andrea:	*[mhm]*
57	Doris:	*aber des is doch auch etwas was*
58		*UNHEIMLICH von der Tradition bestimmt ist*
59		*wenn Frauen nun mal IMMER in dem Bereich gearbeitet habn,*
60		*dann tun sie ihre Fähigkeiten in diesem Bereich ent-WICKELN.*
61		*wenn ich als FRAU immer in einem MÄNNERberuf gearbeitet hab,*
62		*dann entwickle ich meine Fähigkeiten,*
63		*die zu diesem MÄNNERBERUF gehören =*
64	Yang:	*= un ich ich muß sagen, für die MÄNNER es gibt keine Grenze*
65		*für die, für die Arbeit. für die Arbeiten. für die Frauen es gibt Grenze.*
66	Doris:	*welche Grenze?*
67	Yang:	*zum Beispiel die (0.3) körperliche*
86	Doris:	this is not a natural difference in my [eyes]
87	Yang:	[mhm yes.] mhm
88	Doris:	where do YOU see NATURAL differences? (-)
89		because you mentioned something about natural differ[ences]
90	Yang:	[per]haps
91		I have these eh: (1.0) eh it's difficult to say

. . . .

8	Doris:	[you] are now talking about purely physical?
9	Yang:	not physical eh now well
10	Doris:	concerning physical strength? << p > or what do you mean? >
11	Yang:	(not clear?) for example the police
12	Doris:	POLICE?
13	Yang:	CRIMINAL investigators. this is not physical.
14	Doris:	no. this is NOT physical. but it does have to do' with
15		the status of women in the society.
16		MEN are represented as authoritative figures in the society
17		who have MORE to say than WOMEN.

```
18  Yang:    yes.
19  Doris:   and wh- THEN it becomes of course problematic
20           when there is such an UNequal concept of society,
21           then then it becomes difficult to suddenly place
             WOMEN in the same position
22           as men (most of the time?) but if men and women
23           had the same roles
24  Yang:    yes.
25  Doris:   so that eh' when a woman says something, it is treated
             just
26           AS (-) AUTHORITATIVE as when a man would say it
27  Yang:    yes.
28  Doris:   then it wouldn't be a problem.
29           this is a SOCIAL difference then
30           and not a (-) NATURAL.
31  Yang:    yes (.hh) (hi) (.hh)
32  Doris:   yes. I do think so. so. this is no difference then.
33           what what might be true is
34           [or what]
35  Yang:    [and and also] I also think the
36           WAY OF THINKING of women and of men
37  Doris:   try it eh what kind of difference
38           is [this?]
39  Yang:       [way] of thinking.
40  Doris:   what kind of difference do you mean? (0.6)
41  Doris:   how women think, [how men (???) think]?
42  Yang:                     [(? ? ? ? ? ? ? ? ? ? ? )]
43  Tan:                      [I believe that ] already (-) also (-) eh:
44           because of the tra(-)dition because of THE tradition
             or = something = like = that
45  Doris:   well [I]
46  Yang:        [per]haps because of [the tradition]
47  Andrea:                           [well] women cannot
48  Andrea:  well women are not stupider than men.
49  Yang:    no. (-) [this is right]
50  Doris:           [or think differently]
51  Andrea:  you mean they are more em[OTIONAL or what]
52  Yang:                            [I believe eh]
53  Yang:    sometimes in certain areas they are better than men.
54           and the MEN work better in certain areas
55           than [wo]men
56  Andrea:       [mhm]
```

57 Doris: but this is also something that is
58   VERY STRONGLY determined by tradition
59   suppose women have ALWAYS worked in one area
60   then they DEVELOP their abilities in this area.
61   when I as a WOMAN have always worked in a typical
         MALE profession
62   then I develop the abilities,
63   which belong to this MALE PROFESSION =
64 Yang: = and I I must say, for MEN there is no limit
65   for the, for the work. for the jobs. for women there is a
         limit.
66 Doris: what sort of limit?
67 Yang: for example (0.3) physical

We shall first concentrate on Yang's strategies to support his
position. First of all, Doris rejects his example of the 'CRIMINAL
investigators' as a socially constructed difference between women and
men. Yang's recipient signals, which are produced while Doris holds
the floor, are interpreted by her as 'continuers', and so she proceeds
with her utterance. His 'yes hh' and the giggling in line 31 initiates a
repair on Doris' part. First she reconfirms her opinion 'yes. I do
think so. so. this is no difference then.'; then she starts to formulate a
possible qualification to her statement. Instead of signalling his
dissent directly and marking it formally as a disagreement, Yang just
provides a semantic discordant statement (35–36). His disagreeing
utterance is tied to the prior one, indicating a concordant evaluation:

35 Yang: [and and also] I also think the
36   WAY OF THINKING of women and of men

Instead of taking up parts of the prior turn and opposing it, Yang lists
further aspects of his position. The additive conjunction 'and' as well
as the particle 'also' suggest consent. This phenomenon of producing
an utterance that demonstrates dissent on the content level without
formally marking it as disagreement can also be found in lines 52–55:

52 Yang: [I believe eh]
53   sometimes in certain areas they are better than men.
54   and the MEN work better in certain areas
55   than [wo]men

Doris' counter-argument (about the influence of tradition) is met
with a disagreement on Yang's part; however, he contextualizes a
thematic progression of Doris' statement:

64 Yang: = and I I must say, for MEN there is no limit
65   for the, for the work. for the jobs. for women there is a
          limit.

Yang neither reproduces parts of his co-participants' prior turns in order to attack or deconstruct them, nor does he quote their utterances in order to explicitly distance himself from them.

So far the analysis demonstrates that the Chinese and German students make use of different argumentative styles and different ways of signalling dissent.[7]

10.4 Strategies to end the confrontational frame

With the exception of the first 35 minutes of small talk, the conversation is characterized by a confrontational frame. Verbal conflict ends when the oppositional turns cease and other activities are taken up (Vuchinich 1990: 118). As Schegloff and Sacks (1973: 297) point out, when one speaker signals his intent to close the topic, his co-participant can demonstrate in his next turn 'that he understood what a prior [speaker] aimed at, and that he is willing to go along with that'. The termination of verbal conflict also requires a consensus of the participants to go along with the closing down and to change the speech activity.

When Yang and Tan continuously employ techniques to close the verbal conflict, their German co-participants do not join these attempts, and thus the argumentation continues. We shall now consider the strategies used by the Chinese speakers to close the confrontational frame.

10.4.1 Concessions

A verbal conflict may be terminated when one participant 'gives in' and accepts the opponent's position. Since concessions signal that the speaker is not able to defend her/his position, they are potentially face-threatening acts. If the opponent accepts the concession, the conflict ends. In this conversation, the German participants, however, take the concessions of the Chinese speakers as an opportunity to focus on the contradiction between the conceding utterance and the former position of the opponent:

YANG 30
45 Yang: *ich ich bin für Ihre Meinung. (-) daß die Frauen*
         WIRKLICH also:: also:

46		*nach der eh Hochschulabschluß oder (-) also: ehm:*
47		*schon als eine Er- Erwachsene und sie haben weniger Chancen oder weniger (-)*
48		*Möglichkeiten' als die Männer*
49	Doris:	*mhm*
50	Yang:	*und auch die Zukunft (0.3) ist also nich so herrlich wie die Männer.*
51	Doris:	*warum sagst DU, (-) daß daß du meinst eh die Frauen haben GENÜGEND Rechte.*
52		*es reicht. warum SA[GST DU DAS?]*
53	Yang:	*[(? ? ? ?)(hihi)]*

45	Yang:	I I agree with your opinion. (-) that women REALLY we::ll we:ll
46		after they graduate from university or (-) we:ll ehm: as a- adults
47		they have less chances or (-)
48		less opportunities' than men
49	Doris:	mhm
50	Yang:	and also the future (0.3) is not as marvellous as the men's.
51	Doris:	why do YOU say, (-) that that you think eh women have ENOUGH rights.
52		it's enough. why DO [YOU SAY THIS?]
53	Yang:	[(? ? ? ? ? ? ?)(hihi)]

Yang (lines 45ff) agrees with Doris' position. She, however, does not accept his concession but uses it to point out the contradiction with his former position and to bring him into the situation of incompatibility. Instead of participating in the process of closing the confrontational frame, Doris thus takes the concession as an opportunity to challenge her opponent.

10.4.2 Compromises

Providing a compromise is another technique for closing down a verbal conflict. Here, the speaker offers 'a position that is *between* the opposing positions that define the dispute' (Vuchinich 1990: 126). Instead of giving in to the opponent's thesis, the speaker moves towards the other party's position and proposes a possible 'middle ground'. As the speaker neither accepts the opponent's position totally nor completely gives up her/his former opinion, compromises turn out to be less face-threatening than concessions. The opposing party can either accept the proposed compromise and thus the verbal conflict can be brought to an end, or s/he can reject the compromising offer.

In the following transcript segment, Yang offers a compromise between his former position that 'in Germany the women's problem is bigger than in China' and his opponents' argument that 'women in China are just not conscious about their discrimination'. He now states that 'women and men in China have thought little about these issues so far':

YANG 33

4	Yang:	*sie haben auch sehr wenig darüber gedacht = überlegt =*
		DESHALB
5		*es gibt vielleicht in Schina ein bißchen (ruhig?)*
6		*in diese Problem. in die Frauen Problem.*
7		*das kann sein. (0.2) wir eh das' meine* [*zweite*]
8	Andrea:	[*mhm*]
9	Yang:	*zweite zweite Meinung. dass heißt wir können*
10		*noch viel viel tun. viel viel besser tun als* [*jetzt*]
11	Andrea:	[*mhm*]
12		(0.5)
13	Doris:	*mhm. also ich find es probleMATISCH ehm: ich*
14		*eh: weil ich eh es is ne' also du denkst vielleicht*
15		*Emanzipation bedeutet (-) Frau und Mann angleichen*
16		*und daß Frau und Mann gleich SEIN*
17		*SOLLEN, aber Emanzipation bedeutet nicht (-) DAS*
18		*für mich. Emanzipation bedeutet*

4	Yang:	they also have thought very little about this = reflected
		= on = this = THEREFORE
5		it is a little bit more (quiet?) in China
6		concerning this problem. concerning the women's
		problem.
7		this might be. (0.2) we eh the' my [second]
8	Andrea:	[mhm]
9	Yang:	second second opinion. that is there is still a lot
10		a very lot to do for us. to improve very much from
		[now]
11	Andrea:	[mhm]
12		(0.5)
13	Doris:	mhm. well I think it is probleMATIC ehm: I
14		eh: because I eh it is well' you might think
15		emancipation means (-) women and men become
		similar

16		and that women and men SHOULD BE the same
17		however THIS is not emancipation (-)
18		for me. emancipation means

Yang's statement (6) moves towards his opponents' position. However, instead of accepting Yang's compromising offer, Doris expands the argumentation by providing a disagreement.

10.4.3 Change of activity

One further technique to end the confrontational frame is to introduce a 'frame break' (Goffman 1986) and focus on a new verbal activity. One can achieve this for example by focusing on the local situation at hand (e.g. by inquiring 'what kind of tea is this?') or by focusing on a background aspect of the prior utterance. In the following example Tan initiates a frame break (4) by asking for personal information and thus focusing on a background aspect of the prior speaker's turn:

YANG 19

96	Andrea:	*wenn man die Arbeitkraft BRAUCHT,*
97		*dann sagt man die Frauen können*
98		*das AUCH. (-) und wenn man sie*
99		*nich [WILL] dann sagt man sie haben*
1	Tan:	[*mhm*]
2	Andrea:	*keine KRAFT. es (-) eh du siehst an anderen*
3		[*Ländern*]
4	Tan:	[*WARST*] *DU SCHON MAL IN TIBET?*
5	Andrea:	*ja.*
6		*(0.2)*
7		*un in Kina.*
8	Tan:	*eh (hihi)*

13	Andrea:	*mhm. ich HAB ES gesehn daß daß es immer darauf ankommt,*
14		*wenn (0.2) wenn in ei'm Land eh viel harte Arbeit zu machen is*
15		*vom Klima her oder so, dann müssen alle Menschen zusammen*
16		*JEDE Arbeit machen.*

96	Andrea:	when you NEED their work force,
97		then you say that women can do the SAME job.
98		(-) and when you don't WANT

99   [them] then you say that they lack
1 Tan: [mhm]
2 Andrea: physical ENERGY. it (-) eh you can look at other
3   [countries]
4 Tan: [HAVE] YOU BEEN TO TIBET?
5 Andrea: yes.
6   (0.2)
7   and to China.
8 Tan: eh (hihi)

13 Andrea: mhm.I SAW IT it always depends,
14   when (0.2) when in a country eh a lot of hard work
           needs to be done
15   due to the climate or so, then all people together
16   have to do ALL sort of work.

For a frame break to succeed, all participants have to orient their activities to this change of frame. In this case, the frame break is only successful for a short while: Andrea accepts it temporarily, and returns in line 13 to the argumentation.

The continuous efforts of Yang and Tan to change to a more personal conversation all fail because of the German participants' lack of cooperation. The Germans respond to the concessions by focusing on the contradiction, reject the offers of compromise and only temporarily accept the change of activities. Thus, the negotiation of a common ground of rapport fails.

10.5 Concluding remarks

The analysis above demonstrates how different discursive practices and diverging strategies of rapport management can influence social contact situations. The four students, who were very willing to meet each other, were confronted with culturally different conversational conventions and expectations ('pragmatic conventions': see Chapter 2).[8] The two German students valued overt expressions of their opinions and cherished the idea of having a 'good argumentative exchange' – a rather typical expectation within German student culture. In this culture 'getting to know someone' means finding out what the others' opinions and positions on different issues are and perhaps debating with them. When I interviewed the participants after the interaction, Doris and Andrea mentioned that the conversation 'was not very interesting', their co-participants 'don't really have own opinions', and therefore it was rather 'awkward and dragging'. The two Chinese students, however, had different expectations of such a meeting and of showing rapport in the situation at hand. Yang and Tan emphasized in the interview 'the much too strong willingness of the Germans to argue'. Tan explained that in China a conversation between people who meet for the first time and want to get to know each other would be totally different. Instead of 'discussing and contradicting each other all the time', one would talk about oneself and the family and ask the others about their families. Only when this kind of rapport is well established may one start to discuss social and political issues. However, Tan emphasized that both she and Yang are considered to be 'very very open' by Chinese standards. This was also the reason why the discourse style of the two Germans 'was not too much of a problem' to them.

Besides different expectations concerning the social situation, the analysis shows that the participants had differing conventions for selecting strategies in the given context, such as different ways of signalling dissent (cf. 'pragmalinguistic conventions': see Chapter 2). Furthermore, they had differing norms for attributing social meaning to discursive strategies in the particular context. Whereas the direct way of disagreeing was interpreted as 'very rude and inconsiderate behaviour' by the Chinese participants, the German students interpreted these strategies as a sign of showing argumentative 'involvement' (see Chapter 8).

Can we now conclude that the Chinese discourse style is more harmonious and indirect than the German style? Although this interaction, as well as other data stemming from informal discussions among colleagues and acquaintances, seems to confirm this[9] it would be too simple to postulate in a context-free manner that Chinese speakers are indirect and avoid open confrontation. Likewise, it would be too general to assert that German speakers always use very direct strategies and are openly confrontational.[10] There are of course other contexts where Chinese participants demonstrate high directness, which German participants consider inappropriate (e.g. personal questions about one's income, one's marital status or asking for reasons why the German acquaintances 'do not have children'). Furthermore, for Chinese interactants who do not 'share human feelings' (*ganqing, renqing*), that is, who are not relatives, friends, acquaintances or members of the same 'unit' (*danwei*) (i.e. are out-group rather than in-group members – see Chapter 14), other discourse conventions, directness strategies and rapport-management rules apply (Pieke 1992). Thus, it is essential to ask in what communicative contexts interactants use which strategies and which contextualization cues. The interactive setting (institutional or non-institutional, degree of formality, interactive roles etc.), the communicative genre (formal or informal discussion, political debate, small talk, quarrelling among friends, etc.) as well as the particular speech activity (disagreement, stating an opinion, presenting a personal question, etc.) all play vital roles in the ways in which rapport is managed and thus have to be taken into account.

Discussion questions

1 In your opinion, what is the strongest factor that made the German and Chinese participants react as they did to the meeting?
2 If Doris had not been such a self-conscious feminist, do you think the outcome of the meeting might have been different? Why/why not?
3 How do you think you would have felt if you had been present? Would you have been happy to debate women's issues freely, or would you have preferred discussion of a 'safer', less controversial topic?
4 In your opinion (and according to your norms), in what kind of communicative contexts is it usually appropriate to initiate and maintain a heated discussion, and in what kind of contexts is it usually inappropriate to do so?
5 What advice would you give (a) to the German students and (b) to the Chinese students, to help them become more effective/sensitive intercultural communicators?

Notes

1. As these Chinese are either teachers of German at Chinese universities or Chinese students studying at German universities their German is at an advanced level.
2. The argumentative strategies used by Chinese and German participants, which will be outlined in some detail, are also found in the other conversations; cf. Günthner (1994), where I analysed three argumentative conversations between Germans and Chinese and two between Chinese.
3. Cf. also Kotthoff 1993.
4. Cf. Goodwin (1983: 669) for children's aggravated forms of arguing.
5. As Falk (1979: 22) states, 'duet partners are speaking as if they were one person. The second's utterance is often even syntactically, lexically and prosodically a continuation of the first's.'
6. Classical rhetoric lists this among the 'dishonest argumentative strategies' (Oliver 1971).

7. It is difficult to speculate about the role of language proficiency in this interaction. However, what is striking is that in my data – contrary to assumptions that learner languages show 'politeness reductions' and lack face-saving strategies – German native speakers tend to show a more direct (and less polite) argumentative style than the Chinese learners, who show more off-record strategies.

8. Cf. Scollon and Scollon/Wong-Scollon (1991, 1995).

9. Cf. Günthner (1993); cf. also Zhan's (1992) work on politeness strategies in Chinese; Young's (1994) analysis of Chinese-American interactions; Liao's (1994; 1997) studies of directives and refusals used by Americans and Chinese.

10. As women's issues and the issue of 'men's contribution to women's oppression' are highly controversial, these topics tend to result in a highly argumentative style among German academics. Thus, I would argue that the main topic of the interaction, 'women's situation in Chinese and Western societies', contributes to the confrontational style among the German participants.

11

Negative Assessments in Japanese–American Workplace Interaction

Laura Miller

11.1 Introduction

In the Japanese television mini-series 'Concerto' (*Kyôsôkyoku*), sultry pop idol Takuya Kimura plays the role of a struggling architect named Kakeru. In one scene Kakeru has been injured and is at home being looked after by a female neighbour when his ex-lover, who is now his boss's wife, arrives at his apartment with groceries. Surprised to find another woman there cooking for him, she leaves. The cute neighbour, Kyoko, wants Kakeru to test the dish she is busy preparing. She says:

> *Chotto shôyu ga irimasen? Ajimi shite itadakimasu ka?*
> $Doesn't it need a little soy sauce? Won't you taste it?$

Kyoko extends a bite on a pair of chopsticks, which Kakeru obediently takes into his mouth. He immediately looks away and chews contemplatively for several seconds before answering. Finally, uttering '*gû gû*' (good good),[1] Kakeru makes the American 'OK' gesture and walks into another room. On the face of it this seems to be a positive endorsement. At least it isn't a negative assessment along the lines of 'Thy food is such as hath been belched on by infected lungs'.[2] Even so, the sense one gets is that Kakeru is trying hard not to hurt Kyoko's feelings by expressing his honest opinion. His delay before answering her, and the avoidance of eye contact, suggest that he's frantically searching for something kind to say. Our suspicions are confirmed in a later scene in which the ex-girlfriend describes the helpful neighbour: 'She was cooking a *really* tasteless-looking *nikujaga* [a potato and meat dish],' she informs her husband. Kakeru's problem of how to deliver an evaluation or assessment is a conversational landmine speakers in all societies face on a daily basis.

11.2 Negative assessments

In a provocative discussion of a major problem in intercultural communication, Rubin (1983) outlined the difficulties in determining when someone from another culture is saying 'no'. There is not only the issue of recognizing when denials, refusals, and other negative actions are being given, but also of figuring out which of the many possible manifestations of 'no' might be appropriate to particular social situations. Saying 'no' and similar interactional sticky-patches, such as the one that confronted Kakeru, are sometimes referred to with the technical label 'dispreferred response' by conversation analysts (Levinson 1983, Pomerantz 1984). This chapter will focus on negative assessments, which are just one type of dispreferred response.

In almost any conversation a speaker might offer evaluations of the topic of talk, their interlocutor, or another person or thing. C. Goodwin and M. Goodwin (1987) caution us that the term 'assessment' may refer to a variety of phenomena. It might be used to name a structural unit of talk such as an adjective (Kakeru's *'gû gû'* (good good) in the above scene). Assessments are not limited to just lexical or syntactic units, so may be displayed through nonsegmental behaviour such as intonation or gesture (Kakeru's 'OK' hand sign). Lastly, the term 'assessment' can be used to designate a type of speech act that offers an evaluation (all the features of Kakeru's response). It is this last sense that I have in mind when I examine negative assessments in interactions between Japanese and American co-workers.

Contrary to many folklinguistic theories about the respective languages, the discourse strategies most commonly used when giving negative assessments in English and Japanese are quite similar. In both languages, speakers regularly employ prefaces, qualifiers, token agreements, accounts, and pausing to mute disagreements or disapproval. Yet paradoxically, this is an aspect of conversation that sometimes results in uncomfortable encounters and intercultural misunderstanding. Before examining some instances of negative assessments found in Japanese and American co-worker interactions, let me first review the common structure underlying speech acts that offer evaluations.

Pomerantz (1975, 1984) was one of the first analysts to produce a meticulous description of the structure of assessments (and second assessments) in American English conversation. She discovered that when assessments are positive, they are usually stated clearly without delay or pausing. Negative assessments, by contrast, are delivered with all sorts of devices which serve to minimize potential conflict, risk of offence, or 'loss of face' (see Chapter 2). Instead of offering nakedly blunt evaluations, speakers typically employ one or more of the following features when doing a negative assessment:

(1) delay: responses follow silences and gaps, within a turn or between turns;
(2) repair: request for a clarification or a repeat;
(3) hesitation markers or fillers (uh, well, e::r);
(4) prefaces: markers that preface the response (sure but, let me see, sorta, kinda);
(5) token agreements: response framed as partial agreement followed by an assessment that modifies or downgrades it.

For example, in the following segment from Pomerantz (1984: 78) speaker D prefaces her negative assessment with a token agreement in one turn, and later with a hesitation marker in another turn:

A: D'yuh like it =
D: = (hhh) Yes I DO like it =
       = although I rreally:: =
       (Few seconds of intervening talk)
D: (hhh) Well I don't – I'm not a great fan of this type of a:rt

Although rarely linking their descriptions to Pomerantz's (1975, 1984) model, many scholars nevertheless point out that certain words or interjections in Japanese are routinely used to dilute negative responses or comments (Mizutani and Mizutani 1977, 1979, Neustupný 1987, Matsumoto 1985, Kinjo 1987). Rather than categorizing these as markers or prefaces to dispreferred actions in conversation, they are described as lexical hedges or speech act qualifications that deflect the force of a sentence. Examples of hesitation markers or fillers in Japanese are *anô* (well, e::r), *mâ* (somehow, well), *sâ* (well), and *â* (uh). A paralinguistic hesitation marker characteristic of Japanese is the inbreathed fricative, (.hss), which generally indicates an inability to agree with something or an unwillingness to express one's negative opinion (L. Miller 1991).

Typical Japanese prefaces to dispreferred actions are phrases such as *dô deshô ne* (I wonder), *sore mo kekkô desu ga* (that's fine too, but..), and *itcha nan da kedo* (a palatalized form of *itte wa nani da kado*, I hate to say it, but....). Perhaps the word most frequently used as a preface is *chotto* (a bit, a little, somewhat). Matsumoto (1985) has examined *chotto* in detail, observing that it may have the same function as English *sorta* or *kinda*. Often, *chotto* allows the speaker to avoid saying the negative descriptor altogether, as in:

> *Kare wa suteki kedo, koibito ni wa chotto...*
> $He's cool, but as a boyfriend he's sorta....$

Mizutani and Mizutani (1979) and Matsumoto (1985) also point out that a solitary *chotto* given as a response will function as a refusal or negative appraisal, as in:

> A: *dô omou?*
> $What do you think?$
> B: *chotto...*
> $It's a bit...$

Although the same structure for giving a negative assessment is found in English and in Japanese, speakers of one language may not always recognize the prefaces and hesitation markers of the other language. (Chapter 3 discusses Yeung's comparison of Cantonese and English indirectness in which there is similarly the use of different linguistic markers for the same linguistic function.) The result is that interactants, oblivious to these seemingly petty but actually critical fragments of language, may only hear the negative content of a message without the apparatus intended to soften it. Formulaic expressions that immediately signal an underlying or forthcoming negative assessment are not always recognized by non-native speakers, or else don't carry over into the target language when translated. In Japanese conversation, a few of these set phrases include *kangaete okimashô* (let's think about it) and *sore wa dô deshô ne* (I wonder about that). When speaking English, Japanese speakers may use the translated English versions of these expressions as if they had the same communicative functions, and assume that they will be interpreted as the prefacing moves to negative assessments they are intended to be. Likewise, American speakers of Japanese may also deploy inappropriate prefaces or hesitation markers when conveying negative assessments. For example, Neustupný (1987: 149) states that 'A frequent bad habit of foreigners is to hesitate by using the first person pronoun, something like *watashi wa....*'. Instead of indicating hesitation, *watashi wa* (as for me) as a floor-holder sounds excessively forceful and direct. It is possible, therefore, that these differences in the particular modes used to pave the way for negative assessments could very well account for a few of the pitfalls in intercultural interactions.

11.3 Researching intercultural interaction

One outcome of Japan's economic prosperity in the 1970s and the 1980s was a deluge of papers on communication between Japanese and non-Japanese. These papers, primarily directed at an American audience, prototypically took the form of dichotomized lists of dos and don'ts or oppositional traits. The authors often based their description on remembered personal experiences or narratives collected from others. Yet a fundamental lesson learned from the field of descriptive linguistics is that much of our knowledge and use of language are below the level of conscious awareness. Consequently, most speakers cannot be expected to reliably produce accurate descriptions of their own or others' communicative behaviour. This fact was revealed in early sociolinguistic studies by scholars such as Labov (1966), who looked at the use of /r/ in New York City, and Gumperz (1970), who examined the linguistic behaviour of Puerto Ricans in Jersey City. For instance, when Gumperz (1970) asked participants in his study whether they spoke Spanish or English at home, they claimed to exclusively use Spanish in that setting. However, when he tape-recorded their naturally-occurring speech there, he found that there was considerable, yet unconscious, 'code-switching' to English. (Code-switching is the alternation from one language to another within a single utterance or turn by one speaker, or by two or more speakers within a conversation.)

Dependence on data from consciously remembered or hypothesized instances of speech also colours many studies of intercultural communication, where we find numerous reified stereotypes, particularly of Japanese and American communication (Miller 1998). Research on Japanese and American refusals and methods for giving a negative response (Beebe *et al.* 1990, Ikoma and Shimura 1994, Imai 1981, Kinjo 1987, Saeki and O'Keefe 1994, Ueda 1974) has usually taken the form of comparative studies which rely on interview elicitation, questionnaires, and role-play rather than authentic intercultural interactions. One popular method for comparing negative answers or refusals is the 'Discourse Completion Task' (also known as a Production Questionnaire; see Chapter 15). Subjects are given a description of a situation to read and a sample conversation between two people, and are then asked to decide what they themselves might say in such a situation by filling in some blanks. Beebe *et al.* (1990) used this method for Japanese learners of English, and Ikoma and Shimura (1994) used it to compare refusals by American learners of Japanese with those by native Japanese speakers.

While such approaches are valuable in telling us about folk models of 'proper' language, they do not necessarily describe how speakers actually use language. In an effort to remedy this, LoCastro (1986) based her contrastive study of disagreements on data from actual conversations. She had a native-speaking Japanese assistant secretly record himself asking other native speakers about food preferences, specifically whether or not they liked avocados. LoCastro then asked other native English speakers about avocados in English, and later wrote down the answers. Aside from the ethical problem of recording people without their awareness, and the faultiness of memory as a source for accurate description of contexted language use, the study is still one step away from the real locus of our present concern: conversations that actually take place *between* Japanese and non-Japanese.

Simply collecting examples of conversations between Japanese and Americans will not guarantee that instances of negative assessment will surface. Luckily, I was able to record naturally-occurring talk at two advertising agencies in Tokyo, workplaces in which we would expect that co-workers will sometimes offer opinions of work in progress.[3] These conversations were audiotaped or videotaped openly with the full knowledge and consent of participants, who will be identified in the following data segments with pseudonyms. All of the participants spoke each other's languages with various degrees of proficiency. The tapes provide empirical documentation of what, in fact, actually happens in these intercultural interactions.[4] By 'naturally-occurring' talk I mean that people were not in artificial speech situations, but were in their normal work habitats doing their usual routines. I did not create or elicit any particular type of talk, but rather taped workers engaged in everyday business with each other. As Kottak (1999: 8) states about those people anthropologists attempt to study, 'It is not part of ethnographic procedure to manipulate them, control their environments, or experimentally induce certain behaviours.' The value of having such recordings is that they may reveal instances of problematic talk that will go unnoticed by participants, and therefore remain inaccessible through self-report methods of data collection.

11.4 Negative assessment in the intercultural workplace

The snippets of talk which follow illustrate co-workers who use the linguistic resources available to them to accomplish mutual work. Even when they have disagreements to resolve or complaints to air, all of them are ultimately working toward cooperation, consensus and resolution. These are not adversaries at the trade negotiation table or joint venture meeting, but fellow members of the same firm who sit next to each other day by day. Too much of our prior research on Japanese–American communication focuses on what happens between virtual strangers trying to wrangle deals out of each other. The result is a list of 'cultural' traits or behaviours which are supposed to characterize members of each group. But a model like that falls very short of describing what is actually seen and heard in authentic encounters. These social actors are embedded in a work environment in which all of them, Japanese and American alike, equivocate and waffle, or alternatively blurt out cheeky asides and direct requests or complaints. What concerns us about their identities as Japanese or American is whether or not they hold different linguistic and/or cultural assumptions about specific settings, tasks, or behaviours which will produce interpretations that differ from other interactants.

For instance, in addition to the problems associated with recognition of the linguistic forms in which negative assessments are delivered, cultural assumptions about the nature of an interaction, and the social relationships of the participants, will add other dimensions of complexity. In this first segment we see how all these possibilities come together to produce mutually negative interpretations. In this conversation an American copywriter named Ember (E) and one of his Japanese co-workers named Nakada (N) are reviewing some advertisements for which Ember has provided the English copy. As an account executive, Nakada is in a position of more authority in this firm. Here they are talking about one ad in particular:

Extract 1

```
1   E      I mean yuh can see through it right
2          you don't have to use your imagination you can
3          see every little thing so-(it's?) right
4          (it?) plays off of the-the visual
5          (leaves?) nothing << wh > to the imagination >
6               (0.5)
7   N      (.hss) is that so?
8               (0.2)
9   N       idea is cl-very clear to me [now]
10  E                                  [no:w]
11  N      this video can do everything =
12  E      = do everything
```

```
13          (0.8)
14 N        but too much pitch for the vi(hihi)sual
15 E        too (hihi) much? [no no no no]
16 N                        [too much visual] no?
17 E        no (.) no I don't think so
18               (0.2)
19 N        {smacks lips} (.hhh) maybe
20 E        (maybe?)
21 N        ye[ahh]
22 E          [I thin] I think it's okay
```

After Ember describes what the advertisement is about in lines 1–5, we would expect an assessment of some sort from Nakada. Instead, there is a silence in line 6, followed in line 7 by Nakada giving an inbreathed fricative or (.hss), and a repair initiator 'is that so?' This in turn is followed by a weak agreement preface in lines 9 and 11, after which he actually gives his negative assessment in line 14. Here we have a classic example of a negative assessment as proposed by Pomerantz (1984). So why is there a problem?

At the conclusion of this conversation (not transcribed here) Nakada tells Ember to 'think about' this ad copy a little longer. As mentioned already, *kangaete okimashô* (let's think about it) is a formulaic preface in Japanese for a negative assessment that, when used alone, signals that something 'won't do' or 'isn't right'. By telling Ember to 'think about it' Nakada is using this English phrase as if it has the same communicative function as it does in Japanese, and that it will be interpreted accordingly (as a rejection). Yet a few days later Ember was surprised when he found out that this particular copy had been excluded from the campaign. He had most likely understood Nakada's 'maybe' in line 19 and 'yeah' of line 21 as showing a type of agreement, and therefore didn't identify Nakada's negative assessment to 'think about it' as a type of refusal.

Nakada's comment to Ember also brings to light another misinterpretation present during their conversation. This relates to what sort of communicative task each participant assumes is in progress. I spoke with the participants later, and found out that Ember thought the meeting with Nakada was simply in order for him to explain his ideas for the ads. Nakada, on the other hand, saw the meeting as an occasion for a senior (himself) to tell a subordinate (Ember) which ad copy had been selected for use and which had been retracted. Because of Ember's assumptions about the situation, he gave his personal opinions freely, disagreeing with Nakada's negative assessment and producing his own assessment in line 22, 'I think it's okay'. From Nakada's perspective, Ember's expression of a differing opinion would be inappropriate, not seen as the exchange of ideas intended but as an uncooperative reluctance to accept his decision. Nakada interpreted Ember's behaviour as churlishly argumentative, while Ember thought Nakada had deliberately misled him by not stating his wishes clearly.

Interpretations of negative assessments, even when offered in 'correctly' encoded forms, will critically depend on whether or not the offering of a disagreement or disapproval is even considered appropriate at all in that setting, or between those participants. In the next segment we find that an American who offers a negative assessment to his Japanese co-workers, although delicately coded in hedged forms, is still interpreted as 'too direct'. Another copywriter named Moran has been asked to edit and check the English translation of a Japanese script for use in subtitling a television commercial. He is explaining to the two creators of the commercial and a division head why he has changed their direct translation of the Japanese text. Here Moran is concerned about the line in the translation that says 'We brush our teeth together but we use different toothpaste'. When delivering his negative assessment of this scene, which contains images and text pertaining to teeth-brushing in a commercial which is not about toothpaste, Moran delicately dances around the problem.

Extract 2
1 ....so you see the shot of the toothbrush with the
2 different kinds of toothpaste on them and you talk
3 about that and you immediately understand but
4 you've never said 'well we brush our teeth differently'
5 ahh which is kinda a s::tra::nge-I mean its jus not a-
6 (0.3)
7 (hhh)
8 (0.2)
9 it's not a pleasant image (hhh) to start a commercial
10 with necessarily ahh so: I ahh don't say it directly
11 since you have a visual but

He prefaces his negative evaluation of this image with many pauses, qualifiers ('kinda' and 'necessarily'), outbreaths, stretched syllables ('s::tra::nge' and 'so:'), hesitation markers and self-interruptions. Even so, his Japanese co-workers later characterized him as directly expressing inappropriate disagreement because they had a different assumption about why they were meeting. They thought the conference with Moran was simply to have him check the grammatical correctness of their English, not to offer his advice on a better or more culturally appropriate translation. His offering of a negative assessment, no matter that it was indirectly produced, was therefore seen as too straightforward an expression of opinion.

The next two segments concern 'second assessments' (Pomerantz 1984), wherein a speaker's assessment of something or someone invites a second assessment from the recipient. In each of the following cases, the Americans use a form of sarcasm for their second assessments, strategies that do not function in the ways intended. Sarcasm is here understood in Haiman's (1998) sense of communication which encodes the metamessage 'I don't mean this'. According to both Haiman (1998) and Adachi (1996), Japanese and English employ many of the same linguistic strategies for marking an utterance in the sarcastive modality. For instance, both languages use hyperformality, exaggerated pitch, repetition, stylized intonation, and other indexing features. Even so, speakers of one language do not necessarily recognize when sarcasm is being performed in another language. Sarcastic assessments such as 'whatever', commonly found in American English, are often interpreted literally. In addition, sarcasm, like compliments and other speech actions, are not always used the same way in both cultures. In this segment a clerk named Fuji (F) approaches two co-workers, a Japanese, Makino (M) and an American, Crane (C), to get advice on how to write a wedding salutation in English for someone who is getting married. She asks them 'what's a cute and cool thing to say in English?'

Extract 3

1 M	*are okurun no? dempô?*	
	$are you sending that? telegram?$	
2 F	*ya-anô kâdo kaiten no, ima*	
	$ah-well I'm writing a card now$	
3 M	congratulations *de iin ja nai*	
	$Isn't 'congratulations' okay?$	
4 F	congratulations *nan ka sa ajikenai ja nai*	
	$But isn't it that something like um 'congratulations' is bland?$	
5 C	whaddiya want, poetry?	
6 F	poetry, un	

After Makino suggests 'congratulations', Fuji gives a negative assessment of this candidate greeting as lacking flavour (line 4).

Crane then gives a sarcastic assessment of her display of disapproval, as if she's expecting too much for something as trivial as a card. Yet Fuji accepts his formulation innocently with the agreement token 'un' as if he's posing a legitimate question rather than the sarcasm intended. After her happy response Crane must have regretted his wisecrack, because he immediately crafted a detailed greeting for her to use. The next example of American sarcasm, however, simply added to the already existing tension and confusion.

In this next segment an American account executive named Penn (P) is the recipient of implied criticism from another account executive, Muramoto (M), who has more seniority in the firm and often 'checks' his work. A third co-worker named Aoyama had previously complained to Muramoto that Penn is spending too much time with the client from one account (Mr Jones), while neglecting their client from another account (Mr Adams), so Muramoto talks to Penn about modifying his behaviour. After Penn receives Muramoto's critique, he produces a sarcastic quip disguised as gratitude.

Extract 4

1	M	it's OK to go in an around with Mr Jones, but now
2		also now you should, na-be good friends with Mr
3		Adams at K-company
4	P	oh
5	M	so, un, don't focus on Mr Jones only, *wakatta*? ($got it$)?
6	P	Thank Aoyama-*san* ($Mr.$) for arranging my social
7		calendar for me

Penn does not respond to Muramoto's negative assessment and request with an agreement token or compliance token, but rather with a flat, free-standing 'oh'. This 'oh' simply acknowledges receipt of Muramoto's words, but does not invite further explanation or elaboration (Heritage 1984). Muramoto pursues a compliance response from Penn by upgrading the suggestion (now you should ...) into something like an order (don't focus on ...) in line 4. The Japanese tag here, *wakatta*? ('got it?'), especially when issued by a senior, is intended to elicit strong compliance such as 'yes'. Instead, using a completely flat intonation and a deadpan facial expression, Penn produces his oblique dig. This sarcasm deflects and masks his discomfort at both Aoyama for snitching on him, and Muramoto for criticizing him and telling him what to do, all of which may be seen as threats to his face (both his 'quality face' and his 'identity face' – see Chapter 2). Muramoto, too, was left feeling frustrated that the issue was unresolved. She was annoyed by Penn's lack of consciousness and respect for the hierarchical relations between them, which would be a threat to her 'identity face' (see also Chapter 13).

An interesting and more successful tactic for dealing with negative assessments unique to settings like these in which two languages are available for communication is to switch from one language to the other language. Those unaccustomed to it may find the constant code-switching between Japanese and English odd or discordant. Yet both intersentential and intrasentential switching are very common, and serve a multitude of functions. For instance, code-switching may help buttress solidarity and identity (Miller 1995). In the next bit of talk, Crane (C) and Ono (O) are looking over a heap of photographs for use in an advertisement layout. Ono selects one from the pile and sets it in front of Crane, who examines it and then rejects it as 'a bit boring'.

Extract 5a

1 C   *kono shashin wa chotto tsumaranai*
             $this photo is a bit boring$
2 O   *tsumaranai?*
             $boring?$
3 C   *unn*
4 O   *kochi wa ii ja nai*
             $here is nice isn't it?$

Crane's first negative assessment *tsumaranai* (boring) is mitigated nicely with the preface marker *chotto* (a bit). Ono doesn't really agree with him (she does a repeat), but the two of them continue to look through the pile, searching for more candidate photos. Ono picks out another and suggests a specific placement in the layout for it (line 5). Crane rejects this photo too, but switches to English when giving this second negative assessment:

Extract 5b

5 O   *ja kochi mô ii wa? kore to kore to (.) kochi no hô ga ii yo*
             $ah then here is also okay? this and this and (.) HERE is better$
6 C   it's easy to see the cracks on the cover

Crane nixes Ono's selection of the first photo in Japanese, while he rejects the second selection in English. The code-switching serves to distance or buffer the subsequent negative observation. Speakers display a reluctance to deliver too many negative assessments in a row, and so, in essence, begin a new series in the other language. This pattern is also characteristic of the next example.

In this segment, members of an account team are talking about what media markets to use in order to reach an audience of upscale young women. The possible media under consideration are train station posters, radio spots and magazines. Tanaka (T) prefers the magazine choices, Cosmo (Cosmopolitan) or Abbey Road, over the other two options. The American, Penn (P), however, is attracted to the idea of spending money on train station posters.

Extract 6

1 P	OK you guys figure it out please recommend magazine Cosmo or Abbey Road	
2 T	Cosmo or Abbey Road, *hai*	
	$right$	
3 P	or radio or more posters	
4 T	poster enough I think enough	
5 P	maybe Nagoya	
6 T	*Nagoya mô ii*	
	$Nagoya is fine already$	
7 P	*dame?*	
	$no good?$	
8 T	Nagoya is country town	

In line 4, Tanaka gives a negative assessment of the idea of more train station posters in English, but when Penn suggests adding Nagoya station in line 5, Tanaka switches to Japanese to deliver his next negative assessment. When Penn challenges this with a repair initiator in line 7, Tanaka code-switches back to English. His use of 'country town' is how he translated the Japanese word *inaka*, which means something closer to 'outback' or 'boondocks'. Speakers in both instances have 'used up' their opportunities for delivering a series of negative assessments in one language, and switch to the other language in order to maintain goodwill.

I might also note that in these segments, as well as in other intercultural conversations in the data, participants' speech sometimes shades into 'foreigner talk',[5] a simplified form of language produced for non-native speakers. One potential for further study is to determine whether or not the use of a foreigner talk register results in stripped-down utterances in which crucial bits such as prefaces and hesitation markers are refined away as dross, leaving the remaining assessments and other dispreferred speech actions unnaturally bald.

11.5 Conclusion

As the last two examples illustrate, talk between Japanese and American co-workers is not always fraught with difficulty and misunderstanding. The exchange of negative assessments may seamlessly unfold without participants becoming miffed or uncomfortable. But when there are misunderstandings, folk theory and popular stereotypes would lead us to blame Clint Eastwood-style Americans who blast their way through every conversation, or compromisingly ambiguous Japanese who produce a trail of uncertainty in their wakes. But none of the humans who speak in these tapes refrain from expressing their ideas or opinions, and each of them struggles to produce speech in which negative assessments are moderated or cushioned. Even so, misinterpretations sometimes bubble up into the tiny crevices of talk. Prefaces and hesitation markers intended to pillow negative assessments are not 'heard' as such by colleagues, or else there is a mismatch in cultural assumptions about when or to whom assessments should be offered at all. It is here in the finely-tuned traces of everyday talk that recurring misinterpretations and patterned misunderstandings arise and, eventually, assume the guise of grand characterizations of entire populations and ethnic groups.

Discussion questions

1 Why are negative assessments potentially face-threatening? What aspect(s) of face do they threaten?
2 Under what circumstances do you find it particularly difficult to give a negative assessment? Under what circumstances (if any) do you find it relatively easy to give a negative assessment? Try to explain the factors that give rise to the difference.
3 Look again at Extracts 1 and 2, and consider the cultural factors that led to the communicative problems. How do these differences correspond to the description given in Chapter 2, section 2.9, of potential areas of cultural variation that can affect rapport?
4 During the course of one day, consciously attend to and keep track of every time you refuse a request or invitation, or someone else refuses a request or invitation you issue. Are any of the strategies you find similar to those used in negative assessments (e.g. delay, pausing, hesitation markers, prefaces, repair)?

Notes

1. The Japanese word *gû* (good) is a loanword borrowed from English. For a review and analysis of the incorporation of English into the Japanese language, see Miller (1997).
2. From Shakespeare's *Pericles: Prince of Tyre*, Act 4 Scene 6.
3. Moeran (1996) has written an excellent ethnographic description of a Japanese advertising agency.
4. Discussion of these naturally-occurring interactions are also found in L. Miller 1995, 1994a, 1994b and 1991. Although a few of the transcribed segments presented here are also found in these prior studies, the remainder were recently transcribed and analysed for this chapter.
5. The concept of a foreigner talk register was first proposed by Ferguson (1971). Studies of foreigner talk in Japanese include Iino (1996) and Skoutarides (1986).

12

Impression Management in East and West German Job Interviews

Karin Birkner and Friederike Kern

12.1 Introduction

What happens if someone who until very recently belonged to a separate speech community suddenly has to compete with members of a different, (more or less) unknown speech community in a highly competitive labour market (defined by the rules of the latter) and is confronted with stylistic and interpretative patterns of a largely unfamiliar communicative genre? Based on a selection of authentic job interviews, as well as eleven narrative interviews with personnel managers conducted by us, we investigate differences in impression management between applicants from the former GDR and FRG.[1]

This chapter will explore several aspects of German–German communication in job interviews with regard to their cultural specificity. Firstly, we will give an overview of the theoretical and methodological approach that our study is based on. Secondly, we will consider some features typical of job interviews. We will then discuss two main areas of differences in language use between East and West Germans: personal perspectives and disagreement in job interviews.

12.2 Theoretical and methodological preliminaries

Our approach is largely inspired by conversation analysis (henceforth CA; for an overview see Levinson 1983). CA postulates that no external categories should be used in analysis. Instead, analytical categories are obtained empirically and derived directly from data, and need to correspond as closely as possible to those that the participants themselves can be proved to orient to in interaction (participation categories). Forms and structures of language are understood to be intersubjectively produced in discourse and are investigated in terms of their interactive function. As a consequence, much attention is paid to the course of interaction and the participants' contribution to it.

However, there are limits to data analysis if CA's postulates are followed strictly. For example, it is difficult to include in the analysis situational factors such as the role of participants, distribution of speakers' rights, and so on, which could explain the participants' selection of specific communicative styles. Hence, we have included the notion of communicative genre (see Chapter 2) to account for such situational elements. Furthermore, we considered it appropriate to include ethnographic information such as interviewers' accounts and interpretations of specific verbal behaviour, since we consider these to be part of their knowledge as competent speech community members.

12.3 Data

The study described here is based on two types of data.[2] Firstly, 41 authentic job interviews (22 with East and 19 with West Germans) were recorded in seven companies in 1994–5. Secondly, we interviewed 11 staff members from personnel departments of different companies to gain a certain understanding of job interviews and to collect ethnographic data on common stereotypes of East and West Germans and their respective linguistic behaviour. We also recorded several discussions of interviewer teams evaluating candidates immediately after a job interview.

12.4 Typical features of job interviews

One of the main reasons why job interviews were chosen as the focus of this study is that they were a comparatively unknown communicative genre in East Germany. In the former GDR the allocation of jobs, especially for leading positions, was based on different selection procedures. In the West job interviews are important gatekeeping situations and determine social participation or marginalization – even more so in times of increasing unemployment and economic crisis. In the Western social and cultural context, they are closely associated with rules of Western economic discourse in which existing hierarchies are often downplayed and the notion of competition plays an important role. However, the changing social realities in Germany 'after the wall' have forced Eastern speakers to adjust to such new forms of communication to at least a certain extent.

Impression management and positive self-presentation are the applicant's main goals in a job interview. We understand strategies of self-presentation as elements of positive facework and part of the construction of a speaker's social identity. In job interviews constructions of identity are at least partly coordinated with genre-specific goals and function to present the applicants as suitable candidates for the job in question. However, applicants want to present themselves not only as suitable candidates, but also as friendly and likeable people. Likewise, interviewers evaluate the applicants' answers not only by what is being said but also by how it is said (cf. Adelswärd 1988).

The sharp asymmetry between applicant and interviewer is reflected in one of the main features of job interviews: their so-called 'hidden agenda' (Adelswärd 1988: 77: 'the explicit and implicit criterion of success'; cf. Roberts 1985). Interviewers often have some sort of checklist of job allocation criteria which the applicants are not told about: 'So the whole interviewer's "agenda" is hidden from the candidate. The interviewer's line of questioning has a hidden purpose that the candidate may not pick up on' (Roberts 1985: 37). While questioning the applicants the interviewers try to elicit statements relevant to the hidden agenda without making this explicit.

Nevertheless interviewers make an effort to let job interviews seem relaxed, informal and equal conversations. This can be seen in the formulations at the beginning of many interviews where participants are informed about what is going to follow (e.g. 'let's keep this informal and just get to know one another'). However, applicants have to be aware that they are the sole object of an omnipresent evaluation. They try to present themselves as positively as possible in order to gain a favourable decision, while the interviewers have the initiative of choice. On the other hand, the interviewer's main concern is to find out 'if it is put on, ... is he just a good actor and pulling the wool over our eyes, or is he for real?' (in the words of one personnel manager). Consequently, we must distinguish two seman-tic levels: a surface level with an explicit agenda, where the interlocutors talk about facts and dates (biographies, qualifications, the enterprise etc.), and a hidden level, where the utterances are always related to hidden aims, messages and interpretative foils.

Because of the hidden agenda, experienced applicants have a clear advantage over inexperienced ones (cf. Roberts 1985; Sarangi 1994: 171: 'situational literacy'). And indeed studies by Gumperz *et al.*

(1979), Gumperz (1992b), Akinnaso and Seabrook Ajirotutu (1982) and Sarangi (1994) demonstrate that lack of knowledge of the rules of the genre, and especially of the hidden dimensions, may contribute to discrimination against minority members: 'The job interview is one of the most culture-specific events we all have to face' (Roberts and Sayers 1987: 114).

Knowing what makes a job interview a job interview, i.e. familiarity with the genre's special conditions and constraints, is part of the shared knowledge of a community. The Western genre follows Western linguistic norms of positive self-presentation, and frequently these norms are not shared by East German applicants. In our study divergent understandings of the genre prove to be a major factor in the different courses which job interviews take with East and West German applicants.

12.5 Linguistic differences between East and West Germans in job interviews

There are many facets to impression management and positive self-presentation in job interviews, and these vary according to levels of linguistic choice. In the following sections, we will take a closer look at two strategies of self-presentation. One will concern the constitution of subjective and objective perspectives in talk and their pragmatic impact. The second will have to do with the discursive organization of agreement and disagreement.

12.5.1 Perspectives on self-presentation

In our project, we compared similar question/answer sequences to gain an understanding of the ways cultural factors constitute perspectives of East and West German candidates and West German interviewers.

The notion of perspective refers to somebody's standpoint, or point of view, or mode of perception (cf. Graumann 1989). Common to all conceptions of 'perspective' is the view that sensual and cognitive perception is constituted in relation to a person's spatio-temporal or cognitive standpoint. In language, the ability to set and take perspectives (or standpoints) is understood to be a basic communicative competence (cf. Graumann 1989). Interlocutors mutually produce and fix subjective and objective perspectives in the course of interaction; they share and/or negotiate them.

In contextualized dialogue, the use of perspectives depends

furthermore on general, genre-specific goals and intentions on the one hand (cf. Linell and Jönsson 1991) and on various local context conditions on the other. Adelswärd (1988: 116) argues that candidates' ability to take specific perspectives on themselves is one of the main criteria for their success or failure in job interviews: 'A successful applicant positions herself when telling her life-story at the perfect distance, she is neither too impersonal nor too personal'.

More specifically, candidates should clearly set their personal perspectives on certain issues so as to inform the interviewer of their interests and preferences, especially when asked for their motive for applying. Thus, positive self-presentation is partially dependent on foregrounding the individual and stating personal views on certain topics.

In what follows, we will look closely at the various ways speakers verbally express and focus on subjective and objective perspectives.

Example 1: Eastern applicant

1	I:	*WAS: war der ANlaß; daß sie sich (.) grade auf diese*
2		*stelle bewERben? (.) und eh: wi:e eh was GLAUben sie*
3		*aufgrund ihrer bisherigen tätigkeit (.) eh für dieses*
4		*stelle MITbringen zu können.*
5		*{Auslassung 9 Zeilen}*
6	A:	*ja und von den QUELlen her, und von den (.)*
7		*archiVArien die im stadtarchiv liegen, (.) << acc > doch*
8		*das IS (also/eine?) DACHte ich mir is eine sehr*
9		*interessante > AUFgabe? (.) SEIN KOEnnte? (.) für*
10		*JEmanden der das archiv = beARbeitet? (1) das*
11		*SCHRIFTgut?*

1	I:	WHY have you appLIED for this job of all jobs? (.)
2		and how eh: wha:t eh do you THINK you can
3		BRING to this job because of your present work?
5		{9 lines left out}
6	A:	well and because of the SOUrces and because of the (.)
7		ARchive files that are in the archive (.) << acc > indeed
8		that is (well/a?) I THOUGHT to myself is a very
9		interesting > JOB? (.) COULD be? (.) for SOMEone
10		who WORKS at the archive?
11		(1) the WRItings?

The interviewer explicitly asked for the applicant's perspective on the matter ('why have you applied for this job of all jobs'). However, by shifting to a different perspective, the candidate does not answer the question from the requested point of view.

First, the candidate's self-repair from 'is' (*realis*) to 'could be' (*irrealis*) turns an objective fact ('is a very interesting job') into a hypothesis. He places himself in this hypothetical world by setting his own perspective ('I thought to myself') but then initiates a significant perspectival shift by using the impersonal pronoun 'someone'. Consequently, the candidate expresses his personal perspective on the subject, that is to say that the job would be interesting for an archivist, only by indirect reference to himself. He backgrounds his own personal perspective more and more, and replaces it by an unspecified other's perspective. His account is consequently transferred from an individual, personal mode of presentation to a general one.

The candidate's presentation of his reasons for the application has remarkable consequences for the interview. In his next turn, the interviewer immediately challenges the applicant's suitability for the job in a face-threatening way. His reaction indicates that the candidate's self-presentation has not succeeded in convincing him of his suitability.

As the next example shows, perspectives are not always discussed explicitly but are nevertheless oriented to and therefore of interactive importance to both speaker and listener. In the following extract the interviewer asks the candidate to give a hypothetical other-evaluation of her positive qualities.

Example 2: Eastern applicant

```
1   I2:   und wie haben = sie = sich mit ihren kollEgen und
2         kollEginnen denn verstanden?
2   I3:   {räuspert sich}
3   B1:   sehr GUT.
4   I2:   ja,
5   B1:   ja.
6         (1)
7   I2:   was: (.) konnten die so; (0.5) oder was würden DIE
9         SAgen, wenn wir sie FRAgen würden, was sie besonders
10        an ihnen SCHÄtzen?
```

```
1   I2:   and how did you get on then with your
2         COlleagues?
3   I3:   {clears her throat}
4   A:    very WELL
```

5	I2:	yes,
6	A:	yes.
7	A:	(1)
8	I2:	<u>wha:t (.) did they; (0.5) or what would they</u>
9		<u>SAY if we ASKed them what they particularly</u>
10		<u>LIKE about you?</u>

The interviewer carefully constructs a hypothetical scene in which the candidate's former colleagues' perspective is asked for, not her own perspective. So instead of asking 'what do you think makes you an amiable colleague?', she is asked what her former colleagues thought of her. It is now the interviewee's interactively established task to adopt this hypothetical perspective and discuss her own qualities from her former colleagues' standpoint. However, the applicant does not do this. Instead she initiates a complex perspectival shift that allows her to answer the question from a different point of view. Let's take a look at her response:

Example 3: Eastern applicant (continues Example 2)

11	A:	*(hh) (0.5) joa. (1) das is(=ne) gute FRAge; (1)*
12		*schnalzt} man muß EIgentlich, wie jesacht,*
13		*wie alle anderen AUch, PÜNKTlich sein,*
14		*man muß na [türlich, (hh)*
15	I2:	*[<<p> mhm,>*
16		*(0.5) wie jeSACHT, weil ja auch jeder seine*
17		*arbeit HAT, seine KUNden, daß man*
18		*dran intressIERT is, diese alle ANzurufen,*

11	A:	(hh) (0.5) well (1) that's a good QUESTion; (1)
12		{clicks tongue} one has to be, as I said,
13		LIKE everybody ELse, be ON TIME,
14		one has to of [course (hh)]
15	I2:	[<<p> mhm,>]
16		(0.5) as I SAID, because everybody HAS
17		their job, their CLIents, and one is
18		INterested, wants to RING them all,

After an introductory remark ('that's a good question'), the candidate introduces a change of perspective by shifting to the impersonal pronoun 'one'. The applicant does not speak from her colleagues' point of view, rather she refers to generalized 'common-sense knowledge' about intergroup behaviour and relates this to a sense of moral obligation ('one has to'). Thus, the candidate does not take up the specific 'other' perspective of her former colleagues as requested, but instead draws on some higher authority to take an unspecified third person perspective. This shift in perspective allows her to discuss her own positive qualities indirectly and more generally.

During the next few minutes, the interviewer attempts several more times to elicit 'other' perspectives on the candidate's qualities. Again, the candidate shifts to a general perspective by introducing some higher moral authority as a reference point: one does not ask other people what they think about oneself. Thus, she refuses more or less directly to answer the question. A dramatic divergence of perspectives develops until finally the interviewer drops the topic.

The cultural dimension of the constitution and expression of perspectives in the job interviews has already been hinted at. The results show that West and East German candidates' conversational styles differ with respect to perspectivization when they present themselves in job interviews. The examples point to a recurrent pattern in establishing perspectives in dialogue that is possibly culturally bound. Eastern candidates display a tendency to shift to unspecified, generalized perspectives in a variety of contexts. The examples given illustrate that (a) the subjective perspective is replaced by an unspecified impersonal one and (b) requests for an individual perspective are answered with a generalized one referring to a higher authority.

If we look at the West German use of perspectives in similar contexts, a different picture emerges. Even though, in comparable contexts, West Germans do not always establish their personal views directly and also refer to others' perspectives,[3] they do not shift to impersonalized, general perspectives based upon common sense to back up their argument.

Interviews with members from personnel departments confirm the observed differences. Many interviewees took the candidates' openness concerning especially private topics (such as one's qualities and weaknesses) to be one of the striking distinctions between East and West Germans. They found East German applicants to be more evasive on the matter, talking in 'general phrases' and in 'expressions concerning the collective', whereas they considered the West Germans to be more accurate 'saying more precisely that and that I want and I mean it'.

Assuming we are dealing with two distinct cultural perspectives here, we can construct two sets of perspectivization rules. As far as East Germans are concerned, a rule might exist according to which questions about personal qualities, goals or ambitions are answered by reference to impersonalized perspectives. West German applicants, on the contrary, might be said to follow a rule that allows them to state their subjective perspectives more openly or, alternatively, relate to individualized others' perspectives. However, such rules only concern linguistic practices; even though they might be shaped by a sociocultural norm about the value of modesty, it is difficult to find evidence in the data alone for genuine differences in values. In any case, the analyst must be careful when using such external categories as explanatory devices for linguistic differences.

12.5.2 Disagreement

We will now look at how applicants deal with agreement and disagreement in job interviews (see Chapter 10 for dissent organization of (West) Germans). Overt disagreement on the part of an applicant is not very common in a job interview; however, interviewers are more likely to disturb the harmony and to express disagreement. This can be related to the participants' differing goals: the applicant aims to give a positive impression, while the interviewer wants to evaluate candidates and select the best.

To ensure a certain comparability of East and West Germans we looked at applicants' reactions to 'critical questions' by interviewers. By 'critical questions', as you will see in the examples, interviewers implicitly or explicitly bring out an inconsistency in the applicant's self-presentation. In order to not jeopardize their goal of presenting themselves as suitable candidates, applicants must disagree. Expressing disagreement, however, is conversationally precarious since it contradicts the preference system for agreement (cf. Sacks 1987, Pomerantz 1984, Kotthoff 1993). How applicants react to the conflicting demands of global agreement versus local disagreement is illustrated by the following two examples.

Example 4: Eastern applicant
{Kontext: der Bewerber macht sein Abitur in Abendkursen nach}
1   I1:   << p > mhm, > (3) beLAStet das nich? also so (.) so
2   abiTUR und AR [beiten?
3   A: [(gut?) der (.) TACH is ziemlich
4   VOLLjepackt; aber ich WOHne noch zuhause, un[d
5   I1:   [mhm;

6 A: (1) *gehe MORgens aus = dem haus, und komme ABbends;*
7 (0.5) *gegen ZEHN wieder,* (2)
8 *ESse noch was;*
9 I1: << *p* > *abends [um zehn wieder* > *ach so* << *f* > *dann;*
10 A: [(???)
11 I1: (0.5) *von der SCHUle* > *dann [schon.*
12 A: [*ja ja geNAU.*
13 [(????)
14 I1: [*is das JEden abend.*
15 A: *JEden abend.*
16 I1: (1) << *p* > *oijoijoi.* (1.5) *puh* (0.5) *MEIne GÜte.* > (0.5)
17 *eh* (0.5) *MEInen sie nicht; daß das vielleicht* (.)
18 *probLEme bereiten könnte, wenn man sich irgendwo neu*
19 *EINarbeitet.* (2) *also jetzt in SO einer phase zu*
20 *WECHseln.*
21 A: *wäre* (.) *MÖGlich. ja.*
22 (2)
23 I1: << *p* > *mhm* >
24 A: *(aber?) eh:*
25 I1: (0.5) {*schnalzt*} *also daß letztendlich dann durch*
26 *dadurch ihr abiTUR leidet.*
27 A: *neu EINarbeiten* (0.5) *würd ich* (0.5) *verGLEIchen mit*
28 *der entwicklung eines* (.) *komplexen neuen proJEKtes.*
29 (0.5) *wie ich = s letztes jahr geMACHT habe.*
30 (1.2)
31 I1: << *p* > *mhm.* > (1) (*hh*) (1) *ja GUT. aber das is eh* (0.5)
32 *so oder SO.* (0.5) *es is natürlich immer beLAStung.*
33 *nich,*
34 A: << *pp* > *mhm,* >
35 I1: *und es geht immer nur auf KOSten* (.) *oder es geht MEIst*
36 *immer auf kosten von irgndeiner sache dann.* (*hh*) (2)
37 << *pp* > *mhm* > (2.2) {*schnalzt*} *eh:* (0.5)
38 *zu WANN* (.) *würden sie denn zur verFÜgung stehn.*

{context: the applicant is preparing for his Abitur (University entrance examinations) in evening classes}

1 I1: << p > mhm, > (3) isn't that STRESSful? I mean (.)
2 Abitur and WORK[ing?
3 A: [(okay?) the (.) DAY is pretty
FULL; but I still LIVE at home, an[d
5 I1: [mhm;
6 A: (1) leave the house in the MORNing, and come back

```
7              again in the evening; (0.5) at about TEN, (2)
8              have something to eat;
9    I1:       << p > in the evening [at ten > oh I see << f > then;
10   A:                            [(? ? ?)
11   I1:       (0.5) SCHO [ol >
12   A:                     [yes yes right.
13             [(? ? ?)
14   I1:       [that's EVery evening.
15   A:        EVery evening.
16   I1:       (1) << p > wow (1.5) huh (0.5) MY GOODness. > (0.5)
17             eh (0.5) don't you THINK; that could possibly (.)
18             cause problems, if you're just starting
19             on a new JOB somewhere. (2) I mean to
20             CHANGE jobs in a situation like that.
21   A:        might do (.) POSSible. yes.
22             (2)
23   I1:       << p > mhm >
24   A:        (but?) eh:
25   I1:       (0.5) {clicks tongue} I mean that ultimately
26             your A levels would suffer.
27   A:        starting out on a new JOB (0.5) I would (0.5) comPARE
28             to developing a (.) complex new PROject.
29             (0.5) like I DID last year.
30             (1.2)
31   I1:       << p > mhm. > (1) (hh) (1) oKAY. but it's either eh (0.5)
32             one thing or another. (0.5) of course it's always stressful.
33             isn't it,
34   A:        << pp > mhm, >
35   I1        and something is always going to SUffer (.) or ALmost
36             always something's going to suffer. (hh) (2)
37             << pp > mhm > (2.2) {clicks tongue} eh: (0.5)
38             WHEN (.) would you be aVAIlable then.
```

Upon being asked about his employment goals, the East German
applicant mentions that he is taking evening classes (data not shown).
The leading question 'isn't that stressful? I mean (.) Abitur and
working?' could prima facie express empathy, whereas in fact the
interviewer is trying to find out if his future employee will be able to
start a new job involving additional strain. In this context a clear
expression of disagreement from the applicant is needed. But instead
he produces an agreement preface (cf. Pomerantz 1978: 99) '(okay)
the (.) day is pretty full', followed by an adversative 'but', which

introduces a contrasting statement. This contrast, however, remains implicit: 'but I still live at home'. Then he goes on to outline his daily routine. Even though he is making an effort to express the opposite, he seems to lead a rather stressful lifestyle, especially if you take into account the importance that many interviewers assign to hobbies and recreational activities.

The emphatic reaction of the interviewer signals his disagreeing conclusion 'wow (1.5) huh (0.5) my goodness'. In the next leading question the interviewer's doubts about the candidate's suitability are more apparent. But again, instead of a clear contradiction the applicant produces a 'weak agreement': 'might do (.) possible. yes.'. The falling final intonation indicates that he has nothing to add, but the interviewer's reactions (a quiet continuer, produced after a pause of 2 seconds, and a precision) show that he is not satisfied with the answer. The applicant continues: 'starting out on a new job (0.5) I would (0.5) compare to developing a (.) complex new project. (0.5) like I did last year'. Again, the argumentative reference remains implicit and he fails to explain that despite evening classes he managed the job well; nor does he refute the negative implications of the interviewer's leading question.

The interviewer's final comment indicates that his doubts have not been dispelled. What he previously articulated as questions ('isn't that stressful?' and 'don't you think; that could possibly (.) cause problems', he now asserts directly: 'of course it's always stressful' and 'something is always going to suffer (.) or ALmost always'. The subject then changes, and the applicant's opportunities for a counter-argument are exhausted.

If we review the applicant's answers as a whole, we detect a tendency to avoid disagreement and to communicate indirectly. Possibly he does not relate the interviewer's questions to the job on offer, but rather interprets them as everyday topics. He clearly does not foresee the negative implications of his utterances and even when the interviewer becomes more explicit about them, he fails to clarify his position.

The next example illustrates a conversational strategy of a different kind.

Example 5: Western applicant

{*Der Bewerber berichtet von einem Gespräch mit potentiellen Vorgesetzten während einer Betriebsführung*}

1   B: *und dann << all > die ham mich natürlich AUCH gefragt;*
2   *ob ich mich das > mir das vorstellen könnte;*

3 I2:   *mhm,*
4 B: *= << p > sowas zu tun; >*
5 I2:   *(0.5) und da ham sie gesagt SELbstverständlich.*
6   *<< all > produkTION ANwendungstechnik und*
7   *MARketing mach ich. (0.5) abersie können ja*
8   *nich ALles machen. >*
9 B: *(0.5) nee; des hab ich NICH gesagt.*
10 I2:   *was HAM sie gesagt?*
11 B: *(0.5) ich hab gesagt daß ich mir im AUgenblick, (.) nich*
12   *so gut vorstellenkann. (0.5) << all > sondern daß*
13   *ich = s eigentlich ganz GUT finde; daß man hier*
14   *zuNÄchst in der forschung eingestellt wird. > {fährt fort}*

{the applicant is telling about a conversation he had with potential superiors during a tour through the plant}

1 B: and then << all > naturally they ALso asked me
2   if I > could imagine that;
3 I2:   mhm,
4 B: = << p > to do something like that >
5 I2:   (0.5) and then you said of COURSE.
6   << all > I do technical proDUCTion application and
7   MARketing. (0.5) but you can't
8   do EVerything. >
9 B: (0.5) no; I didn't say that.
10 I2:   what did you say?
11 B: (0.5) I said that at the moment, I really can't
12   imagine, (0.5) << all > but what I
13   I find GOOD is that one is
14   inITially hired for research. > {continues}

In this 'critical question' the interviewer contrasts two positions: one that is presented as an applicant's statement about his prospective fields of activity and another one that doubts the practicability of these aspirations. This contradiction should be resolved by the applicant in order to avoid damaging a consistent self-presentation.

In fact, the applicant counters with a strong disagreement. He rejects the claim 'put into his mouth' by the interviewer, using a 'contrastive opposite', which has been described by M.H. Goodwin (1983: 672, see also Pomerantz 1978: 93) as the most aggravated form of disagreement. It is characterized by showing neither dispreference markers nor accounts or justifications, but solely displaying a position of opposition (note the opposition preface 'no'). Strong cohesion is obtained by using the 'opposition format' rhetorical device (Kotthoff 1993: 201ff; M.H. Goodwin and C. Goodwin 1987), which consists of citing the preceding utterance in great part but negating it at the same time. The concatenation of several syntagmas 'then you said' – 'I didn't say' – 'what did you say' – I said' (even more obvious in the German original) intensifies the disagreement format. This form of 'dissent-tying' (see Chapter 10) is thematically reminiscent of the 'he-said-she-said' events which M.H. Goodwin (1980) described in a group of adolescent girls. But despite being such a strong counter reaction, it does not lead into overt dissent between the interactants; rather the applicant gains the floor for a self repair and to formulate his own point of view.

In our material we observed a general tendency for negative impressions to result from applicants agreeing with 'critical questions'. The East German applicants, who mostly make use of this conversational style, have difficulty afterwards in maintaining a positive self-presentation. With the West Germans, however, who more frequently use conversational strategies characterized by overt disagreement, the critical topic is typically dropped. The ethnographic data seem to confirm these findings. In one ethnographic interview, for example, a personnel manager (who also took part in the job interviews) commented: 'If we count assertiveness and conflict management as elements of team work, it's true that they are a bit more reserved, the East Germans.' Later he assesses East Germans as 'very submissive, at times, what the boss says goes and you don't question it'. Asked for the causes he assumes 'because they never had to or it wasn't allowed'. This indicates that some interviewers perceive East Germans as submissive and servile and even assume that they lack the ability to deal with conflict successfully. West Germans, on the other hand, are considered more self-confident and better prepared to handle conflict. From an analytical point of view, this judgement of East German employees could be a result of differences in conversational style. If we take into account that most employers consider assertiveness a key qualification because of its association with teamwork, we could argue that East Germans have to make greater effort to achieve successful self-presentations than West Germans do, because of the East German conversational preference for downgrading disagreement.

However, in job interviews candidates' assertiveness is not only judged by their linguistic behaviour; it is also discussed explicitly. In our data we find an example of an Eastern applicant who is asked if she has ever had an argument with a superior.

Example 6: Eastern applicant

```
1   I2:    and mit ihrem CHEF? ham = se auch mal, (0.5) so = n
2          paar_
3   A:     {empört} NE:IN
4   I2:    (0.5) disKURse gehabt, NEIN?
5   A:     = nie.
6   I2:    weil s = sich so gut mit dem verSTANden haben.
7   A:     (0.5) nee das hat damit nischt zu
8          [TUN; (da hab ich?) reschPEKT.
9   I2:     [nee,
10  A:     (hi[hi)
11  I2:    [sie haben resPEKT.
12  A:     ja; resPEKT;
```

```
1   I2:    and with your BOSS? did you ever, have (0.5) well
2          any_
3   A:     {indignant} NO:
4   I2:    (0.5) ARgument, {lit. 'discourses'} NO?
5   A:     = never.
6   I2:    because you got ON with him so well.
7   A:     (0.5) no that's got nothing to
8          DO with [it; (I'm?) resPECTful.
9   I2:            [no,
10  A:     (hi[hi)
11  I2:           [you are resPECTful.
12  A:     yes; resPECTful;
```

The applicant emphatically denies having had any conflicts with a superior, and gives 'respect' as the reason. The team of interviewers come back to this in their post-interview evaluation, and it seems to be an important factor in their judgement of her:

Example 7: Interviewers' evaluation

I2: Conflicts are something she has problems with, because she also has (0.5) as we have seen in the course of the interviews, the Eastern mentality, that she keeps quiet about them, no question.

I1: ... she probably isn't able to cope with conflicts with her team colleagues. We have clear evidence that she can't easily handle conflict with management

The interviewers' assessment of the applicant corresponds with our findings in the ethnographic interviews. However, looking more closely at the job interview with the applicant concerned, we find a narrative later on where, discussing something else, she gives a detailed account of how she once confronted her boss who had been criticizing her performance behind her back. It is a perfect example of using initiative in dealing with conflict with a superior.

This suggests that although Eastern applicants' communicative norms differ from Western ones in job interviews, their behaviour in real life may in fact be quite similar. In the interviews, Eastern applicants seem to orient much more to the asymmetry of the encounter, whereas West Germans (interviewers as well as applicants) tend to downplay it. This would account for the lack of disagreement shown by East Germans in the interview situation as well as for their apparent rejection of assertiveness. Example 7 also points to another observation: in job interviews the candidates do not seem to get a second chance, as the interviewers obviously missed her narrative about a successfully handled conflict with a boss. Yet this might also suggest that interviewers are blinded by stereotypical expectations about the East German way of dealing with conflicts.

Discussion questions

1   Find a job advertisement that could be interesting for you and imagine being invited for an interview. The interviewer asks 'Why have you applied for this job of all jobs?'

1.1 Note down five possible answers.

1.2 Compare them with the answers your fellow students have found. Order them according to semantic similarity. Can you recognize argumentative patterns?

1.3 Discuss the pros and cons of the respective argumentative patterns.

2   The next question you are asked is 'What are your strong points and what are your weak points?'

2.1 Note down two or three possible strong and two or three possible weak points.

2.2 Collect the answers in class and make a list of frequency. Can you recognize what sort of answers people prefer to give?

2.3 What sort of answers do people tend to avoid giving, and why?

3   Read the following extract from an authentic job interview.

Example 8: Application for telephone marketing

1   I3:   what do you enjoy about retailing;
2   B: (1) well (.) enjoy (.) hm - (.h) what do I enjoy;

```
 3  I3:     (1) because you just said I would like that
 4          (somehow?).
 5  B:      yes I want to earn money; yes, (.) well if one
 6          (has has to?) earn money in a wa:y [what ] (.)
 7  I3                                         [mhm,]
 8  B       I can't go [there] and (stand there?)
 9  I3:                [mhm,
10  B:      and say (-) well folks I'm just doing it for fun. –
11          I certainly [won't do that.
12  I3:                 [mhm,
13  B:      e:h eh just (.) for fun. I wanna earn somethin too. 'h –
```

3.1 Evaluate the answer from the perspective of an employer.
Now read the next example.

Example 9: Application for telephone marketing
```
1  I2:     = mhm, (-) what was especially attractive to you in
2          selling; what did you enjoy about it;
3  B:      (1) if someone didn't want to buy anything;
4          and did in the end anyway
5  I2:     aha,
```

3.2 Evaluate the answer from the perspective of an employer and compare it with the first applicant's answer. Which of the two would you hire? Why?

3.3 Ask people with different cultural backgrounds how they evaluate the two answers. Does everybody agree that the reason 'enjoying your work' is a convincing argument to show positive motivation?

3.4 To what extent might the use of specific arguments (e.g. strong and weak points) be linked to culturally bound linguistic practices?

Notes

1. The findings presented are drawn from the research project 'Impression Management in East and West German Job Interviews' funded by the German Research Foundation.
2. We also collected 27 role-played interviews in both East and West Germany for the project. Those data are not considered here.
3. A Western candidate is asked the same question as the Eastern candidate in Example 2 with the same complex play of perspectives. She replies from the required point of view, giving her colleagues' hypothetical views on herself.

13

A Problematic Chinese Business Visit to Britain: Issues of Face

Helen Spencer-Oatey and Jianyu Xing

13.1 Introduction

This chapter explores the face issues that arose during a ten-day visit to a British company by a group of six Chinese business people who were customers of the British company. The British company had previously hosted many such delegations, yet this particular visit turned out to be particularly problematic: the visitors cancelled all the training sessions that had been arranged, they asked to change hotels twice, and they were dissatisfied with the sightseeing programme. On the last day of the visit, they challenged their hosts over the spending money they were given and argued that the British company had broken the terms of the contract. What should have been a harmonious and enjoyable visit turned out to be acrimonious and unpleasant.

Needless to say, neither side was pleased. The Chinese felt that they had not been hosted appropriately, while the British felt that the visitors were very 'demanding', 'hadn't any ethics' and 'had no due respect for their hosts'.

What actually went wrong? This chapter explores the events from a face perspective.

13.2 Background information

13.2.1 The business background

The British company designs, manufactures and sells an engineering product that is used in industrial plants throughout the world. In every contract signed in China, they agree to host a delegation of up to six people who are involved in some way in the deal. The official purpose of the visit is to inspect the products purchased, to receive technical training, and to have a good time sightseeing. In reality, though, the products have typically already been shipped and installed, so the visitors are unable to inspect the goods. The British company handles all the administration associated with the visit, and prepares a programme of events which includes a welcome meeting, training sessions, local business visits, sightseeing, shopping and social activities, and ends with a close-out meeting.

The costs of the visit are paid by the Chinese, and included in the contract as a package deal. If the expenses incurred during the visit are less than the sum paid, then the balance is given to the visitors as 'pocket money' at the end of the visit.

13.2.2 Research procedure

Two types of data were collected for analysis: (1) video-recordings of all the official meetings between the British and Chinese business people, and (2) comments made by the participants during follow-up interviews and playback sessions. The British and Chinese participants were interviewed separately, and were asked to watch the recordings and to comment on anything they found strange or annoying. All these sessions were audio-recorded.

In all aspects of the data collection, we endeavoured to maximize the validity and reliability of the data. Over the last few years, we have developed very good relations with staff at the host company. During the visit, one of us spent as much time as possible socially with the Chinese visitors in order to build up a good rapport with them (e.g. accompanying them on sightseeing trips). We did this deliberately, so that both British and Chinese participants would have confidence in us, so that they would not feel too uneasy about the recording, and so that they would be honest and open with us in the interviews and playback sessions. We were very satisfied with the ways in which they seemed to 'conduct their business as normal' and with their cooperation during the follow-up sessions.

Note: Translations of Chinese extracts are by Jianyu Xing.

13.3 Problematic occurrences

During the first twenty-four hours of the visit, a number of problems arose, and as a result negative attitudes began to emerge.

13.3.1 Hotel arrangements

The British company took the visiting delegation to an inexpensive hotel which they had previously used with other Chinese delegations. They assumed that the visitors would prefer to stay in relatively cheap accommodation so that they would have more pocket money at the end of the trip. However, the Chinese visitors felt the hotel was not good enough, and complained that the rooms were small and the carpets old and worn-out. They claimed that when they were on business trips in China, they would stay in at least four-star hotels, and felt that this poor-quality hotel was beneath their status. They asked the host company there and then to arrange for them to stay in a different hotel, and were moved to a better-quality family-run hotel the next morning.

13.3.2 The welcome meeting: seating arrangements

The welcome meeting took place that next morning in the host company's conference room. Six Chinese visitors were present, and six British hosts, along with a local interpreter (of Chinese nationality). The room was rather small in size, and had a large oblong table placed in the middle of the room. There were four chairs on either side, and a fifth at one end of the table (the end that was further away from the door). Four Chinese visitors sat on one side (facing the door) and two sat on the other side with the interpreter. One seat was left empty. The British chairman of the meeting sat at the end of the table, and the other British staff were located away from the table, with most either standing or sitting behind the Chinese visitors (see Figure 13.1).

The room arrangements made it physically difficult for people to move around to shake hands and to present business cards, and both British and Chinese participants felt that the venue for the meeting was inappropriate. However, while the British chairman noted that it was 'bad organization' and 'genuine chaos', the Chinese attributed much greater significance to the seating arrangements. In the follow-up interview, the delegation leader commented as follows, with other members chorusing agreement:

Comment 1 (Chinese Delegation Leader)
... it shouldn't have been that he was the chair and we were seated along the sides of the table. With equal status, they should sit along this side and we should sit along that side ...

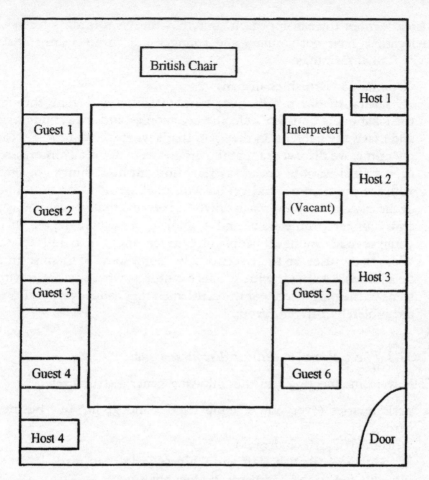

Figure 13.1 Seating arrangements at the meetings

In other words, the Chinese felt that since the two teams were of equal status, they should have sat on opposite sides of the table, with the heads of each side sitting in the middle. They interpreted the different arrangements as conveying a significant 'status' message:

> Comment 2 (Chinese Delegation Leader)
> ... they were chairing, and we were audience, which naturally means that you do what you are told to... They were, right from the start, they were commanding, in control, contemptuous. In actual fact we should have been given equal status ...

The British, on the other hand, clearly had no idea that this was the impression they had conveyed. While they acknowledged that the room was too small, the chairman explained that they had previously

taken a more formal approach, but that the visitors on successive
delegations have got younger and younger and do not want to have
very formal meetings:

Comment 3 (British chairman)
... several of our people have been to China and gone through
their banquets and the welcome ceremonies and everything else,
and that's the perception they got, that's what we replicated. Now
over time, we discovered that the groups were not really interested,
er, they just want to get in say [???] find out how things go, agree
with the programme, and get on with it. It seems to be a lot more
of the cash in their approach now. ... It seems that we get younger
and younger people now, and I think to a certain degree these
younger and younger people are much more exposed to say
Western cultures, so there seems to be more, some of them seem to
be a lot more familiar with Western cultures, where to begin with,
some of the party, some of the gentlemen that came over, er, it was
a completely different group.

13.3.3 The welcome meeting: discourse issues

The welcome meeting had the following general structure:

- preliminaries (everyone shaking hands, and giving out business
  cards)
- welcome (British chairman)
- introductions (British staff and Chinese visitors in turn)
- introduction to the company (British chairman)

In his welcome comments, the British chairman drew attention to
the importance of the Chinese contracts to his company, and
expressed his company's hope that the good relationship between
the two parties would continue in the future:

Extract 1 (Welcome Meeting)
It is extremely important for us at [company] to make a special
effort to welcome all of our Chinese friends and colleagues, as you
and your company are very important to us. We we've over the last
probably four or five years had quite quite a good relationship with
with China, and have people from [company] and [place] and and
the the various [industrial plants] in the various provinces of
China, and we hope this will continue in the future.

Later on, he gave some background information on his company, and made the following comments:

Extract 2 (Welcome Meeting)
So we are obviously very experienced eh in the design and the manufacture of these products. ... A lot of our trade now obviously goes to China and to the other Eastern countries, because that is obviously where a lot of the world trade now is and will be in the future.

In the follow-up interview with the British chairman, he pointed out that his company wanted to make the visit memorable for the Chinese visitors, so that they would have a good impression of his company and remember them on their return. The Chinese, on the other hand, felt that his comments on the Sino-British relationship had not been weighty enough. They had heard on the Chinese grapevine that the British company was in serious financial difficulties, and they believed it was the Chinese contracts that had saved them from bankruptcy. (This was denied by the British company.) So they felt that the British hosts should have expressed their sincere gratitude to them for helping them so significantly.

Comment 4 (Chinese Sales Manager)
It is understandable for them to praise their own products, but by doing so they in fact made a big mistake. Why? Because, you see, because for a company when they haven't got new orders for their products for several years it is a serious problem, to them, but they didn't talk about it. ... he should have said that you have made great efforts regarding [the sale of] our products, right? And hope you continue. They should have said more in this respect. He didn't mention our orders. So in fact this is a very important matter. It is not just a matter of receiving us.

After the chairman finished giving his welcome comments, the British staff introduced themselves, and then the chairman asked the Chinese delegation members to introduce themselves. The head of the delegation took it as an invitation to deliver a return speech, and started to express the group's appreciation to the hosts. However, he was cut short by the interpreter, who explained that they had been asked to introduce themselves, not give a return speech. After several minutes of uncomfortable discussion in Chinese by the visitors, each delegation member introduced himself.

Once again, the British and Chinese participants interpreted the issue very differently. In the follow-up interview with the Chinese, they all argued that it was normal and polite for the head of the delegation to 'say a few words of appreciation', and then introduce himself and each member of the delegation. The head of the Chinese delegation explained it as follows:

Comment 5 (Head of Chinese Delegation)
According to our home customs and protocol, speech is delivered on the basis of reciprocity. He has made his speech and I am expected to say something ... Condescension was implied. In fact I was reluctant to speak, and I had nothing to say. But I had to, to say a few words. Right for the occasion, right? But he had finished his speech, and he didn't give me the opportunity, and they each introduced themselves, wasn't this clearly implied that they do look down upon us Chinese.

Clearly, he and his colleagues were bitterly hurt by not being given the chance to deliver a return speech. Yet in the interview with the British chairman, he once again claimed that current delegations are different from earlier ones, saying that they used to have return speeches, but that as the Chinese have become more familiar with them, 'formalities have really eroded and sort of drifted away'.

13.3.4 Programme of activities

The original programme included one and a half days' on-site training (a manufacturing review, an engineering review, and a quality assurance review), and six days' local sightseeing trips and shopping tours. However, the visitors cancelled the training sessions, saying that they wanted more time for sightseeing and shopping. Yet they showed little interest in the tourist attractions they were taken to, and became impatient for more opportunities for shopping.

The British hosts were offended by this, and in the follow-up interview commented that the group showed no interest at all in their products and manufacturing, and that 'they haven't any ethics, had no due respect for their hosts'.

13.3.5 Attempts to meet with the China Sales Manager

After a few days, the visitors decided they wanted to have more time in London, and to stay in London for a night. They had asked the staff accompanying them on different trips about this, but had received no definite response. This irritated them, and so they decided to try and talk with LJ, the China Sales Manager. Two of the visitors regarded LJ as a friend, as they had previously met him during his visits to China, and they thought he would make the arrangements for them.

LJ was away on an overseas trip when the visitors arrived, and was due back during the middle of their visit. The Chinese visitors expected that, since he was their friend, he would make contact with them immediately after he got back, either officially in the office, or unofficially at their hotel, or at least telephone them. But when LJ made no contact with them on the day of his return, they were annoyed. They repeatedly asked, and at one stage even demanded, the accompanying personnel to contact LJ, and for his home telephone number. This continued for the next few days, including the weekend.

Eventually, LJ arranged a meeting with them the following Monday, one day before their departure. In the follow-up interview, LJ explained that he needed to spend time with his family, since he had been away on a long trip. But from the Chinese point of view, he had failed to act as a genuine friend.

13.4 A face perspective on the problematic occurrences

As argued in Chapter 2, face is a universal phenomenon that is concerned with people's sense of worth, dignity and identity, and that is associated with issues such as respect, honour, status, reputation and competence (cf. Ting-Toomey and Kurogi 1998). In this section, we examine the problematic occurrences from a face perspective.

13.4.1 Aspects of face

Brown and Levinson (1987), in their classic work on politeness, maintain that there are two main types of face concern: desire for autonomy, independence and freedom from imposition (negative face) and desire for approval and appreciation (positive face). However, other theorists (e.g. Matsumoto 1988, 1989, Lim and Bowers 1991, Lim 1994, Mao 1994) have criticized this specification, and argued that face also has an important social identity element that is omitted from Brown and Levinson's model. In line with this, it was argued in Chapter 2 that Brown and Levinson's conceptualization of positive face has been underspecified, and that people have two fundamental desires for approval: a desire for positive evaluation in terms of personal qualities such as competence, abilities etc. (quality face), and a desire for positive evaluation in terms of social identity, such as standing within a group (identity face).

How, then, do these aspects of face relate to the concerns of the Chinese and British business people in this case study?

During the ten-day visit it seems that, for the Chinese, the problematic events primarily revolved around their concerns over identity face, especially their status. They regarded themselves as being extremely important to the British company, and thus as having high status, but felt that the British hosts failed to acknowledge this sufficiently, and thus failed to give them the face they deserved.

- When they were taken to a cheap hotel, their identity face was threatened, because they were used to staying in four-star hotels, and expected to receive at least comparable treatment in Britain.
- When they were welcomed in a cramped room in which they were seated in a 'superior–subordinate' arrangement (from their perspective), their identity face was threatened once again, because they regarded themselves as being at least equal with their hosts.
- When the British chairman failed to express deep-felt gratitude towards them for helping to save his company financially, they felt that their importance to the company had been underestimated and unacknowledged, and that their identity face had thus been insufficiently honoured.
- When the chairman omitted to allow the Chinese delegation leader to give a return speech, they felt that they had been regarded with disdain and treated as inferiors, thus threatening their identity face once more.
- When the China Sales Manager failed to make contact with them as soon as he arrived back from his trip, they felt that he had not fulfilled his obligations of friendship towards them, and this threatened their identity face in terms of their role as friends.

All of these problematic events (apart from the last one) took place within the delegation's first twenty-four hours in Britain, so it is not really surprising that negative attitudes began to arise so early. The cancellation of the training sessions, the demanding approach over arrangements for sightseeing and shopping, and the arguments over money and costs were presumably the Chinese visitors' ways of attempting to redress the balance. Unfortunately, however, the British hosts were oblivious (apart from knowing that they were dissatisfied with the hotel) to the Chinese concerns over status and to the offence they felt from the threats to their identity face.

13.4.2 Group as well as individual face

In defining face, most theorists seem to emphasize the individual scope of face through using terms such as 'image of self' (Goffman 1972), 'self-image' (Brown and Levinson 1987), and 'self-worth' (Ting-Toomey and Kurogi 1998).

However, face concerns are not always individual; sometimes they can be group concerns as well. Gao (1996: 96), for example, argues as follows:

'Face need' is not only a personal concern but, more important, a collective concern (King and Bond 1985). As King and Myers (1977) indicate, face is more a concern to the family than to the person and face-losing or face-gaining acts reflect both on persons themselves and on their families. To illustrate, one's failure threatens the face of the family; one's accomplishment, however, gains face for the family.

During the delegation visit, the face concerns of both the British and the Chinese participants seemed to be group-oriented. The British were concerned about their company's reputation: they wanted the visitors to learn more about their company, and to go back to China with a deep and positive impression, firstly of the company and secondly of Britain. Although this naturally involved individual staff members behaving appropriately, the focus of concern seemed to be more on the company than on people's individual face. See, for example, Extract 1 (above) and Extract 3:

Extract 3 (British administrator, Close-out Meeting)
Would you explain to them that [company] has entertained many groups here. It is very difficult to guess to make provision for them various visits. We could only I would assume that this would be best for them.

Similarly, the Chinese delegation presented themselves as a group, and were concerned about the group's face, and the reputation of Chinese people in general:

Extract 4 (Chinese delegation member, Close-out Meeting)
You just tell him. Is it so easy to bully us Chinese so easy to fool us? This money is what we've been saving on our food. We've had instant noodles every day just to save money and now they've grabbed it. Is that fair?

13.5 Discussion

Although the British hosts were keen to create a positive impression on their Chinese visitors, they inadvertently threatened the visitors' face and the consequences were very negative. Why then did the British hosts' positive intentions (their rapport-enhancement and rapport-maintenance orientation) result in a negative interpretation (rapport neglect and rapport threat)?

13.5.1 Anticipating preferences

The British hosts had formed the impression from previous delegations that the visitors' preferences would be as follows:

- to stay in a cheaper hotel so that they could have more personal 'pocket money' at the end of the visit;
- to have an informal atmosphere in the meetings;
- to have a mixture of training, sightseeing and shopping.

During earlier visits that we recorded and analysed, it seems that the Chinese were fairly satisfied with the arrangements made for them. So the British hosts' anticipation of preferences seems to have been reasonable. Perhaps, though, this group was different in composition from earlier groups.

13.5.2 Judging the importance of the visitors

To the British company, this delegation's ten-day stay was just another customary visit under a standard contract. They did not regard the group as being any different from previous groups, and commented that although the Chinese visitors regarded themselves as important, 'they were not much higher ranking' than other visitors. The British believed that most of the delegation members were engineers, and that they would therefore be interested in receiving technical training. In fact, however, unlike most previous delegations, nearly all of these visitors were sales managers. In China sales managers are much richer than engineers, and also typically regard themselves as much more important. So from a Chinese perspective, this delegation was significantly different from previous groups.

It seems, therefore, that the British had difficulty identifying the roles/positions of the visitors, and assessing their relative importance. One reason for this could be the way in which jobs and positions are often identified in Chinese and translated into English.

Table 13.1 The Chinese visitors' 'expertise' and 'position' titles

Name	'Expertise' title	'Position' title
Mr FJY	Senior Engineer	Head of Delegation [position title not given on card]. Design Department, [W] Company
Mr YZY	Engineer	Sales Manager, International Sales and Planning, [W] Company
Mr XZB	Senior Engineer	Director, [X] Project
Mr LT	Engineer	Director of [Y] Company; Manager of [Z] Company
Mr WFS	Assistant Economist	Head of Equipment Section, [X] Project
Mr HP	Economist	General Manager of [A] Company and [B] Company

It is common practice in China for a person to have two titles on his/her name card, an 'expertise' (technical) title, and a 'position' (job) title. The former shows the area/field that the person is skilled or trained in, and the latter shows the position s/he holds within the organization. So someone may, for example, be trained as an engineer but working as a sales manager. The British hosts were only given information on the delegation members' 'expertise' titles, not their 'position' titles. In other words, they did not receive the full information given in Table 13.1; they only received that shown in the first two columns (along with company affiliations).

It is not surprising, therefore, that the British hosts thought the visitors would be interested in technical training, and failed to realize the important roles they played in concluding contracts. However, the British chairman did sense there was something a little strange, as can be seen from one of his comments in the follow-up interview. When he was asked whether he realized that most of the guests were involved in sales, he replied as follows:

Comment 6 (British chairman)
...one of the things that happened is that when you read their job titles, and explain what they do within the company sometimes it doesn't seem to stack up. Sometimes it doesn't seem to be believable, eh, because sometimes you'll get for example a title like senior project engineer and a project engineer, but you'll find the project engineer is actually more senior than the senior project engineer. So sometimes their titles and their job descriptions don't actually tie up with what they do. So maybe I didn't pick up the fact that they were all in sales...

Clearly, it was difficult for the British company to judge accurately the status, decision-making power, and professional interests of the delegation members.

13.5.3 Managing practical constraints

However, even if the British hosts had gained an accurate understanding of the relative importance of the visitors, they would still have faced difficulties, because there were practical constraints on them, both in terms of the venue and the resources.

13.5.3.1 The venue

The only large room which the company could use for formal welcome and close-out meetings was the cafeteria. During this particular visit, the cafeteria was not available for use, so even if they had wanted to provide a better setting, they would have had difficulty doing so.

13.5.3.2 Resources (financial and staff)

In terms of the financial as well as the staff resources, the hosts had little room to manoeuvre. Under the terms of the contract, the Chinese side had paid a fixed sum of money to cover the expenses incurred by each member of the visiting group. Unlike in China where members of staff involved in receiving foreign visitors normally each have an entertainment budget, the British staff had no such extra allowance. They had to stay strictly within the fixed sum included in the contract and at the same time allow a certain amount to be given back to the visitors as spending money.

The hosts were also under great pressure to provide staff to accompany the visitors on sightseeing and shopping trips. It meant people having to take time off from busy schedules; it meant starting early in the morning, getting back late in the evenings, and going out at weekends. Many people were reluctant to be involved, and this put the hosts under great pressure; in fact, they had to ask retired former employees to help out.

13.5.4 Understanding cultural conventions

Another major source of problems was the lack of mutual understanding of cultural conventions.

In Britain, there is an increasing move towards informality (for example, in the use of terms of address and the conduct of meetings), and an implicit assumption that everyone finds informality more comfortable than formality. Moreover, there is a preference for minimizing hierarchical differences and for stressing equality (at least superficially). However, in China people more normally regard formal protocol as natural, and as a way of displaying respect for all concerned, especially for those with high status. And, as is common in societies with high power distance (see Chapter 14, and Spencer-Oatey 1997), status differences are usually explicitly acknowledged. So people may pay great attention to issues such as seating arrangements, the use of formal titles, the appropriate presentation of business cards, and speech turn-taking. Clearly, both British and Chinese participants were unaware of each other's different conventions regarding preferences for formality/informality and the management of hierarchy issues in relationships.

Another area of unfamiliarity concerns the rights and obligations of the host–guest relationship. Gao and Ting-Toomey (1998: 46) claim that in the Chinese host–guest relationship, 'the host demonstrates *ke qi* (politeness) by doing everything to make the guest "feel at home", and the guest returns *ke qi* by not imposing on the host'. During this visit, however, the visitors clearly thought the British had failed in their responsibilities as hosts. They knew that their airfare and hotel bills would be taken out of the money that they had paid, but they assumed that the cost of other events, such as welcome dinners, sightseeing trips, and so on, would be met by the hosts from a different budget. They could not understand how the British could be 'hosts' if the Chinese had to pay for everything, including the expenses (such as meals) of accompanying British staff. As soon as they realized at the close-out meeting that this was how the costs had been calculated, they protested vehemently, and demanded that the figures be re-calculated. While these host–guest obligations are understandable to British people for 'personal' visits, in a British business context, it is normal to add them in to the contract price, because the hosting costs have to be recovered from somewhere. Once again, each side seemed unable to grasp each other's cultural norms in this respect.

13.6 Implications for face and rapport management theory

Tracy and Baratz (1994: 293) argue for a case study approach to the study of face and facework:

A case study approach would enable researchers to develop a better understanding of the following: How do interactants in a particular setting want to be seen or *not* want to be seen? How do these interactants get this across or try to get this across? What is the relationship between certain communicative behaviors and attributions of identity? What misunderstandings, problems, and/or contradictions arise in the setting that relate to facework?

What implications, then, does this case study have for face theory/ rapport management theory?

13.6.1 Social identity and face

Firstly, this case study offers support for the arguments that social identity can be an important face issue. During this particular business visit, 'status' seems to have been the key issue that was at stake, and we suggest that this can be seen as a component of identity face.

Ide (1989) accepts the validity of a twofold model of face (positive and negative face), but maintains that social relationships are signalled through a component called 'discernment' (*wakimae*). Elsewhere she and her colleagues argue that in Japanese, once a particular status relationship has been identified, speakers 'submit passively to the requirements of the system' (Hill *et al.* 1986: 348) and signal that relationship in the language they use. They contrast 'discernment' with 'volition', which they claim is the strategic use of language to manage face concerns.

However, as Kasper (1996) and Tsuruta (1998) point out, people's use of honorifics in Japanese is by no means entirely predetermined; there is still a strong element of sociolinguistic choice. So it seems more reasonable to argue that their unmarked use is simply a reflection of a rapport-maintenance orientation (see Chapter 2), and any unexpected use is strategic (e.g. a reflection of a rapport-enhancement or rapport-challenge orientation). We believe that the particular importance of social indexing (especially in Asian countries such as Japan, China and Korea) reflects the relative importance of identity face in those countries, rather than the operation of a separate system, discernment–volition.

13.6.2 Independent and interdependent face

Ting-Toomey and Kurogi (1998) argue for a distinction between 'I-identity' and 'We-identity' facework, which derives from the difference between independent self-construal and interdependent self-construal. They argue that independent/interdependent self-construal is the mediating factor between individualism–collectivism (a culture-level factor: see Chapter 14) and behaviour (e.g. facework), and they explain independent and interdependent self-construal as follows:

> Individuals with high independent self-construals tend to view themselves as unique and distinctive from others. They use their own personal attributes and abilities as motivational bases for action rather than the thoughts and feelings of others. Individuals who view themselves as independents value 'I-identity', personal achievement, self-direction and competition. When communicating with others, high independents believe in striving for personal goals, being in control of the agenda and expressing their positions assertively. Overall, independent self-construal types tend to be more self-face oriented than other-face oriented. ...
>
> The interdependent construal of self, on the other hand, involves an emphasis on the importance of relational connectedness (Markus and Kitayama 1991). People who have an interdependent self-construal want to fit in with others, act appropriately, promote others' goals and value relational collaboration. The self-in-relation guides the behavior of high interdependents in social situations. When communicating with others, high interdependents value other-face and mutual-face concerns. They are eager to appeal to other-face concerns in vulnerable interpersonal situations in order to preserve relational harmony. (Ting-Toomey and Kurogi 1998: 196–7)

Ting-Toomey and Kurogi's discussion revolves round the distinction between individual rights/interests/concerns, and group rights/interests/concerns. However, there is no mention of multiparty intergroup communication, and how this fits into their characterization.

In our case study, as explained in section 13.4.2, we found group face to be an important concept. Both groups (British hosts and Chinese visitors) seemed to be more concerned about group face than individual face, and so, to use Ting-Toomey and Kurogi's terminology, they each had interdependent face concerns. However, their group concerns seem slightly different from the concept of independence/interdependence discussed by Ting-Toomey and Kurogi (1998). It seems that Accommodation Theory (see Chapter 9, and Gallois et al. 1995) provides a clearer set of concepts for describing their orientations. The British and Chinese participants seemed to take an intergroup orientation, rather than an interpersonal orientation (in other words, they each had a kind of corporate identity), and because of this their concerns were primarily for group face rather than individual face.

Ting-Toomey and Kurogi's (1998) explanation of independence/ interdependence relates to another issue that is included in Accommodation Theory: socio-psychological orientation. Interdependent self-construal seems associated with a convergent orientation, while independent self-construal seems associated with a divergent or maintainance orientation. People with a convergent orientation show concern for mutual face (mutual interpersonal and/or intergroup face), while people with a divergent (or maintenance) orientation show concern for self-face (individual and/or own in-group face).

Clearly rapport-management theory needs more case studies which explore the genuine concerns about face and sociality rights that arise in different types of interactions and different cultural settings. Such studies are necessary in order to check and validate theoretical concepts, and they may also help (where appropriate) to integrate different theoretical perspectives.

Discussion questions

1   List all the problems that occurred between the hosts and the visitors during the visit (from both British and Chinese perspectives). For each of them, consider:

1.1 How far do you think the British hosts were responsible and how far do you think the Chinese visitors were responsible for the problem occurring?

1.2 How upsetting or annoying was the problem for the people concerned? Do you think it was an infringement of social expectancies (equity and/or association rights) and/or a threat to face (quality and/or identity face) (see Chapter 2)?

2   Identify the background assumptions of (a) the hosts and (b) the visitors which played important roles in the misunderstandings (see Chapter 8). Write a summary of the way in which the background assumptions you identified led to miscommunication.

3   To what extent can the problems that arose during the visit be explained in terms of negative pragmatic transfer (see Chapter 8), and to what extent can they be explained in terms of under- or contra-accommodation (see Chapter 9)? (Do not expect to find clear-cut answers to these questions!)

4   How do you think the problems described in this chapter can best be overcome and/or avoided on future occasions?

Suggestions for Further Reading for Part Four

Studies which analyse intercultural interactions

Bailey, B. (1997 Communication of respect in interethnic service encounters. *Language in Society*, 26: 327–56.

Clyne, M. (1994) *Inter-cultural Communication at Work*. Cambridge: Cambridge University Press.

Halmari, H. (1993) Intercultural business telephone conversations: a case of Finns vs. Anglo-Americans. *Applied Linguistics*, 4(4): 408–30.

Marriott, H.E. (1990) Intercultural business negotiations: the problem of norm discrepancy. *ARAL Series S*, 7: 33–65.

Miller, L. (1991) Verbal listening behaviour in conversations between Japanese and Americans. In J. Blommaert and J. Verschueren (eds), *The Pragmatics of Intercultural and International Communication*, Amsterdam: John Benjamins, 111–30.

Miller, L. (1995) Two aspects of Japanese and American co-worker interaction: giving instructions and creating rapport. *Journal of Applied Behavioural Science*, 31(2): 141–61.

Sarangi, S. (1994) Accounting for mismatches in intercultural selection interviews. *Multilingua*, 13(1/2): 163–94.

Tyler, A. (1995) The coconstruction of cross-cultural miscommunication. *Studies in Second Language Acquisition*, 17(2): 129–52.

Ulijn, J.M. and Li, X. (1995) Is interrupting impolite? Some temporal aspects of turn-taking in Chinese–Western and other intercultural business encounters. *Text*, 15(4): 589–627.

PART FIVE

METHODOLOGICAL ISSUES

Methodological Issues in Conducting Theory-Based Cross-Cultural Research[1]

William B. Gudykunst

Over the years, an extensive body of knowledge about conducting cross-cultural research has been generated (e.g. Berry *et al*. 1997, Brislin *et al*. 1973, Lonner and Berry 1986, Triandis and Berry 1980, van de Vijver and Leung 1997a). Most of the work written on cross-cultural research focuses on specific methods of data collection and analysis (e.g. field research, surveys). Hitherto, the vast majority of writing on cross-cultural research methods has not placed cross-cultural research in the context of theories designed to explain variability in behaviour across cultures. My purpose in this chapter is to outline some of the issues that are important in conducting theory-based cross-cultural research. I, therefore, focus on broad methodological issues, not specific research methods.

This chapter is divided into five sections. First, I examine the distinction between emic and etic approaches to research. Second, I discuss how culture can be treated as a theoretical variable in cross-cultural research. Third, I examine some of the methodological issues necessary for conducting sound theory-based cross-cultural research. Fourth, I isolate several problems in the current cross-cultural research that hinder theoretical advances. Finally, I conclude by integrating the issues discussed in the chapter.

14.1 Emic versus etic approaches to research

The distinction between the emic and etic approaches to studying culture and behaviour can be traced to Pike's (1966) discussion of phonemics (culturally specific vocal utterances) and phonetics (vocal utterances which are universal). Brislin (1983) argues that in current usage the distinction is employed basically as a metaphor for differences between the culture-specific approach (emic, single-culture) and cultural general (etic, universal) approaches to research. Understanding the distinction, however, is critical for conducting methodologically sound cross-cultural research.[2]

Berry (1980: 11–12) presents a succinct summary of the distinction between the emic and etic approaches to research:

Emic approach	Etic approach
studies behaviour from within the system	studies behaviour from a position outside the system
examines only one culture	examines many cultures, comparing them
structure discovered by the analyst	structure created by the analyst
criteria are relative to internal characteristics	criteria are considered absolute or universal

Researchers tend to use one of the two approaches exclusively, and the two approaches often are linked to the qualitative and quantitative debate in the social sciences.

Emic analyses often are equated with the use of qualitative methods of research and etic analyses often are equated with the use of quantitative methods of research. More generally, an emic approach often is associated with subjectivist metatheoretical assumptions (e.g. nominalism, antipositivism, volunteerism: Burrell and Morgan 1979) and etic research often is associated with objectivist metatheoretical assumptions (e.g. realism, positivism, determinism: Burrell and Morgan 1979). Neither the extreme subjectivist nor the extreme objectivist assumptions, however, are defensible. I believe the only reasonable metatheoretical assumptions are between the two extremes.

Just as making extreme subjectivist or objectivist metatheoretical assumptions can be counterproductive, using only an emic or an etic approach to research is problematic. Both emic and etic approaches are needed for methodologically sound cross-cultural research. The approach used *must* depend upon the research question being posed. I believe that the questions researchers pose should drive their methods; the methods should not drive the questions posed.

14.2 Treating culture theoretically in cross-cultural research

I believe that cross-cultural research should be theoretically based; i.e. cross-cultural research should be designed to test theoretical predictions about similarities and differences in behaviour across cultures. Incorporating culture in theory requires a way to treat culture as a theoretical variable. Foschi and Hales (1979: 246), for example, point out that when culture is treated as a theoretical variable 'culture x and culture y serve to operationally define a characteristic a, which the two cultures exhibit to different degrees'. There are dimensions on which cultures can be different or similar that can be used to explain behaviour across cultures (e.g. Hofstede's (1980) dimensions of cultural variability; Kluckhohn and Strodtbeck's (1961) value orientations; Parsons and Shils' (1951) pattern variables).

At the outset, it is important to recognize that behaviour is unique within each culture and, at the same time, there are systematic similarities and differences. The similarities and differences can be explained and predicted theoretically using dimensions of cultural variability such as individualism–collectivism (henceforth I–C). In individualistic cultures, for example, individuals take precedence over groups, while in collectivistic cultures, groups take precedence over individuals (Triandis 1988). There are systematic variations in behaviour that can be explained by cultural differences in I–C. To illustrate, members of individualistic cultures emphasize person-based information to predict each other's behaviours, and members of collectivistic cultures emphasize group-based information to predict each other's behaviours (Gudykunst and Nishida 1986).

There are general patterns of behaviour that are consistent with I–C, but I–C is manifested in unique ways in each culture. In the Japanese culture, for example, collectivism involves a focus on contextualism (Hamaguchi 1980). The concepts of *wa* (roughly translated as harmony), *amae* (roughly translated as dependency), and *enryo* (roughly translated as reserve or restraint) also are critical to understanding Japanese collectivism (Gudykunst and Nishida 1994). Other collectivistic cultures emphasize different cultural constructs as part of their collectivistic tendencies (e.g. Latin cultures emphasize the family, African cultures emphasize the community). Understanding communication in any culture, therefore, requires culture-general information (i.e. where the culture falls on the various dimensions of cultural variability) and culture-specific information (i.e. the specific cultural constructs associated with the dimension of cultural variability).

In this chapter, I overview the dimensions of cultural variability that I have found most useful in understanding similarities and differences in behaviour across cultures: I–C and low- and high-context communication.[3] I also briefly discuss three other dimensions of cultural variability that influence our behaviour: uncertainty avoidance (UA), power distance (PD), and masculinity–femininity (M–F) (Hofstede 1980).

14.2.1 Individualism–Collectivism

I–C is the major dimension of cultural variability used to explain cross-cultural differences in behaviour. This dimension of cultural variability has been isolated by theorists across disciplines, and by theorists in Eastern and Western cultures (see Hofstede 1980, Kluckhohn and Strodtbeck 1961, Triandis 1995, Chinese Culture Connection 1987).

14.2.1.1 Cultural I–C
At the cultural level, the cultural norms/rules emphasize individuals' goals over group goals in individualistic cultures, and group goals over individuals' goals in collectivistic cultures (Triandis 1988). In individualistic cultures, 'people are supposed to look after themselves and their immediate family only', and in collectivistic cultures, 'people belong to in-groups or collectivities which are supposed to look after them in exchange for loyalty' (Hofstede and Bond 1984: 419).

I–C exists in all cultures, but one tends to predominate. Cultures in which individualism tends to be emphasized include the USA, Canada, Australia, New Zealand, and northern European countries. Cultures in which collectivism is emphasized include most Asian, Latin, Arab and African cultures (Hofstede 1980).

14.2.1.2 Individual-level mediators of cultural-level I–C
Cultural I–C has a direct effect on behaviours in that it affects the norms and rules that are used to guide behaviours. Cultural I–C also has an indirect effect on behaviour in that it influences the way that individuals are socialized. Since members of a specific culture are not all socialized in the same way, they do not all learn the same general tendencies. There are at least three different individual characteristics that mediate the influence of I–C on behaviour: personalities, values, and self-construals. Figure 14.1 illustrates how the influence of cultural I–C on behaviour is mediated by these factors.

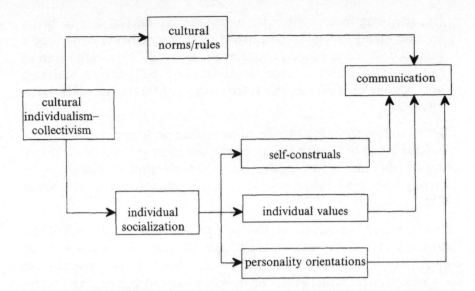

Figure 14.1 Cultural- and individual-level influences of individualism–collectivism on communication
Source: W.B. Gudykunst, *Bridging Differences*, Sage, 1998

The effect of cultural I–C is mediated by our personalities. Idiocentrism and allocentrism, for example, can be viewed as the personality orientations we learn as a function of I–C (Triandis *et al.* 1985).

The second way that the influence of cultural I–C on behaviour is mediated is through the values we hold. Value domains specify the structure of values and consist of specific values (Schwartz 1992). The interests served by value domains can be individualistic, collectivistic or mixed. The value domains of stimulation, hedonism, power, achievement, and self-direction serve individual interests; the value domains of tradition, conformity, and benevolence serve collective interests; and the value domains of security, universalism, and spirituality serve mixed interests.

The third way the influence of cultural I–C on behaviour is mediated is through the way we conceive of (think about) ourselves (see e.g. Kashima 1989, Markus and Kitayama 1991, 1998, Triandis 1989). The independent construal of self involves the view that an individual's self is a unique, independent entity. The important tasks for people emphasizing an independent self-construal are to be unique, strive for their own goals, express themselves, and be direct (e.g. 'say what you mean': Markus and Kitayama 1991).

Experiencing interdependence entails seeing oneself as part of an encompassing social relationship and recognizing that one's behavior is determined, contingent on, and, to a large extent organized by what the actor perceives to be the thoughts, feelings, and actions of *others* in the relationship. (Markus and Kitayama 1991: 227).

The important tasks for people emphasizing an interdependent self-construal are to fit in with the in-group, act in an appropriate fashion, promote the in-group's goals, occupy their proper place, to be indirect, and read other people's minds (Markus and Kitayama 1991).

Independent construals of the self *predominate* in individualistic cultures and interdependent construals of the self *predominate* in collectivistic cultures (Gudykunst *et al.* 1996). It is important to recognize, however, that everyone uses both an independent and inter-dependent construals of the self. Further, people who emphasize interdependent construals of the self exist in individualistic cultures and people who emphasize independent construals of the self exist in collectivistic cultures. The critical issue is which self-construal predominates to influence individuals' behaviours and which self-construal individuals use in guiding their behaviours in a particular situation.

14.2.2 Low- and high-context communication

I–C defines broad differences between cultures, and Hall's (1976) low- and high-context scheme focuses upon cultural differences in communication processes. A high-context (HC) message is one in which 'most of the information is either in the physical context or internalized in the person, while very little is in the coded, explicit, transmitted part of the message' (Hall 1976: 79). A low-context (LC) message, in contrast, is one in which 'the mass of information is vested in the explicit code' (Hall 1976: 70). Cultures in which HC messages tend to predominate include Japanese, Arab and Latin American cultures. Those in which LC messages tend to predomi-nate include Swiss-German, German and Scandinavian cultures.

14.2.3 Uncertainty avoidance

In comparison to members of cultures low in UA, members of cultures high in UA have a lower tolerance 'for uncertainty and ambiguity, which expresses itself in higher levels of anxiety and energy release, greater need for formal rules and absolute truth, and less tolerance for people or groups with deviant ideas or behavior' (Hofstede 1979: 395).

Low and high UA exist in all cultures, but one tends to predominate. Cultures in which high UA are emphasized include Argentina, Belgium, Chile, Egypt, France, Greece, Guatemala, Japan, Mexico, Peru, and Spain. Cultures in which low UA tends to be emphasized include Britain, Canada, Denmark, Hong Kong, India, Jamaica, Sweden, and the USA (Hofstede 1980).

14.2.4 Power distance

PD is 'the extent to which the less powerful members of institutions and organizations accept that power is distributed unequally' (Hofstede and Bond 1984: 419). Individuals from high PD cultures accept power as part of society, and individuals from low PD cultures do not.

Low and high PD exist in all cultures, but one tends to predominate. Cultures in which high PD is emphasized include Egypt, Ethiopia, Ghana, Guatemala, India, Malaysia, Nigeria, Saudi Arabia, and Venezuela. Cultures in which low PD is emphasized include Austria, Canada, Denmark, Germany, Ireland, Israel, New Zealand, Sweden, and the USA (Hofstede 1980).

14.2.5 Masculinity–femininity

Cultural M–F focuses on the equality in gender roles in a culture, and the behaviours associated with these gender roles.

> *Masculinity* pertains to societies in which social gender roles are clearly distinct (i.e., men are supposed to be assertive, tough, and focused on material success whereas women are supposed to be more modest, tender, and concerned with the quality of life); *femininity* pertains to societies in which social gender roles overlap (i.e., both men and women are supposed to be modest, tender, and concerned with the quality of life). (Hofstede 1991: 82–3)

People in highly masculine cultures value things, power, and assertiveness, and people in cultures high on femininity value quality of life and nurturance (Hofstede 1980).

M–F exists in all cultures, but one tends to predominate. Cultures in which masculinity is emphasized include Austria, Italy, Jamaica,

Japan, Mexico, Switzerland, and Venezuela. Cultures in which femininity is emphasized include Chile, Costa Rica, Denmark, Finland, the Netherlands, Norway, and Sweden (Hofstede 1980).

14.2.6 Making theoretical predictions

The dimensions of cultural variability and the individual-level factors that mediate their influence can (should) be used to make theoretical predictions in cross-cultural research. There are several issues that must be kept in mind when making these predictions.

It is critical that cultural- and individual-level effects be differentiated. Cultural-level effects must be derived from the norms and rules of the culture. This means that specific norms and rules should be isolated and these norms and rules must be linked to the dimensions of cultural variability in order to make the cultural-level predictions. The prediction must involve behaviour that results from the cultural norms or rules. To illustrate, there are cultural-level rules guiding reward allocation (Leung and Bond 1984). Members of collectivistic cultures, for example, prefer to use 'equality' rules (i.e. divide rewards equally) with in-group members, but not with out-group members. Members of individualistic cultures, in contrast, use the 'equity' rule (i.e. make rewards based on performance) with both in-group and out-group members.

Individual-level effects are linked to factors that mediate the effect of cultural dimensions (e.g. self-construals mediate the effect of cultural I–C). To illustrate, specific communication styles that individuals use are not linked to cultural norms or rules, rather they are a function of individuals' self-construals (see Gudykunst et al. 1996).

In making predictions at the cultural level, it also must be kept in mind that specific behaviours may not be a function of only one dimension of cultural variability. To illustrate, interaction with strangers may be a function of I–C and UA. Individuals from collective cultures would be expected to differ in how they interact with strangers depending on whether their culture is low or high in UA. Those from high UA cultures would probably avoid strangers as much as possible because they see strangers' behaviours as unpredictable and cultural norms require avoiding ambiguity. Those from low UA cultures, in contrast, might be inclined to interact with strangers because they view ambiguity as 'interesting'.

14.3 Methodological issues in conducting theory-based research

There are several books that specifically address 'methods' for cross-cultural research in psychology (e.g. Berry *et al.* 1997, Brislin *et al.* 1973, Lonner and Berry 1986, Triandis and Berry 1980, van de Vijver and Leung 1997a). It is impossible to present all of the 'methods' discussed in these volumes in this chapter. I focus, therefore, on central methodological issues (not specific methods) critical to conducting sound theory-based cross-cultural research: designing the research, isolating the effects to be studied, establishing equivalence, and developing derived etic measures.

14.3.1 Designing the research

Cross-cultural studies are not 'true experiments' (see Campbell and Stanley 1966). True experiments require that individuals be assigned randomly to conditions of the independent variable(s). Obviously cultures cannot be assigned randomly to dimensions of cultural variability and individuals cannot be assigned randomly to cultures. Cross-cultural studies generally fit the design that Campbell and Stanley refer to as a non-equivalent control group design or a static group comparison (see Malpass and Poortinga 1986 for a discussion of specific designs used in cross-cultural research). This design has numerous threats to internal validity. Analysing data from cross-cultural studies as true experiments can yield misleading results (see Poortinga and Malpass 1986 for a discussion of the problems in making inferences). Differences that emerge in cross-cultural studies may be due to the dimensions of culture being studied, or there may be rival hypotheses based on education, literacy, issues of equivalence, etc. (Campbell and Stanley 1966).

In designing a cross-cultural study, it is important to isolate potential rival hypotheses in advance and design the study in such a way that they can be ruled out. 'A feasible strategy is to identify the most likely variables that may account for expected cultural differences and measure these variables in the study' (van de Vijver and Leung 1997b: 260–1).

The method used to sample the cultures in which data are collected is an important design issue. Van de Vijver and Leung (1997b) isolate three possible sampling methods: convenience, systematic, and random. Most cross-cultural studies use convenience sampling. Cultures are selected because researchers have contacts in the culture, or they will be visiting the cultures. The cultures selected, however, may not be ideal representatives of the dimensions of cultural variability being studied. Systematic sampling involves selecting cultures in a theory-driven way. Ideally, cultures as far apart as possible on the cultural dimensions being studied are selected. If I–C is being studied, for example, cultures that are highly individualistic and highly collectivistic are selected. Random sampling involves selected samples in a random way. Using this approach makes it difficult to test dimensions of cultural variability, but it is useful for testing universals or pan-cultural theories.

Even though individuals cannot be assigned randomly to cultures, they can be assigned randomly to other conditions within cultures. This may be important in testing theoretical predictions based on dimensions of cultural variability. To illustrate, if researchers are interested in the influence of cultural I–C on behaviour, they need to collect data in individualistic and collectivistic cultures. In addition, they may want to 'manipulate' interaction with members of in-groups and out-groups within cultures in a laboratory experiment or on a survey because predictions based on I–C would suggest that there is more variability in in-group–out-group behaviour in collectivistic cultures than in individualistic cultures.[4]

14.3.2 Isolating the effect being studied

Closely related to issues of research design is isolating the specific effect being studied. Researchers often mistakenly assume that culture has only one type of effect on behaviour. This is not the case. If responses to a set of items are considered, culture can have two different types of effects (Leung and Bond 1989). First, culture can affect the relationships among the items. Two items, for example, may be uncorrelated in one culture, positively correlated in another culture, and negatively correlated in a third. This is referred to as the 'patterning' effect of culture. If the correlations are similar across cultures, the relationship has cross-cultural generalizability. If the correlations are different, explanations for the differences must be generated. Second, culture can affect how 'average' members of different cultures respond to items. This is referred to as the 'location' effect of culture. The same correlations may exist between two items in two cultures, but average members of the culture may respond differently to the items.

To establish dimensions of variation at the cultural level, mean scores for cultures on a series of items from individuals from a large number of cultures are either factor analysed or clustered using nonmetric multidimensional scaling. These procedures isolate a location effect for culture, and only a location effect (Leung and Bond 1989). Alternatively, a pan-cultural analysis can be conducted. This type of analysis can yield both a location and a patterning effect for culture. Neither procedure allows for dimensions at the individual level to be isolated.

In order to isolate dimensions at the individual level an 'iso-region' analysis must be conducted (Leung and Bond 1989). To conduct an iso-region analysis, the data are first standardized within individuals – i.e. they are mathematically transformed so that all an individual's responses have zero mean and unit variance. The within-individual standardized scores are then standardized within cultures to eliminate the location effect for culture. If the resulting data are factor analysed, the factors are 'pure' because there is no location effect for culture. There is, however, still a patterning effect for culture in the data. This procedure allows researchers to examine cultural differences at the individual level or to ignore culture and look for universals at the individual level.

The effects that researchers need to isolate depend on the research questions or hypotheses they posed. If the question/hypothesis focuses on universal patterns of behaviour, the pattern effect must be the focus. If, on the other hand, researchers are interested in how behaviour differs in individualistic and collectivistic cultures, the location effect must be the focus.

14.3.3 Equivalence

'If comparisons are to be legitimately made across cultural boundaries, it is first necessary to establish equivalent bases upon which to make comparisons' (Lonner 1979: 27). Equivalence refers to equality in quantity, value, meaning, and so forth. At least five types of equivalence must be addressed: functional, conceptual, linguistic, metric, and sample equivalence. Lack of equivalence in any of these areas can provide rival hypotheses to explain results in cross-cultural studies.

14.3.3.1 Functional equivalence
Functional equivalence involves the relationship between specific observations and the inferences that are made from the observations. Goldschmidt (1966) argues that activities must have similar functions if they are to be used for purposes of comparison. Berry (1969: 122) elaborates:

Functional equivalence of behaviour exists when the behaviour in question has developed in response to a problem shared by two or more societal/cultural groups, even though the behaviour in one society does not appear to be related to its counterpart in another society. These functional equivalences must pre-exist as naturally occurring phenomena; they are discovered and cannot be created or manipulated.

Without equivalent functions, behaviour across cultures cannot be compared.

To illustrate, one area of research in which functional equivalence is of concern is research on communication apprehension (e.g. fear of communication: see Klopf and Cambra 1979). While communication apprehension is viewed as undesirable in the United States where the concept originated, this view is not shared in Japan or Korea where reticence is valued. Any comparisons of this phenomenon must take these functional differences into account. Lack of functional equivalence is a rival hypothesis to the dimension(s) of cultural variability being studied in explaining the results of a cross-cultural study.

14.3.3.2 Conceptual equivalence

Functional equivalence involves equivalence at the macro or cultural level. Conceptual equivalence, in contrast, 'focuses upon the presence (or absence) of meanings that individuals attach to specific stimuli' (Lonner 1979: 27). Sears (1961) argues that researchers must discover the meaning of concepts to individuals within the cognitive systems of the members of the culture(s) being examined.

When studying concepts that first appear unique to one culture (e.g. *amae, sasshi, ishin denshin, enryo, tatemae-honne,* or *omote-ura,* in Japan; assertiveness, communication apprehension, empathy, in the USA), for example, it is necessary to begin by looking at emic conceptualizations of the concepts. Once the concepts have been analysed emically, cross-cultural studies can begin. It is critical, however, to take one additional step and to generate etic conceptualizations of concepts that are compatible with culturally-specific emic conceptualizations (i.e., derived etic conceptualizations).

To illustrate the process being suggested here consider the concept of face. Some writers suggest that face is a universal construct (e.g. Brown and Levinson 1987, Ho 1976) and others argue that the conceptualization of face is culture-specific (e.g. Hofstede 1984, Morisaki and Gudykunst 1994). Morisaki and Gudykunst, for example, argue that face is based on the interdependent self-construal in Japan and based on the independent self-construal in the USA. Hofstede also points out that 'preserving face – that is, preserving the respect from one's reference groups – is the collectivistic alternative to preserving self-respect in the individualistic culture' (1984: 394). Given the differences in conceptualizing face, one must be careful in comparing face across collectivistic and individualistic cultures. Since the referents are different, simple translations cannot be used to study cultural differences in face.

To study face across cultures, a derived etic conceptualization is needed. To capture the conceptualization of face that is shared across cultures it is necessary to isolate the emic conceptualizations and look for commonalities. The commonality in Japanese and US American conceptualizations of face, for example, involves claimed public images. The referents and who is included in the public image differ, but there are sufficient commonalities on which to base etic research (Gudykunst *et al.* 1993). Given the derived etic conceptualization, face would be operationalized using procedures to develop derived etic measures (see below).

An alternative approach is to use emic operationalizations of concepts to test etic models. Triandis *et al.* (1973), for example, suggest that a three-stage process be used in cross-cultural studies. First, researchers develop etic constructs that appear to be universal. Second, researchers develop emic measures of the constructs and validate them. Third, they use the emic operationalizations to study the etic constructs across cultures. This procedure works well for constructs that are 'universal', but it does not work as well in studying constructs that at first glance appear to be culturally-specific. For these constructs, the procedure outlined earlier (i.e. developing derived etic conceptualizations) is needed. Lack of conceptual equivalence becomes a rival hypothesis to the dimension(s) of cultural variability being studied in explaining the results in a cross-cultural study.

14.3.3.3 Linguistic equivalence

Linguistic (or translation) equivalence focuses on the language used in questionnaires, interviews, field observations, or instructions used in research (see Brislin 1976 for a discussion of translation issues). Administration of research instruments in a language of one culture to people in another culture for whom this language is not a native language yields data that are not equivalent. Even if the respondents are bilingual in the original language of the research instrument, the data are not equivalent. Research instruments must be administered in the respondents' native language and the forms used in different cultures must be linguistically equivalent. Lack of linguistic equivalence is a rival hypothesis to the dimension(s) of cultural variability being studied in explaining the results of cross-cultural research.

The most widely used method to establish linguistic equivalence is backtranslation. This procedure generally involves one bilingual translating the instrument from the first language into the second and another bilingual backtranslating the instrument into the first language. Variations in original wording and the backtranslation must then be reconciled.

Brislin (1976: 222) argues that research instruments need to be decentred where

> material in one language is changed so that there will be a smooth, natural sounding version in the second language. The result of decentering contrasts with the awkward, stilted versions common when material in one language is taken as the final content that must be translated with minimal change into another language.

This can be very difficult when multiple cultures are involved.

14.3.3.4 Metric equivalence

Closely related to linguistic equivalence is the issue of metric equivalence, establishing that the score levels obtained in one culture are equivalent to score levels obtained in another culture. To illustrate, research suggests that Japanese do not use extreme scores (e.g. strongly agree or strongly disagree) as much as US Americans. Japanese, therefore, may score lower on scales constructed from questionnaires because of their response tendency, not because of real cultural differences.

Poortinga (1975) argues that there are at least three alternative interpretations of differences in scores between two cultures: (1) the differences exist and are real, (2) the test measures qualitatively different aspects of the concept (this is related to conceptual and linguistic equivalence), and (3) the test measures quantitatively different aspects of the concept. Without establishing metric equivalence, the second and third interpretations become rival hypotheses to explain differences observed across cultures. Minimally both raw and standardized scores should be examined in cross-cultural studies to ensure metric equivalence. Lack of metric equivalence is a rival hypothesis to the dimension(s) of cultural variability being studied in explaining the results of cross-cultural studies.

14.3.3.5 Sample equivalence

The final equivalence is sample equivalence. It is important that comparable samples are used when cross-cultural comparisons are made. Brislin and Baumgardner (1971) point out that most cross-cultural studies use samples of convenience, rather than random samples. Since random samples generally are not feasible in cross-cultural research, steps need to be taken to ensure that samples are as equivalent as possible.

One way to demonstrate the samples are as equivalent as possible is to gather as much data as possible on the respondents that is relevant to the study and compare the data across samples. To illustrate, basic demographic information on the samples (e.g. sex, age, education, social class, etc.) can help establish equivalence. Also, other variables that might be related to the dependent variables could be collected. If, for example, communication in in-groups and out-groups is being studied, the intimacy of the relationships and frequency of contact should be assessed. Lack of sample equivalence is a rival hypothesis to the dimension(s) of cultural variability being studied in explaining the results of cross-cultural studies.

Related to sample equivalence is the issue of whether the samples used actually represent the dimensions of cultural variability being studied (this issue is discussed in more detail below). Samples from Japan, for example, should be checked to ensure that the respondents are collectivistic and samples from the USA need to be checked to ensure they are individualistic. Gudykunst and Nishida (in press) argue that this often is problematic since Japanese college students demonstrate high levels of individualism and when selected 'manipulation check' items are used Japanese samples may be more individualistic than United States samples. Researchers using etic approaches must be careful to ensure that their samples are indeed representative of the dimensions they are studying.

14.3.4 Developing derived etic measures

Often when researchers study behaviour across cultures, they assume that a concept from one culture exists in another culture and that it is similar. These researchers then may use a measure developed in one culture (e.g. a measure of communication apprehension developed in the USA) in the other culture without any changes. This procedure often is referred to as an 'imposed' etic (Berry 1969) or 'pseudo' etic (Triandis et al. 1973). Imposed or pseudo etic measurement can create problems (see issues of equivalence discussed earlier). To develop equivalent measures the 'derived' etic (Berry 1969) measurement is necessary.

Developing derived etic measures is a time-consuming process. Emic aspects of the concept under study must be generated in each culture in which data are being collected (e.g. by intensive interviews or open-ended surveys). The culture-specific and the universal aspects of the concept must be integrated into one measure, translated, and pre-tested in each culture. Based on the pre-test, items that are inappropriate in one or more cultures are discarded and a final measure developed (for an example, see Hasegawa and Gudykunst's 1998 study of silence). The final instrument is presented to a new sample in all of the cultures.

To isolate possible dimensions of the concept being studied, the resulting data must be standardized within cultures before they are factor analysed (to remove the location effect). To illustrate, if researchers are studying self-construals across cultures, they would expect two factors to emerge in the analysis: independent and interdependent self-construals. When the within-culture standardized data are factor analysed, the factors that emerge are the derived etic measure. These factors will be common to all of the cultures. Culture-specific items will not load on the factors isolated. Within-culture factor analysis can be performed to isolate culture-specific factors. The dimensions that emerge from factor analyses should be assessed for reliability and validity (a within-culture analysis, not across cultures, even for derived etics).

As indicated earlier, developing derived etic measures is a time-consuming process. The larger the number of cultures, the longer it will take. One alternative to developing derived etic measures is to use comparable emic measures to test etic models (see Davidson *et al.* 1976, and Triandis and Marin 1983).

14.4 Problems in testing theory in current cross-cultural research

There are numerous problems in the current cross-cultural research being conducted. The space available does not allow a discussion of all of these problems. I therefore focus on problems in conducting theory-based cross-cultural research.[5]

14.4.1 Cultures studied

The vast majority of cross-cultural research involves comparisons of

Asian and Western cultures. One reason for this is that there are more Asian scholars trained in psychology and communication to serve as collaborators than there are researchers in other collectivistic cultures (e.g. Arab, Latin and African cultures). Clearly, there is a need for more research examining behaviour in non-Asian collectivistic cultures. To make generalizations about the dimensions of cultural variability, cultures from many different world regions must be studied.

Generalizations made regarding Asian collectivists may or may not apply to non-Asian collectivistic cultures. Similarly, generalizations from the United States, Britain and Australia may not generalize to other individualistic cultures (e.g. Germany, Norway). There is a clear need for studies of behaviour in a variety of individualistic and collectivistic cultures. Without such studies, it is impossible to make firm generalizations about the effects of cultural I–C (or other dimensions of cultural variability). Isolating the effect of cultural I–C on behaviour also depends on the number of cultures studied and whether that behaviour may be a function of more than one dimension.

14.4.2 Use of only one dimension of cultural variability

Most cross-cultural studies use only one dimension of cultural variability to explain behaviour across cultures. I–C is the dimension used most widely in cross-cultural research. I–C is often used when there is *not* a clear linkage between I–C and the specific behaviour under study. I–C is used so frequently that many researchers have begun to view it as monolithic. In fact, it is probably only behaviour linked to the in-group–out-group distinction that is related to cultural I–C. However, behaviour linked to the in-group–out-group distinction may also be related to other dimensions of cultural variability. If individuals are of unequal status, for example, cultural PD should also affect behaviour. Also, if the individuals' genders differ, cultural M–F should influence the behaviour.

Many aspects of behaviour are affected by more than one dimension of cultural variability (Gudykunst and Ting-Toomey 1988). To illustrate, to understand interaction with strangers it is probably necessary to use both I–C and UA. Members of collectivistic cultures, for example, respond differently to strangers depending on whether they come from low UA or high UA cultures (see Gudykunst and Matsumoto 1996). Further, when Asian cultures are studied, it is particularly important to use multiple dimensions of cultural variability. Asian cultures tend to be collectivistic, but some of the differences among them are a function of differences in UA (see Gudykunst and Bond 1997).

14.4.3 Number of cultures studied

The vast majority of cross-cultural studies involve comparing behaviour in only two cultures. One reason for this trend is the difficulty of forming research teams involving more than two cultures. Another difficulty involves problems in developing derived etic measures in multiple cultures. Also, the more cultures in which data are collected, the longer it takes to complete the research.

To test the effect of dimensions of cultural variability on communication, however, it is necessary to study behaviour in more than two cultures. To illustrate, to ensure that behaviour is due to cultural I–C, at least four cultures are needed (two predominately individualistic and two predominately collectivistic). There must be consistency of responses within at least two individualistic and two collectivistic cultures, and differences between the individualistic and collectivistic cultures. Without at least four cultures, the results may be due to unique aspects of the cultures studied rather than the dimensions of cultural variability studied. This is complicated when the behaviour is a function of more than one dimension of cultural variability.

If the behaviour is a function of more than one dimension of cultural variability, at least eight cultures are needed to adequately test theoretical hypotheses. To illustrate, assume the behaviour is theoretically predicted to be a function of I–C and M–F. To test such predictions, samples from eight cultures are needed: two predominately individualistic, masculine cultures; two predominately individualistic, feminine cultures; two predominately collectivistic, masculine cultures; and two predominately collectivistic, feminine cultures. Also, it must be kept in mind that the behaviour under study needs to be linked clearly to specific cultural norms/rules because I–C and M–F tendencies exist in all cultures.

14.4.4 Ignoring individual-level mediators of cultural-level phenomena

The vast majority of cross-cultural studies do not include individual-level factors that mediate the influence of the cultural dimension(s) under study. The importance of the individual-level factors has only been demonstrated in recent years (around 1995–6), and most current data were collected before this research was published. Future research must, however, begin to take the individual-level factors into consideration.

As indicated earlier, some behaviour is a function of cultural norms and rules, and some is due to individual variability within cultures. The only way that these differential effects can be isolated is if individual-level mediators of the cultural dimension under study are included in the research (this requires derived etic measures of these mediators). Including individual-level mediators is also important because they allow researchers to determine if their samples are representative of the cultural dimension under study.

14.4.5 Representativeness of respondents

Most cross-cultural researchers do not present clear evidence that their respondents are representative of the cultural-level processes studied (this is not an issue in all studies; e.g. studies not involving people, such as those of political advertisements). When samples are collected in individualistic and collectivistic cultures, for example, the respondents in collectivistic cultures are often highly individualistic (see Gudykunst and Nishida in press; Triandis *et al.* 1988). This is especially problematic with student samples.

When the samples are not representative of the cultures from which they were drawn, drawing conclusions regarding dimensions of cultural variability is precarious. Members of collectivistic cultures who emphasize an independent self-construal and do not emphasize an interdependent self-construal will not necessarily follow the in-group norms, and their behaviours, therefore, may not be representative of collectivistic cultures. When the results of a study are inconsistent with theoretical hypotheses, lack of representativeness of the respondents becomes a rival hypothesis for the results that cannot be ruled out unless individual-level mediators are measured. It is imperative that individual-level factors be included in the analyses when samples are not representative of the dimensions of cultural variability under study (e.g. where a sample from Japan is more individualistic than a sample from the United States).

14.4.6 Use of only one method

Most cross-cultural studies use only one type of data (e.g. survey) to test hypotheses. If multiple methods are not used, it is possible that the results are due to the methods used. To illustrate, Asian respondents often do not use the response end-points (e.g. strongly agree or strongly disagree) in surveys. As indicated earlier, in this situation differences in the mean scores obtained may be due to the way Asians respond to surveys rather than being due to cultural differences in behaviour. (Response differences can be taken into consideration in data analysis by using standardized scores). Other problems emerge when respondents in one culture are unfamiliar with stimulus material that members of another culture see regularly (as with many cognitive tests).

Closely related to the use of one method is the use of only etic or emic approaches. To fully understand behaviour across cultures, however, both emic and etic measures are needed. Etic measures allow us to understand commonalities across cultures, while emic measures allow us to understand unique aspects of behaviour within cultures.

Ideally, multiple methods should be used to study behaviour across cultures. Multiple methods allow researchers to rule out methods effects as a rival hypothesis for findings. Multiple methods also allow for 'triangulation' of research findings.

14.5 Conclusion

It is impossible to discuss research methods in isolation from theory. The methods researchers use are based on the metatheoretical assumptions they make and the theories they use to guide their thinking. These assumptions may be either explicit or implicit. Whether they are implicit or explicit, assumptions and theories influence how research is conducted. I believe that research is methodologically sounder when the assumptions and theories are explicit than when they are implicit.

Neither extreme subjectivist nor extreme objectivist metatheoretical assumptions are defensible. Behaviour involves both subjective and objective components. Similarly, the use of only emic or etic approaches to research does not provide sound data for understanding behaviour across cultures. Emic and etic approaches must be combined to give adequate explanations.

Cross-cultural research should be designed to test predictions based on dimensions of cultural variability (Hofstede 1991), value orientations (Kluckhohn and Strodtbeck 1961), and pattern variables (Parsons and Shils 1951), as well as being designed to isolate universals or test pan-cultural theory.[6] At least two cultures representing each 'type' of culture are needed to adequately test hypotheses (e.g. if I–C is being studied, two predominately individualistic and two predominately collectivistic cultures are needed). If there are not at least two cultures, the results cannot be adequately linked to the dimensions of cultural variability under study.

Predictions based on dimensions of cultural variability must be linked clearly to cultural norms and rules associated with the dimension(s) of cultural variability under study.[7] If the behaviour is not linked clearly to cultural norms and rules, it is probably due to the individual-level factors that influence the dimensions of cultural variability (e.g. self-construals mediate the influence of cultural I–C on behaviour), not the cultural dimensions. Even when individual differences are not predicted, individual-level measures should be included in cross-cultural research to establish that the respondents are representative of the dimensions being studied.

When designing cross-cultural studies, care should be taken to include measures of variables that may provide rival hypotheses to the dimensions of cultural variability in explaining the results. To illustrate, self-monitoring (e.g. whether people adapt their behaviours given situational demands or behave similarly across situations) may provide an alternative explanation to I–C in explaining why individuals differ in the ways they interact with in-group and out-group members (see Gudykunst *et al.* 1992). In this case, derived etic measures of self-monitoring should be included in the study. If the rival hypotheses are not ruled out, establishing that the results are due to the dimension(s) of cultural variability under study is impossible.

The data collected to test predictions can be quantitative, qualitative, or some combination of the two. It is possible, for example, to test hypotheses based on I–C using conversational analysis and a laboratory experiment. In fact, using multiple methods to test hypotheses is highly desirable. The important thing is that the data provide reliable and valid measures of the concepts being studied (e.g. the 'dependent' variables). This can be accomplished only when imposed or pseudo-etic measurement is *not* used.

To conclude, conducting methodologically-sound cross-cultural research requires the cooperation of culturally diverse research teams. The research teams need to be committed to working together on common lines of research over a period of time, not just one study. Only when a team of researchers work together over a period of time can they develop methodologically-sound procedures for conducting cross-cultural research that will contribute to our theoretical understanding of culture and behaviour.

Discussion questions

1 What are the advantages of treating culture theoretically when conducting cross-cultural research?
2 Why is it necessary to differentiate the cultural and individual levels when conducting cross-cultural research?
3 Why are cross-cultural studies not 'true experiments'?
4 How does lack of metric equivalence (and other forms of equivalence) affect the way in which results of cross-cultural studies must be interpreted?
5 What are the problems in using imposed etic measures in cross-cultural studies?

Suggestions for further reading

Alasuutari, P. (1995) *Researching Culture: Qualitative Method and Cultural Studies*. London: Sage.
Matsumoto, D. (1996) *Culture and Psychology*. Pacific Grove, CA: Brooks/ Cole, chapter 4.
Triandis, H.C. (1994) *Culture and Social Behavior*. New York: McGraw-Hill, chapter 3.
van de Vijver, F. and Leung, K. (1997) *Methods and Data Analysis for Cross-Cultural Research*. Thousand Oaks, CA: Sage.

Notes

1. I want to thank Helen Spencer-Oatey for her suggestions to make this chapter more understandable to linguists.
2. 'Cross-cultural' and 'intercultural' are often regarded as interchangeable. They are, nevertheless, different. Cross-cultural research involves comparing behaviour in two or more cultures (e.g. comparing self-disclosure in Japan, the USA, and Iran when individuals interact with members of their own culture). Intercultural research involves examining behaviour when members of two or more cultures interact (e.g. examining self-disclosure when Japanese and Iranians communicate with each other). Intercultural behaviour is often compared to intracultural behaviour (e.g. behaviour within a culture). To illustrate, Iranian self-disclosure when communicating with Japanese might be compared with Iranian communication with other Iranians. Understanding cross-cultural differences in behaviour is a prerequisite for understanding intercultural behaviour. I therefore focus on issues of conducting cross-cultural research in this chapter.

3. Space does not permit an elaborate discussion of the various dimensions of cultural variability. For a complete discussion of the various dimensions that could be used see Gudykunst and Ting-Toomey (1988). I discuss individual-level factors that mediate I–C, but do not discuss these for other dimensions (see Gudykunst 1995).
4. Obviously, there should be a 'manipulation check' for the manipulated variable.
5. All research involves trade-offs. One problem may be accepted to control for another. There are few, if any, studies that are problem-free, including my own.
6. Van de Vijver and Leung (1997a, 1997b) suggest other non-theoretical rationales for research.
7. It is important to remember that both aspects of each dimension exist in all cultures (e.g. individualism and collectivism exist in all cultures). Care, therefore, must be taken to ensure that the norms and rules are based on the predominant tendencies being used to make predictions.

15

Data Collection in Pragmatics Research

Gabriele Kasper

Social scientists in any discipline struggle with the issue of how to gather appropriate data to answer their research questions. In this chapter, I will review the types of data collection most commonly used in pragmatics to date (summarized in Table 15.1). Since pragmatics is a fairly new field and is practised by scholars educated in different research traditions, its procedures for collecting data draw on the methods and techniques developed in many of the older and better established social sciences, such as anthropology, sociology, psychology, and linguistics.

The columns under 'Focus' in Table 15.1 specify whether the data mainly inform about different aspects of language in use – interaction, comprehension, or production – or about the participant's metaprag-

Table 15.1 Focus and procedure in some data collection formats

| | Focus | | | | Procedure | |
	interaction	comprehension	production	metapragmatic	online/ offline	interaction with researcher
Authentic discourse	+	+	+	−	on	−/+
Elicited conversation	+	+	+	−	on	+/−
Role-play	+	+	+	−	on	−
Production questionnaire	−	−	+	−	off	−
Multiple choice	−	+	+	+	off/on	−
Scales	−	−	−	+	off	−
Interview	−	−	−	+	off	+
Diary	−	−	−	+	off	−
Think-aloud protocols	−	+	+	+	on	−

matic knowledge and subjective theories. In the 'Procedure' columns, 'online/offline' indicates whether data are collected while the participant is engaged in an activity involving language use ('online') or whether the participant is prompted to recall pragmatic information from memory and report rather than use it ('offline'). 'Interaction with researcher' refers to whether or not researcher–participant interaction is an inherent part of the procedure, as in interviews. Even in the data types marked minus interaction, researcher and participant will have some form of contact prior to and sometimes during the data collection, and this interaction may well influence the data. *Authentic discourse, elicited conversation,* and *role-play* are types of spoken interaction; *production questionnaires, multiple choice,* and *scaled response instruments* are survey methods and thus obtain written responses when self-administered; *interviews* are a specific type of spoken interaction that may or may not be structured by a questionnaire; in less structured forms, interviews produce narrative self-reports and are thus akin to *diaries* as a story-telling genre. *Think-aloud protocols* can be related to interviews and diaries in that they, too, produce narrative self-reports; however, in their classic form, they are online verbalizations of thought processes rather than stories. Verbal protocols have their home in experimental psychology and are thus furthest removed from the conversational interaction in authentic talk activities that opened the list of data collection procedures in pragmatics. I shall now consider each procedure in turn.

15.1 Spoken interaction

The common denominator of authentic discourse, elicited conversation, and open-ended role-play or simulation is that the data are oral, interactive productions and thus allow examination of a wide range of discourse features, including the overall structuring of talk exchanges, the distribution of turns at talk, sequencing of conversational contributions, speaker–listener coordination, and participants' joint achievement of transactional and interpersonal goals. They shed light on participants' production of communicative action and their (mis)comprehension of interlocutors' contributions. The obvious difference between the three types of spoken interaction is that authentic discourse is motivated and structured by participants' rather than the researcher's goals whereas elicited conversation and role-play are brought into being for research purposes. From a sociolinguistic and pragmatic perspective, this underscores the fact that neither of the two elicited data types can ever be 'the same' as authentic conversation since the overall purpose of an interaction is its most powerful structuring force – hence designations such as 'communicative activity' as a unit of analysis for studying contextualized talk exchanges. But very much unlike the popular perception that 'inauthentic' equals 'invalid', interactions arranged for research purposes can be most useful data collection procedures if used judiciously.

15.1.1 Authentic discourse

There are two approaches to collecting authentic spoken discourse data in pragmatics: taking field notes and audio- or video-recording. Data on individual communicative acts have been gathered by note-taking (e.g. on compliments: Herbert 1989; apologies: Holmes 1990; invitations: Wolfson et al. 1983) or audio-recording (e.g. on compliments: Pomerantz 1978; apologies: Owen 1983). Studies of extended speech events, by contrast, require electronic recording. Research on authentic speech events with non-native speaker participants has predominantly focused on discourse in institutional settings, such as business negotiations (Ehlich and Wagner 1995), academic advising sessions (Bardovi-Harlig and Hartford 1996), and oral proficiency interviews (Young and He 1998), to name but a few. This choice is motivated by a number of reasons. Institutional discourse lends itself well to demonstrating the interrelation of text and context, for instance, how institutional structures influence communicative action and are reproduced by it. The relationship between communicative action and social power is thus particularly evident in institutional discourse. Compared to interpersonal conversation, institutional talk has the advantage of being more highly structured, routinized, and recurrent, a direct consequence of the purpose of the institution, role distribution between actors (institutional representative versus client), and actors' goals. In research methodological perspective, this is greatly advantageous because the institutional patterning allows researchers to observe speakers from different sociocultural groups in the same social roles, usually that of a client (one interesting exception being the international teaching assistant, who is an institutional representative). Thus studies of institutional discourse often include an in-built control group (see e.g. Bardovi-Harlig and Hartford 1996).

Frequently the most difficult part in gathering extended authentic data is to gain access to the research site. Institutions are often reluctant to allow any form of observation, and if they do, they may not allow recording. Yet without audio- and preferably video-recordings, the entire research enterprise will be in jeopardy. As we know from microanalytic approaches to discourse, such as conversation analysis (e.g. Heritage 1997), interactional sociolinguistics (e.g. Gumperz 1996) and ethnographic microanalysis (e.g. Erickson 1992), discourse features and strategies exhibit finely structured co-occurrences and regularities that escape even the well-trained observer and are impossible to fixate in memory. There is thus a real danger that memorization and taking field notes will result in recording salient and expected (or particularly unexpected) facets of the interaction, at the expense of less salient but perhaps decisive (often indexical) material. Field notes are a valuable source of contextual information and are indispensable in ethnographic studies, yet they cannot replace electronic recordings (see Duranti 1997, who also gives practical suggestions for recording interaction). In fact, this is not only true for the study of extended speech events but may also apply to the investigation of individual speech acts. For instance, note-taking has proved to be a productive method for studying compliments in different varieties of English because compliments are most frequently packaged as single-turn utterances with a simple, short, highly formulaic structure (see e.g. Wolfson 1989). It is, of course, perfectly legitimate to focus on the content, syntactic structure, and lexical items used in complimenting and, as the compliment research shows, these can indeed be recorded via note-taking. But if the research focus centres on the complimenting *event* in its social and discourse context, including compliment responses and their uptake, electronically recorded data is crucial because note-taking from memory might miss important information. Thus one of the most insightful studies on compliment responses (Pomerantz 1978) would not have been possible without the microanalysis afforded by the audio-recorded data.

In discussions of how best to collect authentic conversational data, the observer's paradox (Labov 1972) is often brought up: is the researcher's presence not going to alter the normal course of the interaction, and will this effect not be exacerbated by a video-camera? As Duranti (1997) argues from rich experience with ethnographic studies, the observer effect is usually temporary. The initial disturbance of routine transactions through the presence of an outsider and of video equipment will subside when the novelty effect has worn off and the routines kick in again. Routinized actions (for instance, teachers' and students' classroom practices) are highly overlearned and difficult to change; they will quickly re-emerge once the interaction is under way. However, since initial observer effects are quite possible, researchers should refrain from the get-your-data-and-run type of data collection. In ethnography, prolonged engagement in the field is a fundamental methodological principle for many reasons besides the observer's paradox (see Watson-Gegeo 1988 and Davis 1995 for ethnography in applied linguistics; Davis and Henze 1998 for ethnography and pragmatics), with 'blitzkrieg ethnography' (Rist 1980) amounting to malpractice. In research with a predominantly discourse analytical orientation, it may be helpful if the researchers and their recording devices are present in the setting for some time prior to the data collection so that participants can get used to having them around. This extra time should be calculated as an indispensable part of the data collection and will be rewarded by a better quality of data.

In addition to the problem of gaining access, authentic data may have other drawbacks. Depending on the research purpose, it may take an unreasonable amount of data to obtain sufficient quantities of the pragmatic feature under study – for instance, of a particular speech act. In fact, authentic data may just not be a viable option when an essential component of the research goal is to compare the use of specific pragmatic features by different groups of speakers in a given context (e.g. pragmatic transfer studies which compare how native and non-native speakers respond to compliments under given circumstances). In this very common situation, elicited conversations or role-plays offer an alternative.

15.1.2 Elicited conversation

The term *elicited conversation* refers to any conversation staged for the purpose of data collection. Unlike in role-plays, participants do not take on social roles different from their own; however, they assume discourse roles assigned by the researcher. We can distinguish two varieties of elicited conversation.

In *conversation tasks*, participants are requested to converse about a topic or jointly reach a particular goal determined by the researcher. Instructions can be as vague as asking participants to get to know each other (see e.g. Scarcella 1983, White 1989), or can be more prescriptive, for example requiring them to address the interlocutor's troubles tellings (Kerekes 1992). Data elicited through such conversation tasks have been found useful for studying various aspects of conversational management (Scarcella 1983) such as backchannelling (White 1989), the use of indexicals such as the Japanese sentence-final particle *ne* (Yoshimi 1999) and the effects of pragmatic transfer on the use of discourse markers and strategies. Kerekes (1992) investigated if and how participants respond to troubles tellings by offering advice or expressions of sympathy. Her study thus focused on specific responding speech acts in troubles-telling events. Even though nothing prevents conversation tasks from including differentially symmetric or asymmetric participant configurations, the cited studies featured equal-status encounters with fairly balanced participation structures, as far as one can tell from the reports.

In this regard, conversation tasks are systematically different from the other variety of elicited conversation, the *sociolinguistic interview*. As with any kind of interview, the sociolinguistic interview is an asymmetrical speech event in which 'one party asks the questions and the other party gives the answers' (Schegloff 1992: 118). Unlike the conversation task, sociolinguistic interviews thus have a genre-specific structure. As part of the standard repertoire in sociolinguistic data collection (Labov 1984; Schiffrin 1987), interviewers ask informants about their life history, experiences, and attitudes. In Labov's original design, one important function of the sociolinguistic interview was to ask the informant about highly emotional experiences under the assumption that such topics would trigger vernacular speech. Topic investment has been shown to affect interlanguage performance (Eisenstein and Starbuck 1989), but its effect on learners' L2 pragmatics has not yet been explored. Sociolinguistic interviews with L2 learners have been analysed for conversational management and repair (Færch and Kasper 1982) and the acquisition of the Japanese sentence-final particle *ne* (Sawyer 1992). Tao and Thompson (1991) examined retroactive transfer in the backchannelling patterns of native speakers of Mandarin Chinese from their interlanguage English, whereas Sawyer (1992) compared learners' production of *ne* in four interviews, conducted over the period of one year, in order to determine developmental patterns in the use of the particle. Sawyer's (1992) study, one of the first on non-native speakers' pragmatic development (cf. Kasper and Schmidt 1996; Kasper and Rose 1999, for review), raises an interesting design issue. As native-speaker baseline data, Sawyer used the frequency of *ne* in the discourse contributions of the Japanese interviewer. This presents a potential validity problem because the asymmetrical structure of the interview positions interviewer and informant in different discourse roles and this asymmetry is very likely reflected in, and in fact co-constructed by, the use of *ne*. As a key discourse marker, *ne* has been shown to index epistemic and affective stance (see e.g. Cook 1992, Yoshimi 1999); as an indexical, its use is, by definition, highly context-sensitive. If comparisons to native-speaker use of *ne* are made, they should be to speakers in the same discourse roles as the non-native speakers. In other words, baseline data could have been obtained by conducting interviews with native speakers of Japanese who were otherwise comparable to the non-native informants, allowing the examination of the use of *ne* in the native and non-native informants' interview responses.

Elicited conversations have the capacity to shed light on such discourse aspects as conversational organization and management, the expression of reference and modality, task-specific communicative acts, and narrative structure. But they are also limited in that participant roles cannot be manipulated, and they allow investigation of only a restricted set of communicative acts and activities.

15.1.3 Role-play

This limitation of elicited conversations is overcome in role-plays, i.e. simulations of communicative encounters, usually in dyads, based on role descriptions. Role-play can be defined as 'a social or human activity in which participants "take on" and "act out" specified "roles", often within a predefined social framework or situational blueprint (a "scenario")' (Crookall and Saunders 1989: 15–16).

Different types of role-play can be distinguished according to participant involvement and extent of interaction. In spontaneous role-plays, players retain their own identities. In mimetic-replicating role-plays, they play the role of a visually presented model, while in mimetic-pretending role-plays, actors assume a different identity (Kipper 1988). Useful as these categories are as a first rough distinction, they are too broad to capture other potentially important variables that might affect the quality of role-playing. For instance, a particular type of spontaneous role-play is the idiographic role-play, in which participants recall and re-run specific, recent and relevant extended interactions (Kern 1991).[1] The great advantage of this type of interaction is that people can rely on recent episodic memory (although they do not have to be completely dependent on it), which will reduce the cognitive load associated with having to invent the action online.

Role-plays also differ in the extent of the interaction. In interlanguage pragmatics, a distinction has been suggested between closed and open role-plays (Kasper and Dahl 1991). In closed role-plays, the actor responds to the description of a situation and, depending on the communicative act under study, to an interlocutor's standardized initiation. They are thus organized as single-turn speech acts. This procedure has been used to elicit requests (Rintell 1981; Rintell and Mitchell 1989), suggestions (Rintell 1981), and apologies (Cohen and Olshtain 1981; Rintell and Mitchell 1989). Open role-plays, on the other hand, specify the initial situation and each actor's role and goal(s) on individual role cards, but the course and outcome of the interaction are in no way predetermined. For instance, a fairly complex interaction would be one where actors discover during the interaction that they have conflicting goals and have to negotiate how to manage their goal conflict, as in the following example.

A. You are going to move into a new apartment on Saturday. It is Thursday today, and you have just received a call from a friend of yours who was supposed to help you move house, saying that he is unable to help you move after all. You don't have a car or a driver's licence, so you depend on the help of somebody who does. You decide to ask B, your next door neighbour. The two of you are friends, and you have helped each other out before. You go to see B.

B. It is Thursday. You have just made arrangements with some friends to spend the weekend in the country. You and your friends are planning to go in your car, leaving Saturday morning and coming back Sunday night. You are at home, watching TV, when the door rings. You can see through the peephole that it is your friend and neighbour, A.

Unlike closed role-plays, an open role-play such as one based on these role descriptions will evolve over many turns and different discourse phases. Communicative acts will be organized over multiple turns and their sequencing will be strongly influenced by the interlocutor's uptake. The conversational activity will address interpersonal functions, such as politeness, and interactional functions, such as coordinating speaker and listener contributions through turn-taking and backchannelling. Open role-plays thus allow observation of those aspects of conversation that are fairly independent of particular contexts and goals, but unlike authentic discourse and elicited conversation, they also permit us to design contexts and roles that are likely to elicit specific speech events and communicative acts. Moreover, through the role specifications, they also enable us to observe how context factors, such as power, distance, and imposition in Brown and Levinson's (1987) politeness theory, influence the selection and realization of communicative acts and how the values of these factors may be changed through conversational negotiation. The rich potential of role-plays to elicit pragmatic and sociolinguistic features in their full discourse context is evident from interlanguage pragmatics research on communicative acts such as requests (Hassall 1997), expressions of gratitude (Eisenstein and Bodman 1993), apologies (García 1989), complaints (Trosborg 1995), refusals (Widjaja 1997), and various face-threatening acts (Piirainen-Marsh 1995); (mis)understanding in service encounters and institutional discourse (Bremer *et al.* 1996); discourse cohesion (Stemmer 1981); gambits (Wildner-Bassett 1984, 1994); conversational organization and maintenance (Edmondson *et al.* 1984); routine formulae (Tateyama *et al.* 1997); and pragmatic fluency (House 1996b).

We thus know that role-play produces all aspects of conversation, but we do not know from the use of role-plays alone whether they provide valid representations of conversational practices in authentic contexts. Whereas validity concerns loom large in behavioural assessment and other social sciences using role-play as a research tool, only a few studies have examined the validity of role-play in interlanguage pragmatics. Though not methodological in focus, Eisenstein and Bodman's (1993) study of expression of gratitude by native and non-native speakers of English sheds light on the effects of three data collection procedures – production questionnaires, open-ended role-plays, and field notes – on expressions of gratitude occurring in authentic interactions. All three data types yielded the same words and expressions, yet they differed in length and complexity. The production questionnaire data were the shortest and least complex, the authentic data the longest and most complex, with the role-play data coming in between. The oral data included more restatements of thanks and discussions about the received gift or service. Both role-play and authentic data demonstrated that thanking is collaboratively enacted, involving the giver as much as the receiver.

Three studies that have compared role-play and written production questionnaires are Margalef-Boada (1993), Sasaki (1998) and Edmondson and House (1991). Margalef-Boada (1993) examined the production of refusals by native speakers of German, native speakers of Spanish (including bilinguals in Castilian and Catalan), and German learners of Spanish, using both data collection methods. In the role-plays, native speakers were paired with native speakers and non-native speakers with non-native speakers. The stimulus contexts were the same for the oral and written conditions, each specifying a request, offer, invitation, or suggestion that the participant had to refuse. The analysis showed the same content and range of semantic formulae in both conditions, with most of them occurring with roughly the same frequency. Different distributions were most noticeable in direct refusals, expressions of regret, avoidance, and adjuncts. The main difference between the written responses and the oral interaction was the large number of semantic repetitions in the role-play (Margalef-Boada 1993: 116). Through the interactive nature of the role-play and the multiple turns over which the refusal event evolved, the role-plays were naturally longer, 'richer and more complex' (Margalef-Boada 1993: 153) than the written single-turn responses. However, in both conditions, participants produced less polite refusals than would be appropriate in an authentic setting, suggesting that the absence of social consequences may have relaxed their adherence to politeness norms.

Sasaki's (1998) comparative study of production questionnaires and role-plays differed from Margalef-Boada (1993) in that she investigated two communicative acts, requests and refusals, and administered the two tasks to the same participants, Japanese EFL learners. In the role-plays, confederates were native speakers of American English. Both methods elicited similar head acts and supportive moves for requests, and types and order of semantic formulae for refusals. But responses varied in length and content, the role-play contributions featuring longer utterances and a greater variety of strategies.

Obviously, when conversational interaction and the sequencing of communicative action in conjunction with turn-taking is the research focus, an interactive procedure such as role-play needs to be chosen. On the other hand, if the purpose of an investigation is to inform about the types of strategies by which a communicative act can be implemented, written production questionnaires are an effective means of data collection, as we will see below.

15.2 Questionnaires

Compared with spoken interaction methods, questionnaires may appear far more restricted in the scope of questions they allow us to study. Excluded from investigation are precisely those pragmatic features that are specific to oral interactive discourse – any aspect related to the dynamics of a conversation, turn-taking and the conversational mechanisms related to it, sequencing of action, speaker–listener coordination, features of speech production that may have pragmatic import, such as hesitation, and all paralinguistic and non-verbal elements. Despite these limitations, different forms of questionnaire data are the most commonly used data types in interlanguage pragmatics.

The three types of questionnaire used in pragmatics – production, multiple-choice, and rating-scale questionnaires – differ from each other in the type of response they elicit. Production questionnaires are open-ended in the sense that they require a participant-generated textual response that is coherent with the context specified in the stimulus item. Multiple-choice and scaled-response questionnaires, by contrast, provide fixed response alternatives from which the participant has to choose the most appropriate one. I will examine each of the three types in turn.

15.2.1 Production questionnaires

Items in a production questionnaire include a situational description and a brief dialogue which has one turn as an open slot. The context given in the scenario is designed to constrain the open turn so that a specific communicative act is elicited. Item formats used in different studies vary in a number of ways. In the classic discourse completion format, (a), the exchange is terminated by a provided rejoinder (1 and 2) and can also be prefaced by an interlocutor initiation (1). The rejoinder can be positive as in (1), where Charlie accepts Jim's (expected) apology, or negative as in (2), where Leslie refuses Walter's (expected) request.

(a) 'classic' discourse completion
(1) *In the lobby of a university library*
    Jim and Charlie have agreed to meet at 6 o'clock to work on a joint project. Charlie arrives on time and Jim is an hour late.
    Charlie: I almost gave up on you!
    Jim:_____
    Charlie: O.K. Let's start working.

(2) *After a meeting*
    Walter and Leslie live in the same neighbourhood, but they only know each other by sight. One day, they both attend a meeting held on the other side of town. Walter does not have a car but he knows that Leslie has come in her car.
    Walter:_____

Leslie: I'm sorry but I'm not going home right away.

(Blum-Kulka *et al.* 1989)

This basic format has been variously modified. In dialogue construction, (b), and the open response formats (c) and (d), no rejoinder is provided. Dialogue construction can either be initiated by a provided first pair part (3) or the participant has to provide both (or all) contributions (4).

(b) Dialogue construction
(3) Your advisor suggests that you take a course during the summer. You prefer not to take classes during the summer.
   Advisor: What about taking Testing in the summer?
   You say:_____

(Bardovi-Harlig and Hartford 1993)

(4) *At a restaurant*
   Catherine is having dinner at an expensive restaurant. When she is getting up from the table she bumps into a waiter, who spills a tray of food.
   Catherine:_____
   Waiter:_____

(Bergman and Kasper 1993)

The open response formats differ in requiring a verbal response, as in (c), or, as in (d), allowing a verbal response, a non-verbal response, or no response, that is, to opt out (d). The choice to opt out allows us to identify sociopragmatic differences in the appropriateness of communicative acts (Bonikowska 1988).

(c) open item, verbal response only
(5) It's your birthday, and you're having a few friends over for dinner. A friend brings you a present. You unwrap it and find a blue sweater.
   You say:_____

(Eisenstein and Bodman 1993)

(6) It is not the first time that loud rock music is heard from your neighbour's apartment quite late at night.
   You pick up the phone and say:_____

(Olshtain and Weinbach 1993)

(7) An American classmate offers you a ride to an off-campus

meeting which you are both required to attend. You are planning to go, and you need a ride, but you do not want to ride with her because of her unsafe driving.

Classmate: Since we're both going to that meeting downtown on Thursday, why don't you ride with me? I'd like some company and besides, you could help me find the place we're supposed to go to.

You:_____

(Robinson 1992)

(d) open item, free response

(8) You are a corporate executive. Your assistant submits a proposal for reassignment of secretarial duties in your division. Your assistant describes the benefits of the plan, but you believe it will not work.

You:_____

(Beebe and Takahashi 1989b, Takahashi and Beebe 1993)

(9) You are going shopping with a friend. She is trying on a pink blouse which she is thinking of buying. In your opinion it does not look good on her at all.

You would:_____

(Steinberg Du 1995)

Does item format, specifically, the presence or absence of a rejoinder and, when a rejoinder is included, whether it is positive (1) or negative (2), influence responses? A recent study investigated this issue and found that different item formats have an effect on participants' strategy choices for requests, complaints, and apologies. Results from production questionnaires with different item formats are thus not directly comparable (Johnston *et al.* 1998).

Furthermore, production questionnaire formats differ as to whether they require the participant to imagine how a fictive person would act in the specified situation (1, 2, 4, 8) or how they think they themselves would act (3, 7). In this regard, production questionnaires allow for the same roletaking options as role-plays.

An obvious question to worry about is whether and how the written mode as opposed to spoken production may result in different responses. Rintell and Mitchell (1989) addressed this question by comparing spoken and written requests and apologies from native and non-native speakers of English, elicited by oral (open role-play) and written (open response format) versions of the same production questionnaire. They found that non-native speakers' oral responses were significantly longer than their written responses; however, this was not true for the native speakers, suggesting that language proficiency rather than research procedure was a crucial factor. Moreover, in some situations both groups were more direct in the written than in the spoken mode, suggesting that respondents were more influenced by face and politeness issues in procedures involving face-to-face interaction. However, these differences were outweighed by the similarities of the written and oral responses, suggesting that strategy choice and wording of single-turn responses to production tasks may be fairly stable across modalities. (See also the discussion in section 15.1.3.)

A serious concern is how production questionnaires compare to authentic data. Beebe and Cummings (1996, originally presented 1985) compared refusals elicited through a single-item questionnaire with refusals performed in telephone conversations in response to the same request. Interlocutors in these interchanges were native speakers of American English. The questionnaire responses did *not* represent natural speech with respect to the actual wording, range of refusal strategies, and response length, but they modelled the 'canonical shape' of refusals, shed light on the social and psychological factors that are likely to affect speech act performance, and helped establish an initial classification of refusal strategies.

Hartford and Bardovi-Harlig (1992) examined the rejections by native and non-native graduate students of their academic advisers' suggestions for the students' course schedules. The production questionnaire elicited a narrower range of semantic formulae and fewer status-preserving strategies than the authentic data, yet it proved an adequate instrument to test hypotheses derived from the authentic interactions. The questionnaire data confirmed Hartford and Bardovi-Harlig's (1992) hypothesis that the non-native speakers were more likely to use unacceptable content to reject advice than the native speakers.

When carefully designed, production questionnaires are useful to inform about speakers' pragmalinguistic knowledge of the strategies and linguistic forms by which communicative acts can be implemented, and about their sociopragmatic knowledge of the context factors under which particular strategic and linguistic choices are appropriate. Whether or not speakers use exactly the same strategies and forms in actual discourse is a different matter, but the questionnaire responses indicate what strategic and linguistic options are consonant with pragmatic norms and what contextual factors influence their choices (although recent studies suggest some qualification; see below). In interlanguage pragmatic research, we may be interested in finding out what L2 learners *know* as opposed to what they can *do* under the much more demanding conditions of conversational encounters. For such research purposes, production questionnaires are an effective option.

15.2.2 Multiple choice

Multiple choice is a versatile questionnaire format which can elicit information on production, comprehension, and metapragmatic judgements. Just like production questionnaires, multiple-choice items specify the situational context and include a prompt for a response, but rather than leaving the response selection to the participant, they specify several response alternatives from which one has to be chosen. This is illustrated in an item from a request study.

> You are having dinner with your friend's family. The food that your friend's mother has prepared is delicious, and you want some more. What would you say or do?
> A. I would wait until the mother saw my empty plate and offered more food.
> B. 'Please give me more food.'
> C. 'This food sure is delicious.'
> D. 'Could I have some more please?' (Rose 1994)

Comparison of responses to production questionnaires and multiple choice have indicated differences in the requests provided by native speakers of Japanese in Japanese (Rose 1994, Rose and Ono 1995) and advice-giving by Chinese ESL learners and native speakers of American English (Hinkel 1997). In all three studies, the multiple-choice results were more consistent with reports on preferences for pragmatic strategies in authentic settings, although no direct comparisons with authentic data were made. The reasons for these differences are far from being well understood, but they call for more research into the validity of both questionnaire types. From a cognitive perspective, the two questionnaire formats impose quite different processing demands: the open-ended production question-naire presents a free-recall task, whereas the closed format of the multiple choice presents a recognition task (Schwarz and Hippler 1991). Multiple-choice responses require that subjects evaluate a very small number of presented alternatives against their memory structures of compatible events, a much less demanding task than having to conduct a free memory search and make an appropriate selection from a wide array of possible solutions. Moreover, as far as opting out goes, tasks may not be compatible unless the possibility for opting out is expressly specified as a legitimate option in the production questionnaire.

In designing multiple-choice tasks, it is important to rely on previous research on the communicative act in question, in order to make principled selections of the response alternatives. It is not good enough to invent responses intuitively because pragmatic strategies might escape the researcher's attention. Valid sources to select response alternatives from are speech act realization strategies collected through production questionnaires (Rose and Ono 1995) or from spoken discourse (authentic or elicited), and free responses to comprehension questionnaires (Bouton 1988).

15.2.3 Rating scales

Pragmaticists are often interested in knowing how appropriate, polite, deferential, and so forth, people assess strategies of communicative action and their linguistic realizations (usually in specific contexts) to be. In addition, they may want to know how people assess the values and weights of the contextual variables that influence strategic and linguistic choices, such as participants' relative power, social distance, and the degree of imposition involved in a linguistic act. The first question raises a pragmalinguistic issue, derived from Hymes' theory of communicative competence (see Hinkel 1996 for a recent study comparing the pragmalinguistic perceptions of ESL learners and native speakers of American English). The second question poses a sociopragmatic problem, addressed in Brown and Levinson's politeness theory (see Spencer-Oatey 1996 for a comprehensive discussion of participant variables and Spencer-Oatey 1993 for a cross-cultural study). As in formal linguistics, the most common method of obtaining metapragmatic assessments is by eliciting scaled category responses. Such responses represent a form of self-report data, a common data type throughout the social sciences.

Metapragmatic assessments can be obtained for several purposes: as a research issue in its own right; as an additional resource to help interpret performance data; as a preliminary step towards developing the instrument for the main study; or as a combination of the above. In studies using any kind of data elicitation format, such as role-plays, production questionnaires, or multiple choice, researchers need to know how respondents assess the contextual variables built into the stimulus situations. Such crucial information cannot be obtained by relying on researcher's intuition. Sociopragmatic assessments of candidate contexts elicited in a pre-study enable researchers to ground their contextual constructions empirically and thus to improve control over context variables. Unfortunately, most cross-cultural and inter-language pragmatic studies lack such careful preparation; hence results are difficult to interpret. One exemplary investigation in which the instrument for the main study was developed through a sequence of pre-studies using sociopragmatic and pragmalinguistic assessments is Takahashi (1995). (See also Chapter 5 for a questionnaire with pragmalinguistic oriented rating scales, and Chapter 4 for a questionnaire with sociopragmatic oriented rating scales.)

In constructing scaled response instruments, it is essential to heed the design principles specified in the sociometric and psychometric literature (e.g. D.C. Miller 1991, Bryman and Cramer 1994). Informativeness, reliability, and validity will be maximized if the following principles are followed: (1) Composite constructs (such as 'power' or 'imposition') are unfolded into their underlying dimensions (e.g. for 'imposition' in apologizing: severity of offence, obligation to apologize, likelihood of apology acceptance, offender's face-loss). (2) Each dimension is operationalized by at least two indicators (e.g. for severity of offence: 'How serious is John's offence?', 'How upset is Paul by John's damaging his car?', 'How great is the damage done to Paul by John?', 'How inconvenient is John's offence to Paul?', 'How costly is John's offence to Paul?'). (3) Rating scales are divided into five to seven steps. (4) The linguistic material used in items is cross-linguistically equivalent. This is achieved by backtranslation, an indispensable process in cross-cultural and interlanguage pragmatics research when any kind of linguistic stimulus material is used (see discussion in Chapter 14).

Scaled response instruments such as rating scales, Likert scales, and semantic differential scales presuppose that the constructs under study are known and well-defined. When this is not the case, more participant-directed, open-ended types of self-report are preferable, such as narrative interviews, diaries, and verbal protocols.

15.3 Interviews

In exploratory research, the modes of inquiry need to be open and inclusive, and unpredetermined. But even for hypothesis-testing and triangulation purposes, researchers may prefer a dynamic, context-

and respondent-sensitive procedure such as narrative self-reports. The most common procedure for obtaining such reports is the research interview.

In pragmatics, 'offline' interviews (i.e. interviews not related to a specific immediately preceding activity) have served as the following: as an initial exploration of a research issue, to triangulate the researcher's interpretation of authentic discourse data, as one among several data types in a multi-method approach, and as the main data source. Different types and applications of interviews in research on communicative acts can be illustrated by studies by Knapp et al. (1984) and Miles (1994) on compliments in American English. Knapp et al. used a large-scale survey interview with partly closed-ended questions and brief responses, focusing primarily on the forms of compliments and compliment responses. Data were content-analysed and frequencies reported. Miles (1994) is a qualitative study, based on observation of compliment exchanges occurring in authentic discourse for information about compliment forms and their distribution and on interviews for community members' emic views on the social meanings and functions of complimenting. Questions were open-ended and respondents engaged in extensive narratives and commentary. Data were analysed interpretatively, with particular attention to respondents' discourse. The report includes extensive quotes from interviewees' comments. These methodological differences resulted in major discrepancies in substantive outcomes. One such difference is the preferred response pattern identified in the two studies. According to the observational part of Miles' study, only 7 per cent of the recipients expressed agreement with the compliment. In contrast, in Knapp et al.'s study, 46 per cent of the compliment responses registered as agreements and only 16 per cent were minimized. Further, Knapp et al.'s interview subjects reported without exception that they felt satisfied with the compliment experience, whereas Miles' interview participants reported feelings of embarrassment and face-threat.

What are we to make of these different findings? As far as the response patterns go, the convergent outcomes of observational studies on complimenting in American English suggest that the problem lies with the self-report data. In a reporting context, subjects are more likely to abide by the prescriptive pragmatic norm of agreeing with compliments or accepting them without mitigation. This explanation is supported by the other discrepancy between Knapp et al. (1984) and Miles (1994), the absence or presence of reports of negative affect associated with complimenting. Once subjects report substantive agreement with a compliment, it would be inconsistent to express negative feelings about the same compliment event, whereas reports of experiencing such an event as emotionally gratifying agree with the reported behavioural practice. Interview subjects thus seem to engage in reconstructive memory activity in order to tell consistent stories. While these stories are intriguing material in their own right, their validity is compromised if the research goal is to establish actual practices of communicative action.

If the research goal is to establish communicative practices (as opposed to what members believe these practices to be), interviews are the wrong choice, because interview subjects' reports are affected by memory constraints and prescriptive orientations. The right choice is observation, as the converging results of many observation-based studies on compliments demonstrate. However, interviews are useful and often indispensable when the research goal is to establish the cultural meanings that communicative practices have for community members, because such emic meanings can only be inferred from observation. Narrative interviews have unique potential for obtaining such in-depth information from native speakers; and similarly, qualitative and ethnographic interviews hold substantial promise for investigating the meanings of communicative practices in the perception of the non-native. But pragmaticists have to resist the temptation of interviewing without thorough preparation. In addition to Briggs' (1986) book, two excellent guidelines for the theory and methodology of narrative interviews are Spradley (1979), another classic on ethnographic interviewing, and Kvale (1996) on qualitative interviewing.

As the comparison of Knapp et al.'s (1984) and Miles' (1994) studies has demonstrated, different genres of research interview yield different information. However, one important feature shared by such diverse interview genres as the interview pre-structured by a detailed schedule (questionnaire) and the open-ended, narrative interview is that they tap respondents' long-term memories of generalized knowledge states, attitudes, or past events. By contrast, another interview genre, often referred to as the retrospective interview, informs about participants' thoughts while they are engaged in a specific activity. This interview genre is usually categorized as a form of think-aloud protocol and will be discussed in the section on this topic below.

15.4 Diaries

Diary studies are investigations whose primary data are one or several persons' journal entries about their experiences relating to the topic of the study. Diaries are the least pre-structured of all types of self-report, and it is precisely this property that allows them to combine most of the features characteristic of the self-report categories discussed in the preceding sections. They share with scaled response instruments and interviews their focus on past experiences and subjective theories while also permitting retrospective reports on specific attended information in the input or in the diarist's mind during an activity. They distinguish themselves from any other form of self-report in that they are – in the self-study variety at least – entirely participant-directed, since the diarist decides on the substance, form, and timing of entries without being constrained by a particular task, response format, or social interaction.

Because of the in-built emic perspective of personal journals, diary studies in second language research have primarily investigated individual differences, learner strategies, teachers' and students' experiences of second language classroom learning and teaching, and sojourners' and immigrants' perceptions of second language learning and communication in particular social and institutional contexts. Two types of diary study can be distinguished: the self-study, in which the diarist and the researcher are the same person, and the commissioned diary study, in which the researcher requests participants (often language learners or teachers) to keep a journal that is then submitted to and analysed by the researcher (with or without participant collaboration).

At the time of writing, investigations with a focus on L2 pragmatics and learner diaries as a main data source amounted to one published study (Cohen 1997), one unpublished conference paper (LoCastro 1998), and one unpublished dissertation (DuFon 1999). One common feature of the three studies is their focus on target languages other than English, two examining pragmatic development in L2 Japanese and one in L2 Indonesian. Cohen and LoCastro report on self-studies, whereas DuFon's investigation is based on commissioned diaries as one data source.

The personal position that second and foreign language learners hold towards the target language and culture, and their opportunities for interaction and input in different societal domains, are increasingly recognized as a significant force in L2 learning. As a prime data source for learners' own perspective on their language learning experience, diary studies have a particularly rich potential for translating this theoretical orientation into research methodology.

15.5 Think-aloud protocols

Diaries, interviews, and scaled response instruments all elicit self-report data in isolation from the contexts in which the reported event occurs. Subjects retrieve pertinent information from long-term memory in order to decide on their response, but they are not currently engaged in an activity requiring online use of the information. In contrast, think-aloud protocols (TAP) are verbalizations of thought processes during engagement in a task.

Anyone wishing to learn about TAP is strongly advised to read the expanded edition of Ericsson's and Simon's 1984 book, published in 1993 under the same title, *Protocol Analysis: Verbal Reports as Data.* The book not only provides the theoretical framework for predicting under which conditions a verbal report should be a valid account of thought processes, but also when and why valid accounts cannot be expected.

A minimalist version of the theory goes as follows. Information processed in short-term memory while a subject is carrying out a task is reportable and veridical. Information not processed in short-term memory, such as perceptual processes, motor processes, and all automated processes, are not available for report. Veridical report is also possible immediately after task completion, when the attended information, or traces of it, is/are still in short-term memory. Once out of short-term memory, information will be lost or encoded in long-term memory, but storage in and retrieval from long-term memory always entails further processing. Therefore, the best reports are concurrent or immediately consecutive verbalizations. Delayed retrospective protocols may only have a tenuous relationship to the original attended information. In addition to type of information and recency of processing, the instruction to subjects for verbalization is crucial. Prompts should only request subjects to say what they are thinking. Subjects should not be asked to describe, explain, or hypothesize because such requests will prompt different cognitive processes than those required by the task and will interfere with the task-related processes.

Studies using various types of verbal protocols in second language research have been reviewed in various places, for instance in Cohen's recent book on learner strategies (1998). Cohen (1996) also reviewed the verbal report studies on interlanguage pragmatics published at the time of writing. I will comment on one published study which illustrates different types of verbal protocol and raises design issues.

Robinson (1992) asked six intermediate and six advanced Japanese learners of English to think aloud while completing a production questionnaire on refusals. In accordance with Ericsson and Simon's (1993) prescriptions, subjects were requested to verbalize whatever they were thinking while focusing on the task, in the language they were thinking in; they were given a practice session. Immediately after they finished the task, the tape-recorded think-aloud protocol was played back to subjects in a retrospective interview. Coding categories were developed inductively from the protocols and an interrater reliability check was run on the coding of one entire protocol by three coders. Methodologically, one of the interesting outcomes of Robinson's study is the different information provided in the concurrent and consecutive reports. The concurrent reports were entirely task-focused, evincing what information in the stimulus subjects attended to, their planning decisions, considerations of alternatives, the consulted pragmalinguistic and sociopragmatic knowledge, and the difficulties subjects experienced in deciding on their response. In the consecutive reports, despite the stimulated recall, subjects often had difficulties remembering their task-related thoughts, which was predictable since they completed the entire questionnaire before the retrospective interview. But in some cases, subjects provided more complete reports than in the concurrent verbalization and very informative details about the reasoning underlying their planning decisions and the sources of the L1 and L2 pragmatic knowledge they drew on. In the following example, the concurrent report sheds light on the response alternatives that the learner considered, whereas the retrospective report informs about the learner's views of social relationships that guided her decision-making.

An American classmate sometimes sleeps late and misses a class that you share with her. This happened again today and she asks if she can borrow your lecture notes. You have the notes but you don't want to lend them to her.

Classmate: I missed class again today. Do you think you could lend me your lecture notes? I'm really getting behind in that class and I'd sure appreciate your help!

You: *I don't have it with me now. Well, you may want to ask someone else because my notes are terrible and I would feel embarrassed to show it to you. Please ask someone else.*

Concurrent report:

well um - for now I should s tell her that - I don't have it with me - and uh – um - um and so that she she will ask somebody else - hm – mm [R: what are you thinking?] but um - she may ask again - what should I say - um - I cannot tell her that I - I I was absent from the class - I did attend - um - what I'm gonna say - it's really hard - um - well - how can I refuse - mm - I can I can just - well I'll just tell her that I don't have it with me - and I have to - tell her that - my my notes are - are not good - um - it's not sufficient for her - oh okay I I I should tell her that we- she should ask someone else - = um - well - I don't I have to ex explain that my notes are good - are not good =

Retrospective report:

R: what was important about this situation?

S: mm - well - I I I don't want to lend a lazy person uh my notes [laughs] [R: hmm] but like I said before it's also important to make other people happy - as long as I can do things for them - so - it's it's easy for me to um to to let other people use my notes - but since I have to refuse um - I just have to say that my notes are not good [R: hmm] yeah - or uh because in as long as uh - notes go um I - have a hard time no uh writing down what my professor says and stuff so I may need some help from someone so - as long as I can help I'd like to um - let the people use my no see my notes so that I can expect someone else to help me some other time. (Robinson 1992)

In verbal report studies involving non-native speakers, the question arises in what language the verbal protocol should be delivered. In Cohen and Olshtain's (1993) and Widjaja's (1997) retrospective interviews, the language of reporting was the participants' native language or language of daily communication. Robinson's retrospective reports, on the other hand, were elicited in participants' L2. Even though Robinson's respondents were explicitly instructed to use either Japanese or English during the concurrent think-aloud (p. 81), they reported only in English (p. 65), presumably out of courtesy to the researcher, who spoke no Japanese. Future studies must ensure that participants actually use whatever language comes to their minds during concurrent verbalization, to minimize the additional processing involved in recoding. For the same reason, immediate retrospection should be initiated in the language used during the think-aloud. Unless participants are advanced enough to think and speak effortlessly in the target language, the experimenter should be bilingual in the L2 and participants' primary language of communication (which can be, but doesn't have to be, their native language). A schematic decision to ask for reports in participants' native language would be psycholinguistically unsound because the native language may not be the language with the lowest activation threshold and thus may not be the language of thought.

The combination of authentic or simulated interaction with retrospective interviews is a common procedure in interactional sociolinguistics. For studies of miscommunication in interethnic encounters, Gumperz and Cook-Gumperz (1982: 19) recommended commentary elicited through playback of a preceding recorded conversation as a technique for evaluating 'how participants reflexively address the social activity that is being constituted by their ongoing talk'. In the European Science Foundation Project on Second Language Acquisition by Adult Immigrants, different types of authentic and simulated spoken discourse were supplemented by feedback sessions, which informed about participants' understanding of the recorded interaction, their attitudes, intentions, and experience (Bremer et al. 1996).

In her study of intercultural gatekeeping interviews, Fiksdal (1990) used microanalysis and focused playback to examine uncomfortable moments and the temporal dimension. Participants first watched the videotaped interaction they participated in and provided any commentary they wished to make. In a second viewing, the researcher then stopped the tape and asked the participants for comments 'at all moments that seemed uncomfortable because of the topic or because of specific comments of the subjects while viewing it; and ... at all moments of postural change' (Fiksdal 1990: 66–7). The comments during the playback session provided a crucial source of information about participants' understanding and intent at those particular points in the discourse. In several respects, the use of retrospective interviews in interactional sociolinguistics and ethnographic microanalysis is more akin to analytic induction than to protocol analysis in the information processing approach (cf. Smagorinsky 1998 and Ericsson and Simon 1998 for a recent discussion).

15.6 Conclusion

For reasons of exposition, this chapter has focused on the design features of individual data collection procedures and their applications in pragmatic research. But as I mentioned several times in passing, studies often combine two or more methods. Retrospective interviews will always be recorded in conjunction with data on the participant's completion of the primary task. In ethnographic studies, a multi-method approach is standard, including participant observation, interviews, audio- and video-recordings of interactions, and collection of documents. In fact, researchers in different disciplinary traditions advocate the use of multiple data collection procedures as a means to offset the instrument or observer bias that is necessarily involved in each technique. Material collected by means of complementary techniques and from different sources allows triangulation, which may be necessary or desirable in order to increase the validity/credibility of a study.

All of the data collection methods discussed in this chapter have usefully illuminated different aspects of pragmatics and will continue to do so. Very likely, we will soon see new techniques, especially those utilizing innovations in computer technology. In a field as complex as cross-cultural and intercultural pragmatics, researchers have to borrow from neighbour disciplines as well as design their own methodologies suitable for studying different research objects and questions. Given the decisive impact of data collection on substantive findings and theory construction, research into adequate data gathering methodology remains a lasting concern in pragmatics research.

Discussion questions

1   In empirical studies, how (and to what extent) does the procedure for collecting spoken data influence the language that is produced?

2   If you want to investigate spoken interaction, what are the relative strengths and weaknesses of using the following types of data: authentic discourse, elicited conversation, role-play and production questionnaires?

3   What issues should you take into account when devising a production questionnaire for cross-cultural research?

4   Audiotape a conversation between yourself and another person, first obtaining permission to do so. Try to transcribe a few minutes of talk on the tape. What are some of the problems you have in your efforts to make a transcription? Are there aspects of the talk you find on the tape which surprise you? Were there features of your own speech you were not previously aware of?[2]

5   After a few weeks, listen to the tape again and compare what you hear with your transcription. Are there differences? Revise your

transcript, being careful not to 'normalize' it. In other words, don't change what you hear into something that makes better sense or is grammatically correct. How is this authentic talk different from what you might find in a novel as an example of 'conversation'?[2]

6   Look at each of the empirical chapters in this volume and, for each one, note the data collection procedure(s) that were used. Why do you think the researchers chose those methods? What are the strengths and weaknesses of these procedures for the research issue(s) they were designed to investigate?

Suggestions for further reading

Beebe, L.M. and Cummings, M.C. (1996) Natural speech act data versus written questionnaire data: how data collection method affects speech act performance. In S. M. Gass and J. Neu (eds), *Speech Acts across Cultures*. Berlin: Mouton de Gruyter, 65–86.

Coupland, N. and Jaworksi, A. (eds) (1997) *Sociolinguistics: A Reader and Coursebook*. Basingstoke: Macmillan, Part II: Methods for studying language in society.

Du Bois, J.W. (1991) Transcription design principles for spoken discourse research. *Pragmatics*, 1(1): 71–106.

Stubbs, M. (1983) *Discourse Analysis*. Oxford: Blackwell, chapter 11, Collecting conversational data.

Notes

1. John Twitchin (personal communication) argues that it is misleading to call these interactions role-plays since people are reproducing their own role behaviour rather than taking on and acting out other roles. He suggests that the term 're-creations' would portray the characteristics of such interactions more clearly.
2. Discussion questions 4 and 5 were contributed by Laura Miller.

References

Adachi, T. (1996) Sarcasm in Japanese. *Studies in Language*, 20(1): 1–36.

Adelswärd, V. (1988) *Styles of Success: On Impression Management as Collaborative Action in Job Interviews*. Linköping University, Sweden: VTT-Grafiska Vimmerby, Linköping Studies in Arts and Science.

Aitchison, J. and Carter, H. (1994) *A Geography of the Welsh Language 1961–1991*. Cardiff: University of Wales Press.

Akinnaso, F.N. and Seabrook Ajirotutu, C. (1982) Performance and ethnic style in job interviews. In J.J. Gumperz (ed.), *Language and Social Identity*. Cambridge: Cambridge University Press, 119–44.

Apte, M. (1994) Language in sociocultural context. In R.E. Asher (ed.), *The Encyclopedia of Language and Linguistics*. Oxford: Pergamon Press, Vol 4: 2000–2010.

Argyle, M., Henderson, M., Bond, M.H., Iizuka, Y. and Contarello, A. (1986) Cross-cultural variations in relationship rules. *International Journal of Psychology*, 21: 287–315.

Ashcroft, B., Griffiths, G. and Tiffin, H. (1998) *Key Concepts in Post-Colonial Studies*. London: Routledge.

Bach, K. and Harnish, R.M. (1979/1982) *Linguistic Communication and Speech Acts*. Cambridge, MA: MIT Press.

Bailey, B. (1997) Communication of respect in interethnic service encounters. *Language in Society*, 26: 327–56.

Bakakou-Orfanou, A. (1990) [in Greek]. Telephone communication: utterance variation of requests forgetting connected with the person called. *Glossologia* 7–8: 33–50.

Ball, P., Giles, H., Byrne, J.L. and Berechree, P. (1984) Situational constraints on the evaluative significance of speech accommodation: some Australian data. *International Journal of the Sociology of Language*, 46: 115–30.

Bardovi-Harlig, K. and Hartford, B.S. (1993) Refining the DCT: comparing open questionnaires and dialogue completion tasks. In L.F. Bouton and Y. Kachru (eds), *Pragmatics and Language Learning, Monograph Series, Vol. 4*. Urbana, IL: Division of English as an International Language, University of Illinois at Urbana-Champaign, 143–65.

Bardovi-Harlig, K. and Hartford, B.S. (1996) Input in an institutional setting. *Studies in Second Language Acquisition*, 18: 171–88.

Barnlund, D.C. and Araki, S. (1985) Intercultural encounters: the management of compliments by Japanese and Americans. *Journal of Cross-Cultural Psychology*, 16(1): 9–26.

Barnlund, D.C. and Yoshioka, M. (1990) Apologies: Japanese and American styles. *International Journal of Intercultural Relations*, 14: 193–206.

Baxter, L.A. (1984) An investigation of compliance-gaining as politeness. *Human Communication Research*, 10(3): 427–56.

Beebe, L. (1981) Social and situational factors affecting communicative strategy of dialect code-switching. *International Journal of the Sociology of Language*, 32: 139–49.

Beebe, L.M. and Cummings, M.C. (1996) Natural speech act data versus written questionnaire data: how data collection method affects speech act performance. In S.M. Gass and J. Neu (eds), *Speech Acts across Cultures*. Berlin: Mouton de Gruyter, 65–86 (original version 1985).

Beebe, L.M. and Takahashi, T. (1989a) Do you have a bag?: social status and patterned variation in second language acquisition. In S. Gass, C. Madden, D. Preston and L. Selinker (eds), *Variation in Second Language Acquisition, Vol. 1: Discourse and Pragmatics*. Clevedon: Multilingual Matters, 103–25.

Beebe, L.M. and Takahashi, T. (1989b) Sociolinguistic variation in face-threatening speech acts. In M. Eisenstein (ed.), *The Dynamic Interlanguage*. New York: Plenum, 199–218.

Beebe, L.M., Takahashi, T. and Uliss-Weltz, R. (1990) Pragmatic transfer in ESL refusals. In R.C. Scarella, E. Anderson and S.C. Krashen (eds), *On the Development of Communicative Competence in a Second Language*. New York: Newbury House, 55–73.

Berens, F.J. (1981) Dialogeröffnung in Telefongesprächen: Handlungen und Handlungsschemata der Herstellung sozialer und kommunikativer Beziehungen. In P. Schröder and H. Steger (eds), *Jahrbuch 1980 des Instituts für Deutsche Sprache*, Düsseldorf: Schwann, 402–17.

Bergman, M.L. and Kasper, G. (1993) Perception and performance in native and nonnative apology. In G. Kasper and S. Blum-Kulka (eds), *Interlanguage Pragmatics*. New York: Oxford University Press, 82–107.

Berry, J. (1969) On cross-cultural comparability. *International Journal of Psychology*, 4: 119–28.

Berry, J. (1980) Introduction to *Methodology*. In H.C. Triandis and J. Berry (eds), *Handbook of Cross-Cultural Psychology*. Boston: Allyn and Bacon, Vol 2: 1–28.

Berry, J., Poortinga, Y. and Pandey, J. (eds) (1997) *Handbook of Cross-Cultural Psychology: Theory and Method, Vol. 1* (2nd edn). Boston: Allyn and Bacon.

Besnier, N. (1990) Language and affect. *Annual Review of Anthropology*, 19: 419–51.

Bhabha, H.K. (1988) The commitment to theory. *New Foundations*, 5: 5–23.

Bhabha, H.K. (1994) *The Location of Culture*. London: Routledge.

Bilbow, G.T. (1997) Spoken discourse in the multicultural workplace in Hong Kong: applying a model of discourse as 'impression management'. In S. Harris and F. Bargiela (eds), *The Language of Business: An International Perspective*. Edinburgh: Edinburgh University Press, 21–48.

Bilous, F.R. and Krauss, R.M. (1988) Dominance and accommodation in the conversational behaviours of same- and mixed-gender dyads. *Language and Communication*, 8: 183–94.

Blakemore, D. (1992) *Understanding Utterances: An Introduction to Pragmatics*. Oxford: Blackwell.

Bloch, C. (1996) Emotions and discourse. *Text*, 16: 323–41.

Bloch, M.E.F. (1998) *How We Think They Think*. Oxford: Westview Press.

Blum-Kulka, S., Danet, B. and Gherson, R. (1985) The language of requesting in Israeli society. In J.P. Forgas (ed.), *Language and Social Situations*. New York: Springer-Verlag, 113–39.

Blum-Kulka, S., House, J. and Kasper, G. (eds) (1989) *Cross-Cultural Pragmatics: Requests and Apologies*. Norwood, NJ: Ablex.

Blum-Kulka, S. and Weizman, E. (1988) The inevitability of misunderstanding: discourse ambiguities. *Text*, 8: 219–41.

Bond, M.H. (1988) Finding universal dimensions of individual variation in multicultural studies of values: the Rokeach and Chinese value surveys. *Journal of Personality and Social Psychology*, 55: 1009–1015.

Bond, M.H. (1991) *Beyond the Chinese Face*. Hong Kong: Oxford University Press.

Bond, M.H. (1996) Chinese values. In M.H. Bond (ed.), *The Handbook of Chinese Psychology*. Hong Kong: Oxford University Press, 208–26.

Bond, M.H. (1998) Managing culture in studies of communication: a futurescape. *Journal of Asian Pacific Communication*, 8(1): 31–49.

Bond, M.H. and Chan, S.C.N. (1995) Country values and country health. Paper presented at the 7th European Congress of Psychology, Athens, Greece, July.

Bond, M.H., Wan, K.C., Leung, K. and Giacalone, R. (1985) How are responses to verbal insult related to cultural collectivism and power distance? *Journal of Cross-Cultural Psychology*, 16: 111–27.

Bonikowska, M.P. (1988) The choice of opting out. *Applied Linguistics*, 9: 69–181.

Bourhis, R.Y. and Giles, H. (1977) The language of intergroup distinctiveness. In H. Giles (ed.), *Language, Ethnicity and Intergroup Relations*. London: Academic Press in co-operation with European Association of Experimental Social Psychology, 119–35.

Bourhis, R.Y., Giles, H., Leyens, J.P. and Tajfel, H. (1979) Psycholinguistic distinctiveness: language divergence in Belgium. In H. Giles and R.St. Clair (eds), *Language and Social Psychology*. Oxford: Blackwell, 158–85.

Bouton, L.F. (1988) A cross-cultural study of ability to interpret implicatures in English. *World Englishes*, 17: 183–96.

Bremer, K., Roberts, C., Vasseur, M.-T., Simonot, M. and Broeder, P. (1996) *Achieving Understanding*. London: Longman.

Briggs, C.L. (1986) *Learning How to Ask*. Cambridge: Cambridge University Press.

Brinker, K. and Sager, S.E. (1989) *Linguistische Gesprächsanalyse: Eine Einführung*. Berlin: Erich Schmidt.

Brislin, R. (1976) *Translation: Application and Research*. New York: Gardner.

Brislin, R. (1983) Cross-cultural research in psychology. *Annual Review of Psychology*, 34: 363–400.

Brislin, R. and Baumgardner, S. (1971) Non-random sampling of individuals in cross-cultural research. *Journal of Cross-Cultural Psychology*, 2: 397–400.

Brislin, R., Lonner, W. and Thorndike, R. (1973) *Cross-Cultural Research Methods*. New York: Wiley.

Brons-Albert, R. (1984) *Gesprochenes Standarddeutsch: Telefondialoge*. Tübingen: Günter Narr.

Brown, G. and Yule, G. (1983) *Teaching the Spoken Language*. Cambridge: Cambridge University Press.

Brown, P. and Levinson, S.C. (1987) *Politeness: Some Universals in Language Usage*. Cambridge: Cambridge University Press. Originally published as 'Universals in language usage: politeness phenomena' in J. Goody (ed.), (1978) *Questions and Politeness: Strategies in Social Interaction*. Cambridge: Cambridge University Press.

Brown, R. and Gilman, A. (1960/1972) Pronouns of power and solidarity. In T.A. Sebeok (ed.), *Style in Language*. Cambridge, MA: MIT Press, 253–76. Reprinted in P. Giglioli (ed.), *Language and Social Context*. Harmondsworth: Penguin Books, 252–82.

Brown, R. and Gilman, A. (1989) Politeness theory and Shakespeare's four major tragedies. *Language in Society*, 18: 159–212.

Bryman, A. and Cramer, D. (1994) *Quantitative Data for Social Scientists*. London: Routledge.

Burgoon, J.K., Stern, L.A. and Dillman, L. (1995) *Interpersonal Adaptation Patterns*. Cambridge: Cambridge University Press.

Burrell, G. and Morgan, G. (1979) *Sociological Paradigms and Organizational Analysis*. London: Heinemann.

Button, G. (1987) Moving out of closings. In G. Button and J.R.E. Lee (eds), *Talk and Social Organization*. Clevedon: Multilingual Matters, 101–51.

Button, G. (1990) On varieties of closings. In G. Psathas (ed.), *Studies in Ethnomethodology and Conversation Analysis*. Lanham: University Press of America, 93–148.

Byrne, D. (1971) *The Attraction Paradigm*. New York: Academic Press.

Byrnes, H. (1986) Interactional style in German and American conversation. *Text*, 6(2): 189–206.

Caffi, C. and Janney, R. (1994) Toward a pragmatics of emotive communication. *Journal of Pragmatics*, 22: 325–73.

Campbell, D. and Stanley, J. (1966) *Experimental and Quasi-Experimental Designs for Research*. Chicago: Rand McNally.

Carlsmith, J.M., Ellsworth, P.C. and Aronson, E. (1976) *Research Methods in Social Psychology*. Reading, MA: Addison Wesley.

Chen, R. (1993) Responding to compliments: a contrastive study of politeness strategies between American English and Chinese speakers. *Journal of Pragmatics*, 20: 49–75.

Chinese Culture Connection (1987) Chinese values and the search for culture-free dimensions of culture. *Journal of Cross-Cultural Psychology*, 18(2): 143–64.

Clark, H.H. (1996) *Using Language*. Cambridge: Cambridge University Press.

Clark, H.H. and French, W.J. (1981) Telephone *goodbyes*. *Language in Society*, 10: 1–19.

Clyne, M. (1987) Cultural differences in the organization of academic texts: English and German. *Journal of Pragmatics*, 11: 211–47.

Cohen, A.D. (1996) Developing the ability to perform speech acts. *Studies in Second Language Acquisition*, 18: 253–67.

Cohen, A.D. (1997) Developing pragmatic ability: insights from the accelerated study of Japanese. In H.M. Cook, K. Hijirida and M. Tahara (eds), *New Trends and Issues in Teaching Japanese Language and Culture* (Technical Report no. 15). Honolulu: University of Hawaii, Second Language Teaching and Curriculum Center, 133–59.

Cohen, A.D. (1998) *Strategies in Learning and Using a Second Language*. London: Longman.

Cohen, A.D. and Olshtain, E. (1981) Developing a measure of sociocultural competence: the case of apology. *Language Learning*, 31: 113–34.

Cohen, A.D. and Olshtain, E. (1993) The production of speech acts by EFL learners. *TESOL Quarterly*, 27: 33–56.

Cook, H.M. (1992) Meanings of non-referential indexes: a case study of the Japanese sentence-final particle 'ne'. *Text*, 12: 507–39.

Coupland, J., Coupland, N. and Robinson, J.D. (1992) 'How are you?': negotiating phatic communion. *Language in Society*, 21: 207–30.

Coupland, N. (1995) Accommodation theory. In J. Verschueren, J.-O. Östman and J. Blommaert (eds), *Handbook of Pragmatics Manual*. Antwerp: International Pragmatics Association, 21–6.

Coupland, N., Coupland, J., Giles, H. and Henwood, K. (1988) Accommodating the elderly: invoking and extending a theory. *Language in Society*, 17: 1–41.

Coupland, N., Coupland, J. and Giles, H. (1991a) *Language, Society and the Elderly: Discourse, Identity and Ageing*. Oxford: Blackwell.

Coupland, N., Giles, H. and Wiemann, J.M. (eds) (1991b) *'Miscommunication' and Problematic Talk*. Newbury Park, CA: Sage.

Crookall, D. and Saunders, D. (1989) *Communication and Simulation*. Clevedon: Multilingual Matters.

Culpepper, J. (1996) Towards an anatomy of impoliteness. *Journal of Pragmatics*, 25: 349–67.

Dascal, M. (1985) The relevance of misunderstanding. In M. Dascal (ed.), *Dialogue: An Interdisciplinary Approach*. Amsterdam: Benjamins, 441–59.

Davidson, A., Jaccard, J., Triandis, H., Morales, M. and Diaz-Guerrero, R. (1976) Cross-cultural model testing. *International Journal of Psychology*, 11: 1–13.

Davis, K.A. (1995) Qualitative theory and methods in applied linguistics research. *TESOL Quarterly*, 29: 428–53.

Davis, K.A. and Henze, R.C. (1998) Applying ethnographic perspectives to issues in cross-cultural pragmatics. *Journal of Pragmatics*, 30: 399–419.

DuFon, M.A. (1999) The acquisition of linguistic politeness in Indonesian as a second language in a naturalistic context. Unpublished PhD dissertation, University of Hawaii at Manoa.

Duranti, A. (1997) *Linguistic Anthropology*. Cambridge: Cambridge University Press.

Edmondson, W.J. (1981) *Spoken Discourse: A Model for Analysis*. London: Longman.

Edmondson, W.J. (1987) 'Aquisition' and 'learning': the discourse system integration hypothesis. In W. Lörscher and R. Schulze (eds), *Perspectives on Language in Performance*. Tübingen: Narr, 1070–1089.

Edmondson, W.J. (1989) Discourse production, routines, and language learning. In P. Bierbaumer *et al.* (eds), *Englisch als Zweitsprache*, Tübingen: Narr, 287–302.

Edmondson, W.J. and House, J. (1981) *Let's Talk and Talk About It: A Pedagogic Interactional Grammar of English*. Munich: Urban and Schwarzenberg.

Edmondson, W.J. and House, J. (1991) Do learners talk too much?: the waffle phenomenon in interlanguage pragmatics. In R. Phillipson, E. Kellerman, L. Selinker, M.S. Smith and M. Swain (eds), *Foreign/Second Language Pedagogy Research*. Clevedon: Multilingual Matters, 273–86.

Edmondson, W.J., House, J., Kasper, G. and Stemmer, B. (1984) Learning the pragmatics of discourse: a project report. *Applied Linguistics*, 5: 113–27.

Ehlich, K. and Wagner, J. (1995) *The Discourse of Business Negotiation*. Berlin: Mouton de Gruyter.

Ehrman, M. (1993) Ego boundaries revisited: toward a model of personality and learning. In J. Alatis (ed.), *Georgetown University Round Table on Languages and Linguistics: Strategic Interaction and Language Acquisition*. Washington, DC: Georgetown University Press, 330–62.

Eisenstein, M. and Bodman, J.W. (1986) 'I very appreciate': expressions of gratitude by native and non-native speakers of American English. *Applied Linguistics*, 7(2): 167–85.

Eisenstein, M. and Bodman, J.W. (1993) Expressing gratitude in American English. In G. Kasper and S. Blum-Kulka (eds), *Interlanguage Pragmatics*. New York: Oxford University Press, 64–81.

Eisenstein, M. and Starbuck, R.J. (1989) The effect of emotional investment on L2 production. In S. Gass, C. Madden, D. Preston and L. Selinker (eds), *Variation in Second Language Acquisition, Vol. 2: Psycholinguistics Issues*. Clevedon: Multilingual Matters, 125–37.

Erickson, F. (1992) Ethnographic microanalysis of interaction. In M.D. LeCompte, W. Millroy and J. Preissle (eds), *The Handbook of Qualitative Research in Education*. New York: Academic Press, 201–25.

Ericsson, K.A. and Simon, H.A. (1993) *Protocol Analysis: Verbal Reports as Data*. Cambridge, MA: Bradford/MIT Press (1st edn 1984).

Ericsson, K.A. and Simon, H.A. (1998) How to study thinking in everyday life: contrasting think-aloud protocols with descriptions and explanations of thinking. *Mind, Culture, and Activity*, 5: 178–86.

Færch, C. and Kasper, G. (1982) Phatic, metalingual and metacommunicative functions in discourse: gambits and repair. In N.E. Enkvist (ed.), *Impromptu Speech*. Åbo: Åbo Akademi, 71–103.

Falk, J. (1979) The duet as a conversational process. Unpublished PhD dissertation, Princeton University.

Feather, N.T. (1982) *Expectations and Actions: Expectancy-Value Models in Psychology*. Hillsdale, NJ: Erlbaum.

Ferguson, C. (1971) Absence of copula and the notion of simplicity: a study of normal speech, baby talk, foreigner talk, and pidgins. In D. Hymes (ed.), *Pidginization and Creolization of Languages*. Cambridge: Cambridge University Press, 141–50.

Ferguson, C. (1975) Towards a characterization of English foreigner talk. *Anthropological Linguistics*, 17: 1–14.

Ferguson, C. (1996) *Sociolinguistic Perspectives: Papers on Language in Society, 1959–1994*, ed. T. Huebner. New York: Oxford University Press.

Fiksdal, S. (1990) *The Right Time and Place: A Microanalysis of Cross-Cultural Gatekeeping Interviews*. Norwood, NJ: Ablex.

Forgas, J.P. and Bond, M.H. (1985) Cultural influences on perceptions of interaction episodes. *Personality and Social Psychology Bulletin*, 11: 75–88.

Foschi, M. and Hales, W. (1979) The theoretical role of cross-cultural comparisons in experimental social psychology. In L. Eckensberger, W. Lonner and Y. Poortinga (eds), *Cross-Cultural Contributions to Psychology*. Amsterdam: Swets and Zeitlinger, 244–54.

Fraser, B. (1990) Perspectives on politeness. *Journal of Pragmatics*, 14(2): 219–36.

Fraser, B. and Nolan, W. (1981) The association of deference with linguistic form. In J. Walters (ed.), *The Sociolinguistics of Deference and Politeness*, The Hague: Mouton, 93–111. Special issue (27) of the *International Journal of the Sociology of Language*.

French, J.R.P. and Raven, B. (1959) The bases of social power. In D. Cartwright (ed.), *Studies in Social Power*. Ann Arbor: University of Michigan Press, 150–67.

Gabrenya, W.K.J. and Hwang, K.K. (1996) Chinese social interaction: harmony and hierarchy on the good earth. In M.H. Bond (ed.), *The*

Handbook of Chinese Psychology. Hong Kong: Oxford University Press, 295–307.

Gal, S. (1978/1997) Language change and sex roles in a bilingual community. In N. Coupland and A. Jaworski (eds) (1997), *Sociolinguistics: A Reader and Coursebook*. Basingstoke: Macmillan, 376–90. (A shortened version of S. Gal. (1978) Peasant men can't get wives: language change and roles in a bilingual community. *Language in Society*, 7(1): 1–16.)

Gallois, C. and Giles, H. (1998) Accommodating mutual influence in intergroup encounters. In M.T. Palmer and G.A. Barnett (eds), *Mutual Influence in Interpersonal Communication: Theory and Research in Cognition, Affect, and Behavior (Progress in Communication Sciences, Vol. 14)*. Stamford, CT: Ablex, 135–62.

Gallois, C., Franklyn-Stokes, A., Giles, H. and Coupland, N. (1988) Communication accommodation in intercultural encounters. In Y.Y. Kim and W.B. Gudykunst (eds), *Theories in Intercultural Communication*. Newbury Park: Sage, 157–85.

Gallois, C., Giles, H., Jones, E., Cargile, A.C. and Ota, H. (1995) Accommodating intercultural encounters: Elaborations and extensions. In R.L. Wiseman (ed.), *Intercultural Communication Theory: International and Intercultural Communication Annual, Vol. 19*. Thousand Oaks, CA: Sage, 115–47.

Gao, G. (1996) Self and other: a Chinese perspective on interpersonal relationships. In W.B. Gudykunst, S. Ting-Toomey and T. Nishida (eds), *Communication in Personal Relationships across Cultures*. London: Sage, 81–101.

Gao, G. and Ting-Toomey, S. (1998) *Communicating Effectively with the Chinese*. London: Sage.

Gao, G., Ting-Toomey, S. and Gudykunst, W.B. (1996) Chinese communication processes. In M.H. Bond (ed.), *The Handbook of Chinese Psychology*. Hong Kong: Oxford University Press, 280–93.

García, C. (1989) Apologizing in English: politeness strategies used by native and non-native speakers. *Multilingua*, 8: 3–20.

Garrett, P., Coupland, N. and Williams, A. (1999) Evaluating dialect in discourse: teachers' and teenagers' responses to young English speakers in Wales. *Language in Society*, 28 (3): 321–54.

Gibbs, R. (1981) Your wish is my command: convention and context in interpreting indirect requests. *Journal of Verbal Learning and Verbal Behaviour*, 20: 431–44.

Gibbs, R. (1986) What makes some indirect speech acts conventional? *Journal of Memory and Language*, 25: 181–96.

Giddens, A. (1991) *Modernity and Self-Identity: Self and Society in the Late Modern Age*. Cambridge: Polity Press.

Giles, H. (1973) Accent mobility: a model and some data. *Anthropological Linguistics*, 15: 87–105.

Giles, H. and Coupland, N. (1991) *Language: Contexts and Consequences.* Milton Keynes: Open University Press.

Giles, H. and Johnson, P. (1987) Ethnolinguistic identity theory: a social psychological approach to language maintenance. *International Journal of the Sociology of Language,* 68: 69–99.

Giles, H., Taylor, D.M. and Bourhis, R. (1973) Towards a theory of interpersonal accommodation through language: some Canadian data. *Language in Society,* 2: 177–92.

Giles, H., Coupland, J. and Coupland, N. (eds) (1991) *Contexts of Accommodation: Developments in Applied Sociolinguistics.* Cambridge: Cambridge University Press.

Godard, D. (1977) Same setting, different norms: phone call beginnings in France and the United States. *Language in Society,* 6: 209–19.

Goddard, C. (1997) Cultural values and 'cultural scripts' of Malay (Bahasa Melayu). *Journal of Pragmatics,* 27: 183–201.

Goffman, E. (1963) *Behavior in Public Places.* New York: Free Press.

Goffman, E. (1972) *Interaction Ritual: Essays on Face-to-Face Behavior.* Harmondsworth: Penguin.

Goffman, E. (1986) *Frame Analysis: An Essay on the Organization of Experience.* Boston: Northeastern University Press.

Goldschmidt, W. (1966) *Comparative Functionalism.* Berkeley: University of California Press.

Goodwin, C. and Goodwin, M.H. (1987) Concurrent operations on talk: notes on the interactive organization of assessments. *Papers in Pragmatics,* 1(1): 1–54.

Goodwin, M.H. (1980) 'He-said-she-said': formal cultural procedures for the construction of a gossip dispute activity. *American Ethnologist,* 7(4): 674–95.

Goodwin, M.H. (1983) Aggravated correction and disagreement in children's conversations. *Journal of Pragmatics,* 7: 657–77.

Goodwin, M.H. and Goodwin, C. (1987) Children's arguing. In S.U. Phillips, S. Steele and C. Tanz (eds), *Language, Gender and Sex in Comparative Perspective.* Cambridge: Cambridge University Press, 200–48.

Graumann, C.F. (1989) Perspective setting and taking in verbal interaction. In R. Dietrich and C. Graumann (eds), *Language Processing in Social Context: An Interdisciplinary Account.* Amsterdam: Elsevier, 95–122.

Gregory, M. and Carroll, S. (1978) *Language and Situation: Language Varieties and their Social Contexts.* London: Routledge and Kegan Paul.

Grice, H.P. (1989) Logic and conversation: William James Lectures, 1967. Reprinted in H.P. Grice, *Studies in the Way of Words.* Cambridge, MA: Harvard University Press, 22–40.

Gu, Y. (1990) Politeness phenomena in modern Chinese. *Journal of Pragmatics,* 14: 237–57.

Gu, Y. (1998) Politeness and Chinese face. Lecture given in the Department of Linguistics, University of Luton, Summer 1998.

Gudykunst, W.B. (1995) Anxiety/uncertainty management (AUM) theory: current status. In R. Wiseman (ed.), *Intercultural Communication Theory*. Thousand Oaks, CA: Sage, 8–57.

Gudykunst, W.B. and Bond, M.H. (1997) Intergroup relations. In J. Berry, M. Segall and C. Kagitcibasi (eds), *Handbook of Cross-Cultural Psychology* (2nd edn). Boston: Allyn and Bacon, Vol. 3: 119–61.

Gudykunst, W.B. and Matsumoto, Y. (1996) Cross-cultural variability of communication in personal relationships. In W.B. Gudykunst, S. Ting-Toomey and T. Nishida (eds), *Communication in Personal Relationships across Cultures*. Thousand Oaks, CA: Sage, 19–56.

Gudykunst, W.B. and Nishida, T. (1986) Attributional confidence in low- and high-context cultures. *Human Communication Research*, 12: 525–49.

Gudykunst, W.B. and Nishida, T. (1994) *Bridging Japanese/North American Differences*. Thousand Oaks, CA: Sage.

Gudykunst, W.B. and Nishida, T. (in press) The influence of culture and strength of cultural identity on individual values in Japan and the United States. Paper presented at the Intercultural Communication Studies Conference.

Gudykunst, W.B. and Ting-Toomey, S. (1988) *Culture and Interpersonal Communication*. Newbury Park, CA: Sage.

Gudykunst, W.B., Gao, G., Nishida, T., Nadamitsu, Y. and Sakai, J. (1992) Self-monitoring in Japan and the United States. In S. Iwawaki, Y. Kashima and K. Leung (eds), *Innovations in Cross-Cultural Psychology*. Amsterdam: Swets and Zeitlinger, 185–94.

Gudykunst, W.B., Guzley, R. and Ota, H. (1993) Issues for future research on communication in Japan and the United States. In W.B. Gudykunst (ed.), *Communication in Japan and the United States*. Albany: SUNY Press, 291–332.

Gudykunst, W.B., Matsumoto, Y., Ting-Toomey, S., Nishida, T., Kim, K. and Heyman, S. (1996) The influence of cultural individualism–collectivism, self construals, and individual values on communication styles across cultures. *Human Communication Research*, 22: 510–43.

Guiora, A., Paluszny, M., Beit-Hallahmi, B., Catford, J., Cooley, R. and Dull, C. (1975) Language and person: studies in language behavior. *Language Learning*, 25: 43–61.

Gumperz, J.J. (1970) Verbal strategies in multilingual communication. In J.E. Alatis (ed.), *Bilingualism and Language Contact*. Washington, DC: Georgetown University Press, 129–47.

Gumperz, J.J. (1982a) *Discourse Strategies*. Cambridge: Cambridge University Press.

Gumperz, J.J. (ed.) (1982b) *Language and Social Identity*. Cambridge: Cambridge University Press.

Gumperz, J.J. (1992a) Contextualization and understanding. In A. Duranti and C. Goodwin (eds), *Rethinking Context: Language as an Interactive Phenomenon*. Cambridge: Cambridge University Press, 229–52.

Gumperz, J.J. (1992b) Interviewing in intercultural situations. In J. Heritage and P. Drew (eds), *Talk at Work*. Cambridge: Cambridge University Press, 302–30.

Gumperz, J.J. (1996) The linguistic and cultural relativity of conversational inference. In J.J. Gumperz and S.L. Levinson (eds), *Rethinking Linguistic Relativity*. Cambridge: Cambridge University Press, 1–21.

Gumperz, J.J. and Cook-Gumperz, J. (1982) Introduction: language and the communication of social identity. In J.J. Gumperz (ed.), *Language and Social Identity*. Cambridge: Cambridge University Press, 1–21.

Gumperz, J.J. and Levinson, S.C. (1996) *Rethinking Linguistic Relativity*. Cambridge: Cambridge University Press.

Gumperz, J.J., Jupp, T.C. and Roberts, C. (1979) *Crosstalk: A Study of Cross-Cultural Communication*. Southall: National Center for Industrial Language Training.

Günthner, S. (1993) *Diskursstrategien in der interkulturellen Kommunikation. Analysen Deutsch–Chinesischer Gespräche*. Tübingen: Niemeyer.

Günthner, S. (1994) 'Also moment SO seh ich das NICHT'– Informelle Diskussionen im interkulturellen Kontext. *LiLi*, 24: 97–122.

Günthner, S. and Knoblauch, H. (1995) Culturally patterned speaking practices: the analysis of communicative genres. *Pragmatics*, 5(1): 1–32.

Haberland, H. (1996) Communion or communication? A historical note on one of the 'founding fathers' of pragmatics. In R. Sackman (ed.), *Theoretical Linguistics and Grammatical Description: Papers in Honour of Hans-Heinrich Lieb*. Amsterdam: Benjamins, 163–66.

Haiman, J. (1998) *Talk is Cheap: Sarcasm, Alienation, and the Evolution of Language*. Oxford: Oxford University Press.

Hall, E.T. (1976) *Beyond Culture*. New York: Doubleday.

Hall, S. (1994) Cultural identity and diaspora. In P. Williams and L. Chrisman (eds), *Colonial Discourse and Post-Colonial Theory: A Reader*. New York: Columbia University Press, 392–403.

Halliday, M.A.K. (1973) *Explorations in the Functions of Language*. London: Edward Arnold.

Halliday, M.A.K. (1990) New ways of meaning: a challenge to applied linguistics. *Journal of Applied Linguistics*, 6: 7–36.

Hamaguchi, E. (1980) Nihonjin no rentaiteki jiritsusei: Kanjinshugi to kojinshugi (Japanese connected autonomy: Contextualism and individualism). *Gendai no Esupuri (Contemporary Spirit)*, 160: 127–43.

Hartford, B.S. and Bardovi-Harlig, K. (1992) Experimental and observational data in the study of interlanguage pragmatics. In L.F. Bouton and Y. Kachru (eds), *Pragmatics and Language Learning Monograph Series, Vol. 3*. Urbana, IL: Division of English as an International Language, University of Illinois at Urbana-Champaign, 33–52.

Hasegawa, T. and Gudykunst, W.B. (1998) Silence in Japan and the United States. *Journal of Cross-Cultural Psychology*, 29(5): 668–84.

Hassall, T.J. (1997) Requests by Australian learners of Indonesian.

Unpublished PhD dissertation, Australian National University.

Henne, H. and Rehbock, H. (1979) *Einführung in die Gesprächsanalyse*. Berlin: de Gruyter.

Herbert, R.K. (1989) The ethnography of English compliments and compliment responses: a contrastive sketch. In W. Olesky (ed.), *Contrastive Pragmatics*. Amsterdam: Benjamins, 3–35.

Heritage, J. (1984) A change-of-state token and aspects of its sequential placement. In J.M. Atkinson and J. Heritage (eds), *Structures of Social Action*. Cambridge: Cambridge University Press, 299–395.

Heritage, J. (1997) Conversation analysis and institutional talk: analysing data. In D. Silverman (ed.), *Qualitative Research*. London: Sage, 161–82.

Hill, B., Ide, S., Ikuta, S., Kawasaki, A. and Ogina, T. (1986) Universals of linguistic politeness: quantitative evidence from Japanese and American English. *Journal of Pragmatics*, 10: 347–71.

Hinkel, E. (1996) When in Rome: evaluations of L2 pragmalinguistic behaviors. *Journal of Pragmatics*, 26: 51–70.

Hinkel, E. (1997) Appropriateness of advice: DCT and multiple choice data. *Applied Linguistics*, 18: 1–26.

Ho, D. (1976) On the concept of face. *American Journal of Sociology*, 81: 867–84.

Hofstede, G. (1979) Value systems in forty countries. In L. Eckensberger, W. Lonner and Y. Poortinga (eds), *Cross-Cultural Contributions to Psychology*. Amsterdam: Swets and Zeitlinger, 389–407.

Hofstede, G. (1980) *Culture's Consequences: International Differences in Work-Related Values*. Beverly Hills, CA: Sage.

Hofstede, G. (1984) The cultural relativity of the quality of life concept. *Academy of Management Review*, 9: 389–98.

Hofstede, G. (1991) *Cultures and Organizations: Software of the Mind*. London: McGraw-Hill.

Hofstede, G. (1997) The Archimedes effect: the metamorphosis of an engineer. In M.H. Bond (ed.), *Working at the Interface of Culture: Eighteen Lives in Social Science*. London: Routledge, 47–61.

Hofstede, G. and Bond, M. (1984) Hofstede's culture dimensions. *Journal of Cross-Cultural Psychology*, 15: 417–33.

Holmes, J. (1986) Compliments and compliment responses in New Zealand English. *Anthropological Linguistics*, 28(4): 485–508.

Holmes, J. (1990) Apologies in New Zealand English. *Language in Society*, 19: 155–99.

Holmes, J. (1995) *Women, Men and Politeness*. London: Longman.

Holtgraves, T. and Yang, J.-N. (1990) Politeness as universal: cross-cultural perceptions of request strategies and inferences based on their use. *Journal of Personality and Social Psychology*, 59(4): 719–29.

Holtgraves, T. and Yang, J.-N. (1992) Interpersonal underpinnings of request strategies: general principles and differences due to culture and gender. *Journal of Personality and Social Psychology*, 62: 246–56.

Holtgraves, T., Srull, T.K. and Socall, D. (1989) Conversation memory: the effects of speaker status on memory for the assertiveness of conversation remarks. *Journal of Personality and Social Psychology*, 56(2): 149–60.

Holyoak, K.J. and Thagard, P. (1995) *Mental Leaps: Analogy in Creative Thought*. Cambridge, MA: MIT Press.

Hopper, R. (1992) *Telephone Conversation*. Bloomington: Indiana University Press.

House, J. (1977) *A Model for Translation Quality Assessment*. Tübingen: Narr.

House, J. (1979) Interaktionsnormen in deutschen und englischen Alltagsdialogen. *Linguistische Berichte*, 59: 76–90.

House, J. (1993) Toward a model for the analysis of inappropriate responses in native/non-native interactions. In S. Blum-Kulka and G. Kasper (eds), *Interlanguage Pragmatics*. Oxford: Oxford University Press, 163–84.

House, J. (1996a) Contrastive discourse analysis and misunderstanding: the case of German and English. In M. Hellinger and U. Ammon (eds), *Contrastive Sociolinguistics*. Berlin: Mouton, 345–61.

House, J. (1996b) Developing pragmatic fluency in English as a foreign language: routines and metapragmatic awareness. *Studies in Second Language Acquisition*, 18: 225–52.

House, J. (1997) *Translation Quality Assessment: A Model Revisited*. Tübingen: Narr.

House, J. (1998) Politeness and translation. In L. Hickey (ed.), *The Pragmatics of Translation*. Clevedon: Multilingual Matters, 54–71.

House, J. and Kasper, G. (1981) Politeness markers in English and German. In F. Coulmas (ed.), *Conversational Routine: Explorations in Standardized Communication and Prepatterned Speech*. The Hague: Mouton, 289–304.

Hudson, R.A. (1980) *Sociolinguistics*. Cambridge: Cambridge University Press.

Humana, C. (1992) *World Human Rights Guide*. New York: Oxford University Press.

Hunter, A. (1994) *Etiquette*. Glasgow: HarperCollins.

Hymes, D. (1971) Competence and performance in linguistic theory. In R. Huxley and E. Ingram (eds), *Language Acquisition: Models and Methods*. London: Academic Press, 3–28.

Hymes, D. (1972) Models of the interaction of language and social life. In J. Gumperz and D. Hymes (eds), *Directions in Sociolinguistics*, New York: Holt, Rinehart and Winston, 35–71.

Ide, R. (1998) 'Sorry for your kindness': Japanese interactional ritual in public discourse. *Journal of Pragmatics*, 29: 509–29.

Ide, S. (1989) Formal forms and discernment: two neglected aspects of universals of linguistic politeness. *Multilingua*, 8(2/3): 223–48.

Iino, M. (1996) Excellent foreigner: Gaijinization of Japanese language and culture in contact situations. Unpublished PhD dissertation, University of Pennsylvania, Philadelphia.

Ikoma, T. and Shimura, A. (1994) Pragmatic transfer in the speech act of refusal in Japanese as a second language. *Journal of Asian Pacific Communication*, 5(1–2): 105–29.

Imai, M. (1981) *Sixteen Ways to Avoid Saying No in Japan.* Tokyo: Nihon Keizai Shimbunsha.

Ip, G.W.M. and Bond, M.H. (1995) Culture, values, and the spontaneous self-concept. *Asian Journal of Psychology*, 1: 30–6.

Itani, R. (1996) *Semantics and Pragmatics of Hedges in English and Japanese.* Tokyo: Hituzi Syobo.

Jaszczolt, K. (1996) Relevance and infinity: implications for discourse interpretation. *Journal of Pragmatics*, 25: 703–22.

Johnston, B., Kasper, G. and Ross, S. (1998) The effect of rejoinders in production questionnaires. *Applied Linguistics*, 19: 157–82.

Jones, E., Gallois, C., Callan, V. and Barker, M. (1999) Strategies of accommodation: development of a coding system for conversational interaction. *Journal of Language and Social Psychology*, 18: 123–52.

Karim, H.K. (1997) The historical resilience of primary stereotypes: core images of the Muslim other. In S.H. Riggins (ed.), *The Language and Politics of Exclusion: Others in Discourse.* Thousand Oaks, CA: Sage, 153–82.

Kashima, Y. (1989) Conceptions of persons: implications in individualism/collectivism research. In C. Kagitcibasi (ed.), *Growth and Progress in Cross-Cultural Psychology.* Amsterdam: Swets and Zeitlinger, 104–12.

Kasper, G. (1992) Pragmatic transfer. *Second Language Research*, 8(3): 203–31.

Kasper, G. (1996) Linguistic etiquette. In F. Coulmas (ed.), *Handbook of Sociolinguistics.* Oxford: Blackwell, 374–85.

Kasper, G. and Blum-Kulka, S. (eds) (1993) *Interlanguage Pragmatics.* New York: Oxford University Press.

Kasper, G. and Dahl, M. (1991) Research methods in interlanguage pragmatics. *Studies in Second Language Acquisition*, 13: 215–47.

Kasper, G. and Rose, K.R. (1999) Pragmatics and SLA. *Annual Review of Applied Linguistics*, 19: 81–104.

Kasper, G. and Schmidt, R. (1996) Developmental issues in interlanguage pragmatics. *Studies in Second Language Acquisition*, 18: 149–69.

Kelly, G. (1955) *The Psychology of Personal Constructs, Vols 1 and 2.* New York: Norton.

Kerekes, J. (1992) *Development in Nonnative Speakers' Use and Perception of Assertiveness and Supportiveness in Mixed-Sex Conversations. Occasional Paper No. 21.* Honolulu: University of Hawaii at Manoa, Department of English as a Second Language.

Kern, J.M. (1991) An evaluation of a novel role-play methodology: the standardized idiographic approach. *Behavior Therapy*, 22: 13–29.

Kim, M.S. (1994) Cross-cultural comparisons of the perceived importance of interactive constraints. *Human Communication Research*, 21: 128–51.

King, A.Y. and Bond, M.H. (1985) The Confucian paradigm of man: a sociological view. In W.S. Tseng and D.H. Wu (eds), *Chinese Culture and Mental Health*. Orlando, FL: Academic Press, 29–45.

King, A.Y. and Myers, J.T. (1977) *Shame as an Incomplete Conception of Chinese Culture*. Occasional paper. Hong Kong: Social Research Center, The Chinese University of Hong Kong.

Kinjo, H. (1987) Oral refusals of invitations and requests in English and Japanese. *Journal of Asian Culture*, 11: 83–106.

Kipper, D.A. (1988) The differential effect of role-playing conditions on the accuracy of self-evaluation. *Journal of Group Therapy, Psychodrama, and Sociometry*, 41: 30–5.

Klopf, D. and Cambra, R. (1979) Communication apprehension among college students in America, Australia, Japan, and Korea. *Journal of Psychology*, 102: 27–31.

Kluckhohn, C. (1951) Values and value-orientations in the theory of action: an exploration in definition and classification. In T. Parsons and E.A. Shils (eds), *Toward a General Theory of Action*. Cambridge, MA: Harvard University Press, 388–433.

Kluckhohn, F. and Strodtbeck, R. (1961) *Variations in Value Orientations*. New York: Row, Peterson.

Knapp, M., Hopper, R. and Bell, R. (1984) Compliments: a descriptive taxonomy. *Journal of Communication*, 34: 19–31.

Kotani, M. (1997) Accounting practices of the Japanese in the United States: explorations of their meanings of apology. Paper presented at the 47th Annual Meeting of the International Communication Association, Montreal.

Kottak, C.P. (1999) *Mirror for Humanity* (2nd edn). Boston: McGraw-Hill.

Kotthoff, H. (1989) *Pro und Kontra in der Fremdsprache*. Frankfurt: Lang.

Kotthoff, H. (1993) Disagreement and concessions in disputes. On the context sensitivity of preference structures. *Language in Society*, 22: 193–216.

Kroeber, A.L. and Kluckhohn, C. (1952) *Culture: A Critical Review of Concepts and Definitions* (vol. 47, no.1). Cambridge, MA: Peabody Museum.

Kuhn, M.H. and McPartland, T.S. (1954) An empirical investigation of self-attitudes. *American Sociological Review*, 19: 68–76.

Kuhn, T.S. (1962) *The Structure of Scientific Revolutions*. Chicago: University of Chicago Press.

Kvale, S. (1996) *Interviews: An Introduction to Qualitative Research Interviewing*. Thousand Oaks: Sage.

Labov, W. (1966) *The Social Stratification of English in New York City*. Washington, DC: Center for Applied Linguistics.

Labov, W. (1972) *Sociolinguistic Patterns*. Philadelphia: University of Pennsylvania Press.

Labov, W. (1984) Field methods of the project on linguistic change and variation. In J. Baugh and J. Sherzer (eds), *Language in Use*. Englewood Cliffs, NJ: Prentice Hall, 28–53.

Lado, R. (1957) *Linguistics across Cultures*. Ann Arbor: University of Michigan Press.

Lakoff, R. (1990) *Talking Power*. New York: Basic Books.

Laver, J. (1975) Communicative functions of phatic communion. In A. Kendon, R.M. Harris and M.R. Key (eds), *The Organization of Behavior in Face-to-Face Interaction*. The Hague: Mouton, 215–38.

Laver, J. (1981) Linguistic routines and politeness in greeting and parting. In F. Coulmas (ed.), *Conversational Routine: Explorations in Standardized Communication and Prepatterned Speech*. The Hague: Mouton, 289–304.

Ledoux, J. (1996) *The Emotional Brain*. New York: Simon and Schuster.

Leech, G.N. (1983) *Principles of Pragmatics*. London: Longman.

Leung, K. and Bond, M.H. (1984) The impact of cultural collectivism on reward allocation. *Journal of Personality and Social Psychology*, 49: 793–804.

Leung, K. and Bond, M.H. (1989) On the empirical identification of dimensions for cross-cultural comparisons. *Journal of Cross-Cultural Psychology*, 20: 133–51.

Levine, D.R., Baxter, J. and McNulty, P. (1987) *The Culture Puzzle: Cross-Cultural Communication for English as a Second Language*. Englewood Cliffs: Prentice Hall.

Levinson, S.C. (1983) *Pragmatics*. Cambridge: Cambridge University Press.

Lewandowska-Tomaszczyk, B. (1989) Praising and complimenting. In W. Oleksy (ed.), *Contrastive Pragmatics*. Amsterdam: John Benjamins, 73–100.

Liao, C.-C. (1994) *A Study on the Strategies, Maxims, and Development of Refusals in Mandarin Chinese*. Taipeh: Crane Publishing.

Liao, C.-C. (1997) *Comparing Directives: American English, Mandarin and Taiwanese English*. Taipeh: Crane Publishing.

Liefländer-Koistinen, L. and Neuendorff, D. (1991) Telefongespräche im Deutschen und Finnischen: Unterschiede in ihrer interaktionalen Struktur. Paper presented at the Akten des 8 Internationalen Germanisten-Kongresses, Tokyo 1990, Munich.

Lim, T.-S. (1994) Facework and interpersonal relationships. In S. Ting-Toomey (ed.), *The Challenge of Facework: Cross-Cultural and Interpersonal Issues*. Albany: SUNY Press, 209–29.

Lim, T.-S. and Bowers, J.W. (1991) Facework: solidarity, approbation, and tact. *Human Communication Research*, 17(3): 415–50.

Linell, P. and Jönsson, L. (1991) Suspect stories: perspective setting in an asymmetrical situation. In I. Marková and K. Foppa (eds), *Asymmetries in Dialogue*. Hemel Hempstead: Harvester Wheatsheaf, 75–100.

LoCastro, V. (1986) 'Yes, I agree with you, but' ... : agreement and disagreement in Japanese and American English. Paper presented at the Japan Association of Language Teachers' International Conference on Language Teaching and Learning, Seiri Gakuen, Hamamatsu, Japan.

LoCastro, V. (1998) Learner subjectivity and pragmatic competence development. Paper presented at the American Association of Applied Linguistics conference, Seattle, March 1998.

Loh, W.C.T. (1993) Responses to compliments across languages and cultures: a comparative study of British and Hong Kong Chinese. Department of English, Research Report Series 30: 1–89. City Polytechnic of Hong Kong.

Lonner, W. (1979) Issues in cross-cultural psychology. In A. Marsella, A. Tharp and T. Cibrowski (eds), *Perspectives in Cross-Cultural Psychology*. New York: Academic Press, 17–45.

Lonner, W. (1980) The search for psychological universals. In H.C. Triandis and W.W. Lambert (eds), *The Handbook of Cross-Cultural Psychology*. Boston: Allyn and Bacon, 143–204.

Lonner, W. and Berry, J. (eds) (1986) *Field Methods in Cross-Cultural Research*. Beverly Hills, CA: Sage.

McAuley, P., Bond, M.H. and Kashima, E. (1999) Cross-cultural insights into the neglected, elusive situation: contextually-defined dimensions of role relationships in Hong Kong and Australia. Paper presented at the joint IACCP and ITC Conference on Cultural Diversity and European Integration, Graz, June 29–July 2.

Malinowski, B. (1966 [1923]) The problem of meaning in primitive languages. Supplement to C.K. Ogden and I.A. Richards, *The Meaning of Meaning*. London: Routledge and Kegan Paul, 296–336.

Malpass, R. and Poortinga, Y. (1986) Strategies for design and analysis. In W. Lonner and J. Berry (eds), *Field Methods in Cross-Cultural Research*. Beverly Hills, CA: Sage, 47–84.

Mao, L.R. (1994) Beyond politeness theory: 'face' revisited and renewed. *Journal of Pragmatics*, 21: 451–86.

Margalef-Boada, T. (1993) Research methods in interlanguage pragmatics: an inquiry into data collection procedures. Unpublished PhD dissertation, Indiana University.

Markus, H.R. and Kitayama, S. (1991) Culture and the self: implications for cognition, emotion, and motivation. *Psychological Review*, 98: 224–53.

Markus, H.R. and Kitayama, S. (1998) The cultural psychology of personality. *Journal of Cross-Cultural Psychology*, 29: 63–87.

Marwell, G. and Hage, J. (1970) The organization of role relations: a systematic description. *American Sociological Review*, 35: 884–900.

Massimini, F. and Calegari, P. (1979) *Il Contesto Normativo Sociale*. Milan: Angeli.

Matsumoto, Y. (1985) A sort of speech act qualification in Japanese: chotto. *Journal of Asian Culture*, 9: 143–59.

Matsumoto, Y. (1988) Reexamination of the universality of face: politeness phenomena in Japanese. *Journal of Pragmatics*, 12: 403–26.

Matsumoto, Y. (1989) Politeness and conversational universals: observations from Japanese. *Multilingua*, 8(2/3): 207–21.

Merritt, M. (1994) Repetition in situated discourse: exploring its forms and functions. In B. Johnstone (ed.), *Repetition in Discourse: Interdisciplinary Perspectives, Vol. 1.*, Norwood, NJ: Ablex, 23–36.

Messick, D.M. (1988) On the limitations of cross-cultural research in social psychology. In M.H. Bond (ed.), *The Cross-Cultural Challenge to Social Psychology*. Newbury Park, CA: Sage, 41–7.

Miall, D. (1995) Anticipation and feeling in literary response: a neuro-psychological view. *Poetics*, 23: 275–98.

Miles, P. (1994) Compliments and gender. Paper presented at the *University of Hawaii Occasional Papers Series*, No. 26, 85–137.

Miller, D.C. (1991) *Handbook of Research Design and Social Measurement*, 5th edn. Newbury Park, CA: Sage.

Miller, L. (1991) Verbal listening behavior in conversations between Japanese and Americans. In J. Blommaert and J. Verschueren (eds), *The Pragmatics of Intercultural and International Communication*. Amsterdam: John Benjamins, 110–30.

Miller, L. (1994a) Japanese and American indirectness. *Journal of Asian and Pacific Communication*, 5(1–2): 37–55.

Miller, L. (1994b) Japanese and American meetings and what goes on before them. *Pragmatics*, 4(2): 221–38.

Miller, L. (1995) Two aspects of Japanese and American co-worker interaction: giving instruction and creating rapport. *Journal of Applied Behavioral Science*, 31(2): 141–61.

Miller, L. (1997) Wasei eigo: English 'loanwords' coined in Japan. In J. Hill, P.J. Mistry and L. Campbell (eds), *The Life of Language: Papers in Linguistics in Honor of William Bright*. The Hague: Mouton/de Gruyter, 123–39.

Miller, L. (1998) Stereotype legacy: culture and person in Japanese/American business interactions. In Y.T. Lee, C. McCauley and J. Draguns (eds), *Through the Looking Glass: Personality in Culture*. Mahwah, NJ: Lawrence Erlbaum.

Mizutani, O. and Mizutani, N. (1977) *Nihongo Notes 1*. Tokyo: The Japan Times.

Mizutani, O. and Mizutani, N. (1979) *Nihongo Notes 2*. Tokyo: The Japan Times.

Moeran, B. (1996) *A Japanese Advertising Agency: An Anthropology of Media and Markets*. Honolulu: University of Hawaii Press.

Morgan, J. (1978) Two types of convention in indirect speech acts. In P. Cole (ed.), *Syntax and Semantics 9: Pragmatics*. New York: Academic Press.

Morisaki, S. and Gudykunst, W.B. (1994) Face in Japan and the United States. In S. Ting-Toomey (ed.), *The Challenge of Facework*. Albany: SUNY Press, 47–94.

Mulac, A., Wiemann, J.M., Widenmann, S. and Gibson, T.W. (1988) Male/female language differences and effects in same-sex and mixed-sex dyads: the gender-linked language effect. *Communication Monographs*, 55: 315–35.

Nakamura, H. (1964) *Ways of Thinking of Eastern Peoples: India–China–Tibet–Japan*. Honolulu: University Press of Hawaii.

Naotsuka, R. (1980) *Oobeejin ga chinmoku suru toki: ibunka kan no comyunikeeshon*. Tokyo: Taishuukan-shoten.

Naotsuka, R., Sakamoto, N. *et al.* (1981) *Mutual Understanding of Different Cultures*. Osaka: Taishukan.

Nebashi, R., Ohashi, R., Bresnehan, M.J. and Liu, W.Y. (1997) Individualism and collectivism in Japanese and American response styles. Manuscript submitted for publication.

Neustupný, J.V. (1987) *Communicating with the Japanese*. Tokyo: Japan Times.

Newman, L.S. (1993) How individualists interpret behavior: idiocentrism and spontaneous trait inference. *Social Cognition*, 11: 243–69.

Niedzielski, N. and Giles, H. (1996) Linguistic accommodation. In H. Goebl, P.H. Nelde, Z. Starý and W. Wölk (eds), *Contact Linguistics*. Berlin: Walter de Gruyter, 332–42.

Niemeyer, S. and Dirven, R. (eds) (1997) *The Language of Emotion*. Amsterdam: Benjamins.

Ochs, E. (1989) The pragmatics of affect. Special issue of *Text*, 9: 1.

Odlin, T. (1989) *Language Transfer*. Cambridge: Cambridge University Press.

Oliver, R.T. (1971) *Communication and Culture in Ancient India and China*. Syracuse: Syracuse University Press.

Olshtain, E. (1989) Apologies across languages. In S. Blum-Kulka, J. House and G. Kasper (eds), *Cross-Cultural Pragmatics: Requests and Apologies*. Norwood, NJ: Ablex, 155–73.

Olshtain, E. and Cohen, A.D. (1983) Apology: a speech-act set. In N. Wolfson and E. Judd (eds), *Sociolinguistics and Language Acquisition*, Rowley: Newbury House, 18–35.

Olshtain, E. and Weinbach, L. (1993) Interlanguage features of the speech act of complaining. In G. Kasper and S. Blum-Kulka (eds), *Interlanguage Pragmatics*. New York: Oxford University Press, 108–22.

Owen, M. (1983) *Apologies and Remedial Interchanges*. Berlin: Mouton de Gruyter.

Parsons, T. and Shils, E. (1951) *Toward a General Theory of Action*. Cambridge, MA: Harvard University Press.

Pavlidou, T. (1991) [in Greek]. Politeness on the telephone: contrastive analysis of Greek and German conversations. *Studies in Greek Linguistics*. Proceedings of the 11th Annual Meeting of the Department of Linguistics, Faculty of Philosophy, Aristotle University of Thessaloniki, 26–28 April 1990. Thessaloniki: Kyriakidis, 307–26.

Pavlidou, T. (1994) Contrasting German–Greek politeness and the consequences. *Journal of Pragmatics*, 21: 487–511.

Pavlidou, T. (1995) [in Greek]. Phatic commun(icat)ion and phatic elements. *Studies in Greek Linguistics: A Festschrift for Professor M. Setatos*. Proceedings of the 15th Annual Meeting of the Department of Linguistics, Faculty of Philosophy, Aristotle University of Thessaloniki, 11–14 May 1994. Thessaloniki, 710–21.

Pavlidou, T. (1997) The last five turns: preliminary remarks on closings in Greek and German telephone calls. *International Journal of the Sociology of Language*, 126: 196–220.

Pavlidou, T. (1998a) Greek and German telephone closings: patterns of confirmation and agreement. *Pragmatics*, 8(1): 79–94.

Pavlidou, T. (1998b) Zum Stellenwert der phatischen Kommunion in einer Theorie der Kommunikation. In D. Krallmann and H.W. Schmitz (eds), *Perspektiven einer Kommunikationswissenschaft*. Internationales Gerold Ungeheuer-Symposium, Essen 6-8 April 1995. Vol. 1. Münster: Nodus, 273–84.

Pavlidou, T. (1998c) Moving towards closing: Greek telephone calls between familiars. Paper presented at the XII International Pragmatics Conference, Reims, July 19–25, 1998.

Penman, R. (1990) Facework and politeness: multiple goals in courtroom discourse. *Journal of Language and Social Psychology*, 9 (1–2): 15–38.

Pieke, F.N. (1992) The ordinary and the extraordinary. Unpublished PhD dissertation, University of California at Berkeley.

Piirainen-Marsh, A. (1995) *Face in Second Language Conversation*. Jyväskylä, Finland: University of Jyväskylä.

Pike, K. (1966) *Language in Relation to a Unified Theory of the Structure of Human Behavior*. The Hague: Mouton.

Pomerantz, A. (1975) Second assessments: a study of some features of agreements/disagreements. Unpublished PhD dissertation, University of California at Irvine.

Pomerantz, A. (1978) Compliment responses: notes on the co-operation of multiple constraints. In J. Schenkein (ed.), *Studies in the Organization of Conversational Interaction*. New York: Academic Press, 79–112.

Pomerantz, A. (1984) Agreeing and disagreeing with assessments: some features of preferred/dispreferred turn shapes. In J.M. Atkinson and J. Heritage (eds), *Structures of Social Action: Studies in Conversation Analysis*. Cambridge: Cambridge University Press, 57–101.

Poortinga, Y. (1975) Limitations of intercultural comparisons of psychological data. *Netherlands Tijschrift voor de Psychologie*, 30: 23–39.

Poortinga, Y. and Malpass, R. (1986) Making inferences from cross-cultural data. In W. Lonner and J. Berry (eds), *Field Methods in Cross-Cultural Research*. Beverly Hills, CA: Sage, 17–46.

Population Crisis Committee (1988) *Country Rankings of the Status of Women: Poor, Powerless, and Pregnant*. Population Briefing Paper No. 20, June.

Rampton, B. (1995) *Crossing: Language and Ethnicity Among Adolescents*. London: Longman.

Rampton, B. (1997) *Sociolinguistics and Cultural Studies: New Ethnicities, Liminality and Interaction (CALR Occasional Papers in Language and Urban Culture No. 4)*. London: Thames Valley University, Centre for Applied Linguistic Research.

Richards, J.C. and Sukwiwat, M. (1983) Language transfer and conversational competence. *Applied Linguistics*, 4(2): 113–25.

Riggins, S.H. (ed.) (1997) *The Language and Politics of Exclusion: Others in Discourse*. Thousand Oaks, CA: Sage.

Ringland, G.A. and Duce, D.A. (1988) *Approaches to Knowledge Representation*. Taunton: Research Studies Press.

Rintell, E. (1981) Sociolinguistic variation and pragmatic ability: a look at learners. *International Journal of the Sociology of Language*, 27: 11–34.

Rintell, E. and Mitchell, C.J. (1989) Studying requests and apologies: an inquiry into method. In S. Blum-Kulka, J. House and G. Kasper (eds), *Cross-Cultural Pragmatics*. Norwood, NJ: Ablex, 248–72.

Rist, R. (1980) Blitzkrieg ethnography: on the transformation of a method into a movement. *Educational Researcher*, 9(2): 8–10.

Roberts, C. (1985) *The Interview Game and How It's Played*. London: BBC.

Roberts, C. and Sayers, P. (1987) Keeping the gate: how judgements are made in intercultural interviews. In K. Knapp, W. Enninger and A. Knapp-Potthoff (eds), *Analyzing Intercultural Communication*. Berlin: Mouton de Gruyter, 111–35.

Roberts, C., Davies, E. and Jupp, T. (1992) *Language and Discrimination: A Study of Communication in Multi-ethnic Workplaces*. London: Longman.

Robinson, M. (1992) Introspective methodology in interlanguage pragmatics research. In G. Kasper (ed.), *Pragmatics of Japanese as Native and Target Language. Technical Report No. 3*. Second Language Teaching and Curriculum Center, University of Hawaii at Manoa, 27–82.

Robinson, W.P. (ed.) (1996) *Social Groups and Identities: Developing the Legacy of Henri Tajfel*. Oxford: Butterworth Heinemann.

Rose, K.R. (1994) On the validity of discourse completion tests in non-Western contexts. *Applied Linguistics*, 15: 1–14.

Rose, K.R. and Ono, R. (1995) Eliciting speech act data in Japanese: the effect of questionnaire type. *Language Learning*, 45: 191–223.

Rubin, J. (1983) How to tell when someone is saying 'no' revisited. In N. Wolfson and E. Judd (eds), *Sociolinguistics and Language Acquisition*. Rowley: Newbury House, 10–17.

Sacks, H. (1987) On the preference for agreement and contiguity in sequences in conversation. In G. Button and J.R.E. Lee (eds), *Talk and Social Organisation*. Clevedon: Multilingual Matters, 54–69.

Saeki, M. and O'Keefe, B. (1994) Refusals and rejections: designing messages to serve multiple goals. *Human Communication Research*, 2(2): 67–102.

Said, E. (1978) *Orientalism*. New York: Vintage.

Sarangi, S. (1994) Accounting for mismatches in intercultural selection interviews. *Multilingua (Cross Cultural Communication in the Professions*, Special Issue, edited by Anne Pauwels), 13(1/2): 163–94.

Sasaki, M. (1998) Investigating EFL students' production of speech acts: a comparison of production questionnaires and role plays. *Journal of Pragmatics*, 30: 457–84.

Sawyer, M. (1992) The development of pragmatics in Japanese as a second language: the sentence-final particle 'ne'. In G. Kasper (ed.), *Pragmatics of Japanese as a Native and Foreign Language: Technical Report No. 3*. Second Language Teaching and Curriculum Center, University of Hawaii at Manoa, 83–125.

Scarcella, R. (1983) Discourse accent in second language performance. In S. Gass and L. Selinker (eds), *Language Transfer in Language Learning*. Rowley, MA: Newbury House, 306–26.

Schegloff, E. (1972) Sequencing in conversational openings. In J. Gumperz and D. Hymes (eds), *Directions in Sociolinguistics*. New York: Holt, Rinehart and Winston, 346–80.

Schegloff, E. (1992) On talk and its institutional occasions. In P. Drew and J. Heritage (eds), *Talk at Work*. Cambridge: Cambridge University Press, 101–34.

Schegloff, E. (1994) Telephone conversation. In R.E. Asher (ed.), *The Encyclopedia of Language and Linguistics*. Oxford: Pergamon, Vol. 9: 4547–9.

Schegloff, E. and Sacks, H. (1973) Opening up closings. *Semiotica*, 8: 289–327.

Schiffrin, D. (1987) *Discourse Markers*. Cambridge: Cambridge University Press.

Schiffrin, D. (1994) *Approaches to Discourse*. Oxford: Blackwell.

Schwartz, S.H. (1992) Universals in the content and structure of values. In M. Zanna (ed.), *Advances in Experimental Social Psychology, Vol. 25*. New York: Academic Press, 1–65.

Schwartz, S.H. (1994) Beyond individualism/collectivism: new cultural dimensions of values. In U. Kim, H.C. Triandis, C. Kagitcibasi, S.C. Choi and G. Yoon (eds), *Individualism and Collectivism: Theory, Method, and Applications*. Newbury Park, CA: Sage, 85–119.

Schwarz, N. and Hippler, H.-J. (1991) Response alternatives: the impact of their choice and presentation order. In P.P. Biemer, R.M. Groves, L.E. Lyberg, N.A. Mathiowetz and S. Sudman (eds), *Measurement Errors in Surveys*. New York: Wiley, 41–56.

Scollon, R. and Scollon, S.W. (1995) *Intercultural Communication: A Discourse Approach*. Oxford: Blackwell.

Scollon, R. and Wong-Scollon, S. (1991) Topic confusion in English–Asian discourse. *World Englishes*, 10 (2): 113–25.

Searle, J. (1983) *Intentionality*. Cambridge: Cambridge University Press.

Searle, J.R. (1996) *The Construction of Social Reality*. London: Penguin Books.

Sears, R. (1961) Transcultural variables and conceptual equivalence. In B. Kaplan (ed.), *Studying Personality Cross-Culturally*. Evanston, IL: Row and Petersen, 445–55.

Seeman, M. (1997) The elusive situation in social psychology. *Social Psychology Quarterly*, 60: 4–13.

Selting, M., Auer, P., Barden, B., Couper-Kuhlen, E., Günther, S., Quasthoff, U., Schlobinski, P. and Uhmann, S. (1998) Gesprächsanalytisches Transkriptionssystem (GAT). *Linguistische Berichte*, 173: 91–122.

Shimanoff, S. (1987) Types of emotional disclosure and request compliance between spouses. *Communication Monographs*, 54: 85–100.

Sifianou, M. (1989) On the telephone again! differences in telephone behaviour: England vs. Greece. *Language in Society*, 18: 524–44.

Sifianou, M. (1992a) *Politeness Phenomena in England and Greece: A Cross-Cultural Perspective*. Oxford: Clarendon.

Sifianou, M. (1992b) The use of diminutives in expressing politeness: modern Greek versus English. *Journal of Pragmatics*, 17: 155–73.

Singelis, T.M. and Brown, W.J. (1995) Culture, self, and collectivist communication: linking culture to individual behavior. *Human Communication Research*, 21: 354–89.

Skoutarides, A. (1986) Foreigner talk in Japanese. Unpublished PhD dissertation, Monash University.

Slugoski, B.R. and Turnbull, W. (1988) Cruel to be kind and kind to be cruel: sarcasm, banter, and social relations. *Journal of Language and Social Psychology*, 7: 101–21.

Smagorinsky, P. (1998) Thinking and speech and protocol analysis. *Mind, Culture, and Activity*, 5: 157–77.

Smith, P.B. and Bond, M.H. (1998) *Social Psychology across Cultures*, 2nd edn. London: Prentice Hall.

Spencer-Oatey, H. (1993) Conceptions of social relations and pragmatics research. *Journal of Pragmatics*, 20: 27–47.

Spencer-Oatey, H. (1996) Reconsidering power and distance. *Journal of Pragmatics*, 26: 1–24.

Spencer-Oatey, H. (1997) Unequal relationships in high and low power distance societies. A comparative study of tutor–student role relations in Britain and China. *Journal of Cross-Cultural Psychology*, 28(3): 284–302.

Spencer-Oatey, H. and Xing, J. (1998) Relational management in Chinese–British business meetings. In S. Hunston (ed.), *Language at Work*. Clevedon: British Association for Applied Linguistics in association with Multilingual Matters Ltd, 31–46.

Sperber, D. (1996) *Explaining Culture*. Oxford: Blackwell.

Sperber, D. and Wilson, D. (1986/1995) *Relevance: Communication and Cognition*. Oxford: Blackwell.

Sperber, D., Premack, D. and Premack, A.J. (1995) *Causal Cognition: A Multidisciplinary Debate*. Oxford: Oxford University Press.

Spradley, J.P. (1979) *The Ethnographic Interview*. New York: Holt, Rinehart and Winston.

Steinberg Du, J. (1995) The performance of face-threatening acts in Chinese. In G. Kasper (ed.), *Pragmatics of Chinese as Native and Target Language: Technical Report No. 5*, Honolulu: University of Hawaii, Second Language Teaching and Curriculum Center, 165–206.

Stemmer, B. (1981) *Kohäsion im gesprochenen Diskurs deutscher Lerner des Englischen. Manuskripte zur Sprachlehrforschung*, 18, Bochum, Germany.

Sternberg, R.J. (1995) *In Search of the Human Mind*. Fort Worth: Harcourt Brace.

Stiles, W.B. (1980) Comparison of dimensions derived from rating versus coding of dialogue. *Journal of Personality and Social Psychology*, 38(3): 359–74.

Storti, C. (1990) *The Art of Crossing Cultures*. Yarmouth, ME: Intercultural Press.

Street, R.L.J. (1982) Evaluation of noncontent speech accommodation. *Language and Communication*, 2: 13–31.

Sugimoto, N. (1998) Norms of apology depicted in U.S. American and Japanese literature on manners and etiquette. *International Journal of Intercultural Relations*, 22(3): 251–76.

Tajfel, H. (1974) Social identity and intergroup behaviour. *Social Science Information*, 13: 65–93.

Tajfel, H. (ed.) (1978) *Differentiation between Social Groups*. London: Academic Press.

Takahashi, S. (1995) Pragmatic transferability of L1 indirect request strategies perceived by Japanese learners of English. Unpublished PhD dissertation, University of Hawaii at Manoa.

Takahashi, T. and Beebe, L.M. (1993) Cross-linguistic influence in the speech act of correction. In G. Kasper and S. Blum-Kulka (eds), *Interlanguage Pragmatics*. New York: Oxford University Press, 138–57.

Tanaka, N. (1991) An investigation of apology: Japanese in comparison with Australian. *Meikai Journal*, 4: 35–53.

Tanaka, N. (1999) 'Apology' re-visited: some cultural differences between English and Japanese. *Meikai Journal*, 11: 23–44.

Tannen, D. (1979) What's in a frame? In R. Freedle (ed.), *New Directions in Discourse Processing*. Norwood, NJ: Ablex, 137–81.

Tao, H. and Thompson, S.A. (1991) English backchannels in Mandarin conversation: a case study of superstratum pragmatic 'interference'. *Journal of Pragmatics*, 16: 209–23.

Tateyama, Y., Kasper, G., Mui, L., Tay, H.-M. and Thananart, O. (1997) Explicit and implicit teaching of pragmatic routines. In L. Bouton (ed.), *Pragmatics and Language Learning, Monograph Series Vol. 8*. Urbana: University of Illinois at Urbana-Champaign, 163–77.

Thakerar, J.N., Giles, H. and Cheshire, J. (1982) Psychological and linguistic parameters of speech accommodation theory. In C. Fraser and K.R. Scherer (eds), *Advances in the Social Psychology of Language*. Cambridge: Cambridge University Press, 205–55.

Thomas, J. (1983) Cross-cultural pragmatic failure. *Applied Linguistics*, 4(2): 91–112.

Thomas, J. (1995) *Meaning in Interaction: An Introduction to Pragmatics*. London: Longman.

Ting-Toomey, S. and Cocroft, B.-A. (1994) Face and facework: theoretical and research issues. In S. Ting-Toomey (ed.), *The Challenge of Facework*. Albany: SUNY Press, 307–40.

Ting-Toomey, S. and Kurogi, A. (1998) Facework competence in intercultural conflict: an updated face-negotiation theory. *International Journal of Intercultural Relations*, 22(2): 187–225.

Tracy, K. (1990) The many faces of facework. In H. Giles and W.P. Robinson (eds), *Handbook of Language and Social Psychology*. Chichester: Wiley, 209–26.

Tracy, K. and Baratz, S. (1994) The case for case studies of facework. In S. Ting-Toomey (ed.), *The Challenge of Facework*. Albany: SUNY Press, 287–305.

Triandis, H.C. (1978) Some universals of social behavior. *Personality and Social Psychology Bulletin*, 4: 1–16.

Triandis, H.C. (1988) Collectivism vs. individualism: a reconceptualization of a basic concept in cross-cultural psychology. In G. Verma and C. Bagley (eds), *Cross-Cultural Studies of Personality, Attitudes and Cognition*. London: Macmillan, 60–95.

Triandis, H.C. (1989) The self and social behavior in differing cultural contexts. *Psychological Review*, 96: 506–17.

Triandis, H.C. (1995) *Individualism and Collectivism*. Boulder, CO: Westview.

Triandis, H.C. and Berry, J. (eds) (1980) *Handbook of Cross-Cultural Psychology, Vol. 2: Methodology*. Boston: Allyn and Bacon.

Triandis, H.C. and Marin, G. (1983) Etic plus emic versus pseudoetic. *Journal of Cross-Cultural Psychology*, 14: 489–500.

Triandis, H.C., Malpass, R. and Davidson, A. (1973) Cross-cultural psychology. *Biennial Review of Anthropology*, 24: 1–84.

Triandis, H.C., Leung, K., Villareal, M. and Clack, F. (1985) Allocentric versus idiocentric tendencies. *Journal of Research in Personality*, 19: 395–415.

Triandis, H.C., Bontempo, R., Villareal, M., Asai, M. and Lucca, N. (1988) Individualism–collectivism: cross-cultural studies on self-ingroup relationships. *Journal of Personality and Social Psychology*, 54: 323–38.

Trompenaars, F. and Hampden-Turner, C. (1997) *Riding the Waves of Culture: Understanding Cultural Diversity in Business*, 2nd edn. London: Nicholas Brealey.

Trosborg, A. (1995) *Interlanguage Pragmatics*. Berlin: Mouton de Gruyter.

TSG (1975) *Texte Gesprochener Sprache, Band III*. Erarbeitet im Institut für Deutsche Sprache. Forschungsstelle Freiburg. Munich: Hueber.

Tsuruta, Y. (1998) Politeness, the Japanese style: an investigation into the use of honorific forms and people's attitudes towards such use. Unpublished PhD dissertation, University of Luton.

Turner, K. (1996) The principal principles of pragmatic inference: politeness. *Language Teaching*, 29: 1–13.

Tyler, A. (1995) The coconstruction of cross-cultural miscommunication: conflicts in perception, negotiation, and enactment of participant role and status. *Studies in Second Language Acquisition*, 17(2): 129–52.

Ueda, K. (1974) Sixteen ways to avoid saying 'no' in Japan. In J. Condon and M. Saito (eds), *Intercultural Encounters with Japan: Communication-Contact and Conflict*. Tokyo: Simul Press, 185–92.

van de Vijver, F. and Leung, K. (1997a) *Methods and Data Analysis for Cross-Cultural Research*. Thousand Oaks, CA: Sage.

van de Vijver, F. and Leung, K. (1997b) Methods and data analysis of comparative research. In J. Berry, Y. Poortinga and J. Pandey (eds), *Handbook of Cross-Cultural Psychology, Vol. 1: Theory and Methods* (2nd edn). Boston: Allyn and Bacon, 257–300.

Victor, D.A. (1992) *International Business Communication*. London: HarperCollins.

Vollmer, H.J. and Olshtain, E. (1989) The language of apologies in German. In S. Blum-Kulka, J. House and G. Kasper (eds), *Cross-Cultural Pragmatics: Requests and Apologies*. Norwood, NJ: Ablex, 197–218.

Vuchinich, S. (1990) The sequential organization of closing in verbal family conflict. In A.D. Grimshaw (ed.), *Conflict Talk*. Cambridge: Cambridge University Press, 118–38.

Watson-Gegeo, K.A. (1988) Ethnography in ESL: defining essentials. *TESOL Quarterly*, 22: 575–92.

Watts, R.J. (1989) Relevance and relational work: linguistic politeness as politic behavior. *Multilingua*, 8: 131–66.

Watzlawick, P., Beavin, J.B. and Jackson, D. (1967) *Pragmatics of Human Communication: A Study of Interactional Patterns, Pathologies, and Paradoxes*. London: Norton.

Werlen, I. (1984) *Ritual und Sprache: Zum Verhältnis von Sprechen und Handeln in Ritualen*. Tübingen: Günter Narr.

Wetherell, M. (1996) Constructing social identities: the individual/social binary in Henri Tajfel's social psychology. In W.P. Robinson (ed.), *Social Groups and Identities: Developing the Legacy of Henri Tajfel*. Oxford: Butterworth Heinemann, 269–83.

White, S. (1989) Backchannels across cultures: a study of Americans and Japanese. *Language in Society*, 18: 59–76.

Whiting, B.B. (1976) The problem of the unpackaged variable. In K.F.

Reigel and J.A. Meacham (eds), *The Developing Individual in a Changing World*. The Hague: Mouton, 303–309.

Widjaja, C.S. (1997) A study of data refusal: Taiwanese vs. American females. *University of Hawai'i Working Papers in ESL*, 15(2): 1–43.

Wieland, M. (1991) Turn-taking structure as a source of misunderstanding in French–American cross-cultural conversation. In L.F. Bouton and Y. Kachru (eds), *Pragmatics and Language Learning, Monograph Series, Vol. 2*. Urbana: Division of English as an International Language, University of Illinois at Urbana-Champaign, 101–18.

Wierzbicka, A. (1994) Cultural scripts: a semantic approach to cultural analysis and cross-cultural communication. In M. Pütz (ed.), *Language Contact, Language Conflict*. Amsterdam: John Benjamins, 69–87.

Wildner-Bassett, M. (1984) *Improving Pragmatic Aspects of Learners' Interlanguage*. Tübingen: Narr.

Wildner-Bassett, M. (1994) Intercultural pragmatics and proficiency: 'polite' noises for cultural appropriateness. *International Review of Applied Linguistics*, 32: 3–17.

Williams, C.H. (1987) Location and context in Welsh language reproduction: a geographic interpretation. *International Journal of the Sociology of Language*, 66: 61–83.

Wilson, D. and Sperber, D. (1986) An outline of relevance theory. In *Encontro de Liguistas Actas*: University of Minho, Braga, Portugal, 21–41. Also published in *Notes on Linguistics*, 1987, 39: 5–24. Dallas: SIL.

Wish, M., Deutsch, M. and Kaplan, S.J. (1976) Perceived dimensions of interpersonal relations. *Journal of Personality and Social Psychology*, 33: 409–20.

Wolfson, N. (1981) Compliments in cross-cultural perspective. *TESOL Quarterly*, 15(2): 117–24.

Wolfson, N. (1989) *Perspectives: Sociolinguistics and TESOL*. Rowley, MA: Newbury House.

Wolfson, N., d'Amico-Reisner, L. and Huber, L. (1983) How to arrange for social commitments in American English: the invitation. In N. Wolfson and E. Judd (eds), *Sociolinguistics and Second Language Acquisition*. Rowley, MA: Newbury House, 116–28.

Wood, L.A. and Kroger, R.O. (1991) Politeness and forms of address. *Journal of Language and Social Psychology*, 10(3): 145–68.

Ye, L. (1995) Complimenting in Mandarin Chinese. In G. Kasper (ed.), *Pragmatics of Chinese as Native and Target Language*. Honolulu: University of Hawaii Press, 207–95.

Yeung, L.N.T. (in press) The question of indirection: a comparison of Chinese and English participative decision-making discourse. *Multilingua*.

Ylänne-McEwen, V. (1993) Complimenting behaviour. *Journal of Multilingual and Multicultural Development*, 14(6): 499–508.

Yoon, K.K. (1991) Bilingual pragmatic transfer in speech acts: bi-directional responses to a compliment. In L.F. Bouton and Y. Kachru (eds), *Pragmatics and Language Learning. Vol. 2.* Urbana: Division of English as a Second Language, University of Illinois at Urbana-Champaign, 75–100.

Yoshimi, D.R. (1999) L1 language socialization as a variable in the use of '*ne*' by L2 learners of Japanese. *Journal of Pragmatics*, 31: 1513–25.

Young, L.W.L. (1994) *Crosstalk and Culture in Sino–American Communication.* Cambridge: Cambridge University Press.

Young, R. (1988) Variation and the interlanguage hypothesis. *Studies in Second Language Acquisition*, 10: 281–302.

Young, R. and He, A.W. (eds) (1998) *Talking and Testing.* Amsterdam: Benjamins.

Yuan, Y. (1996) Responding to compliments: a contrastive study on the English pragmatics of advanced speakers of English. *BUILD 20 Proceedings*: 861–72.

Žegarac, V. (1998) What is 'phatic communication'? In V. Rouchota and A. Jucker (eds), *Current Issues in Relevance Theory.* Amsterdam: Benjamins, 327–61.

Zhan, K. (1992) *The Strategies of Politeness in the Chinese Language.* Berkeley: Institute of East Asian Studies.

Index